Moby-Dick as Philosophy

Other books by Mark Anderson

Pure: Modernity, Philosophy, and the One
The Thinker-Artist (Sophia and Philosophia)
Plato and Nietzsche: Their Philosophical Art

Moby-Dick as Philosophy
Plato – Melville – Nietzsche

Mark Anderson

S.Ph.

S.Ph. Press
Nashville, TN

ISBN-13: 978-0-9967725-0-1
ISBN-10: 0-9967725-0-2

Library of Congress Control Number: 2015914307

Cover art by Matt Kish,
design by Mark Anderson

www.sphpress.com

Table of Contents

Etymology

The ancient Greek word φιλοσοφία, "philosophy," derives from the word φιλόσοφος, "philosopher," which is itself a compound of two other words, φίλος and σοφία. The word φίλος is a noun that denotes a friend, one who is fond of, one who loves, someone or something. The word σοφία, also a noun, translates as "wisdom." The philosopher, then, is one who loves wisdom; and philosophy, as everyone knows, is the love of wisdom. Yet it is not so easy to elaborate on this simple definition. What exactly is wisdom? And what is the proper mode of the philosopher's love? A philosopher grounds his self-conception on his answers to these questions. What is he as a philosopher? What does she do, how does she live, as a lover of wisdom? It seems to me that we have lost sight of the relevance of these questions, and that our conception of philosophy has suffered as a result. Hence this study of Plato, Melville, and Nietzsche, which is in a way a meditation on wisdom and the love of wisdom, and thereby also an attempt to revise our contemporary conception of the philosopher.

The history of this book begins with two other books. The first of these I was writing myself, or anyway trying to write. *Wisdom and the Love of Wisdom: Plato – Michelangelo – Melville – Nietzsche*. This was to be the title. The substance of the work I envisioned as similar to the substance of this present book, which I explain below. I say that I was *trying* to write the book: I had drawn up a detailed outline; I had even written a few thousand words. But I could not begin to write in earnest. I was stalled at the preliminary stage of thinking, planning, taking notes, and composing paragraphs or sections here and there, more or less at random. One can infer from the title that Melville was central to my project, but also that I had not thought to structure the book around a reading of *Moby-Dick*. And here the second book is relevant—a chapter-by-chapter commentary on *Moby-Dick* I happened across one day by accident. It did not occur to me then that the book might be relevant to my own work, at least not directly. I simply wanted to read it, as I want to read most every book on Melville in general and *Moby-Dick* in particular. Unfortunately, I didn't much like it. The title led one to expect a deep dive into Melville's mind, but the book really only skimmed the surface. Moreover, the chapters often had little or no connection to the deepest layers of the content of the corresponding chapters of the novel, nor did they hang together to form an overarching account, story, or portrait of either Melville's masterpiece or the man himself. *Moby-Dick* is a profoundly philosophical work, but the author of the commentary seemed determined to discuss everything but the philosophical substance of the novel. So one afternoon as I was reading the book and brooding on my disappointment, not long after exploring the idea of dropping Michelangelo from my own book to concentrate exclusively on Plato, Melville, and Nietzsche, it occurred to me that I could produce the book I'd been trying to write by adopting this format of a chapter-by-chapter commentary on *Moby-Dick*. I knew that Melville had read Plato's dialogues, the *Phaedo* in particular, also that he mentions Plato and the *Phaedo* explicitly in *Moby-Dick*, and alludes throughout the novel to themes in Platonic philosophy. I had moreover long been struck by his anticipation in *Moby-Dick* of elements of Nietzsche's philosophy, the death of God, for example, and the potentially nihilistic consequences of this event. Now everything fell into place. I could see my work laid out before my mind's eye, at least in its general contours. I began writing in earnest the following day and did not stop until I completed a draft six months later.

Regarding the substance of this book, I should state here at the start that it is not quite a straightforward commentary on *Moby-Dick*. Think of it as a series of reflections on the novel's philosophical content (also the philosophically relevant historical, spiritual, and mythological content), with something like an argument surfacing and sounding here and there throughout the length of the work. I say *something like* an argument because I employ the word in part as is standard in recent usage, according to which an argument is a sequence of statements or premises set out to support or justify a conclusion, but also in the somewhat more antiquated sense according to which an argument is the primary subject matter or theme of a discussion or story. As to the structure or form of my argument, it emerges gradually, a section here and there, in an order more suited to a digressive essay than to the concise formulation of a proof. Although I do intend to ground reasoned and reasonable assertions on actual facts, and thereby to elaborate an original new reading of *Moby-Dick*, my primary objective is to fashion a fresh image of the philosopher—or, really, to return to an image that I think more nearly resembles the original—by superimposing portraits of Plato, Melville, and Nietzsche—the thinkers themselves, their ideas and their lives—to produce a composite image through the overlaying and interblending of figures. And this brings me to the content of my argument, which has to do with the nature of philosophy and its relation to wisdom, and the relation of creative artistry to both. I develop this theme by situating these matters in the context of the history of philosophy conceived as the rise and fall of a certain influential variety of Platonism, which rise and fall we may characterize in Nietzschean terms as the life and death of God; and I explore all this with reference to the different reactions, as exemplified particularly by Melville and Nietzsche, to the nihilism that looms on the horizon of these intellectual and spiritual revolutions.

Since among all else that it is, this is a book about philosophy, I might have called it "Philosophy as *Moby-Dick*." The idea behind such a title would be to stress that one may practice philosophy legitimately through creative thinking and writing, that philosophy need not take the form of a meticulously logical treatise striving above all for clarity. The philosopher may explore and experiment with substance, style, and form precisely as Melville did when he conceived and composed *Moby-Dick*. Plato and Nietzsche are exemplary practitioners of this manner of creative philosophizing, and their positions in the philosophical canon are secure; and although I do not intend to make a case for including Melville in this canon, I do hope to persuade at least some readers that the broadly similar approach to philosophical activity as a practice infused with artistry, as exemplified in the lives and works of Plato, Melville, and Nietzsche, is not only serious but perhaps even superior to the constricted modes of professionalized thinking and writing that predominate today. This depends in part on taking philosophy seriously as the love of *wisdom*, rather than the love of *truth*, and so dissociating wisdom from truth to at least some extent, particularly from truth understood in accordance with the presuppositions of academic scholarship, modern logic, and a narrowly materialist science. But I shall have more to say about these matters in the body of the text. For now I add that I have written this book as an act of creative philosophizing, and I have tried to reflect the unconventional style and form of *Moby-Dick* in the book's tone and structure. To read this book aright, then, one should approach it as a work informed by scholarship but as on the whole an experimental endeavor, in short as a work of philosophy allied with art.

Finally, to restate concisely with a metaphor the substance of much that I have just written, the commentary form of this book is the warp through which I thread the weft of a selective history of philosophy, and the woven fabric of the whole is meant to display a portrait of the philosopher.

Extracts

"The unexamined life is not worth living."

Plato, Apology

"And yet self-knowledge is thought by some not so easy. Who knows … but for a time you may have taken yourself for somebody else? Stranger things have happened."

Melville, The Confidence-Man

"I am not yet able, in accord with the Delphic inscription, to know myself."

Plato, Phaedrus

"Active, successful natures do not act according to the maxim, 'know yourself,' but instead as if there hovered before them the command: *will* a self, and you *become* a self."

Nietzsche, Mixed Opinions and Maxims

"Those who philosophize correctly are training to die."

Plato, Phaedo

"All that philosophers have handled for thousands of years have been concept-mummies; nothing real escaped their grasp alive."

Nietzsche, Twilight of the Idols

"Death, though in a worm, is majestic; while life, though in a king, is contemptible. So talk not against mummies. It is part of my mission to teach mankind a due reverence for mummies."

Melville, The Confidence-Man

"Plato, I think, was sick."

Plato, Phaedo

"A sick philosopher is incurable."

Melville, *The Confidence-Man*

"And as for my long sickness, do I not owe it indescribably more than I owe to my health? I owe it a *higher* health—one which is made stronger by whatever does not kill it. *I also owe my philosophy to it.*"

Nietzsche, *Nietzsche Contra Wagner*

"Those who are not sham but real philosophers, looking down from above on the life of those below, and who seem to some to be of no value but to others to be worth everything, sometimes they appear to be sophists, sometimes statesmen, and sometimes they might give to some the impression that they are mad."

Plato, *Sophist*

"Oh, this mad old fool of a wisdom!"

Nietzsche, *Thus Spoke Zarathustra*

"Life is not by square and line: / Wisdom's stupid without folly."

Melville, *Clarel*

"For folly's sake, wisdom is mixed in with all things."

Nietzsche, *Thus Spoke Zarathustra*

"Nor was his philosophy to be despised; it abounded in wisdom."

Melville, *White-Jacket*

"If the things I say happen to be true, it is noble to believe them."

Socrates, in Plato's *Phaedo*

"But truth is ever incoherent."

Melville, in a letter to Hawthorne

Moby-Dick as Philosophy

"Nothing is true, all is permitted."

Zarathustra's shadow, in *Thus Spoke Zarathustra*

"Philosopher, probe not too deep. All you say is very fine, but very dark."

Melville, *Mardi*

"This experience of wondering is particularly characteristic of the philosopher, for there is no other source of philosophy than this."

Plato, *Theaetetus*

"Profound aversion to reposing once and for all in any one total view of the world. Fascination of the opposing point of view: refusal to be deprived of the stimulus of the enigmatic."

Nietzsche, *The Will to Power*

"Common consistency implies unchangeableness; but much of the wisdom here below lives in a state of transition."

Melville, *Mardi*

"And you shall learn solely in order to create."

Nietzsche, *Thus Spoke Zarathustra*

"In a written discourse on any subject there is necessarily much play."

Plato, *Phaedrus*

"No man can read a fine author, and relish him to his very bones, while he reads, without subsequently fancying to himself some ideal image of the man and his mind. And if you rightly look for it, you will almost always find that the author himself has somewhere furnished you with his own picture."

Melville, "Hawthorne and His Mosses"

"And so I tell my life to myself."

Nietzsche, *Ecce Homo*

vi

Moby-Dick as Philosophy

Chapter 1: Loomings

This first chapter provides an introduction to Ishmael, narrator of *Moby-Dick*. We learn about the man as much through our encounter with his perspective on the world as through the autobiographical details he chooses to share. We learn, for example, that he was in despair when he went to sea—certainly he was full of "spleen," and he may well have been suicidal. But we learn also that he is in high spirits and good humor when relating the story of all that he experienced there. Ishmael as narrator exhibits tendencies of mood and mind more vigorous, playful, and life-affirming than the dreamy but morose intellectuality of Ishmael as sailor. The existential transformation indicated by this contrast, unexpressed but always on display, is the secret heart of *Moby-Dick*. It is also the aspiration of the philosopher. Pre-philosophical man abides in peaceful harmony with his gods and the world around him. The philosopher is an exile from this Eden, and seeking a way to return, he is somber and agitated. The sage, though still a harborless wanderer, has attained to a state of playful serenity. Ishmael as sailor represents a certain type of philosopher; as narrator he is wise; and his story provides an account of his transformation from melancholy philosopher to joyful sage. But Ishmael's story is not just his own: his story is the medium through which Melville relates his own story, for Ishmael is an expression of Melville's higher self, and *Moby-Dick* as a whole is Melville's intellectual-spiritual autobiography projected in prose as a symbolical self-portrait.

Melville was throughout his life preoccupied by those barbed enigmas that Dostoevsky refers to as the *accursed questions*, and in his greatest work he disports with them like a man well accustomed to playing what Nietzsche calls the *wicked* game. Divinity or atheism? Morality or immoralism? Knowledge or skepticism? Purpose and meaning or nihilism? Hope or despair? Melville, who liked to refer to himself as "a pondering man," has left us in his *Moby-Dick* a record of his youthful wanderings through the labyrinth of these questions. The novel is a portrait in words of the cosmic and microcosmic mystery that Ishmael calls "the ungraspable phantom of life." That we ourselves, as reflected within and to ourselves, are this phantom—this is indeed, as Ishmael says, "the key to it all." Unfortunately, it is a key of alien design; we have no idea what use to make of it.

Melville understood this all-too-human condition of troubled wonderment; its darkness drew him in, seduced him. His Ishmael describes himself as "tormented with an everlasting itch for things remote." He "love[s] to sail forbidden seas," and he is drawn to "a horror" as to a potential friend. Through these words we catch a glimpse of Melville himself as reflected in his artist's mirror. It is an image his friend Nathaniel Hawthorne once captured by portraying Melville as obsessed intellectually with "everything that lies beyond human ken." And when we read Melville's letter inviting Hawthorne to his home for another bout of "heroic" drinking and "ontological heroics," we experience something of the Ishmaelean exuberance that characterized him at the height of his intellectual and creative powers. Melville probed the gloomiest of depths with a spirit enkindled by the sun. He asked the accursed questions without regarding them *as* accursed, which is to say without suffering from them.

Melville himself does not employ the expression "accursed questions," preferring instead a formulation borrowed from Milton's *Paradise Lost*: "Fixed Fate, Free-will, and foreknowledge absolute." But as these were matters discussed by Satan's infernal legion of fallen angels, they are in a sense accursed. Like his Ishmael, Melville believed every man is buffeted by the "universal thump" that began its rounds against us humans as punishment for the primordial error committed by "the two orchard thieves." The struggle is unavoidable, and whether it emanates from divine decree, cosmic law, or natural causal processes, we must submit. Yet taking a lesson from "Seneca and the Stoics," we may learn to "grin and bear it." Or taking a lesson from Ishmael and Melville, we may learn to do even more—we may learn to *affirm* our destiny. Ishmael knows that "those stage managers, the Fates," are responsible for his adventure on the sea, and that in this instance any notion of "unbiased free will and discriminating judgment" is only a "delusion." Yet in his telling we sense no brooding feelings of helplessness or resentment. In even his lowest moments Ishmael expresses nothing baser than a good-natured ironic detachment; at his best he exhibits a form of Dionysian cheerfulness. Nietzsche calls this *amor fati*, love of fate; and a similar idea appears in Plato as well, expressed at times through his accounts of reincarnation, or through his depiction in the *Republic* of Odysseus in the after-world "well-pleased" to select a quiet life from among the lots of lives made available by the Fates, a "life to which he will be joined by necessity." By thinking on fate Melville was led into every philosophical abyss, but he was not darkened by his deep surroundings. He coruscates when exploring the murky fundaments of the world.

Democritus of Abdera insisted that "truth is in the deep." Whether or not we can make sense of the canonical notion of truth as correspondence to reality, and perhaps especially if we can *not* make sense of it, Democritus would seem to have been onto something that Melville also felt. Best thoughts are *deep* thoughts. Melville's intuition is manifest in his reflections on the propensity of every "metaphysical professor" to seek out a lake or stream when set to wandering in the appropriate landscape. "Meditation and water," Ishmael says, "are wedded for ever." Plato and Nietzsche would likely agree. Plato set his greatest work, the *Republic*, in the harbor town of Peiraias, his *Phaedrus* on the banks of the flowing Ilisos. Nietzsche loved to walk and think with "mountains for company, but not dead ones, mountains with *eyes* (that is, with lakes)"; and his Zarathustra insists that "everything is in the sea." Whatever precisely this word "truth" might signify, only those who *dive* may hope to learn.

Plato, Melville, and Nietzsche loved to dive. Their deepest soundings were expressions of their lives as creative pondering men who seek in the depths an undersea route to a mountain on whose peak one stands no longer as an agitated or melancholy philosopher, but rather as the possessor of a joyful wisdom, *la gaya scienza*—as, in short, a Zarathustran sage.

Chapter 2: The Carpet-Bag

Like the greatest of Plato's and Nietzsche's works, *Moby-Dick* addresses many subjects simultaneously. And like Plato's *Phaedo* and Nietzsche's *Thus Spoke Zarathustra*, it is at least in part concerned with life after death—not, however, in the traditional sense of this expression. Nietzsche's afterlife is not really *after* at all; it is rather a repetition of one's present life, identical in every detail, including its temporal properties. Life eternally recurs, *ad infinitum* in the past and future alike. Plato for his part describes in several dialogues an otherworldly scheme of reincarnation, but the most philosophical elements of the *Phaedo* in particular deal with a *living imitation* of death, with philosophy as "training for death." By death Plato means the separation of the soul from the body, and the philosopher while alive engages in a similar separation, striving through a process called "purification" (*katharsis* in the Greek) to transcend mundane intellectuality into metaphysical wisdom. This is Plato's philosophical reformulation of those ancient Greek mystery rites that centered on spiritual-psychic descents into the underworld. As his Socrates stresses throughout the *Phaedo*, the living philosopher sojourns in Hades by separating his higher from his lower self through purification, dying to the world as experienced by his superficial corporeal elements.

Ishmael descends into the underworld himself. In the present chapter he arrives in New Bedford, Massachusetts, with the intention to travel from there to Nantucket, the original home of American whaling. But the cunning "springs and motives" set in action by the Fates, as described in the previous chapter, conspire to detain him in the town: the ferry on which he had planned to sail has already left for the island. He was correct as to his "destined port"—he will make his way to Nantucket—but he mistook for an inconsequential transit point a town in which he will make a friend fated through death to save his life.

Melville describes New Bedford in terms calculated to evoke the most primal of images and moods: here is Tyre of the mysterious ancient East, there the "aboriginal … Red-Men" pursuing their prey, the prodigious Leviathan. We glimpse dim figures moving in the mist, shadows of ominous significance later revealed to be emissaries of hell. Ishmael himself is hardly more than a living shade: having little money and wrapped in tattered clothes, he avoids the few refined establishments and makes his way down "dreary streets" alone, wading deeper and deeper into "blocks of blackness," drifting through deserted precincts where the occasional flicker of illumination appears to his funereal mind "a candle moving about in a tomb."

Eventually Ishmael comes upon an open door. Crossing the threshold he steps into a haze of dimly illuminated swirling smoke. If he entered expecting succor or solace, his hopes are immediately dashed. He topples over an ash-box and imagines its unsettled contents the detritus of Gomorrah in smoldering ruins. And upon stepping through an interior door he finds himself in the midst of a hellish black-mass, an "Angel of Doom" at the pulpit sermonizing on "the blackness of darkness, and the weeping and wailing and teeth-gnashing there."

Withdrawing from the infernal hall, Ishmael steps once again into the enshrouding veil of night. He makes his way toward the docks and arrives at a building that strikes him as potentially suitable, even though its condition is such that he imagines it having been "carted here from the ruins of some burnt district." This is the Spouter-Inn, and the proprietor is identified ominously as Peter Coffin. Ishmael knows that the surname is common in the area, yet he cannot ignore its morbid connotations. Immediately he thinks of death. He sees a freezing vagabond and thinks of Lazarus and Dives, the destitute man who at death ascends to heaven and the rich man who descends into hell. He recalls the story of Saint Paul as a prisoner on a ship bound for Rome, tossed about by high winds and tempestuous seas. He imagines his own body the house of his self or soul, his eyes the windows glazed by death. Considered together these images recall Plato's Pythagorean account in the *Phaedo* of the body encasing the soul like a prison-house, from which the true philosopher endeavors to liberate himself through a living enactment of death, which is to say through the activity of intellect independent of the seductions of bodily pleasure and the manifold deceptions of the senses.

As we shall see, later in the novel Ishmael dies before his death, and in the end he is saved for life by an accessory of death, a coffin ascending from the depths of the sea. Ishmael's life is a training for death, a living enactment of death and rebirth by way of various mystical sympathies. The relevant differences in this regard between *Moby-Dick* and the *Phaedo* stem from Melville's idiosyncratic philosophical perspective, which is characterized by an overlay of proto-Nietzschean, inverted-Platonic elements. Ishmael separates his soul from his body, if not by communing with metaphysical truth, then at least by transforming every surface reality into material for the exploration of deep and ever deeper strata of thought. And if his soul does not undergo a Platonic transmigration from one corporeal incarnation to another, we may nevertheless say of him, as Nietzsche used to say of himself, that some men are born posthumously.

Chapter 3: The Spouter-Inn

Recall Ishmael's earlier boast that he can be social with a horror. To this he had added that it's good to befriend "all the inmates of the place one lodges in." Here then is Ishmael lodging in Hades, and more specifically in a low, darkened chamber therein. We should not be surprised, then, if he encounters demons. Nor should we start, given his earlier remarks, if he makes a bosom friend of a particularly frightful denizen of this underworld.

Immediately on entering Mr. Coffin's establishment, Ishmael encounters a mysterious painting. His description of the canvas, and his various attempts to identify the subject and comprehend "its purpose," provide Melville the occasion to limn the perspective through which his Ishmael regards the universe around and within him. His first thought is that the work descends from the era of the Salem witches, and that the artist has endeavored to depict "chaos bewitched." A deep word, "chaos." It first appears in western literature as the name of a primordial deity-element in Hesiod's *Theogony*, a genealogical account of the origins of the gods and the universe composed by the Boeotian shepherd-poet early in the archaic period, sometime around 700 BCE. In Hesiod's telling Chaos is the originary principle, ontologically primary, the fact of facts from which Darkness and Night are born. Only then does Day appear, itself the offspring of Night. Appearing with Chaos are Gaia, or Earth, and Tartarus, the Underworld, settled deep within Gaia's bowels. Earth engenders Ouranos, the spangled sky above, which in turn produces the Sea and Ocean, Ishmael's own domain. Notice that the heavenly things descend from the chthonic, the light from the bewitched and bewitching dark.

The thought that the painting at issue does in fact represent chaos bewitched, though a "wild" surmise, appeals to Ishmael. Still, he conjures other possibilities as well. Perhaps, he speculates, it is the wind-whipped Black Sea, or a wintry Hyperborean landscape. On the far shores of the Black Sea there once was an oriental Salem of sorts, Colchis, birthplace of the sorceress Medea. Smitten with Jason, whom she helped to seize the Golden Fleece, Medea fled her home and royal father, a wizard himself, aboard the famous Argo. She dismembered her brother and tossed his limbs in the sea to delay her father's pursuit, and wherever she went thereafter, from Iolcus to Corinth, she left in her wake pools of blood as fathers and children succumbed to her spells or her blade. The regions around the Black Sea fascinated the Greeks, and many regarded the area as mysterious, mystical, and terrifying, a suitable setting for ghost stories and tragedies. Similarly enigmatic and enthralling was Hyperborea, where, according to Melville in *Pierre*, "a mind fitted by nature for profound and fearless thought" will see all things "in a dubious, uncertain, and refracting light." And "viewed through that rarefied atmosphere the most immemorially admitted maxims of men begin to slide and fluctuate, and finally become wholly inverted." Melville was himself familiar with such shifting realms of thought, hence his proto-Nietzschean tendencies toward an inverted-Platonism. "Neither by land nor by sea will you find the way to the Hyperboreans," Nietzsche writes in *The*

Antichrist, quoting Pindar, a Boeotian poet like Hesiod; and he adds that Hyperborea is situated beyond the realm of death. He omits the association with Apollo, who wintered there annually. While the god was away, Dionysus took his place at Delphi, navel of the earth and site of Apollo's Pythian oracle. Two maidens from Hyperborea were said to be interred on the island of Apollo's birth, Delos, site of a festival celebrated in his honor. Socrates' execution was delayed while an Athenian embassy was away at this festival, during which time the city by law was to be purified, which process included a prohibition against executions. During this interval Socrates met often with his friends, conversing for example on philosophy as training for death through purification as recorded in Plato's *Phaedo*.

In the *Phaedo* Socrates reports that as a young man he was keen on those ideas that today we classify as Presocratic natural philosophy. From this tradition descends the teaching that the world is composed of earth, water, air, and fire, to which Ishmael alludes when he construes the scene on the enigmatic painting as "the unnatural combat of the four primal elements." The first man to articulate the doctrine of four elements was the Sicilian Greek Empedocles, who besides being a philosopher was also a poet, physician, and prophet. He was, moreover, as he states in his mystifying verses, a *daimôn*, a divine spirit, whose corporeal nature is punishment for the shedding of blood, a Pythagorean notion that appears at least implicitly in the *Phaedo*. Empedocles' elements do indeed engage in a kind of combat, for although at times they are brought together as one by the cosmic force of Love, during another stage in the cycling of the universe the power of Eris, or Strife, dominates, and then the elements transition from a singular state of pure unity to an extreme phase of multiplicity.

But eventually Ishmael abandons these and other interpretations for the theory that the painting portrays an enormous whale suspended in the sky above a dismasted vessel, captured by the artist in a moment just prior to its immolation on the pikes that remain of the ship's three shattered masts. One thinks of a triptych of men on the skull of Golgotha. One thinks, in a word, of death.

The Spouter-Inn is heavy with mementos of death, its walls bedecked with "a heathenish array of monstrous clubs and spears." The bar is situated within the capacious jawbone of a whale, and the wizened old barman operating there appears "another cursed Jonah." The landlord, Mr. Coffin, laughs "diabolically" and frightens Ishmael with intimations of a dreadful secret knowledge—something to do with the man he intends for Ishmael's roommate roaming the night attempting to sell his head. Having arranged to bunk these two strangers in the same quarters, Coffin is also an instrument of fate, for he introduces Ishmael to the pagan harpooner Queequeg, a man Ishmael regards at first sight as an "abominable savage," an "infernal head-peddler," and maybe "the devil himself."

Queequeg is no devil, but he will serve Ishmael as a demon, which is to say as a *daimôn*, or spirit-guide, of the type that in the *Phaedo* leads the soul to which it has been assigned into the interior of Hades, taking most by way of the river Acheron, as Queequeg later sails with Ishmael from New Bedford to Nantucket by way of the river Acushnet. And as the *daimôn* then leads on to the place of judgment, from which the soul in its charge eventually returns to life by climbing out of the Acherousian lake, so Queequeg commissions the coffin later modified to serve as a life-preserver, onto which Ishmael climbs from out of the sea when at the end of the novel the *Pequod* "sink[s] to hell."

Chapter 4: The Counterpane

In the previous chapter I mentioned both the Delian festival in honor of Apollo and the sorceress Medea. We may bring these two together, and relate the pair to Plato's Hades-besotted *Phaedo*, by way of Ishmael's observation that the tattoos on Queequeg's arm resemble "an interminable Cretan labyrinth of a figure." The labyrinth calls to mind the fabled Athenian king, Theseus. When the Athenians participated in the celebrations on Delos they were honoring not just Apollo but Theseus too, Theseus whom Medea had once tried to murder. The interval of time during which the Athenians maintained in their city a state of ritual purity was, specifically, while a ship believed to be the very ship on which Theseus had sailed to Crete was away at the festival. This vessel was evidently quite old, and through the years its deteriorating planks had one by one been replaced. A certain type of philosopher puzzled over the problem whether this was in fact the same ship on which Theseus had sailed, or whether it had become a different and distinct individual due to its material components having been replaced, and if so, at what stage in its repairs and replacements it had changed. This may seem a pedantic debate, and it may well be; but it is bound up with serious questions concerning the effects wrought by change on identity: must every apparent island of Being eventually erode and melt away into the surrounding sea of Becoming?

In any case, to tell the story of Theseus's voyage to Crete we must go back to the founding of Knossos, a city just inland from the island's north-eastern coast. There was once a quarrel among rivals to determine the rightful ruler of Knossos. One of these men, Minos, was a son of Zeus, Zeus who in the form of a white bull had kidnapped and coupled with the Phoenician Europa. Minos claimed the throne on the grounds that he was dear to the gods, Poseidon in particular, and to confirm his credentials he prayed to Poseidon for a bull, vowing to offer it up as sacrifice in the god's honor. Suddenly there appeared an unblemished white bull, shambling onto the beach from the waves of the sea. Minos thus secured for himself the throne, but he sacrificed to Poseidon an inferior bull and retained the bull from the sea for himself. Poseidon was enraged, and for retribution he induced Minos's wife, Pasiphaë, to fall in love with the beautiful white beast. Daedalus, the famed engineer-craftsman, and ancestor of Socrates, constructed for the queen a hollow wooden cow, which she entered and thereby mated with the bull who when mounting and penetrating the artificial animal penetrated Pasiphaë as well. The offspring of this unholy act was the Minotaur, a creature with a man's body and the head of a bull. Minos, appalled, compelled Daedalus to erect a labyrinth in which to imprison the monster, and after one of his sons fell dead while visiting Athens, he forced the city annually to dispatch to Crete seven maidens and seven young boys whom he shut inside the labyrinth for the Minotaur to kill and consume.

Theseus finally put an end to this barbaric ritual. He was the son of the Athenian king Aegeus, born in Troezen in the Peloponnese to Aethra, with whom Aegeus lay one night before returning to his realm unaware that he had engendered a child. When as a young man at his mother's direction Theseus made his way to his father's territory, he encountered Medea in the royal house. She had taken flight from Corinth—literally taken flight, in a chariot pulled by winged dragons—after murdering the king's daughter and her own children, and having settled in Athens as consort of Aegeus, she had borne the king a son. Witch that she was, Medea recognized Theseus upon his arrival, and desiring to reserve the throne for her own young son, she attempted to poison him. When she failed at this and other of her murderous schemes, and after Aegeus finally recognized Theseus as his own, Medea fled Athens to return to her original eastern haunts. Young Theseus later persuaded his father to send him to Crete as one of the seven sacrificial victims, and there he confronted and killed the Minotaur. He succeeded with the assistance of Minos's daughter Ariadne, who had fallen for the handsome young prince. Ariadne forsook her home and family for Theseus, but after their escape from Crete he abandoned her on the island of Naxos. Later she met and married Dionysus. Theseus meanwhile had sailed on to Delos where he celebrated his success with a dance called the Crane. Hence his role in the Delian festival, and hence the Athenian ritual whose purificatory deferral of executions preserved Socrates long enough to discuss philosophy as training for death.

It is fitting that Plato mentions Theseus in the *Phaedo*, not only as a link in the chain of causes that resulted in the delay of Socrates' execution, but also because Theseus himself descended to the underworld while alive. He travelled with a friend who intended to kidnap Persephone, queen of the dead, but the pair sat down in chairs from which they could not stand up again. Theseus was rescued by Heracles, who made his own descent into Hades and was thereby associated with the mystery cult at Eleusis, which centered on Demeter and Persephone. Throughout the early sections of the *Phaedo* Plato alludes to a variety of otherworldly, underworldly, obscure, and irrational events and ideas that taken together cast the discussion at the heart of the work in a primal, murky, and darkly mystical intellectual-psychological atmosphere. Melville has done something similar with *Moby-Dick*. Plato's dialogue is not just a series of proofs of the immortality of the soul; it rather resembles a labyrinth itself, a philosophical-spiritual labyrinth though which initiates ritually pass on their way to joining a Platonic mystery cult whose members are as intimate with dark obscurities as with bright truths. And Melville's novel is no mundane whaling adventure, however exciting; it is instead an investigation into, and a rumination on, the possibility of discovering philosophical heights submerged beneath abysmal depths.

Chapter 5: Breakfast

In the chapters in which he introduces Queequeg, Ishmael makes a point of indicating not only the man's eccentric customs and habits, but also his own psychological and intellectual reactions to them. To label Ishmael a relativist would, I think, be inaccurate; but it might be fair to say that his mind is marked by relativistic tendencies. Melville of course is himself the source of these tendencies, not just in the obvious sense as creator of his protagonist, but more significantly as the intellect that projected and formed Ishmael after the fashion of its own philosophical predilections. And since Melville the man traced in his life a fascinating intellectual-existential trajectory whose course forms part of the theme of this book, it may be of use at this early stage to remark on these matters in some detail.

When Ishmael first lays eyes on Queequeg, as reported in the chapter "The Spouter-Inn," he is terrified of the man. He regards him initially as a diabolical savage, and considering his hawking of shrunken heads, Ishmael fears that he may even be a cannibal. Near the end of the chapter Ishmael describes the "queer proceedings" in which Queequeg engages with a small religious icon, a ritual he is uncomfortable witnessing. Placing the little "Congo idol" in the fireplace, Queequeg lights a sacrificial fire and offers the diminutive figure a biscuit, chanting all the while and distorting his face with strange expressions. Similarly, if more trivially, in "The Counterpane" Ishmael relates Queequeg's unusual manner of bathing, shaving, and dressing, and he adds in the present chapter details as to Queequeg's surprising comportment at table and suggests, moreover, that the man regularly exhibits other "peculiarities" of behavior.

As disturbed as he is upon first hearing tell of and then later encountering Queequeg in person, Ishmael soon grows fond of the man. And to anticipate briefly an episode I consider at length in a later chapter, he even assists Queequeg during the performance of his pagan ritual with his little idol. In his own words, he decides to "turn idolator" himself. Ishmael, then, is broad-minded, or anyway he becomes so through his friendship with Queequeg. Melville had developed his own open mind well before writing *Moby-Dick*, in large part through his activities as a sailor who, by putting in at a variety of exotic locales, harvested a full share of uncommon experiences, some delightful, some terrifying, very few of them available to the average nineteenth-century American youth.

Despite what I have called Ishmael's relativistic tendencies, like Melville he is at some level an objectivist, which is to say that he regards truth as existing independently of the human mind. Beliefs, customs, and traditions depend on personal subjectivities, but objectivism has to do with the source of *truth*, not the source of humans' *beliefs about* the truth. Similarly, relativism is *not* the doctrine that different individuals or cultures have different beliefs

13

about, say, reality or morality, not even if we add that resolution of these differences is difficult or even impossible. This is but a mundane observation concerning human psychology and sociology. Philosophically serious relativism, like serious objectivism, has to do with the truth, truth itself, not our opinions about or perspectives on the truth. The relativist believes that truth is relative to an individual or a culture, that whether there is a truth about this or that matter and, if so, what that truth is, depends on individual or cultural subjectivity, and by "depends on" the relativist means "is generated by." When Protagoras proclaims that "man is the measure of all things," he does not mean only that it takes a human consciousness to perform a measurement, which is just another straightforward empirical observation, hardly worthy of philosophical reflection or debate. No, Protagoras means that man is the measure as *standard*, and his point is that man brings truth into being and gives it its form, literally makes it to be, and makes it be as it is.

I have said that Ishmael and Melville were objectivists *at some level*. I qualify the claim because the epistemological position that exercised the most influence on their worldviews is not objectivism but skepticism. Skepticism, notoriously, may follow from an objectivist realism, for the fact—assuming that it is a fact—that truth is "out there" independently of our minds raises the question whether we can ever make cognitive contact with it. It has seemed to many philosophers that we can know the contents of our minds directly and without mediation, but that our contact with the world beyond our minds is mediated by our perceptual and cognitive systems, which of course raises the question whether these media reveal their objects without addition or distortion. Many philosophers have insisted that our senses and minds do indeed alter external reality in the process of internalizing and transforming it into experience, sometimes radically. Immanuel Kant, for example, argued that the spatial and temporal properties that most every previous philosopher had taken for objective features of external objects are in fact products of our own mental apparatus. According to his version of Transcendental Idealism, all we can say of the external world with certainty is that it exists. But its nature in itself apart from its manifestation as appearance to us—of this we have no idea. The character of the world is a variable (x) whose value we do not, and *cannot*, know. In order to identify external reality as it is in itself we would have to step outside the filtering mechanisms of our own minds, but in this condition we could not perform mental acts such as identification.

Although Kant developed his epistemology in order to determine the limits of reason, and thereby to secure certain knowledge to at least some extent, a good many philosophers elaborated his conclusions in radically skeptical directions. Melville did, as did Nietzsche after him. We know that Melville on his voyage to London in 1849, not long after he first read the *Phaedo*, and not long before he started work on *Moby-Dick*, met George Adler, a professor of German literature with an interest in philosophy who was, according to Melville, "full of the German metaphysics, & discourses of Kant." In company aboard ship the two "talked metaphysics continually, & Hegel, Schlegel, Kant &c were discussed under the influence of the whiskey." For some time on shore they maintained their association and on several occasions "talked high German metaphysics" together. So Melville likely believed in something like "truth," or "reality," but as to its nature, it appears that a combination of natural psychological inclination, life experience, and acquaintance with German idealist metaphysics led him to adopt a complex attitude that for now as a first approximation we may refer to as skeptical.

Chapter 6: The Street

In this chapter Ishmael sees New Bedford for the first time in the sunlight. It is a respite from the hellish gloom and the stink of death through which he has moved so far. The world is bright; Ishmael is invigorated.

In the previous chapter I noted the relativistic tendencies of Ishmael-Melville's mind, but I also insisted that his predominate epistemological attitude is akin to skepticism. In this connection it will be useful to borrow Nietzsche's distinction between the skepticism of the weak mind, which can easily transition into a debilitating form of nihilism, and the healthy skepticism characteristic of the man who is more powerful than the intellectual and spiritual problems that beset him. I shall have more to say about nihilism, for in the years following *Moby-Dick* Melville seems to have suffered from a nihilistic condition. For now I treat the skepticism of his best period, the time of his life when he burned so bright internally that the obscure unknowns of the world, and even the chance that our most pressing questions are unanswerable, could not darken his mood.

Melville went to sea for the first time in the summer of 1839, but this was a relatively short passage to Liverpool and back. His real maritime adventures began in 1841, when at the age of twenty-one he set sail for the Pacific on a whaleship called *Acushnet*. He would not return for nearly four years, and while he was away he enjoyed a wildly adventurous life. To mention just a few of his more outrageous escapades: he deserted from the *Acushnet* on its arrival at the Marquesas Islands, and to ensure his escape he and a confederate tramped deep into the island's interior. The two young men were taken in by the Typee natives, a warrior-tribe of cannibals who were less than eager to see their guests depart. Yet Melville and his friend were not mistreated, and in fact before they began to fear for their own flesh, they thoroughly enjoyed themselves. Melville in particular spent many hours in the company of a captivating young girl whom he called Fayaway; they bathed together in pristine waters, Melville admiring her naked beauty and engaging with her in other more discrete amusements. By writing about this relationship in his first novel, *Typee*, which was a popular success, Melville became something of a sexualized celebrity—when Sophia Hawthorne met him many years later, this is the lens through which she first regarded him: she saw "Fayaway in his face." In any case, Melville eventually managed to escape his captors (his friend having previously fled) and sign onto another ship, but not long thereafter he participated in a mutiny and was punished with a stretch in a Tahitian calaboose. Once more he managed to escape, absconding by moonlight along with several others, and he made his way to Eimeo (or Moorea), where he spent time working, wandering, and beach-combing. He even made a few brazen attempts to meet the local queen. Eventually he enlisted in the American navy for the sole purpose of making the return voyage home.

As a young man at sea Melville encountered a bewildering plurality of exotic worlds and foreign worldviews, which resulted in his developing a facility for inhabiting multiple perspectives. He came to see through the social, cultural, and religious traditions into which he had been born by looking into native paganism in person. This enabled him to cultivate a broad-minded variety of skepticism. In popular usage the skeptic is often the unbeliever, the person who rejects some traditional doctrine and repudiates customary rituals or behaviors. The atheist, for example, is often regarded as a skeptic. But much of contemporary atheism is really just another form of small-mindedness. I intend the word "skepticism" in its ancient Pyrrhonian sense, according to which the skeptic is one who suspends judgment, withholds assent, rather than one who confidently adopts a dissenting judgment. Descending from the ancient Greek Pyrrho (late fourth to early third century BCE) and codified in the work of Sextus Empiricus (second or third century CE), Pyrrhonian skepticism consists at its core of a series of ten arguments, or "modes," intended to persuade us that knowledge is unobtainable and thereby to induce a state of *epochê*, or suspension of judgment. One of these modes, for example, appeals to differences among humans, in both body and soul (or mind), and noting that these differences produce different perceptions of the world, as well as different tastes and capacities, it suggests that we cannot determine which among the various humans is properly attuned to reality. Another mode makes the same point by noting differences between peoples with respect to their laws, customs, ways of life, beliefs, and dogmas. People the world over perceive and think about things in many divergent ways, which leads to their living and acting differently from one another too. Melville experienced this phenomenon directly, and it induced him to subject his own attitudes and assumptions to critical scrutiny. Who lives correctly, the staid New Englander or the carefree Polynesian? Who knows the truth, the Christian or the pagan? To which criterion might we appeal in order to answer such questions? The Pyrrhonian contends that since one can always meet the proposal of a criterion with a counter-proposal, we must withhold judgment even about the standards on which judgments themselves are based.

So just as the "astonishment" that Ishmael experiences upon first seeing "so outlandish an individual as Queequeg" dissipates during his morning promenade through New Bedford, where he witnesses a multitude of foreigners, many of them "savages outright," intermingling with the upstanding townsfolk, Melville too learned to regard the strange world we all inhabit with equanimity, or *ataraxia*, to use the term employed by the Pyrrhonians to indicate the state of mental tranquility at which they aimed as their ultimate end, the *telos* of their activities. And Melville's equanimity is the fact I want to stress here. To admit one's ignorance is no simple feat; to withhold judgment with respect to the deepest and most pressing of life's puzzles, and to do so without *suffering* from the lack of resolution, requires a condition of intellectual and spiritual vitality sufficient to beat back any threat of existential despair. In the years immediately leading up to and during which he wrote *Moby-Dick*, Melville enjoyed an abundance of this vitality rarely matched by any other thinker or artist. It empowered him to thrust into the blackness of the abyss of unknowing the light of his own joyful wisdom.

Chapter 7: The Chapel

The chapter begins with a return to the gloom from which Ishmael had enjoyed a relieving interval of light while strolling through New Bedford in the morning. The clouds descend, a harsh wind blows, and sleet and rain pummel him. Making his way through the town battered and soaking, he enters a chapel to whose walls are affixed marble plaques dedicated to the memories of whale-men lost at sea. Once again his thoughts turn toward death. He reflects as well, ironically and cynically, on traditional notions of the afterlife. But when the thought of his own death creeps over him—"Yes, Ishmael, the same fate may be thine"—then quite suddenly he returns to a "merry" mood. He is not overcome by a suicidal longing for non-existence, the prospect of which cheers him. Instead, his gloom is dispersed by Platonic ruminations on the nature of reality and the immortality of the soul.

We know that Melville was reading Plato around the time he wrote *Moby-Dick*, reading specifically Plato's dialogue on life and death, the *Phaedo*, for in a letter from the spring of 1849 he declares his intention to read the work that summer, and in *Moby-Dick* he mentions the *Phaedo* by name and alludes to several of its most distinctive ideas. For instance, when meditating on the subject of "Life and Death" in the present chapter, Ishmael remarks that "in looking at things spiritual, we are too much like oysters observing the sun through the water, and thinking that thick water the thinnest of air." The image derives directly from the *Phaedo*, which is set on the day that Socrates must drink his hemlock and die. Not long before drinking the poison, while discussing the afterlife with his friends, he insists that popular notions of the nature of reality are mistaken, "just as if someone dwelling in the midst of the depths of the sea should think he lived on its surface, and seeing the sun and the other stars through the water should judge the sea to be the sky."

This bipartite or two-level account of reality is the most distinctive feature of Platonism in general. The significance of the idea is evident in Plato's (and Melville's) analogy: we tend to believe that the material world is reality entire, but like the sea-dweller who manages to ascend to the surface, and peering out from the waves realizes that there is in fact a level of reality previously unknown to him, if we could but expand our minds we too would know that there is more to reality than the material spatial-temporal realm presented to us through our senses. Apart from the physical there is also metaphysical reality, and the metaphysical is more fully real, more knowable, and more valuable than the physical.

There is, then, at one level of reality, that which is, that which always is, that which really and simply is, or to put it another way, the eternal, non-composite, unchanging, and absolutely actual, thoroughly and purely real. Plato refers to this as τὸ ὄν, transliterated as *to on*, the *to* being the neuter singular definite article, or "the," the *on* being the neuter singular participle of the verb εἶναι (*einai*), which means "to be." The *on* by itself we could translate as the circumstantial participle "being," as in the two instances of this word in the previous sentence. But the addition of the definite article transforms the participle into a substantive, a word signifying something—some *thing*—that in its essence is characterized by being. We could translate this *to on* literally, but clumsily, as "the be-ing thing," but it is standard to prefer the formulations "what-is," "that-which-is," or, more simply, "being." Often, in order to bring out the broader and deeper metaphysical import of the expression in Plato's philosophy, the translation is capitalized, thus: Being.

Plato inherited this expression and something of the concept from Parmenides' τὸ ἐόν (*to eon*). In a poem of dactylic hexameter verse—Homer's meter—Parmenides argues that this *to eon*, this Being, is in some sense the one and only existent reality, and that it neither comes to be nor passes away, neither moves nor changes, nor has it any component parts. In short, ultimate reality is an eternal, unchanging, absolutely simple One. The only alternative to this Being would be Non-Being, but according to Parmenides what-is-not necessarily cannot be, nor can it be thought or spoken of. The contrast between Being and Non-Being is exhaustive, and since Non-Being, by definition as well as by fact, *is not*, there is and can be only Being, in the sense detailed above.

Although Plato inherited Parmenides' concept of Being, he rejected Parmenides' conclusion that there is only one *to on*. Plato postulates the existence of many eternal, unchanging, non-composite entities, essences existing independently and separately from the physical objects whose essences they are. These metaphysical essences are known to us as Platonic Forms. There is, for example, a singular metaphysical Form of Beauty over and above the many beautiful physical objects in the material world. These Forms are the objects of knowledge—they are not easy to know, but of every existing type of reality only the Forms are knowable.

Plato also rejected Parmenides' assumption that the only possible alternative to Being is the necessarily non-existent and un-thinkable Non-Being. In a dialogue known as the *Sophist* he develops at length an account of Non-Being as difference, as that which is not this or that, as opposed to what-is-not *simpliciter*. He seems to agree that what-is-not, conceived as absolute nothingness, is necessarily non-existent, but he carves out a conceptual space for that-which-is-not as that-which-is-not-*x*, for example that which is not even, is not round, or is not beautiful. With this he makes sense of the possibility of difference in our conception of the world; and as a thing may thus be conceived as being or becoming different not only from another thing, but even from itself, he makes sense as well of the possibility of change. And with change he is able to add a third category between Being and Non-Being, namely Becoming.

Becoming, γένεσις (*genesis*, as in the first book of the Old Testament, in which we read of the world *coming to be*), is the other aspect or level in Plato's bipartite account of reality. Becoming is that which both is and is not, is ephemeral, composite, changeable, and less than fully real. All that falls under the category of Becoming comes to be and passes away; at one time it is not, at a later time it is, and at a later time still it is not again. I say that at some time it is, by which I mean that it exists, but even as existent it never really fully *is*. As Plato puts it, as long as it exists, it continually rolls around between Being and Non-Being, which is to say that, for example, it is both tall and not-tall (as a man is tall compared to a grain of sand but short compared to a mountain), a double and not a double (as four stones are twice two but half of eight), or beautiful and not beautiful (beautiful to one person but not to another, or beautiful at one time but not at another). The realm of Becoming is the material world of particular physical objects, and since these particulars do not possess stable unchanging properties, they cannot be known; they are the objects of perception or belief.

It is impossible to say exactly how Plato understood this two-fold division of reality. Are we dealing with different levels of reality, different dimensions, different aspects, or different types of thing within one and the same reality? And if the latter, is this one and the same reality a spatial-temporal complex or something altogether different, of which space-time is itself only a part, aspect, or level? Plato himself may have changed his mind about these matters over the course of his long career; and even if we concentrate on a single dialogue it is not easy, perhaps not possible, to specify exactly what he had in mind. We may nevertheless summarize his distinction between Being and Becoming, as it has played out in the Platonic tradition, as a distinction between the metaphysical and the physical, placing on one side of this division such entities (if this word is not itself too confining) as the Platonic Forms, the One, God, the transcendent source of all things, and Soul, and on the other side particular objects, the many, man, the material world of objects, and all that is bodily. Being is necessary, independent, good, beautiful, and true. It is Reality. Becoming is contingent, dependent, a confused mixture of good and evil, beauty and ugliness, truth and falsehood. It is at best appearance; at worst it is an illusion through and through.

This two-level account of reality recurs in many of Plato's texts, in the *Phaedo*, as we have seen, but most famously in the so-called "Allegory of the Cave" in Book 7 of the *Republic*. Wherever it appears the message is the same: we humans tend to mistake the nature of reality. Caught up as we are in the physical world, the sensory information it floods us with, and the pleasures and pains with which it assails us, we are distracted and diverted from attaining insight into the truth. We require a "turning" of the soul away from Becoming toward Being. Only then will we know the True, behold the Beautiful, and do the Good.

Chapter 8: The Pulpit

This short chapter contains little more than a description of the pulpit employed by Father Mapple. This pulpit may well be sufficiently unusual to merit attention, but I focus on one of its features, and Ishmael's comment thereon, to add further details to the account of Platonism provided in the previous chapter. In that chapter I supplied some idea of one core feature of "Platonism in general," but here I elaborate on what I call *Phaedo*-Platonism, which we may think of as a development to extreme limits of certain elements within Platonism. This strand of Platonism has been extraordinarily influential on the western spiritual tradition, including the more spiritual varieties of philosophy, Plotinus's Neoplatonism in particular. When Nietzsche writes in the Preface to *Beyond Good and Evil* that "Christianity is Platonism for 'the people,'" he has what I call *Phaedo*-Platonism in mind.

Father Mapple's pulpit is constructed to resemble the prow of a ship so tall that he requires a ladder to mount its height. He employs a rope-ladder for the purpose, and upon entering the pulpit he draws the ladder up behind him so that he is isolated and unassailable within. Speculating as to the meaning of Mapple's act, Ishmael concludes that it "signifies his spiritual withdrawal ... from all outward worldly ties and connections." This notion of spiritual withdrawal from the world recalls Plato's account in the *Phaedo* of purification. The *Phaedo* is informed throughout by elements borrowed from the Pythagorean tradition, in particular the idea that the body is the prison of the soul, whose true home is the non-material metaphysical dimension of reality, what I have termed Being in the previous chapter. Suffering retribution for some ancient unspecified misdeed, human souls are condemned within recurring cycles of bodily birth, death, and rebirth, and only those who sufficiently purify themselves can hope one day to be freed from their bondage to the physical world. To achieve this release is finally to be liberated (the word *lusis*, deliverance, release, or liberation, recurs throughout the *Phaedo*) and to live in the future forever without a body.

This final release is attainable only at death, which is to say at the literal separation of the soul from the body, and only by the man who has attained the highest condition of purity. But the philosopher while alive engages in a sort of imitation of this separation—hence Plato's famous characterization of philosophy in the *Phaedo* as "training for death"—and this is philosophical purification. It is indeed a "spiritual withdrawal ... from all outward worldly ties," for it involves the withdrawal of the soul from the worldly concerns that rivet the bonds that shackle it to the material world. These worldly concerns include exaggerated desires for honor or wealth, food and drink, expensive clothes, or sex. The philosopher avoids excessive indulgences in such things, and he despises the pleasures that common men derive from them. The philosopher seeks wisdom, which, to the extent it is obtainable in this life, is available only by way of intellectual-spiritual communion with the metaphysical realm of Being; and the physical body with its worldly concerns only interferes with the search. Its pleasures and pains in particular impede the soul's progress toward purity. The philosopher, therefore, must direct his mind—intellectually, psychically, spiritually—toward true reality, must focus his attention at its deepest level on Being. But since Being is knowable by the mind alone, bodily distractions like pleasures and pains, desires and fears, are stumbling blocks the philosopher can avoid only by assiduously cultivating the mind and the things of the mind over the body and its things.

In the previous chapter I noted that the Platonic Forms are objects of knowledge, whereas material things are objects only of perception or belief. This is precisely the inverse of the way we moderns typically think about these matters. Influenced as we are by the assumptions of science (usually a naive understanding of science), we tend to regard physical objects and processes as knowable, and all that is metaphysical or supernatural as, at best, a matter of "faith." Some go further and insist that nothing metaphysical exists at all, that only physical things are real. The former, epistemological, position is known as empiricism—all knowledge is acquired by way of sensory experience. The latter, ontological, position is known as materialism—only material things, the sort of things accessible by sensory experience, exist. These two positions taken together constitute the core of "scientism," which amounts in short to the claims that science alone generates knowledge, and that the realm of the real is exhausted by the actual and possible objects of scientific knowledge. In the *Phaedo* Plato implicitly rejects scientism by explicitly rejecting empiricism and materialism, and in fact he equates the pair with the hatred of reason. The modern worldview, then, which prides itself on its commitment to reason, Plato condemns as anti-rational for its empiricist epistemology and materialist ontology. He labels the doctrine the basest of base things.

Since according to Plato the objects of knowledge are metaphysical entities inaccessible to our senses, the Platonic philosopher seeks knowledge by way of the mind, or soul, alone. His disregard of the senses is his release from the bonds of the body, and this is the central feature of purification. So the Platonic philosopher spiritually withdraws by identifying himself with the soul gathered up alone by itself, just like Father Mapple alone on high in the perch of his pulpit temporarily delivered from the ties that bind men to the world.

Chapter 9: The Sermon

This chapter records Father Mapple's sermon on Jonah and the whale, in which the attentive reader may detect images and ideas reminiscent of Platonic purification. Father Mapple remarks, for example, on the difficulty of disobeying ourselves in order to obey God, which recalls Plato's contrast between the body and soul, and the soul's tendency to be alienated from itself by the lures of the body. He also describes Jonah as confined in the "prison" of the whale and praying for "deliverance," which recalls Plato's notion that the soul is imprisoned in the body and striving for deliverance (*lusis*) though purification. I shall have more to say about purification and *Phaedo*-Platonism throughout the course of this book; but in this present chapter, although I continue to focus on Plato, I base my account on Father Mapple's sermon as an example of the use of stories, or myths, to communicate ideas, which provides the opportunity to move away for the moment from the consideration of Platonism as philosophical doctrine to focus instead on Plato the man as a philosopher.

In the previous two chapters I have provided preliminary sketches of philosophical Platonism, both as a general phenomenon and in the more specialized version that I have called *Phaedo*-Platonism. It is worth noting at this point that it is not at all clear that Plato was confidently committed to any of the ideas that have come down to us under his name. Of course he was most likely the author of those dialogues that scholars agree in attributing to him, and maybe even of two or three others about which there is still some disagreement—I do not mean to deny any of this. I intend rather to stress the fact of Plato's writing *dialogues* rather than treatises. Given his choice of genre, we can no more read his personal beliefs off the page than we can Shakespeare's. We do not know what either man believed about this or that specific subject because he nowhere tells us in his own voice. We know the context in which Plato chose to situate his thinking about particular matters; we know the range of ideas he judged it worthwhile to bring into association; we can identify in general terms positions that recur throughout his corpus, for example that the soul is superior to the body, or that antinomianism and atheism are socially and politically pernicious. But despite all that we can say along these lines, we are unable to determine with any specificity which ideas Plato would have admitted to accepting and positively advocating, and which he would have outright rejected. This is so not only because he wrote dialogues, but also because his career as an author spanned nearly fifty years, a period during which a man might change his mind about any number of things; and, indeed, the dialogues taken as a whole have appeared to many careful scholars to manifest several inconsistencies, which some have taken as evidence that Plato did indeed change his mind, that his thinking developed over the years (from which this position is known as "developmentalism").

Why would Plato choose to communicate his ideas this way? Was it perhaps a deliberate choice *not* to communicate, not directly or frankly anyway? There is evidence that goes back to Aristotle, who studied in Plato's Academy under the master for almost twenty years, that Plato taught "unwritten doctrines," so perhaps after all Plato did not intend to express his final beliefs in his written works. Or is it rather that Plato *does* speak his mind in his works, but that his mind just is not what we have come to expect of the mind of a philosopher? We expect a philosopher, like Aristotle among the ancients or Bertrand Russell more recently, to adopt positions, to specify these positions precisely and explain them thoroughly and clearly, and to defend them with arguments while rebutting rival positions with counter-arguments. Plato's dialogues often include such features (not always, but often), but they come from the mouths of characters rather than in Plato's own voice. At times, moreover, Plato goes out of his way to distance himself from the ideas in a work, as for example in the *Symposium* when he attributes the ideas usually taken as the philosophical core of the work to a woman named Diotima, whose conversation with Socrates was reported by the philosopher to the guests at a drinking party at which Aristodemus was present, and he, Aristodemus, related the speech to Apollodorus, who in the *Symposium* reports the speech to an unnamed interlocutor and thereby also to us, the readers. So Plato intentionally places himself at four removes from the central ideas of the dialogue, as Melville is at three removes from Father Mapple's sermon as reported by Ishmael. What can this mean? I do not intend to imply that Plato regarded the ideas he attributes to Diotima as fiction. He may very well have accepted them, or ideas similar to them, as fact. His style of writing suggests to me, however, that he was concerned with more than just the explicitly expressed ideas, that he intended by way of his form to communicate a different sort of content, this content having to do not with philosophical doctrine but rather with the proper activity of the philosopher. It seems to me that Plato was not a philosopher according to the model to which we are accustomed. He was rather a type that I have elsewhere called a thinker-artist, which for now I define in brief as a creative writer and experimental thinker whose preferred artistic medium is prose and whose preferred subject matter is the discipline we refer to as philosophy. He may well have been a sage who, like other wise men, communicates not through reason rigidly defined but rather through the composition of poems and the writing of laws. The dialogues are prose-poems of a sort, and through them

Plato establishes laws in the Nietzschean sense; and in his last long dialogue, the *Laws*, he actually elaborates a legal code.

This brings us back to Father Mapple's sermon on Jonah and the whale, and the enterprise of communicating ideas indirectly through stories. Early in the *Phaedo* Socrates' friends express their surprise at learning that the old philosopher has been composing poetry while in prison. In the course of explaining himself Socrates remarks that poets compose *mythoi* (myths) rather than *logoi* (arguments) but that he himself is not a *mythologikos*, a teller of myths. This characterization fits nicely with the standard view of Socrates and Plato as paradigmatically *rational* men, as the men in the West most responsible for setting our course away from myth and tradition toward science, logic, and revolution. Nietzsche regards Socrates' rejection of the tragic worldview in favor of an optimistic reliance on reason as the turning point of world history, and Plato's following Socrates in this as preparing the soil for Christianity, which to Nietzsche's mind is a pernicious farrago of untruths and naive wishes mistaken for facts. I shall have much more to say about Nietzsche in later chapters, but for now I set his remarks on Socrates and Christianity to one side and concentrate on Plato. Did Plato suffer from the hypertrophy of the rational faculty that Nietzsche attributes to Socrates? Did his obsession with *logoi* drive *mythoi* and the expression of instinct from the field of human thought and experience? I think not, and I believe that his manner of writing as outlined above demonstrates this.

The *Phaedo* is named for the character Phaedo, who was present in the prison for Socrates' last conversation. The dialogue is his recounting of Socrates' final hours to an admirer eager to learn about the philosopher's end, what he said and how he behaved before he died. At the beginning of the work this man asks Phaedo who among Socrates' friends was there that day, and when listing the names of the Athenians who were present Phaedo adds, "Plato, I think, was ill." So at the beginning of a long, dense work relating in detail Socrates' final conversation, Plato announces through his narrator that he himself was not actually present for the event. Does this mean that we cannot trust his account of all that was said and done that day? And if we cannot take his word for these things, must we not also reject his character Phaedo's word? But if we cannot trust Phaedo's account, can we believe his report that Plato was absent? And since in more than one place Socrates notes that his argument is incomplete and inconclusive, must we not infer that the argument is not the only, nor even the main, point of the dialogue? These problems and meta-problems are generated by Plato himself, and I take them for indications that the *Phaedo* is something other than a straightforward factual account, a *logos*, and that it is instead a *mythos*. It is composed of *mythoi* and *logoi* both, and much else besides, but as a whole it is a creative work, an artistic exploration of ideas, moods, attitudes, and beliefs.

Now let's inspect even more closely Socrates' claim that philosophers are concerned with arguments rather than poetry, stories, or myths. Plato seems intentionally to undermine this point throughout the dialogue by blurring the lines between *mythos* and *logos* and by attributing a degree of seriousness to *mythoi* that we wouldn't expect if myths were nothing more than false tales. For example, just after denying that he is a *mythologikos* Socrates says that it is fitting for a man in his position to *mythologein*, in other words "to relate *mythoi* about," the journey to the underworld. Moreover, he pairs this word with *diaskopein*, which means "to look into" or "to investigate," the same word Plato uses in the *Republic* to transition into the section that begins with the introduction of the Philosopher-King and culminates in a detailed discussion of metaphysics and epistemology. It is, in short, a stereotypically "rational" word, but here it is side by side with a typically "irrational" word. So despite what he has said about the different functions of philosophy and poetry, Plato's Socrates introduces the day's long discussion in a manner that suggests that it is a combination of both. Similarly, near the end of the dialogue Socrates refers to his account of the true nature of the earth as both a *logos* and a *mythos*. Later once again he calls it a *mythos* and says that although no sensible man would insist that his account is absolutely accurate, it is nevertheless "befitting and worthy of a man to run the risk of thinking" that something like his account is true. It is, he adds, "a noble risk."

So the *Phaedo* is not exhausted by the character Socrates' *logoi*. It is rather the author Plato's *mythos*. In other words, the work as a whole is more than just the arguments; it comprises stories, allusions, asides, and atmospherics as well. These irrational or arational poetic elements account for as much of the content of the dialogue as the rational logical elements, and in fact they infuse the arguments themselves.

The point of these remarks is to stress that Plato is not at all above employing poetry and myth to communicate his ideas. Like the *Phaedo*, the *Gorgias* and the *Republic* conclude with mythical accounts of the underworld and the mechanisms of the judgment of souls. The *Protagoras*, the *Phaedrus*, and the *Symposium* include myths as well, each of them addressing different themes. Finally, consider all you have heard about Atlantis—now consider that there is one and only one original source of all you think you know about this fantastic island and its history: Plato, who in his *Timaeus* and *Critias* tells the tale to make a point about the nature of his ideal city as described for example in the *Republic*.

In the course of this chapter I have intimated a difference between the philosopher as rational optimist and the sage as thinker-artist. I shall have more to say about these matters in later chapters. For now I stress the similarities between Plato's work and Melville's: through their writings both of these men engage in a form of indirect communication, Melville through the novel, Plato through his dialogues, which Nietzsche regarded as prefiguring models of the novel. As the creator of the dialogues Plato is much more than a mere philosopher; he works in a grander mode. He is a sage who expresses his wisdom through an artistically embellished mask of philosophy. And as I hope to demonstrate through this work, we should think of Melville in similar terms.

Chapter 10: A Bosom Friend

Following Father Mapple's sermon, Ishmael and Queequeg sit together before the fire in the Spouter-Inn and solidify their friendship. The situation provides Ishmael an opportunity to comment on Queequeg's character and to reflect on the influence his friendship has on him.

Queequeg had been at the chapel earlier but had left before Father Mapple's benediction. When Ishmael returns to the inn he finds him sitting quietly alone, whittling on his wooden idol and turning over the pages of a book. So lost is he in his activities that he does not notice Ishmael enter the room. Ishmael observes him for a time and is struck by the relaxed calmness of his demeanor. Think on this man for a moment: Queequeg earns his living as a harpooner aboard whaleships, so his is not an easy life; nor is he a stranger to violence. Moreover, he is leagues from home, living among people whose customs and beliefs are strange to him. He barely speaks the language. Yet for all this Queequeg is at his ease, maintaining a state of self-possessed tranquility. There is, Ishmael remarks, "something sublime" in his serene self-sufficiency, and he sums up his observations by attributing to Queequeg a "Socratic wisdom."

The wisdom Ishmael has in mind is not the *sophia* typically associated with Socrates in Plato's dialogues. Though Socrates nowhere insists that he knows only one thing, namely that he knows nothing—this is a popular misconception—it is nevertheless the case that he makes only very limited claims to knowledge or confident belief, and he usually admits that he does not have knowledge of the particular matter at issue in a conversation (this is true anyway of the so-called "early dialogues," which typically end in *aporia*, literally a "lack of passage" or "an inability to proceed," which in this instance indicates a failure to solve the problem or answer the question at hand). In the *Apology* Socrates tells the story of his friend Chaerophon's visit to Apollo's oracle at Delphi, to whom Chaerophon put the question whether anyone was wiser than Socrates. The god replied that Socrates was the wisest of men. When Socrates received the report of this judgment he was shocked; he was at a loss to comprehend a god's pronouncing wise—indeed, the *wisest*—a man whose knowledge was really so very meagre. He decided then to investigate the meaning of Apollo's declaration by conversing with those among Athens' citizens who enjoyed a reputation for wisdom. He would, for example, speak with a general about courage, or with a religious authority about piety. Through these trials he discovered something surprising: none of these men possessed the knowledge that others attributed to them, nor even the knowledge they claimed for themselves. As a result of these examinations Socrates concluded that, although neither he nor his interlocutors knew these things, he at least knew that he did not know, whereas the others did not know even this much. Thus, he had this one little bit of knowledge that everyone else seemed to lack. He reasoned, then, that this must be Apollo's meaning: he, Socrates, possessed this merely "human wisdom" that does not mistake ignorance for knowledge.

This, as I say, is not the wisdom Ishmael attributes to Queequeg. The "touch of fine philosophy" he detects in the man has to do rather with his apparent condition of *ataraxia*, that equanimity or mental tranquility I mentioned at the end of chapter six. We are used to thinking of wisdom as the goal of philosophy, and in this we are not altogether mistaken. But many philosophers sought wisdom for the sake of the spiritual, psychological, or, as we might say, the existential benefits that accrue to the sage, a good life (*eudaimonia*) for Aristotle, pleasure (*hêdonê*) for the Epicureans, a minimum of emotions or passions (*apatheia*) for the Stoics, *ataraxia* for the skeptics. Plato, as usual, is another, and a trickier, matter: his highest condition may have been "likeness to god," but I take this up in a later chapter. In any case, the "serenity" Ishmael identifies in Queequeg is one motivation of the philosopher's quest for wisdom.

Recall that Ishmael went to sea primarily as treatment for depression. The voyage was his "substitute for pistol and ball." In this chapter he begins to recover. Through his friendship with Queequeg, even before putting out to sea, Ishmael feels "a melting" within him. "No more," he says, were his "splintered heart and maddened hand ... turned against the wolfish world. This soothing savage had redeemed it." Now it might be something of an exaggeration to regard Ishmael at this point as fully "redeemed." But redemption is indeed a central feature of his story, that philosophical redemption at the core of which is serenity, tranquility, *ataraxia*, and which when achieved is not in itself a philosophical state but is transcendent of philosophy. It is wisdom, wisdom conceived—as I elaborate throughout the course of this book, and to employ a formulation introduced earlier—wisdom conceived as the condition of one who contemplates the accursed questions without regarding them *as* accursed, or, to adapt a Nietzschean formulation, the condition of one who stares into the abyss without the abyss glaring back.

In this chapter, then, Ishmael begins his progress toward becoming the serene sage that we encounter in Ishmael as narrator of *Moby-Dick*. An essential element of his development is his decision to participate with Queequeg in his pagan ritual involving the little black idol. When the two men have returned to their room after dinner, Queequeg takes up his idol, prepares for the rites, and invites Ishmael to join in the proceedings. The logic by which Ishmael decides to assent illustrates an ironic distancing from the beliefs and traditions into which he was born. He reasons that as a good Christian he is committed to following the will of God, which involves doing to his fellow men as he would have them do to him. And what would he have his fellow man Queequeg do to him? To participate in his Christian worship service. He concludes, therefore, that to do the will of God he must participate in Queequeg's own worship rituals. In short, he must "turn idolator."

So Ishmael kindles the sacrificial fire, performs a ritual food-offering, bows before the idol and kisses its nose. These rites performed, he and Queequeg go to bed "at peace with [their] consciences and all the world." The tranquil mood that settles over Ishmael in this chapter is, by his own account, due to his association with Queequeg. Participating in an activity that he had previously regarded as a barbarian's heathenish cavortings with a "little devil" brings him peace. The committed believer could never engage in such activities, nor, doing so, could he be at peace with himself. The typical philosopher might also decline to participate, disdaining such supernaturalist rituals as atavistic recrudescences of our naive unenlightened past. The sage, however, occupies an intellectual position above not only ingenuous belief but above simple unbelief as well. His spiritual freedom is such that he can play with ideas, explore worldviews or thought-worlds, and experiment with and on himself as the artist of his own mind.

Chapter 11: Nightgown

Ishmael and Queequeg, unable to sleep, sit up in bed chatting and smoking from Queequeg's tomahawk pipe. Thinking back on the scene from his position as narrator, Ishmael recalls the pleasure he experienced that night from the contrast between the chilly air in the room and the warmth beneath the covers. He then remarks that "there is no quality in this world that is not what it is merely by contrast. Nothing," he concludes, "exists in itself." This thought we may associate with Socrates' comments on pleasure and pain near the beginning of the *Phaedo* and in this way augment the account presented so far of Platonic metaphysics.

Phaedo's chronicle of Socrates' last day begins in the morning with a group of friends waiting for the prison to open. When finally allowed inside, they find Socrates recently released from his shackles. The word here for release (*lelumenon*) is a participial-form of the very word Socrates employs throughout the dialogue for the philosophical release (*lusis*) of the soul from the prison-house of the body effected through purification. And when Socrates remarks on the pleasure he feels upon being released from his bonds, the word he uses for bonds (*desmos*) is the same he will use to refer to the body as the bonds of the soul. This contrast between Socrates' body confined in the prison and his soul's release from the prison of his body adds emphasis to Socrates' indifference to his physical form. And here in the *Phaedo*, not long before he drinks the hemlock, he stresses that his body is not really him, and that his soul's departing after death will be *his* departure. The physical remains will be a mass of matter with no true identity in itself.

But to return to the contrast of pleasure and pain: Prior to beginning his narration of the day's events, Phaedo recalls experiencing that day a "really strange feeling" of an "unaccustomed mixture of pleasure blended together with pain." But then, near the start of his narration, he reports that Socrates, reflecting on his feelings upon being released from his bonds, commented that pleasure and pain cannot be present in a person at the same time, but that whenever a man pursues and catches hold of the one, he must take the other also, as if they were two creatures sharing a single head. It is so even now with him, he says, the pain he had experienced from the pressure of his bonds has been followed by pleasure upon his release. Just so, we might add, will his soul upon its release from his body be liberated from the polymorphous pains of a human life.

The idea that the world is characterized by opposite properties and states, whether existing simultaneously or necessarily following on one another, is a core component of Platonism. "Nothing exists in itself," says Ishmael, and his opinion conforms to traditional Platonic doctrine, so long as we keep in mind his reference to "this world." In this realm of Becoming, nothing is ever simply what it is; each of the many physical particulars always has opposite properties. Any tall thing is simultaneously short; any collection of things that is double the number of another collection is simultaneously half of some other collection; anything appearing beautiful to me now will not appear beautiful to someone else, nor will it appear beautiful to me later. Here we see the influence on Platonism of Heraclitus, the archaic Ephesian who taught that the cosmos is formed of opposite properties locked forever in constant strife with one another. This unceasing war of all against all is the generative father of reality as we know it, and Heraclitus symbolized his cosmogonical principles through images of the violence of fire, whose flames live through the death of the matter they consume. This world resembles fire also in the ceaselessness of its motions, its elements constantly flowing, streaming, transforming into and out of one another. "All things flow," Heraclitus proclaimed, and in this formula he sums up the idea of Becoming.

Among the ancients it was said that as a young man Plato studied with Cratylus the Heraclitean, a man so taken with the master's philosophy that he pushed it to its most extreme limits. Heraclitus had said that one cannot step into the same river twice, presumably intending to stress the constantly changing state of the river: due to the flowing of its waters the river itself will have changed by the time you attempt to dip your foot a second time. But Cratylus reasoned that if the world really is characterized by opposite properties and constant change, then no thing is ever really any more *this* than it is *that*, never really is an "itself," from which he concluded that one cannot step into the same river *even once*. The doctrine of flux must obliterate identity, and this in turn must destroy the functionality of language. If there are no stable things, then there can be no objects for our words to name. We are told that as a result of his conclusions Cratylus gave up speaking; he communicated solely by wiggling a finger.

Plato develops a similarly radical interpretation of Heraclitus in his dialogue the *Theaetetus*, in which he expresses the doctrine of flux in the formulation that "all things are always changing in every way." But he does not mistake this for a complete account of the whole of reality. He was confident that some at least of our words signify real objects, also that we do, or at least can, identify and know these objects. But since "this world," this material realm of Becoming, is indeed a world of constant flux, there must be another level, dimension, or aspect of reality to which Heraclitus's account does *not* apply and in which exist the real objects of our words and knowledge. This is the metaphysical realm of Being. Contrary to Ishmael's claim that nothing exists in itself, metaphysical entities as conceptualized in Platonism in fact do just that. When referring to a Form, Plato often employs the expression *auto kath' hauto*, "itself as itself," by which he intends to stress the fact that a Form is essentially a thing that "exists in itself." So Ishmael's insight is correct as far as it goes, but as he himself must know as a student of Platonism, reality may very well outstrip the limitations and boundaries of "this world."

Chapter 12: Biographical

In this chapter Ishmael provides a brief biography of Queequeg, including his homeland, his royal lineage, and an account of how he came to leave his family and fellows to adopt the life of a whaleman. Regarding the island from which his subject hails, Ishmael remarks that it is "not down on any map; true places never are." This is an exaggeration, of course; more, it is an outright falsehood. True places are precisely the places down on maps. That is, unless one intends to employ the word "true" to indicate something other than "correspondence to reality."

By placing his apparently false comment about truth at the head of his biography, Ishmael intimates that he is telling a tale, or in Platonic terms, relating a *mythos*. And it is a *mythos* within a *mythos*, as *Moby-Dick* as a whole, including Ishmael's *mythos*, is Melville's *mythos*. Plato's own myths usually have to do with the nature of the underworld, judgment, and reincarnation. There are others, but none that pretends to be the biography of a man. Nor does he introduce his myths with a comment on their truth-status seemingly designed to undercut their reliability. If anything, he usually contextualizes them in such a way as to enhance their credibility. Or so it is with those sections of the dialogues standardly designated "myths." But if we step back and examine the dialogues themselves, then considering the collection as a whole, the corpus does in fact relate the biography of one man's life and death—Socrates'—and his story is marked by a number of features characteristic of myths, including the intervention of a god, heroic deeds, and a remarkable death. And as for the story of the hero's death, recall that at the start of the *Phaedo* Plato announces through the narrator that he was not present for the event, which does tend to diminish the credibility of his tale. The dialogue ends with a *mythos* about the underworld, but it may well be, as I have previously claimed, that the dialogue itself, as a whole, is a broader and deeper *mythos*.

Having said all this, and having said by now much more besides about Platonism as related to *Moby-Dick*, I should make it clear at this point that my account of the novel does not include the assertion that either Ishmael or Melville himself were Platonists. In the previous chapter I described Ishmael as "a student of Platonism," and so he was, as was Melville. But neither of them were adherents. Melville entertained the same reservations regarding Platonic idealism that troubled him about Emerson's Transcendentalism, which was in part grounded in Platonism. Melville read Emerson and had heard him lecture too, and he included him among those men he loved, "men who *dive*." But Melville had a healthy strain of naive-realism in him, also of skepticism and pessimism, which set him against any form of dogmatic optimistic idealism. He clearly had some affinity for Platonism, certainly he was fascinated by it, even if he could not swallow it whole. He also had a tendency to lean away from realism in the other direction, by which I mean that his anti-realist inclinations were motivated less by a bright Platonic idealism than by a darker brand of Nietzschean falsificationism, which we may define in brief for now as a view descending from Kant's Transcendental Idealism that maintains that our perceptual and cognitive faculties present to our minds a falsified view of reality, that the world we experience as an ordered collection of substances, beings, and things, is really in itself an undifferentiated blur of energy, force, power, or of no one knows what exactly. There is no truth as commonly understood because there is no world as commonly experienced with respect to which our thoughts or statements might be true.

Ishmael's introductory remark concerning the truth, then, has more a Nietzschean than a Platonic note, and we will encounter similar sentiments throughout our reading of *Moby-Dick*. Consider, for example, Ishmael's remarking in the previous chapter with respect to identity that it is "as if darkness were indeed the proper element of our essences, though light be more congenial to our clayey part." No orthodox Platonist would say such a thing. Plato regularly associates light with our essential element, the soul that knows truth illuminated by the Good, which in the *Republic* he famously compares to the sun. Our "clayey part," or body, is the shadowy side of ourselves, darkened as it is by ignorance and lustful obsessions. This contrast is pronounced in what I have called *Phaedo*-Platonism, deriving no doubt from the extreme hostility to the body expressed in the *Phaedo* itself, in which "the body and its desires" are made responsible for most every gloomy element of human life, from fears to wars to all sorts of nonsense. Not only is Ishmael's observation not Platonic, it is downright anti-Platonic, and we could with fairness call it an inversion of Platonism. This way of thinking is characteristic of Melville's mind, and it is an intellectual trait he shared with Nietzsche. One scholar has described *Moby-Dick* as an expression of "inverted Platonism"—and he has done so apparently with no idea that Nietzsche himself once used precisely this formulation to characterize his own philosophy.

There are other Nietzschean elements throughout *Moby-Dick*, as for example Ishmael's remarks on Christianity in the present chapter. Although Queequeg had hoped that during his sojourn in Christendom he would learn much to improve his native people upon returning home, he discovered instead "that even Christians could be both miserable and wicked; infinitely more so, than all his father's heathens." Now this is mild compared to Nietzsche's "eternal indictment of Christianity" as "the one great curse" and "the one immortal blemish on mankind," and although Melville had expressed in previous works, and will express later in this one, many harsh words against Christians, he was never so hostile as Nietzsche. Still, he did stand out in his time and place for the rough treatment he gave the religion, and he was often chastised for his acerbic observations by critics and lay-readers alike.

So Melville at heart was more proto-Nietzschean than Platonist, and I will explore this side of the man himself, as well as of his great novel, in the second half of this book. But for now I shall continue, in the course of treating other matters, adding detail to my account of *Phaedo*-Platonism.

Chapter 13: Wheelbarrow

This chapter is named for one of many episodes that Ishmael relates to demonstrate the cultural chasm that separates him from Queequeg; wide, to be sure, but deep too, so deep as to mark not merely a cultural but an existential divide as well. But the fact of there being such differences among men is not the main interest of the chapter. More significant still is the display of Ishmael's intellectual-psychological facility for overleaping the gulf between himself and his eccentric new friend.

As Ishmael tells the story, Queequeg first encountered a wheelbarrow when the owners of a ship on which he had once sailed loaned him one to carry his sea-chest from the harbor to his temporary lodgings ashore. Having no idea what use to make of the thing, Queequeg bound his chest secure inside the tub, then raised the entire bundle onto a shoulder and lugged it away down the street. In reply to Ishmael's speculation that the onlookers must have been much amused, Queequeg shares another story, this one concluding with his own amusement at the expense of a white man. Many years previous, when he was still living on his native island, the captain of a merchant ship came ashore to dine with the royal family. The High Priest being present, he consecrated the common drink by dipping his fingers into the liquid. But the captain misinterpreted the ritual, and mistaking the dish for a finger bowl, he proceeded to clean his hands with the blessed beverage. How the natives laughed!

It is the rare man on either side of a cultural divide who avoids making a fool of himself in the eyes of those who occupy the opposite territory. But Ishmael is, or is becoming, precisely such an experienced and broad-minded man. This is not to say that he has developed a special faculty of insight into the nature of every foreign thought or deed he encounters, but rather that he has learned not to assume that the opinions and rituals contingent on the time and place of his own birth are the only sensible ones. Every people has its way, and it is "a mutual, joint-stock world, in all meridians." We must learn to empathize with one another, and to stretch our minds if need be in order to do so. And in this context the psychic expansion seems more to the point than the empathy.

During his passage with Queequeg from New Bedford to Nantucket, Ishmael learns this lesson directly. On board the ferry are a number of narrow-minded "boobies and bumpkins" who jeer at Queequeg and mock him behind his back. Catching one of these young rogues in the act, Queequeg snatches him up and tosses him into the air, and with a deftly placed smack on his airborne rump ensures that he lands on his feet. The onlookers are appalled and frightened at the sight of this "devil" abusing a robust young American in this way. The captain is called for and soon arrives; he denounces Queequeg as a "cannibal" and threatens to kill him. Queequeg is picked out as a stranger, isolated, misunderstood, and abused.

It happens that during this commotion the ship's boom suddenly comes loose and, swinging wildly, smashes into the mocking young rascal, knocking him overboard into the sea. Pandemonium ensues: everyone is in a frenzy of panic, the captain included. Queequeg alone keeps his head. Squatting down beneath the flailing boom, he manages to grab and secure it; then, heedless of his own safety, he leaps into the icy waters, and after several minutes of searching dives down and resurfaces with the young man in tow. Queequeg is hailed all round as a "noble" specimen of manhood.

We recall that Ishmael himself had previously mistaken Queequeg for a diabolical man-eater, but also that he has since overcome his initial prejudices and befriended the man. This episode on the ferry confirms the soundness of his judgment, not only in Ishmael's own mind but in the mind of the reader as well. In this chapter Ishmael records no fewer than three instances of strangers agog at the friendly relations between himself and Queequeg, and we are meant to gather that whereas the normal man is incapable of escaping his cramped preconceptions, Ishmael's soul is capacious. He is a common sailor with uncommon intellectual potential, and, to adapt an expression that Melville once applied to himself, he is unfolding within himself, maturing into the man who will narrate *Moby-Dick*.

Chapter 14: Nantucket

At the conclusion of the previous chapter I borrowed an expression that Melville employed with respect to himself in a letter to Hawthorn composed while he was writing *Moby-Dick*. From the time he was twenty five, he says, he has "unfolded within myself" every three weeks or so. He is referring to the period beginning with his return from his four wild years at sea, the period during which he became an avid reader of serious literature, a successful author, and a "pondering man."

When Melville wrote to Hawthorne of his internal unfolding, he was at the height of his intellectual and creative powers; existentially he was in his prime. Hershel Parker has captured something of Melville's mood during this period in a sparkling essay entitled "Melville in the Berkshires." In July of 1850 Melville vacationed with his family in Pittsfield, Massachusetts, the Berkshire territory in which he had spent much time as a youth and where he would soon buy the farm on which he would write the bulk of *Moby-Dick*. While on this vacation he accompanied his cousin Robert Melville on his "official tour as chairman of the Berkshire Agricultural Society's committee to award Premiums on Crops." Melville composed the report himself, and the spirit of his prose style prefigures his celebration of Hawthorne in the exuberant "Hawthorne and His Mosses," written the following month, and *Moby-Dick* itself, which he began during this same period. For an indication of Melville's mood, which Parker characterizes aptly as "expansive," consider the following paragraph from the report:

> Swamps and quagmires, in which the only vegetable productions were alders and ferns, with a few cat-tails interspersed among them as decorations, are now covered with a carpet of herds-grass and clover, and afford exuberant crops of hay. The committee would be sorry that any words of theirs should give rise to suspicion that they are deficient in the milk of human kindness, and they profess to have as great an aversion to strife as the most enthusiastic members of the Peace Society; yet they cannot withhold their approbation of the determination manifested by the proprietors of these swamps, to exterminate the tribes of insects and reptiles, which, for aught that we know to the contrary, had held a life estate

thereof from generation to generation, since the day when Noah, with his numerous family, emerged from the Ark.

Melville's mastery of himself—of his mind, his mood, and his talent—is on brilliant display here. He is toying with words, at play like a man unimpededly in command of his matter and material.

Melville was as impressive in person as on paper during this period. He was, to borrow once more from Parker's account, "young and healthy," which expression I gloss as physiologically robust in a Nietzschean sense. This is the summer of the famous trip to Monument Mountain when Melville first met Hawthorne. While on the excursion Melville leapt onto a rock that projected out beyond the cliffs, a feat that made others in the party nervous and queasy. On another occasion he scurried up a tall tree, sat on a precarious branch, and called out to locate the approaching members of his party. He notoriously drove his wagon with wild abandon, and he regularly tramped out for walks and hikes of miles. Melville in his early-thirties was, in short, full of vigor and overflowing with instinctive power. Indeed, despite the high pitch to which his intellect had by this time developed, his conscious mind did not inhibit his unconscious vitality. Melville's friend J. E. A. Smith recalled that Melville in the Berkshires often "threw off thoughts suggested by the locality or the incidents of the day, although he seemed as unconscious of any effort as of his breathing or the beating of his heart. It was," he concluded, "involuntary." This description calls to mind Nietzsche's reflections on the superiority of free-flowing unconscious activity, as in his remark that "Artists … [know] only too well that precisely when they no longer do anything 'voluntarily' but do everything of necessity, their feeling of freedom, subtlety, full power, of creative placing, disposing, and forming reaches its peak."

In the previous chapter Ishmael praised Queequeg's "unconsciousness" with reference to his rescue of the drowning man; he had acted on instinct, without any thought for potential danger or reward. In the present chapter he marvels at the "unconscious power" of the whale, more dreadful even than its intentional attacks. Like Nietzsche, Ishmael understands that the highest type of man (or beast) functions at his best when acting instinctively. And Ishmael understands this because Melville does, and Melville understands this because when writing these words he was himself this type of man. Despite his fascination with the accursed questions, Melville was possessed of the intellectual-spiritual power to confront them playfully, which is not to say unseriously. The cheerfulness with which he confronted life's darkest imponderables displays the joyful wisdom whose presence in the man marks him out as positively Zarathustran.

Chapter 15: Chowder

Recall that in the second chapter Ishmael identified Nantucket as his "destined port" precisely as he was searching for lodgings in New Bedford, a town in which he had planned to spend no time at all. He had arrived there after the ferry to Nantucket had sailed, and the next boat would not depart until after the weekend. A minor inconvenience, perhaps; just a little chance occurrence; but sufficient to determine the course of Ishmael's actual destiny.

Socrates in the *Phaedo* is similarly affected by "some chance occurrence" (*tuchê tis*). As we have seen, his execution is delayed for several days while Theseus's ship is away at the Delian festival, during which time for the sake of purity no prisoners may be killed. The conversation recounted in the *Phaedo* takes place when it does because the ship has finally returned, so everyone knows that this will be Socrates' last day alive.

One wonders what Plato had in mind by designating as "chance" the fact that Socrates' trial took place when it did in relation to the beginning of the Delian festival. The coincidence provides the ideal occasion to introduce into his dialogue the theme of purification. Although Plato nowhere provides an exhaustive analysis of the role chance (*tuchê*) plays in world- and life-events, Aristotle in his *Physics* explicitly denies that chance is a cause; it is rather the name we give to occurrences that in themselves have some other identifiable mundane cause, but that appear to have happened for the sake of the end designated "chance." So, for example, the selection of the day on which to hold Socrates' trial had its causes, as did the events surrounding the beginning of the Delian festival; that they happened to correspond in such a way as to delay Socrates' execution was a matter of "chance." Would Plato accept this account? He seems almost to intimate that the machinations of Fate are behind these events.

The Greeks' view of fate has long struck me as unusual, not to say inconsistent. Consider Achilles' famous decision in the *Iliad*: if he decides to leave Troy and return home, he is fated to have a long but anonymous life. If he chooses instead to remain and fight at Troy, he is fated to die young with immortal glory. He has a choice, but the consequences of his decision are a matter of fate. But if the world works this way, then why is Achilles' apparent choice not itself the fated outcome of some previous apparent choice? If some events are fated, must not all events be?

In a later chapter we shall consider Melville's attempt to weave free will, chance, and fate together into a single fabric, but here he suggests that his Ishmael is caught up in the inexorable workings of fate when he has him say that his whaling adventure was included in the "grand program of Providence that was drawn up a long time ago." His delay in New Bedford was no more a meaningless accident than Socrates' extended time in prison. Just as Socrates has time to share his thoughts about purification as a living death and descent to the underworld for the sake of wisdom and release from the cycle of rebirth, Ishmael during his time in a figurative underworld among images and reminders of death discovers the infernal key to his own future liberation from death, Queequeg.

The theme of finding the light of life in the darkness of the land of the dead is ancient, and it is associated with elements present in the *Phaedo*. I have noted that the dialogue is informed by many Pythagorean ideas, and there is some evidence that Pythagoreans were interested in underworld descents for the sake of illumination in relation to reincarnation. The obscure figure Zalmoxis was said to have been a slave of Pythagoras initiated into the mysteries of wisdom by the master, and perhaps by way of the Eleusinian Mysteries as well. He disappeared underground for so long that he was taken for dead, but then he returned and was believed to have become immortal. Plato identifies this Zalmoxis as a physician and healer of both bodies and souls in the *Charmides*. There is also the practice known as incubation, which was employed particularly for purposes of healing at sites dedicated to Asclepius, son of Apollo, famously mentioned by Socrates at the end of the *Phaedo*, as we shall later see. Healer-priests would descend into caves or enter dark rooms in the temple complex in order to commune through visions with deities who assisted with healing. Parmenides and his followers in ancient Elea may have engaged in incubation rituals, and indeed the beginning of Parmenides' great poem about Being may provide an account of visions received during one such experience.

So Ishmael's chance descent into the dark land of the dead, and his locating there an instrument of life—of his own future life—is a theme that resonates with Plato's *Phaedo*. But Ishmael has not yet attained his goal. At this point in the novel he is still only on his way to the light, still only searching for wisdom. Hence he sees a gallows in the sign of the inn recommended by Mr. Coffin. He was, he remarks, "over sensitive to such impressions at the time." And the collection of the impressions he experiences in these opening chapters he fears for intimations of Hell. But his fears result precisely from his not having yet fully descended, for when he has done so and returned again above ground, into light and life, he will possess the wisdom to see that in the underworld is located the secret key to life above ground, but only for initiates. And *Moby-Dick*, like the *Phaedo*, is itself a symbolic recounting of an initiation ceremony whose literal procedural details are preserved exclusively for those who know.

Chapter 16: The Ship

This chapter begins with Queequeg reporting to Ishmael the words delivered to him by his little idol, Yojo. Today the two men must find a whaler to sign on to, but Yojo has insisted that Ishmael select the ship by himself, without Queequeg's assistance. Yojo claims to know already which ship it must be, and he insists that if left to his own devices Ishmael will "infallibly light upon [it], for all the world as though it had turned out by chance." Here again is the interplay between fate and chance in Ishmael's adventure, as it plays out as well in all our adventures. Events that appear to be accidental occurrences as we encounter them may take on the appearance of necessity when considered as moments generative of a present from which vantage we look back on them as past. Ishmael is telling his story, and in order to be *this* story all the events *must* be in place, and they *must* occur in a specific temporal order and structural relation to one another.

But what to make of the fact that a sort of prophecy regarding this part of Ishmael's destiny issues from Queequeg's wooden figurine? We have seen by now more than one instance of Queequeg's appearing as Socrates, and his communion with Yojo in this chapter strikes me as another. Socrates was infamous for claiming at times to hear in his mind the words of a divinity, which he called his *daimonion*, literally his "little divine being." At the end of Plato's *Apology*, for example, upon the reading of his death sentence, Socrates claims not to be afraid, nor even to regard the sentence as bad, on the grounds that his "prophetic *daimonion*" did not oppose his coming to court that day, even though it regularly opposed him whenever he was about to make a mistake in action. He concludes, then, that death is something good, and he regards the silence of his *daimonion* as "abundant evidence" of this.

We are by now familiar with the emphasis on death as good—as the ultimate goal of the philosopher, in fact, whose life is a training for death—in Plato's *Phaedo*. Death is the soul's release from the prison-house of the body. In the *Gorgias* Socrates reports having heard from a wise man that "the body is our tomb," which expression plays on the alliterative resonances between the words for body (*sôma*) and tomb (*sêma*); and in the *Cratylus* he attributes this doctrine to the followers of Orpheus, by which he (Plato, really) would have meant adherents of a mystical secret doctrine with Pythagorean elements concerning the fate of the soul after death. And to return to the *Phaedo*, besides conceiving of the body as a prison, there are suggestions that it is also a sort of disease, as when Socrates claims that the supposed virtue of those who love the body is really a sham virtue that "has nothing healthy" about it.

In the present chapter of *Moby-Dick* Ishmael dismisses "all mortal greatness" as "disease," which sentiment has the odor of *Phaedo*-Platonism about it. He also remarks that "all men tragically great are made so through a certain morbidness." A contemporary critic, writing about Melville six years after the publication of *Moby-Dick*, complained that the author had "indulged himself in a trick of metaphysical and morbid meditations until he has almost perverted his fine mind from its healthy productive tendencies." Around this same time Hawthorne, after visiting with Melville for the first time in many years, noted in his diary that his friend's works "for a long while past, have indicated a morbid state of mind." Hawthorne may well have been right, and we shall look into Melville's intellectual-spiritual condition in the years following *Moby-Dick* later in this book. But the Melville who conceived and composed this novel was not at all unhealthy. To the contrary, he was at the peak of his health and power, having attained to a condition that we can describe in Nietzsche's terms as Zarathustran.

As we have just seen in the previous chapter, Ishmael at this point in his development is still "over sensitive" to morbid impressions. He still conceptualizes this human life as putting up for a time at an inn whose "grim sign" reads "Thunder Cloud." He is on his way to becoming the Ishmael who narrates *Moby-Dick*, but he is only just setting out on the journey that will eventually lead him there. And if, as I have claimed, Ishmael as narrator represents the sage, then the melancholy and occasionally cynical Ishmael we have had to do with so far is the philosopher in search of wisdom. He has the experience, the broad-mindedness, the intrepid curiosity, and the wit of a philosopher, which traits when combined with psychological-spiritual health (physiological health in Nietzsche's sense) and the appropriate circumstances (the events recounted in *Moby-Dick*, for instance) can lift the philosopher out of his philosophy into wisdom. This is Ishmael's journey, and it is so because it was Melville's journey. Ishmael is the symbolic medium through which Melville recounts his transformation from agitated philosopher to cheerful sage.

But not all philosophers successfully make this transition. Most are variations of a type that I call the *perpetual philosopher*, which is to say the thinking man lost in the labyrinth of his dark thoughts. This is the man who regards the accursed questions *as accursed*, whose ruminations on the problem of the universe cause him to *suffer*. The model of this type in *Moby-Dick* is Captain Ahab. Ahab does not appear in this chapter, but one of the owners of the *Pequod*, which ship Ishmael has selected in accordance with Yojo's prophecy, introduces Ahab into the story as "a grand, ungodly, god-like man." We shall consider this matter of Ahab's being "god-like," but for now I note that the condition has nothing in common with Plato's "likeness to god." It certainly does not imply psychological, spiritual, or intellectual equanimity. No: although Ahab "ain't sick," he "isn't well either." He is, in fact, "kind of moody—desperate moody, and savage sometimes." He is "stricken, blasted," and even if it be true that he "has his humanities," nonetheless his cultured, empathetic nature has been darkened over by the gloominess of his meditations—or rather by the hidden weakness that prevents him from transforming these same meditations from gloomy to bright. This weakness, an impotence arising from different causes in different men, is the mark of the perpetual philosopher.

Chapter 17: The Ramadan

Before we inspect more closely the nature of the perpetual philosopher, a few more words for now on the doctrine characteristic of *Phaedo*-Platonism that the body is a prison or disease. Plato always privileges the soul over the body, but rarely to this extreme. In the *Republic*, for example, the soul is regarded as a person's true self, the seat of one's intellectual and moral virtues; but matters relating to the health and training of the body are given their due. Even the philosophers must meet the physiological demands of a warrior. All this is to say that I doubt that Plato himself subscribed to an unmitigated version of *Phaedo*-Platonism. Melville certainly rejects it, and his attitude comes through in this chapter on Queequeg's meditative religious ritual that has him locked in his room all day unmoving and silent.

Ishmael's broad-mindedness, which is really a manifestation of Melville's ability to "reverse perspectives" (to employ a Nietzschean phrase), is often on display in his dealings with Queequeg's spiritual beliefs and practices. He has "the greatest respect toward everybody's religious obligations," he says, and he elaborates by adding that "we good Presbyterian Christians should be charitable in these things, and not fancy ourselves so vastly superior to other mortals, pagans and what not, because of their half-crazy conceits on these subjects... and Heaven have mercy on us all – Presbyterians and Pagans alike – for we are all somehow dreadfully cracked about the head, and sadly need mending." Ishmael understands that regarding divine matters we humans have little if any unobscured insight into the Truth.

Melville's ability to reverse perspectives in this context is due to his own ironic detachment or distance from the punctilios of personal religious commitment. He has no time for the surface elements of dogma. We experience this aspect of Melville's intellect through Ishmael's explaining to Queequeg the thoroughly Nietzschean point that "all these Lents, Ramadans, and prolonged ham-squattings in cold, cheerless rooms [are] stark nonsense; bad for the health; useless for the soul; opposed, in short, to the obvious laws of Hygiene and common sense." The gloomy and anti-natural character of so much religion is due precisely to this sort of neglect of the body, and the notion of hell, for example, "is an idea first born on an undigested apple-dumpling; and since then perpetuated through the hereditary dyspepsias nurtured by" this neglect. Here we have Melville's comical take on what Nietzsche will later call the "ascetic ideal." And this sentiment, manifested also in Ishmael's earlier remark (in "A Bosom Friend") that any man who "gives himself out for a philosopher" must have, "like the dyspeptic old woman," "'broken his digester,'" is a prefiguring of Zarathustra's observation that the spirit of the pessimistic philosophers is "an upset stomach which counsels death," for, as he puts it, "the spirit *is* a stomach."

But despite his insouciance with respect to dogma and ritual; despite, that is, his broad-minded intellectual free-spiritedness, Ishmael still suffers from melancholy, anxiety, and existential agitation. His reaction to Queequeg's locking himself in his room is frantic. He fears that his friend has been murdered or suffered a stroke. He runs through the inn shouting for an axe, and finally ignoring the protests of the innkeeper's wife, he breaks down the door. The commotion and noise do not disturb Queequeg, who remains calmly sitting, silent and still on the floor. But Ishmael's agitation endures. He tries more than once to distract Queequeg from his ritual, to catch his attention and draw him out of his trance. But Queequeg does not budge; he does not even acknowledge Ishmael's presence. He remains precisely as he is until sunrise the following morning, at which time he revives and goes cheerfully about his business.

Queequeg's manner during his Ramadan is yet another manifestation of his "Socratic wisdom." Socrates was known at times to enter into a sort of meditative trance during which he would stand still in silence, sometimes for hours on end. At the beginning of the *Symposium*, for example, when the philosopher and his friend Aristodemus arrive at Agathon's house, Socrates remains outside "turning his mind toward himself." When questioned about the matter Aristodemus explains that Socrates has this habit of sometimes standing off by himself wherever he happens to be. He will not be moved by appeals to let up; he will not budge. Later in this same dialogue, Alcibiades reports that when he was with Socrates during the military campaign at Potidaea, the philosopher one morning began mulling over some matter and stood still on the same spot from that dawn until the next sunrise thinking it through. Finally he offered a prayer to the sun and went on with his day as usual. Agathon associates this behavior with Socrates' wisdom, and he imagines that Socrates actually acquires wisdom during these episodes.

I do not mean to imply that Queequeg is the model of the sage in *Moby-Dick*. As I have said, Ishmael as narrator fills this role. Queequeg provides the youthful Ishmael insight into the nature of mental tranquility, *ataraxia*. This is his "Socratic wisdom." But Ishmael as narrator, like Melville himself, is wise with a *Platonic* wisdom, that wisdom of the thinker-artist who plays with ideas, constructs and explores new thought-worlds, experiments with his own mind. Ishmaelean-Melvillean wisdom, like this Platonic wisdom, and also like Nietzsche's joyful wisdom, requires both Ishmael's playfully ironic Pyrrhonian broad-mindedness and Queequeg's spiritual equanimity. These are the elements that distinguish the philosopher on his way to wisdom from the perpetual philosopher.

Chapter 18: His Mark

When Ishmael brings Queequeg to the *Pequod* to sign up for the voyage, one of the owners, the sternly pious Captain Bildad, interrogates the pair regarding Queequeg's religious affiliations. He will permit the man to sail only if he is "in communion with [a] Christian church." The situation provides Melville yet another opportunity to express his ironically playful indifference to dogma, which he does by having his Ishmael insist that Queequeg belongs to the First Congregational Church, and that he is moreover a deacon therein. When pressed, Ishmael explains that every man, woman, and child around the world worships in "the same ancient Catholic Church," the only notable divisions within the global congregation resulting from the fact that "some of us cherish some queer crotchets." These crotchets are precisely the particular doctrinal specifics that distinguish one religion, or one denomination within a religion, from all the others. Ishmael's contention that these various beliefs and rituals "noways [touch] the grand belief" displays Melville's own broad-minded, and at least semi-Pyrrhonian, attitude toward spirituality.

The ancient Pyrrhonian skeptics appealed to the ten modes I mentioned earlier to argue that one must withhold judgment about all "non-evident" matters, which is to say matters involving claims about the *true* nature of reality as opposed to its *appearances* to us. It is readily apparent that human beings across diverse societies incline toward belief in a deity or deities, but whether such beings really exist, and whether they exist precisely as this or that person or people conceives them to exist, this is not evident at all. The Pyrrhonian concludes, therefore, that we must withhold judgment (this is the practice of *epochê*). But this is not the final word on the matter. The Pyrrhonians adopted certain standards of action to which they could appeal as guides for daily conduct, and one of these included the traditions and laws of one's society. Plato had worried about the pernicious effects on society of vocal unbelievers, men who openly mocked or advocated the overthrow of traditional religious beliefs or moral values, and it would seem that the Pyrrhonians shared Plato's concerns. So for the practical advantage of each individual skeptic, and for the stability of his society, they advised men to adhere to the traditions into which they were born. The gods are non-evident, but as a practical matter it is best to attend the religious festivals and sacrifices of one's city, just like the average citizen.

Melville seems to have adopted a position not unlike this, up to a point anyway. Whatever he may have believed about the ultimate unity of all religions at their deepest levels, he regarded himself a Christian in some broad sense of the word, or at least as a loyal citizen of Christendom. He did not refrain from needling the faith, nor even from expressing outright criticisms and challenges, and this in public through his writings; and he was notorious among his Pittsfield neighbors for refusing to attend church. Late in life he did request that the pastor put him down as a member of All Souls Unitarian Church in New York City, but this seems to have been the extent of his expressions of sympathy with established Christianity, if "sympathy" we may call it. So perhaps Melville would not have merited the absolute approval of either Plato or the Pyrrhonians on this score, but, as I have said, he was well to this side of the much more radical and vociferous Nietzsche, the harshest of whose anti-Christian pronouncements would have appalled Melville's sense of propriety, even while, I suspect, secretly appealing to his intellect.

Chapter 19: The Prophet

When Ishmael and Queequeg disembark from the *Pequod*, they are accosted by a haggard old stranger on the docks—Elijah, named for the biblical prophet who censured King Ahab and his wife Jezebel for permitting the worship of Baal in Israel. Informed that the two men have registered their names on the ship's roster, he asks whether they have committed their souls as well. Or maybe, he speculates, they have no souls, which would be just as well since a soul is "a sort of fifth wheel to a wagon." Besides, Captain Ahab has more than enough soul to go around.

The soul is the primary subject of the *logoi* in Plato's *Phaedo*. Its nature, its function, and its fate following the death of the body are all discussed at length. So central is this theme that the work has sometimes been known as *On the Soul*. Near the end of the dialogue, in a section commonly referred to as Socrates' "second sailing"—though it may very well recount Plato's own intellectual voyage—the philosopher argues that since the soul is that which when present in a body always causes the body to live, life is of its essence, which in turn implies that the soul is immortal. Soul, in short, is the principle of life. It is also the source of action, particularly in its capacity as rational agent of deliberation. Soul, moreover, is that by which we know. Given this range of activity, it might be useful to think of soul in Plato as a combination of what today we mean by the words "soul" and "mind." The Greek word is *psychê*, which we have retained as "psyche" to indicate our mental nature in a broad sense. Hence, for example, the word "psychology."

But what could it mean to suggest, as Elijah suggests, that some men might have no souls, and that they might be better off for it? In what sense might a soul be a "fifth wheel"? For Plato I think these would simply be false assertions, the "jabbering" (to quote Ishmael) of a madman, a sophist, or one who wants "to look as if he had a great secret in him." A body without a soul would not at all be a steady four-wheeled thing; it would simply be dead, a corpse.

Elijah's rantings, then, are nonsense from the perspective of *Phaedo*-Platonism. From a Christian perspective too, of course. They intimate a challenge to the standard western worldview by undermining assumptions about man and the universe that have served as intellectual foundations for millennia. They hint at a world turned upside down. And this, I believe, is their purpose. Melville does not advocate a materialist metaphysics through the wild figure of Elijah; he is generating an atmosphere of ominous and disorienting gloom in which to envelop the *Pequod* and its Captain. Elijah is the initial source of Ishmael's "vague wonderments and half-apprehensions" about Ahab and his ship, and these wonderings and apprehensions are the conditions of the philosopher. Both Plato and Aristotle identify "wonder" as the source of philosophy; it is the *archê*, the fundamental originary principle, of philosophy as the love of wisdom. And this wonder Aristotle associates with aporia, which in this context signifies a state of uncertainty and perplexity.

Aporia is one source of the agitation and anxiety that I have associated with the philosopher, in contrast to the serenity, the *ataraxia*, of the sage. Ishmael is assailed by "half-apprehensions" concerning "shadowy things" precisely because he represents the philosopher. And Ahab and all that is associated with his sailing (his "second sailing," really, as he lost his leg to Moby Dick on his previous voyage) is the source of Ishmael's philosophical ruminations because Ahab and Ishmael represent two different types of philosopher considered in relation to the sage, one who has transcended philosophy into wisdom, and one who remains an agitated philosopher even unto death. Ishmael as narrator, like Melville as author, is looking back on his former self at a time when he stood at the head of two divergent paths, and he is telling the story of one man who wandered forever lost inside the Minotaur's shadowy maze, and another who found the exit and walked into the light of the sun.

Chapter 20: All Astir

Before the *Pequod* "blindly plunge[s] like fate into the lone Atlantic" (as it will at the end of chapter twenty-two), preparations must be made. The bustle aboard ship, the barking of commands, the loading and storing of supplies—all these things are recounted in the present chapter.

Socrates, too, must prepare for his "fated" journey to Hades in the *Phaedo*. The proper preparation for this departure is a lifetime of purification through philosophy, for the soul descends into the underworld taking with it nothing but its "education and rearing," and its only salvation is "to become as good and wise as possible." Ishmael takes more than just his education and rearing along on his journey, but not much more, and none of his material gear contributes to the salvation of his soul. Only his goodness and approach to wisdom accomplish this.

Socrates' fated day of departure arrives after a lifetime of preparation, but he also takes more immediate steps toward securing for himself a blessed future. At the beginning of the *Phaedo* we learn that he has been composing poems in prison. When asked about this he explains that for years a recurring dream has repeatedly urged him to "make and practice music." The word for "music" here (*mousikê*) signifies any art over which the Muses preside, including instrumental music in our sense of the word, but also, for example, choral dance and lyric poetry. Socrates says that he had always assumed that the dream was encouraging him to persist in his philosophical pursuits, for philosophy is the "greatest music." But since after his trial it occurred to him that the dream might have intended that he practice a more "popular" form of music, he did not want to die without purifying himself of any potentially culpable negligence. Therefore he composed a hymn to Apollo in honor of his festival, and he also set to verse a *mythos* of Aesop he happened to know.

The consideration in this section of the differences among various types of "music" reintroduces the distinction between *logos* and *mythos*. Socrates associates the philosopher with arguments, the poet with stories and fables.

But, as we have seen, Plato subverts this nice distinction throughout the dialogue. Whatever were the facts of the historical Socrates' actual practice of philosophy, Plato himself was no mere logic-chopper. This is evident, for example, in Socrates' admission that no sensible man will take his description of the afterlife literally, and even more in his advice that we should nevertheless chant his *mythos* to ourselves as if it were a sort of incantatory charm. We should *risk* belief.

This sort of trust is beyond Ishmael as he prepares for his own departure. He is disturbed that he hasn't yet encountered Captain Ahab. As narrator he reports that his younger self did not much appreciate "being committed this way to so long a voyage, without once laying my eyes on the man who was to be the absolute dictator of it." As a philosopher rather than a sage, and as a young philosopher at that, Ishmael requires concrete assurances, physical evidence. He will learn that there are more things in heaven and earth than are dreamt of in his philosophy, as Melville himself had learned through personal experience and his avid reading of Shakespeare. As author, Melville is busy with his own sort of preparations, equipping his Ishmael with the characteristics required of the man who when confronted with an immaterial deity (whether good, evil, or beyond the both of them) will recognize it for what it is, square up to it, plunge into the abysmal depths of its being-beyond-being, and finally ascend into the light transformed, amplified, wise.

Chapter 21: Going Aboard

The strangest part of Plato's surpassingly strange *Phaedo* may well be Socrates' likening of himself to Apollo's prophetic swans. Near the terminus of life as he is, he claims special insight into the fate of his soul after death. And in this, he says, he is akin to the god's glorious singing birds.

At the conclusion of the third of his first three arguments for the immortality of the soul, Socrates says that the soul of the philosopher who is properly oriented toward his release (*lusis*) from the body attains a state of *galênê*, which word is used primarily to designate the stillness or calm of the sea. The true philosopher is serene in the face of death. When he suspects that the two Pythagorean philosophers present, Simmias and Cebes, are not yet fully convinced, he admits that his *logoi* are incomplete. There are, he says, still a number of dubious and vulnerable points in his reasoning, especially if one wants to examine the subject thoroughly. Simmias replies that he and Cebes have indeed been perplexed (*aporôn*, being in the condition of *aporia*) for a while, but that they are reluctant to trouble him given his present unfortunate situation. In response to this Socrates gently teases the men, laughing at their concern and insisting that he does not consider his present *tuchê* (chance, fate) a misfortune. He adds that their worries suggest that they consider him inferior to swans with respect to prophecy.

Are swans then prophetic? And is Socrates a prophet too? Yes, they are, swans and Socrates both, at least when death is near. By way of justifying his striking opinion Socrates explains that swans are Apollo's special birds, and as Apollo is a prophetic god (witness his oracle at Delphi, through which the god proclaimed Socrates the wisest of men), so the swan too is a prophet. Like all birds, swans sing throughout their lives, but they sing "most and most beautifully" before they die. Men who fear death imagine that swans before dying sing from dread, but as no birds are moved to sing by pain, neither is the swan. Singing swans on the verge of death are in fact rejoicing, for as Apollo's servants they have foresight of the good things awaiting them in the underworld. Socrates is like the swans in that he too is a servant and devotee of Apollo, and he has received from his master a prophetic skill as powerful as theirs. Therefore he is no more disheartened than they to be released from this life. His final conversation is his swansong, or the *Phaedo* as a whole is the imaginative swansong Plato wrote in honor of his old friend.

Socrates foresees a good afterlife for himself because he has dedicated his earthly life to the practice of philosophy as training for death through purification. He has endeavored to separate his soul from his body for the sake of true virtue and wisdom, and he has approached as near to this goal as a mortal man can hope to do. Therefore he is "unappalled" in the face of death, as Melville puts it in a short story entitled "Cock-A-Doodle-Do!" His Ishmael in *Moby-Dick*, however, is different. Still young and agitated, not yet far along the philosophical road to wisdom, he is no prophet himself; and the prophet he encounters on the docks is no rejoicing swan.

As Ishmael and Queequeg are on their way finally to board the *Pequod*, they are once again accosted by Elijah. As before, the man speaks in riddles, his words portentous with intimations of darkness and death. He alludes to the shadowy figures Ishmael has recently seen approaching the ship as if they were apparitions, spectral beings only "looking like men." The encounter stirs up in Ishmael "no small wonderment," and although he twice refers to Elijah as "cracked," he is himself affected and infected by the man's gloomy mood. He broods on the identity of the figures he has seen, or thinks he has seen, moving in mist near the ship, disconcerting himself to the point that he must struggle to suppress his anxiety. His stress manifests in other ways as well, as for example when he sees a sleeping sailor in the forecastle and imagines the man a corpse. And when the body eventually stirs to life, and the sailor announces that Captain Ahab has at last come aboard, his words only darken Ishmael's forebodings.

Ishmael would have liked to interrogate the sailor on the matter of Captain Ahab, but their exchange is interrupted by activity on deck. The chief mate is awake and at his business, and they must join in the labor. So Ishmael and Queequeg follow the man up the forecastle stairs and into the "clear sunrise" above—but Ishmael's mind ceaselessly revolves around the "invisible" Ahab shut up in his cabin below.

Chapter 22: Merry Christmas

The *Pequod* sets sail on or around Christmas Day, an occasion that prompts a song from Bildad. Standing at the helm he intones a hymn recalling the Israelites' approach to the Promised Land, whose sweet green fields symbolize the promise of future bliss to the Christian faithful. Ishmael is moved by the song, and he dreamily anticipates a paradisiacal voyage through "eternally vernal" climes. It is a hybrid vision of unblemished tropical islands and the pure realm of heaven. But his sanguine mood is fleeting, or superficial, or both. For at one level or another of his mind he broods still on Ahab, the unseen Captain, the hidden master. This grim presence, all the more ominous for its absence, casts a long void-shadow across Ishmael's mood. Hence, despite the spiritual optimism inspired by the season, he conceptualizes the ship's departure as an aimless driving of fate into pitiless seas.

Despite the date, Ishmael is not meditating on the birth of his savior, the living God. To the contrary, he imagines that the man piloting the ship from the harbor is "a devil." This is yet another example of the agitated perplexity that marks young Ishmael's distance from wisdom. Consider the contrast with Socrates in the *Phaedo*. As we have seen, the dialogue is set during the period of the Athenian festival commemorating the birth of Apollo, the deity to whom Socrates is especially dedicated. He has even composed a hymn in the god's honor. And as I have noted in the previous chapter, he is confident that his devotion to Apollo will secure a good afterlife for his soul. Socrates, in short, is appropriately reverential to his god, observing his own sort of Christmas Day. He is a pagan, as is Queequeg; and evidently their piety has to do with their "Socratic wisdom."

Apollo's birth was dated to the seventh day of the Athenian month Thargelion, which corresponds roughly to our month of May. We have seen that Socrates' trial began just before this, on the day after the Athenians sent Theseus's ship to the festival, and that his execution was postponed until the embassy returned to Athens, which interval according to Xenophon lasted thirty days. Among the ancients, Socrates' own birth was dated to the sixth day of Thargelion, which was the birthday of Apollo's sister, Artemis. So his trial was held, and he was sentenced to death, very nearly on his own birthday. The ancients also claimed that Plato was born the day after Socrates (approximately forty years later), and so shared Apollo's birthday. This dating of his birth goes back at least to the second century BCE. Even older is the story that Plato was the son of Apollo. Speusippus, Plato's nephew, student, and successor as head of the Academy, reported the belief popular among his contemporaries that once when the husband of Plato's mother attempted intercourse with his wife, he saw a vision of Apollo and restrained himself, leaving his wife "pure of intercourse" (*katharan gamou*) until she gave birth to a child. Some ancients, including some early Christians, took the phrase "katharan gamou" to indicate that Plato's mother was a virgin at the time of his birth.

It may be that Plato was taken to have had a special relationship to Apollo from the words he wrote for Socrates to speak in the *Phaedo*. Those who regarded the character Socrates a mouthpiece for Plato's own ideas would have attributed to Plato himself Socrates' expressions of dedication to the god. But Plato was called "divine" in his day for the majesty of his ideas and the beauty of his prose style, and as the poets often credited their verses to the Muses, so Plato's intellectual and literary achievements might be explained by the inspiration of Apollo, who some thought to be the father or leader of the Muses. Today of course we cannot entertain such beliefs, and they were certainly incomprehensible to Nietzsche. He did however associate Socrates and Plato with Apollo; but, as we shall see, he did not at all approve of the Apollonian nature of their ideas.

Chapter 23: The Lee Shore

My first exposure to *Moby-Dick* was through this chapter. A friend who was reading the book at the time—he did not finish it then, nor has he completed it since: a common experience with this difficult and unsettling work—this friend showed me "The Lee Shore," and I was mesmerized. "Wonderfullest things are ever the unmentionable." "Bear thee grimly, demigod! Up from the spray of thy ocean-perishing—straight up, leaps thy apotheosis!" The writing struck me as strange and beautiful. Add to this the fact that Melville employs his masterful prose to express such thoughts as that "in landlessness alone resides the highest truth, shoreless, indefinite as God." And all this within a chapter of hardly more than a single page, a chapter Ishmael describes as "a six-inch .... stoneless grave." I have loved *Moby-Dick* ever since, and I have loved Melville for writing it, and even more for *thinking* it.

Short as it is, this chapter has exercised scholars for years. The figure leaping up to his apotheosis, the man whose grave this chapter is, is called Bulkington. He is introduced in the third chapter as a man "in the deep shadows of [whose] eyes floated some reminiscences that did not seem to give him much joy," a man who "interested [Ishmael] at once" and whom "the sea-gods had ordained" to sail with him on the *Pequod*. Yet Bulkington makes no further appearance in the book until the present chapter, in which he falls overboard into the sea, never to be heard from again. Why? Why include in the text so minor a figure who contributes nothing whatever to the action of the story? What was Melville thinking?

Bulkington's presence in the novel, along with various inconsistencies of detail and peculiarities of narrative structure, have led many scholars to conclude that Melville began *Moby-Dick* as an altogether different sort of book than it eventually became, a book with no Queequeg and perhaps no Ahab in it. Melville, they say, set out to write a straightforward maritime adventure, very much like his earlier works (excluding the sprawling, wildly philosophical *Mardi*). Yet under the influence of a close rereading of Shakespeare, and his encounter with Nathaniel Hawthorne, in person and in writing, he was inspired to rethink his intentions and to conceive of *Moby-Dick* as a work of artistic and intellectual depth, of hidden secrets and dark truths. Thus there are two, according to some even three or more, novels interposed upon one another to create the final version of *Moby-Dick*.

The form of Melville's novel is chimeric, agglutinative, Frankensteinian. In June of 1851 Melville wrote to Hawthorne that as he had recently been "building some shanties of houses (connected to the old one)," so had he been adding "some shanties of chapters and essays" to *Moby-Dick*. Like an old farmhouse whose central structure various owners have altered and added to over the years, the simple plot at the center of *Moby-Dick* is infused internally with additional hallways, rooms, and cupboards, and equipped externally with porches, outbuildings, and secret gardens. It is more than, it is in fact something entirely other than, a single story moving forward smoothly in accordance with the classical unites; it is rather an intellectual and narrative labyrinth whose every alcove and corridor (including even the dead-ends) is essential to the form—to the greatness of the form—of the whole.

The structural complexity of *Moby-Dick* is similar to Plato's mature dialogues and Nietzsche's greatest works. The early works of all three men are relatively uncomplicated; they pursue a single subject with single-minded intent. Of course they exhibit prefigurings of the depth and complexity of their authors' later works, but only as intimations, and only when viewed with hindsight. The best of Plato's dialogues—the *Phaedrus*, say, or the *Republic*—are multilayered, allusive, and here and there uncannily enigmatic. Nietzsche's best works are similar: the Third Essay of *On the Genealogy of Morals*, for example—"What is the Meaning of Ascetic Ideals?", to my mind Nietzsche's single greatest piece of writing—addresses several topics simultaneously, constantly leaps ahead and circles back on itself, hides from the reader and reveals its treasures precisely when one is tempted to look away. Similarly, the "shanties of chapters and essays" that Melville constructed for *Moby-Dick* add levels and layers and intricacies that augment the form to such an extent that the content itself is affected. His stylistic experimentations produce an alchemy of substance.

Whether Melville intended from the beginning to create so labyrinthine a work of art, or whether the complexity is a consequence of his reconceiving and rewriting the book after he had already well begun it—either way he ultimately intended the form to be as we have it. He could have smoothed it over, straightened out the crooked turns. He might easily have written Bulkington out of the story. But he elected not to. This requires an explanation, and I cannot believe that having reconceived the book he decided against substantially revising it simply because, "like most professional authors, he was reluctant to throw away something he had already written."

This is to attribute an essential component of the book's originality and greatness—its unparalleled and occasionally baffling structure—almost to laziness. Besides, even during the time he was supposedly writing the early, more conventional version of the novel, Melville referred to it in a letter as "a strange sort of book." He knew what he was doing in shaping the work as he did. He was determined to write a philosophical book, and he understood that the ideas he intended to communicate required a form as confounding as the thoughts themselves.

Chapter 24: The Advocate

One of the most interesting of the ideas referred to in the previous chapter, also the most untimely, is the thought that the "highest truth" resides "in landlessness alone," as "indefinite as God." When I label this idea "untimely" I employ a Nietzschean expression, and I do so because Melville's remarks on truth often have a non-Platonic, and indeed an almost Nietzschean ring to them. Like Nietzsche—like everyone—Melville sometimes uses the words "true" or "truth" to mean, simply, "factual" or "fact," as for example when he writes to a friend that in his depiction of the whaling life in *Moby-Dick* he "mean[s] to give the truth of the thing." But when later that year he writes, in "Hawthorne and His Mosses," that one "must have plenty of sea-room to tell the Truth in," he alludes to deeper meanings. And when in a letter to Hawthorne he praises his friend's "intense feeling of the visable truth," and explains that he has in mind "the apprehension of the absolute condition of present things as they strike the eye of the man who fears them not, though they do their worst to him," his stress is less on the condition of present things, on the facts, than on the boldness with which a deep thinker confronts them. This is evident from his reference in this same letter to "the tragicalness of human thought in its own unbiased, native, and profounder workings" as exhibited by the man who "declares himself a sovereign nature (in himself) amid the powers of heaven, hell, and earth." That we are dealing here with matters more profound than physical courage in the face of mundane forces is suggested by Melville's subsequent reflections on the threat that these "Powers" might "choose to withhold certain secrets," and on these secrets as having to do with "the Problem of the Universe."

The tragedy of a deep mind fearlessly confronting the problem of the universe: this, rather than any Scholastic *adaequatio intellectus ad rem*, captures for Melville what can be grasped by thought of the nature of truth in its profoundest sense. His defense in the present chapter of the respectability of whaling concludes with the famous remark that "a whale-ship was my Yale College and my Harvard," and the lessons he learned during his years of higher education at sea are summed up in Ishmael's exclamation, "what are the comprehensible terrors of man compared with the interlocked terrors and wonders of God!" We need not take the mention of God here literally, or anyway not as exhaustive of Melville's intentions. He is thinking ultimately of the problem of the universe, the great secret, which is all the more uncannily problematic for the possibility that "there is *no* secret," as he puts it in the letter to Hawthorne cited above. This thought that reality is a hollow shell, a nut that when cracked yields no nourishing kernel, this is the abyss that troubled Nietzsche's thoughts, prompting him occasionally to suspect that there is *no* truth. When he advises those who look into the abyss to beware lest the abyss look into them, he might well have had Melville in mind, had he only known of his great predecessor.

The landlessness of truth, then, must relate in Melville's mind to the terrible wonders of the world, the inner- and outer-worlds alike. Melville was a thought-diver, and he explored his own interior depths as doggedly as any scientist investigating the external world of nature. Nietzsche once wrote that "it was on the soil of this *essentially dangerous* form of human existence, the priestly form, that man first became *an interesting animal*, that only here did the human soul in a higher sense acquire *depth* and become *evil*." In other words, the Christian obsession with guilt turned the human animal's mental gaze inward, and our constant self-surveillance carved out our souls by burrowing into the ground-levels of our minds, which descendingly generated ever profounder depths to match our relentlessly probing psychological excavations. These dark interior shafts of the soul were Melville's favorite hunting-grounds, and we may picture the treasure he sought in his own psychic underworld as a gate overgrown and hidden by thorns that stands on the vanishingly narrow threshold between the human spirit and the World Soul, the point of contact between two realms. His awareness that the gate might be locked, or open onto nothingness, or indeed that it might not exist at all, made the quest all the more hazardous, and thus all the more alluring, more seductive, more *tempting*.

Chapter 25: Postscript

As in this short chapter Ishmael merely supplements his defense of the honor of whaling presented in the previous chapter, describing the use of whale oil in the coronations of British monarchs, so I take the opportunity to sum up what I have written in the previous two chapters.

Moby-Dick is an eccentric book because Melville was an untimely author, something other, something more, than an author as authors existed in his time and place. Melville was a type that I like to call a *thinker-artist*, which as I have explained in previous works is a term intended to designate a sage who expresses himself creatively from behind a philosopher's mask or, as in Melville's case, a sage who expresses himself philosophically through the mask of a creative writer. Melville worked in a tradition of writers of straight-forward prose, from Irving and Cooper in fiction to Emerson and Thoreau in philosophical non-fiction. But under the intentionally acquired influence of European authors like Shakespeare, Thomas Browne, and Coleridge, and that rare-bird of his own country, Hawthorne, he developed an appreciation for writers in whose works one encounters "deep far-away things ... occasional flashings-forth of the intuitive Truth ... short, quick probings at the very axis of reality." I take this quote from Melville's "Hawthorne and His Mosses," ostensibly a review-essay of Hawthorne's *Mosses from an Old Manse*, but really in bulk a declaration of Melville's own intellectual and creative liberation from traditional strictures of substance and style. He composed the essay while writing *Moby-Dick*, and one detects traces of self-observation and self-formation throughout. Melville is writing as much of himself as of his subject when he dwells on Hawthorne's "mystical blackness" deriving from a "Calvinistic sense of Innate Depravity and Original Sin." And when he claims with reference to "the blackness of darkness beyond" that "even [Hawthorne's] bright glidings but fringe, and play upon the edges of thunder-clouds," he surely has his *Moby-Dick* in mind as well.

I have noted that Melville described his novel as "a strange sort of book," and I have stated my belief that by this he meant to allude to the structure of the work as well as to its content and tone. He grafted apparently foreign elements onto the simple contours of his early, straight-forward style, and thereby produced a monster of a book whose corporeal form is as extraordinary as the mood that infuses its soul. The result reads like an encyclopedic prose-poem chanted by drunken angels in Hell.

In his review-essay Melville muses on Hawthorne's "blackness of darkness beyond" in association with Shakespeare's Lear speaking "the sane madness of vital truth." I read these expressions as referring to those problems that I have called, following Dostoevsky, the accursed questions. I reference Dostoevsky, though we cannot with certainty identify the man who coined the expression. It has been proposed that the phrase entered the Russians' vocabulary (as *proklyatye voprosy*) by way of Mikhail L. Mikhailov's translation of "der verdammten Fragen" in Heinrich Heine's *Zum Lazarus*. Whether or not this is true, it would be appropriate, for Heine's poem is a rumination on the misfortunes and evils that mar this world supposedly under divine care. Dostoevsky and Melville worried over the same problems, and the several related existential and cosmic conundrums that branch off from them. As artists they thought deeply about the accursed questions in which they knew themselves to be implicated, and they reflected as well on the various ways that other men confront or attempt to evade them. The variations correspond to differences within the type *man*, and they distinguish as well different types of *philosopher*.

Chapter 26: Knights and Squires

There are those who read *Moby-Dick* as a commentary on American political life, taking the *Pequod* and its crew for the nation and her citizens. This sort of reader takes seriously remarks such as those in the present chapter in praise of democracy with reverence for the "great democratic God." I myself find the reading of the novel as an allegorical political treatise unpersuasive; it is a narrow, constricted and constricting interpretation. *Moby-Dick* is throughout too vast a work, too broad and too deep, to represent nothing more than this, or even to represent this primarily. And as for the declarations of devotion to democracy, I have a hard time taking them seriously, but I admit that I may be in the wrong here. Melville's two grandfathers served in the Revolutionary War; his paternal grandfather even participated in the Boston Tea Party and displayed in his home a vial of tea that he carried away from the event. As a child Melville knew and respected both men, and he was proud of his connections to the founding of his country. So he may very well have honored our democratic system without irony. If so, he would have distinguished himself in this from both Plato and Nietzsche.

During Plato's lifetime Athens was a democratic polis more often than not. In the aftermath of the Peloponnesian War between Athens and Sparta, when Plato was in his early- to mid-twenties, the democracy was dismantled and rule by the so-called "Thirty Tyrants" installed in its place. Among these thirty men, and another ten in charge of the harbor town Peiraias, were two relatives of Plato, an uncle and a cousin. So Plato was born into a family with close ties to the anti-democratic faction in Athens, and he seems to have inherited their political biases. To mention just one example of his attitude toward democracy, in Book 8 of the *Republic* he includes a blistering account of the nature of the democratic state and the democratic man. Blistering and stunningly prescient: his description of a society drunk on freedom to such an extent that anarchy infects the citizens' very souls, respect for authority deteriorates, traditions and social conventions collapse, teachers pander to students, and in general youth culture dominates opinion and taste—this description is a frighteningly faithful portrait of our own society. In this work Plato ranks democracy lowest among the traditional forms of government excepting only an outright tyranny.

Nietzsche disdained democracy every bit as much as Plato, perhaps with even more venom. He condemned modern European democratic conventions as the treacly residue of the Christian belief that all souls are equal in the eyes of God. He could not accept democracy because he rejected the metaphysical foundations that support it: he did not believe in God; he denounced Christianity as a dangerous falsehood; he rejected the traditional concept of the soul; and he regarded the social-political notion of equality a weapon of revenge wielded by inferior classes of men against their betters. In short, Nietzsche was sure that belief in such "lies" as are bound up with democracy, equality, and human rights depends on belief in the existence of Melville's "great God absolute," the "just Spirit of Equality," the divine conceived as the "center and circumference of all democracy!"

Melville's understanding of the conceptual underpinnings of democracy might not have diverged too far from Nietzsche's, for the words I have quoted just above that ground democracy in a conception of God as the source and support of human equality are Melville's own, as spoken by Ishmael in the present chapter. If, then, we would like to know whether Melville was indeed an enthusiastic partisan of democracy, we should have to consider whether he did in fact believe in such a God. It is not at all clear to me that he did. And if he did not, I think we cannot be sure of his political sympathies. Of course it is possible that Melville rejected Ishmael's Nietzschean account of the metaphysical assumptions at the heart of democracy, and I suppose it is possible too that he did not intend to imply that Ishmael accepts the account on any literal interpretation, that the words he wrote for his Ishmael to speak were rhetorical expressions of respect for democracy dressed up in figuratively theological language. It is hard to say what Melville had in mind because when Ishmael brings up democracy at this point in the narrative he is motivated by other than social-political considerations.

Ishmael's praise of democracy in this chapter is bound up with his (Melville's, really) justification for depicting humble sailors on occasion as grand, tragic figures. He asks the "great democratic God" to bear him out if "to meanest mariners, and renegades and castaways, I shall hereafter ascribe high qualities" and "weave around them tragic graces." So perhaps after all we are not dealing with a theological justification of democracy, nor even with the rhetoric of theology in support of Ishmael's respect for democracy; perhaps there is only the rhetoric of democracy in support of Melville's narrative style. In any case, I do not intend to settle the matter here. I will instead follow Melville by turning now to an analysis of character types. In the present chapter he introduces the first mate, Starbuck, and in the following chapter he presents the second and third mates as well. I take all three together in the next chapter and, with reference to Ishmael's characterizations, discuss the various ways that different types of men confront the accursed questions, and thereby engage with philosophy.

Chapter 27: Knights and Squires

First mate Starbuck is a pious man, faithful to his family and his God. He is superstitious, though in a manner indicative of intelligence rather than ignorance. He is also a man of action, but though he regularly exhibits physical courage, he "cannot withstand those more terrific, because more spiritual terrors, which sometimes menace you from the concentrating brow of an enraged and mighty man." Stubb, the second mate, is "happy-go-lucky … good-humored, easy, and careless." He is the sort of man who gives no thought to death, not from bravery or defiance of God, but rather from a lack of intellectual curiosity and spiritual depth. Deep thinking would distract him from the corporeal pleasures of his dinner and his pipe. The third mate Flask is all business. He has no "sense of reverence for the many marvels of [the whale's] majestic bulk and mystic ways." He takes his work seriously *as work*, but he does not understand, and does not care to understand, the cosmic and existential implications of the craft that consume a pondering man like Ishmael.

These three mates we may take to represent three different ways of relating to philosophy. Men like Stubb have no use for it at all. They dismiss intellectual activity as a useless waste of time, a morbid distraction from the pleasures of life. Of course they would never read Aristotle, but if they did they would not comprehend his claim that the highest activities are chosen precisely because they have no significant practical consequences. Philosophy is indeed useless; it is chosen for itself because it is good in itself. Pleasure and enjoyment naturally attend the acquisition of philosophical insight, but the philosopher does not seek insight for the sake of pleasure. Other men live for enjoyment, and they find their bliss in physical things. To employ a vocabulary derived from the *Phaedo*, devoted as they are to their desires, they voluntarily imprison themselves to the bonds of the body. Nietzsche would call such men decadent, but those among them who affect sophistication like to refer to themselves as epicures. Their ignorance of Aristotle is matched by their ignorance of Epicurus, who as a hedonist would certainly approve their seeking of pleasure, but as certainly would reproach them for failing to recognize pleasures higher than those connected with the body. The shallow hedonist does not regard the accursed questions *as* accursed, but this is so only because he does not regard them at all.

The intelligent among the religious tend to be aware of the accursed questions. The principles of their faith do after all address these matters. Why do bad things happen to good people? Is the will free? Why is there something rather than nothing, and why do I in particular exist? Is there meaning, a plan or a purpose, within or behind this world and our lives? But men of faith, dedicated exclusively to one specific creed or dogma, cannot really engage with these questions at the deepest, most personal level. They cannot take them seriously, cannot not really *feel* them, because they believe they know the answers, or anyway that someone does, their priest or pastor, or at least their God. Moreover, they trust that the answers are comforting. So the believer does not usually think about the accursed questions in the sense of *thinking through* them. He knows they exist, and he realizes that they would be troubling if they were unanswered or unanswerable, but he rests blissfully in the confidence that God's in his heaven and all is right with the world. This type of man, then, does not regard the accursed questions *as* accursed, but only because he believes in a God who has answered all questions from eternity, and whose answers are balms for his soul.

Similar to the man of religious faith is the man who believes that his philosophy, or that science as a collective enterprise, has answered, or one day will answer, all genuine questions. Some such men even insist that the accursed questions are not actual questions. They appear to be questions because they are grammatically well-formed interrogatives, but since they do not refer to matters subject to empirical verification or falsification, they are only apparent questions. They may in fact be literally meaningless; at best they are misguided. Men of this type typically inhabit the university. They are academics and researchers; they are professionals. Some of these professionals engage with the "big" questions, but their true interests lie elsewhere, in their family, their career, their sports, or their politics. Most work exclusively on a narrow set of professionally sanctioned technical problems, in accord with the methods and perspectives approved by their peers. Whether they be professional philosophers or research scientists, many of these academic professionals adhere to the anti-philosophical, anti-scientific ideology known as scientism, according to which science alone is the source of knowledge about reality, and the boundaries of reality are determined by scientific knowledge. Since science yields knowledge only of physical objects and physical processes, physical objects and processes alone exist. Anyone who claims or implies that reality extends beyond the empirical realm must rely on a backward faith or pseudo-knowledge, or else he must be ignorant. And the man who wonders aloud whether these professionals claim to *know* that scientism is true, and, if so, what means they have employed to verify this empirically—well, let's not think about him. He is trouble.

Trouble he may be, but he might also be a philosopher. Not a *professional* philosopher, mind you; not even if he earns his living as a professor of philosophy. Philosophers in the tradition of Plato, Melville, and Nietzsche are wonderers, pondering men, tempters and attempters. They do not limit their inquiries, or their methods of inquiry, to the subjects and procedures that happen to be fashionable among their contemporaries. Their very lives are involved in the problems that consume them, the questions that confound them. Therefore they take these problems and questions as seriously as they take themselves. They are drawn to the accursed questions because these are

Plato — Melville — Nietzsche

the vital questions, the ultimate problems, provocative of wonder and perplexed anxiety. The men who pursue them are the shoreless explorers who share with Ishmael an "everlasting itch for things remote." Everlasting: the deep thinkers never turn away from the accursed questions; their aim is to continue to regard them, but to cease to regard them *as* accursed. These are the lovers of wisdom.

Chapter 28: Ahab

Ishmael and Ahab are two variations of the authentic philosopher. They confront the accursed questions unflinchingly, and regarding them *as* accursed they suffer from them. The relevant difference between them in this regard is that Ahab will never master his suffering to attain the serenity of the sage; he is the *perpetual philosopher*. Ishmael on the other hand will one day transcend philosophy into wisdom. He will learn to live with the accursed questions without suffering. This is the Ishmael we encounter as narrator of *Moby-Dick*, a man who became who he is in part by taking Ahab as an example of what not to be.

In the present chapter Ahab finally appears on deck, but he does not act or speak for himself. He serves as a screen on which the young Ishmael projects elements of his own interior condition. Still, Ahab is no featureless surface; he is too momentous a man to display only a flat, malleable blankness. His very presence influences Ishmael's subjectivity and affects its externalized manifestation. He shapes as much as he is shaped, even as a mental image in the mind of another man. Nevertheless, we learn in this chapter as much about Ishmael's perception of Ahab as about the man himself; and if for a moment we concentrate on the perception rather than its object, we may catch sight of the movements of Ishmael's soul.

Ishmael characterizes Ahab as something of a divine figure. Before the Captain ascends to reveal himself on deck he is a "supreme lord and dictator" secluded below in a "sacred retreat." He is an "unknown" entity, and his absence appears all the more troublingly mysterious when Ishmael recalls the "diabolical" prophet Elijah's minatory ramblings concerning him. Upon seeing the man at last, Ishmael likens him to Perseus, son of Zeus, slayer of the gorgon Medusa. More, he compares him specifically to Benvenuto Cellini's cast statue of Perseus, which stands in the Loggia della Signoria in

65

Florence, Italy, a self-sufficient hero coolly unmoving amid the touring crowds of sweltering mortals. Melville had not yet seen the statue when he wrote *Moby-Dick*, but he had inspected engravings. Years later he would describe it from first-hand experience as an "astonishing conception," a work "brought to perfection" in living flames after its conception in "the fiery brain of the intense artist." Cellini's Perseus is indeed astonishingly perfect. Prodigiously overwhelming, it is simultaneously breathtaking and inspiring, a true rival to Michelangelo's David. The young man stands on the beheaded body of Medusa, whose contorted limbs beneath his feet are the fleshy dais from atop which he raises the gorgon's bleeding head aloft in awful glory. In his other hand he carries still the severing blade. His contrapuntal pose is expressive at once of relaxation and taut force, his gaze simultaneously determined and content. His muscular body is sinuous as rippling water suddenly congealed into adamant. Nobility and beauty, violence and elegance, divinity and monstrosity: such contrary properties are unified in this more-than-human mortal.

The comparison to Ahab may be apt, but it is ironic as well. Perseus pursued and struggled with a monster whose most lethal weapon was her adversaries' lust to behold her, to know her, to see her face and to understand as no man had done before. Medusa was the abyss who stares back at impetuous observers, and in her gaze was petrified death. But with the assistance of Athena, goddess of wisdom and war, Perseus overcame her. Respecting Medusa's seductive power he approached her indirectly, confronted her image as a reflection in his mirror. He caught the light of her form by turning away from the darkness of her matter. Finally he removed the head, seat of insight swarming with serpents. Prudent and calm, he made off with the dread vessel of wisdom, suitable gift for Athena, who affixed it to her snaky aegis.

Ahab will not fare so well. He cannot look away, not even for a moment, and not even if by temporarily retreating the hunter makes the swiftest progress toward his prey. No pause for impatient Ahab on his road to death, the very road that leads the prudently patient man to life. So although to Ishmael Ahab appears almost a god—courageous, resolute, "fixed and fearless"—mighty as he may be, he is not omnipotent. And besides his fearsome powerfulness, Ishmael observes signs of weakness too, indications almost of death. Ahab looks like "a man cut away from the stake" after having been ravaged by fire. A pale scar extends from under his hairline down the side of his face and neck, disappearing finally under his clothes: it resembles the jagged track of a shock of lightning scorched in the splintered bark of a living tree. Then, of course, there is Ahab's stump of a leg, artificially extended by a "barbaric" prosthetic cut and carved from the jawbone of a whale. Its hideousness contributes to Ahab's grim aspect, marked already by a "crucifixion in his face," and shadowed by clouds upon clouds lowering over his brow. The Captain is "moody"; he is "stricken."

Ahab limps on a false leg; his head and neck are scarred indeed. But that he is a tortured demigod seared by flames, a looming thunder-storm of a man, these are products of Ishmael's perception. He reads into Ahab signs of his own moroseness. He admits to being haunted by wild imaginings regarding the man even before he sets eyes on him. He was apprehensive, uneasy, or perturbed. In fact he cannot quite identify his obscure unsettled feelings: he suffered, he says, from "colorless misgivings." He describes a sort of existential dread, an aimless anxiety, a fear without object. But is the tortured soul at issue here Ahab's fretful inner ghost or Ishmael's?

I do not mean to imply that Ishmael misjudges his captain. But if he sees accurately into the man's obscure interior, it is so because he has explored the similarly twisted shafts of the caverns within his own subterranean self. Although he does not know it, in Ahab the young Ishmael encounters a projected foreshadowing of one possible version of his own intellectual-spiritual future. He sees a man who suffers from the accursed questions, a suffering that has made of him a monumental figure, but which has marked him too with presages of an inexorably approaching doom.

Chapter 29: Enter Ahab; to him, Stubb

With his first words as reported by Ishmael Ahab imaginatively refers to himself as a living corpse. He stays on deck now more than he goes below, for a visit to his cabin is, he says, like "going down into one's tomb," a descent into a "grave-dug berth." The mates and sailors too: their sleeping quarters Ahab calls their "nightly grave," their bedclothes are material anticipations of their burial-shrouds. Ahab's actions are marked by a correspondingly moody aggressiveness. Asked by Stubb to muffle the midnight clanking of his whale-bone leg on the deck, he lashes out wildly, dismissing the mate as a dog. When Stubb objects to being so rudely treated,

Ahab escalates his insults, denouncing him as "ten times a donkey, and a mule, and an ass." He even threatens lethal violence, advancing as if he would kill Stubb where he stood. Hastily retreating in fear, Stubb wonders whether Ahab is insane or in need of prayerful interventions, and this even though he is not a praying man.

Safely away from the furious captain, Stubb ruminates on the encounter; and in doing so he discloses additional facts about Ahab: the Captain does not sleep, and when on occasion he takes to his bed, he so tosses and turns throughout the night that in the morning his sheets are disordered, twisted, and knotted at the foot of the bed, his pillow hot as if his head were a brick baked in an oven. Stubb takes all this for evidence of a troubled conscience, possibly; but after all he cannot be sure, for Ahab is "full of riddles."

Ahab is a mysterious man, this is true. Who can name the visions that worry his sleep? But we do know something of his personality as revealed through the observable facts. The man is restless, ill at ease, tensely vigilant to a point of discomposure. His obsessions have metastasized and amalgamated into a single dangerous mania, a concentrated preoccupation with the beast who took his leg. And unsettled as he is by enraged anguish, his fixation has blurringly distorted into a vindictive stalking of God, whatsoever that abysmal word should mean in the crypt of Ahab's frenzied mind.

In the previous chapter I identified Ahab as the perpetual philosopher, and I believe his behavior as related in this chapter provides some initial indications of his condition. We may find him to be profound, but we will never see him at peace. And if the wisdom of the genuine sage is joyful, then Ahab is no wise man.

Chapter 30: The Pipe

If we could summon the generosity of spirit to think of Ahab as at least on his way to wisdom, we would nevertheless have to admit that the man is his own impediment. Blind as he is to the world around, he has lost himself in the labyrinth of his mind, and his morose constitution is the Minotaur feeding on the flesh of his inmost being.

A self-lacerating man such as Ahab is, before at last destroying himself, may assume an impressive stature in the eyes of unknowing observers. Given a robust physique and the appropriate psychic conditions, particularly intellectual and spiritual depth bound up with a willful resolve toward a single unattainable end, his interior torments may manifest externally as a tragic disposition. There is about such men an air of constrained explosiveness, always the threat of whirlwind and lightning. The combined effects of imagination in the subject and mystery in the object are in this way sophistical, touching the truth while veering away from reality.

So Ahab appears to Ishmael a noble man of fate, enigmatic, foreboding, regal. When he sees the Captain sitting on his ivory stool he thinks of ancient Danish royalty. Ahab is a "Khan," a "king," a "great lord of Leviathans." He is as old as time, deeper than history, a monster-haunted myth.

Now suppose we assume that Ishmael is right, or at least not too far wrong—must we admire Ahab? Does Ahab admire himself? As he knows the world more thoroughly than young Ishmael, and as he is acquainted more deeply with himself as well, I believe he knows better than to admire. Consider his rueful ruminations on his pipe. Sitting on deck astride his monarchial stool, Ahab lights his pipe and smokes. What does he think about then, approaching as he must a contemplative mood induced by his rhythmic respirations? He thinks of death, of course; and only when disturbed by this thought does he notice that the wind blows the smoke directly back into his face. How different from the experience of the thoughtless Stubb: the second mate's pipe, we learn in chapter twenty-seven, filters the air of those of its particles that have been "infected with the nameless miseries of the numberless mortals who have died exhaling it." Ahab's pipe effects no such purification. He inhales the world's miseries, and his "nervous whiffs" resemble to him the dying spoutings of a whale, "strongest and fullest of trouble."

Although Ahab broods on death, he marks as well his presently agitated state. He realizes that he's no man for a pipe, which after all is an instrument "meant for sereneness." Ahab is far from serene, and his "torn iron-grey locks" are but one visible sign of his internal unrest. Therefore he resolves to smoke no more and tosses the pipe overboard. The hissing of its fire in the engulfing waves foreshadows Ahab's own unhappy fate.

I have written that the sage regards the accursed questions without regarding them *as* accursed. He does not suffer from his meditations on the grim facts of human existence; he is serene. Ahab is no sage precisely because he suffers; and what's worse, he seems almost to prefer his suffering to tranquility. In the *Phaedo* Plato writes of the man whose desires respecting pleasure and pain induce him to contribute to his own confinement within the prison of his body. Just so has Ahab locked himself inside a cell of tortured grief. His regard for the accursed questions makes him a philosopher. His inability to regard them as anything other than accursed binds him to the condition of perpetual philosopher.

Chapter 31: Queen Mab

In the *Symposium*, when Socrates finally joins the party after lingering outside in a mystifying kind of contemplative trance, the tragedian Agathon requests that the philosopher sit beside him. He would like, he says, by touching Socrates to have the benefit of the wisdom he acquired on the porch. Socrates replies that it would be good if wisdom could be transmitted between men simply by contact. Not that this would benefit Agathon, however, for Socrates is sure that his wisdom is paltry and as dubious as a dream.

This notion of a dream-like pseudo-wisdom recalls Plato's famous "Allegory of the Cave" from Book 7 of the *Republic*. Here there are men chained in a cave with their heads securely fastened; unable to turn at the neck, they see only the interior wall of the cave directly in front of them. Behind these prisoners are men pacing back and forth on the far side of a low wall, holding various artifacts above their heads like puppeteers raising their puppets above a little stage. And behind these men burns a fire whose flames cast shadows of the artifacts on the wall in front of the prisoners. Since from childhood these chained men have experienced nothing besides these shadows, they mistake them for ultimate reality. They have what they call "wisdom" in their cave, namely the ability to identify the shadows and associate them with one another, remembering for example which ones usually follow or accompany others. Down in this underground realm men contend with one another over these shadows as if they were living in a dream.

Through this allegory Plato makes a point about cognition and reality similar to the image in his *Phaedo* likening our understanding of the world to the experience of men dwelling beneath the sea who mistake the leagues of waters above them for the sky, an image Melville himself employs in *Moby-Dick*. Plato writes specifically that the prisoners are like us, by which he means that as they mistake insubstantial shadows for true things, so we go wrong in taking the material world for ultimate reality. If one of these prisoners were released from his bonds (*lusin … tôn desmôn*, the same language we have encountered in the *Phaedo*) and led up out of the cave, he would come to know true reality. And just so, if we were to receive a properly philosophical education, we would learn that quite apart from physical objects there are metaphysical essences existing independently of space and time, entities that Plato calls Forms. These are the perfect paradigms of which the objects familiar to us in the natural world are imperfect imitations. These unchanging Forms are somehow responsible for the mutable objects that "participate" in them having the essential properties that make them the kinds of things that they are. Every beautiful thing, for example, is beautiful by participating in the Form of Beauty. The Forms, moreover, are objects of intellection and knowledge, whereas physical things are the objects only of perception and belief. Here I restate the differences between Being and Becoming I introduced earlier.

For the Platonist, then, true wisdom consists in the understanding of ultimate reality, knowledge of the metaphysical Forms, which distinguishes the lover of wisdom from the lover of opinion as a waking man is distinguished from a dreamer.

I write in this chapter of wisdom and dreams because in "Queen Mab" Melville has erected a shanty of a chapter concerning these very matters. The chapter's title he has borrowed from Mercutio's account in *Romeo and Juliet* of a fairy-like figure who generates dreams in mortals, but its content involves the second mate Stubb recounting a dream in which Ahab repeatedly kicks him with his ivory leg and thereby transmits wisdom to him. But as Socrates points out in the *Symposium*, wisdom cannot be passed from one man to another through mere physical contact, and Stubb himself imagines it possible only because he has taken the word of a figure appearing in his dream. But what could a dream-image know about wisdom? And such a strange image at that—a humpbacked merman carrying seaweed with marlinspikes protruding from his rear, arrow-ends out.

This image of the merman recalls the figure of Glaucus in Book 10 of Plato's *Republic*. Glaucus was a fisherman who one day leapt into the sea and was transformed into a divine merman whose body eventually was so thoroughly overgrown with shells, seaweed, and rocks that he took on the appearance of a multi-form beast. Pressing a point familiar to us from the

Phaedo, Socrates compares the misshapen figure to the human soul in communion with the body before it has become pure (*katharon*). Neither the *Republic* nor the *Symposium* are as extreme in their condemnation of the body as the *Phaedo* and the broader tradition that I have designated *Phaedo*-Platonism. But they do come close, as demonstrated by this comparison of an embodied soul to a deformed sea-beast in the *Republic*, and also by Diotima's account in the *Symposium* of philosophical progress toward true wisdom involving an ascent from lust for physical bodies toward love of the soul and, ultimately, love of the disembodied Form of Beauty itself.

Chapter 32: Cetology

This chapter is the rock on which many first-time readers of *Moby-Dick* founder. If they have made it this far—some do not—their will to continue sinks right here. The content of the chapter contributes nothing directly to the plot, and although it is only approximately ten pages long, to the wrong sort of reader it can seem interminable. Some people are interested exclusively in the action of the story. These are the people who imagine that *Moby-Dick* can be adequately filmed—for it is after all the straightforward story of a madman hunting a whale. But this is to ignore the fact that a significant element of the book's greatness resides in Melville's prose. The words, the vocabulary and syntax, the asides and philosophical observations, the written evocation of mood and creation of atmosphere—these are as vital as the story; in some ways they are more vital.

In the contribution of Melville's style to the greatness of *Moby-Dick* there is a parallel to Homer's *Iliad*. Homer sometimes is not satisfied to mention merely that, for example, Achilles was angry, nor even that he was as angry as a threatened lion. Instead he will say something along the following lines: Achilles was as angry as a lioness who while sunning with her cubs detects a foreign scent. Lifting her head to scan the horizon, she spies a group of hunters approaching. She recoils and sniffs the air again. The men are stooped low to remain out of sight, moving slowly with spears in hand. They are on the hunt for meat, and also for skins from which their women will fashion winter clothes. They have trekked for miles. They communicate in hushed tones. They mean to kill. The lion now rouses her young and leads them off to shelter out of the way. Her blood boils and her tail twitches erratically; her lips curl back to reveal lethal fangs. She is stalking back toward the invaders. Drawing near the men, she roars, an angry, bellowing wail... And so on and one for many lines, concluding at last with "thus was Achilles angry."

Now if as a reader one is interested only in Achilles' emotional state, Homer has provided far too much irrelevant information; he has interrupted the plot to tell a pointless mini-story within the actual story of interest. But this is not the proper way to approach the *Iliad*. It is after all a poem, and the beauty of the work is often less in the details of the story than in the telling. So it is with *Moby-Dick*. The novel in a way is something of a prose-poem. Therefore, to appreciate it fully one must approach it as more than—as something altogether other than—a simple story with an unswerving plot-line. One must read it as a multifaceted work of art.

This chapter on cetology, the study of whales, functions as a semi-scientific introduction to all the known varieties of whale. It is a naturalist's taxonomy of the order of cetaceans by species—or anyway it is an ironic playing with such an undertaking, and in order really to appreciate the chapter one must take it for the play that it is. Melville does not ask his audience to commit the information to memory; there will be no exam. He asks only that we read and enjoy. Anyone who loves language for its own sake, who is willing to deviate temporarily from the straight line of the plot in search of more poetic adventures, should have no trouble granting Melville's request. Read and enjoy.

One last note on this theme: the unusual nature of "Cetology," the appearance the chapter presents of being an excerpt from an encyclopedia mistakenly grafted into the book by an absent-minded printer, this contributes to what I have called the chimeric, the Frankensteinian, form of the book. The poetry of *Moby-Dick* is not only in the language; the structure of the work is itself a form of poetry. Melville has intentionally constructed his book from many different types of material: the whole is of written words, to be sure; but these words are compounded into different genres, and these genres in turn are interwoven to form a strange but beautiful fabric.

Having said all this, I do not wish to leave the impression that there is nothing of philosophical interest in this chapter. In fact it concludes with a famous reflection on the essentially fragmentary nature of all great undertakings. At the end of the chapter Ishmael admits to presenting only an imperfect taxonomy of the whale, but, he adds, he is content to leave his work as incomplete as the Cologne Cathedral, which for hundreds of years supported a crane atop its unfinished south tower. Ishmael justifies his carefree attitude by remarking that although "small erections may be finished by their first architects; grand ones, true ones, ever leave the copestone to posterity." He then exclaims "God keep me from ever completing anything," and I take it that Melville intends to offer insight into his own ideas about philosophy and truth when Ishmael adds that the whole of *Moby-Dick* is "but a draught—nay, but the draught of a draught."

From the content of the present chapter we may infer still more about Melville's notions of philosophy and truth, more that relates to my discussion of wisdom in the previous chapter. But as it relates as well to the content of the chapter to follow, I reserve it for inclusion immediately below.

Chapter 33: The Specksynder

In the previous chapter Ishmael describes his taxonomical efforts as the "classification of the constituents of a chaos." The implication is that the task is impossible, for an actual chaos may not even present one with objects to classify. According to the original meaning, a chaos is a chasm, a void or abyss; at best it would be a collection so disordered that none of its elements has any specifiable identity. Any systematic ordering of a chaos, then, must be arbitrary. Yet Ishmael takes this problem lightly, for the taxonomy is his undertaking *as narrator*, which is to say as the serenely playful sage that he is as opposed to the agitated young philosopher he was at the time of the story he is telling. So even though it is "a fearful thing" to "have one's hands among the unspeakable foundations, ribs, and very pelvis of the world," Ishmael is not himself afraid. And this is another way of saying that Ishmael addresses the accursed questions without regarding them *as* accursed.

The stereotypical philosopher seeks the truth, the final and absolute truth. This is what monomaniacal Ahab is after. But Ishmael understands that "any human thing supposed to be complete, must for that very reason infallibly be faulty." Ishmael is no stereotypical philosopher. As narrator he has transcended philosophy, as I have said; and he has accomplished this not by acquiring knowledge of the truth, but rather by attaining to wisdom. Philosophy is by definition the love of wisdom, and it may very well be a mistake—a venerable mistake, but a mistake nonetheless—to identify wisdom exclusively with knowledge of truth.

In the first chapter of Book 6 of the *Nicomachean Ethics* Aristotle identifies wisdom (*sophia*) as the proper excellence, or the virtue, of that part of the rational human soul that he calls *to epistêmonikon*. It is common to translate this as "the scientific part," but the translation is somewhat misleading since the Greek *epistêmê* means something closer to "certain knowledge" than to "scientific knowledge" in our sense of this expression. With this part of the soul we "contemplate beings of the sort whose fundamental principles do not admit of being otherwise," or necessary beings, which is far from what we imagine the business of contemporary science to be. In any case, Aristotle states in chapter seven that *sophia*, the virtue of this highest part of the soul, is itself a compound of *nous* and *epistêmê*, the former defined as the intellectual apprehension of indemonstrable first principles, the latter as certain knowledge of the conclusions that follow from these principles. In chapter two we learn that the function or naturally proper activity of each of these parts of the soul is the acquisition of truth.

I relate Aristotle's account in some detail to stress the emphasis on truth in his conception of wisdom. I myself am not convinced, and I suspect that Plato, Melville, and Nietzsche would share my doubts. Many, probably most, of those philosophers who identify with the tradition of Platonism, and some of the characters who appear in the Platonic dialogues—Socrates in particular—might well have accepted Aristotle's identification of wisdom with knowledge of truth. But I doubt that Plato himself did. This is not to say that he denied the very existence of truth, nor that he ranked truth among the lowest of values. But I take the ambiguous, playful, indirect, and sphinx-like nature of the dialogues to suggest that Plato was after something grander than the truth. Nor do I admit that the dialogues were mere expressions of Plato's intellectual-creative impulses ancillary and subordinate to his purely philosophical activities, or pedagogical tools for the communication of the truths he discovered through these activities. Plato must have spent as much time conceiving and composing the dialogues as he spent doing anything else, and I believe that during this time he regarded himself as engaged in philosophical activity, or, better, in an activity expressing wisdom that manifests as philosophy.

In the present chapter Ishmael remarks that Ahab "sometimes masked himself," employing the "forms and usages" that coordinate relations between captain and crew for "other and more private ends" than was customary. I believe that the dialogues were themselves a sort of mask for Plato, indeed that Platonism itself is one of Plato's most enduring masks. Nietzsche once referred to "Platonism in Europe" as a "monstrous and frightening mask" behind which lurks some great thing that one day will inscribe itself "in the hearts of humanity with eternal demands." And later in the same book he wrote that "every profound spirit needs a mask: even more, around every profound spirit a mask is growing continually, owing to the constantly false, namely *shallow*, interpretation of every word, every step, every sign of life he gives." It seems to me that Nietzsche is right, and that the profundity of Plato's wisdom was misread by those around him as an ultimate concern for truth, that Plato the philosophical seeker of truth is the mask that grew up around Plato the sage.

Chapter 34: The Cabin-Table

I have by now written at some length about Ahab as the perpetual philosopher. The Captain is too agitated to qualify as a sage. He is as much a stranger to Plato's playfulness as to Nietzsche's Zarathustran cheerfulness. Worse, he is a voluntary exile from wisdom. He prefers his suffering to the tranquility of *ataraxia*, and as Nietzsche says, that man is corrupt who chooses, who prefers, that which is disadvantageous for him.

Ahab is also far too obsessed with seeking the truth. And to echo Nietzsche once again, why not rather untruth? Through his obsession with the white whale Ahab reveals his distance from wisdom, and thus his alienation from the essence of philosophy, which at its core is the love of wisdom, not the love of truth. Conceived as the love of wisdom, and depending on one's understanding of "love" in this case, philosophy may be either a way of ascent toward its own transcendence into the superior state of wisdom, or one manifestation of the sage's expression of wisdom. I shall have more to say about this distinction later, but for now I contrast this conception of philosophy with philosophy conceived as the love of truth. This latter is the perpetual philosopher's conception, and it makes of philosophy a labyrinth, an inescapable maze whose dead-ends and shadows darken the mood of the man locked and lost inside.

Even worse than Ahab's obsession with truth, from the perspective of *Phaedo*-Platonism, is his "supposing that those things are true which the body says" are so. Men like Ahab who feel pleasures and pains excessively tend to believe that whatever produces these states must be "most distinct and most true." And since physical things produce bodily pleasures and pains, this sort of man tends to identify truth with physical reality. He is, in short, a materialist, like the prisoners chained in the cave, only in this image the body itself is the cave, and instead of chains it binds the soul with nails.

At the end of the present chapter Ishmael describes "Ahab's soul" as "shut up in the caved trunk of his body," like a bear hibernating in an old tree. Ahab asks the right questions, but he has so thoroughly identified the whale, a physical object, with the answers, that he has reduced philosophy to a corporeal pursuit. He is locked inside a philosophical labyrinth because he is shut inside his body. And as this explains his lack of wisdom, it explains as well his concomitant lack of tranquility. I have noted that the genuine philosopher who escapes from the bonds of the body through purification is thereby liberated from excessive pleasures and pains; he becomes as tranquil as a calm sea. But Ahab's existential seas are tempestuous. Ishmael refers to him as "moody," "awful," "black terrific," and "inclement." And what does Ahab's soul do inside the imprisoning trunk of his body? It gnaws on "the sullen paws of its gloom!" So despite the fact that Ahab rules his ship like a lord, a khan, or a king, these are earthly, and therefore ephemeral and ultimately trivial, titles. And though the man who receives the benefits that accrue from such powerful positions may enjoy his pleasures, he will also suffer excruciating pains; and in either case these are mere physical states, inferior to the nobler intellectual-spiritual condition of wisdom. In the hierarchy of reincarnated beings as laid out in Plato's *Phaedrus*, the tyrant occupies the lowest rank; and although the king ranks second, the philosopher stands above him in first place.

Ahab's soul is gloomy because although it would like to ascend to wisdom—the desire of every soul—Ahab has tethered it to philosophy conceived as the pursuit of truth, and truth conceived as a phenomenon embodied exclusively in the natural world. In short, Ahab seeks the metaphysical while restricting his search to the physical realm. As a result he is a grotesque intellectual crossbreed: deep in his soul he longs to be a sage, but his body has hammered his spirit into the alien shape of a materialist scientist. The result is a morbid contradiction, a monster at war with itself.

Chapter 35: The Mast-Head

The philosophical tradition that I have designated *Phaedo*-Platonism is composed of ideas drawn from dialogues other than just the *Phaedo*, but all of them are consistent with the *Phaedo*'s radical otherworldliness. I have mentioned the *Republic* and *Symposium*; there is also the *Theaetetus*, the locus classicus of the notion of likeness to god (ὁμοίωσις θεῷ, *homoiôsis theôi*). I introduce the idea at this point because in this chapter Ishmael relates the experience of standing aloft on the mast-head scanning the ocean below to losing one's identity and unifying with that "bottomless soul, pervading mankind and nature," which phenomenon he associates with pantheism.

Purification in the *Phaedo* is likened to separation of the soul from the body, the soul's release (*lusis*) from the imprisoning bonds of corporeality. This separation and release is also described as a flight or escape, as when Socrates explains the notion of philosophy as training for death by saying that just as in death the soul separates from the body, so the soul of the philosopher who would acquire knowledge of the incorporeal Forms must separate from the influence of the senses by fleeing from the body. Later he explicitly identifies the proper practice of philosophy as training for death with purity, separation, and flight.

Plato also associates the philosopher with flight in the *Theaetetus*. In this dialogue Socrates says that since it is not possible to eliminate from the earth all those bad things opposed to the good, "one must try to fly from here ... as quickly as possible," and this flight, he adds, is "likeness to god." This likeness consists in "becoming just and pious with wisdom," which recalls Socrates' discussion of virtue in the *Phaedo*, during which he associates purification with the sum of all true virtue existing together "with wisdom." In this same section of the *Phaedo* Socrates employs the familiar image of purification as release from the bonds of the body, and this recalls similar language in the *Republic*, specifically in that part of the Allegory of the Cave that describes the prisoner leaving the cave after his release from his bonds (*lusis ... tôn ... desmôn*). And later, with reference to this same allegory, Socrates calls ascent from the cave a turning away of the soul from the shadowy images of the physical realm toward the reality of the Forms, and he describes this as a "release from bonds" (*lusis ... apo tôn desmôn*). The man who is properly oriented to the Forms, the philosopher, likens himself to them as nearly as he can and thereby becomes as divine (*theios*) as a human may.

Near the end of the *Republic* Plato returns to the idea of human approximation to the divine, and his Socrates opines that the gods will never neglect the man who through the practice of virtue becomes as like god as possible (*homoiousthai theôi*).

In his later works Plato moderates his account by placing less stress on separation and flight from the world as components of god-likeness. In this he is motivated in part by a conception of the divine as *nous*, or intellect, which is not wholly other than the physical realm but is in fact the ordering principle of the world. The result is that in the *Laws*, for example, a late work (many would say his last), "assimilation to god takes on new meaning..., involving concern for the order of human affairs rather than a dismissive flight from them." But even here, in a work of Plato's fullest maturity, traces of *Phaedo*-Platonism remain. In Book 8, the god of the underworld, representing death, is said to be "always best for the race of humans," and the union of soul with body is said to be no better than their dissociation. The Greek word I have rendered as "dissociation" is *dialusis*, which is composed of the preposition *dia* prefixed to the *lusis* familiar from the *Phaedo*.

In this chapter describing his experiences on the *Pequod*'s mast-head, Ishmael explicitly mentions the *Phaedo*. He warns all owners of ships against enlisting any young man "who offers to ship with the Phædon ... in his head." Why? Because a "sunken-eyed young Platonist," left to himself at a "thought-engendering altitude" atop a mast-head, will so withdraw into meditative reveries on deep, eternal, and otherworldly matters that he will spot no whales. With his mind's eye focused exclusively on metaphysical realities, the eyes in his head will be of little use for seeing even the bulkiest of physical objects. This is the condition that Plato describes in the Allegory of the Cave: if the man who has left the cave to gaze on true reality returns to the realm of shadows below, he will not see well for the darkness; he will appear to the chained inhabitants a fool with faulty vision, a good-for-nothing deserving of ridicule or reprimand.

Ishmael's comparison of the "mystic ocean" to a soul that pervades all the world reminds one of the World Soul introduced by Plato in the *Timaeus*, and later identified by Plotinus (205-270 CE) as one of the three fundamental principles of reality. As an emanation of the One, the ultimate source of all things physical and metaphysical, by way of the second principle, Mind, in which the Forms reside as thoughts within an impersonal but divine intellect, the World Soul pervades and animates nature, manifesting in each human being as his or her individual soul. At our core, then, each of us is an emanation of the One, which Plotinus identifies with a principle that Plato in the *Republic* cryptically describes as the Good "beyond being," which is somehow responsible for the intelligibility and perhaps even the very existence of the Forms. Plotinus also calls this principle God, and by radicalizing Plato he says that our highest state is not merely to be *like* God but rather to *be God*. And since for Plotinus the divine is the All-Pure, we become God through purification. Becoming God is the ultimate human *telos*, our final goal, our fullest state of being and the condition of our highest happiness (*eudaimonia*). In Neoplatonism—which is the term contemporary scholars employ for Plotinus's variation of Platonism—the ontologically primary principle is so often called the One rather than God that Plato's "becoming like God" is called *henôsis* (from the fact that the word for "one" in Greek is ἕν, *hen*) or, more simply, unification.

Unification with the One, or *henôsis*, is discussed by Plotinus's student Porphyry and by Porphyry's student Iamblichus. It is a major element of Neoplatonism even during its revival among those Renaissance Christian Platonists in Florence who gathered around Marsilio Ficino, center of the so-called Florentine Academy and the first man to translate all of Plato and Plotinus into Latin. And as the Neoplatonic tradition influenced the development of early Christian theology (St. Augustine, for instance, was a Neoplatonist before converting to Christianity), the goal of unification is taken up by Greek Orthodox thought and various strains of Christian mysticism under the label *theôsis* (which derives from the Greek word for god, *theos*).

This brief intellectual history will, I hope, make clear the enormous influence of *Phaedo*-Platonism on western philosophical and theological thought. This is what Nietzsche had in mind when he identified the "gloomy religio-moral pathos" and "Platonic slander of the senses" as a "preparation of the soil for Christianity." It is also an element within Emersonian transcendentalism that Melville could never abide. As susceptible as his Ishmael is to intellectual distractions while ostensibly looking out for whales on the mast-head, he does not quite declare himself one of the "absent-minded" Platonists described in this chapter. Nevertheless, he quite obviously shares much in common with them. He has, he says, "the problem of the universe revolving" in him, and in this he is like Melville himself. He is drawn to the accursed questions, and if he does not attend to them as a committed Platonist, he is much closer to the serenity engendered by "Socratic wisdom" than is the raging Captain Ahab.

Chapter 36: The Quarter-Deck

Ahab admits that he is enraged. More, he insists on it. In this chapter, in which he discloses to the crew his intention to hunt and kill the white whale, swearing the men to join him in this one pursuit above all else, he announces that to sate his appetite for vengeance he will chase Moby Dick even through the fires of hell, and he invokes God's wrath against everyone present if they do not finally destroy the beast.

The contrast between Ahab's troubled anxiety and Ishmael's serenity could not be drawn more starkly than Melville has done in the previous chapter and this one. No mellow melting into the World Soul for Captain Ahab; no unification with the imperturbable divine. If Ahab resembles any god at all, it is some ghastly counter-deity to the Platonic god of purity and goodness. "Death and devils!" he shouts to his men, and with this he seems to summon the idols to which he has dedicated whatever remains of his haunted life. When Ahab speaks of the whale's taking his leg, he groans like a sickly, wounded animal; and as if he were brooding on the sum of the problematic questions embodied for him by Moby Dick, he calls the white whale "accursed."

Ahab's unwillingness to master himself in the face of the accursed questions, his incapacity to transcend, not the questions themselves, but the desperate anxieties they stir up in the souls of thoughtful but impotent men, clouds his thinking about the ultimate matters that obsess him. As I have said, he confuses the physical with the metaphysical, always seeking the one in the other's proper place. He is, really, a metaphysician infected with an inchoate nihilism. Consider his analysis of reality. He says that all "visible objects" are as "pasteboard masks" behind which there moves and acts "some unknown but still reasoning thing." Here we have the insight of a mind inclined to metaphysics: it is a general expression compatible with philosophies that advocate according to their own idiosyncratic specifics a two-level account of reality. In Platonism, as we have seen, the Forms are intelligible—and, for some, intelligent—entities that express their natures through physical objects; for men like Spinoza or Hegel the material world is the external, visible side of God or the immaterial World Spirit; while according to Schopenhauer this world is the physical objectification of the metaphysical Will that infuses all things and acts in and through them. Even according to traditional Christian theology God is behind this world and at work through it, if not quite literally one with it as the invisible interior of every visible object.

But Ahab regards physicality, his body included, not just as a mask but as a prison. In this he agrees with *Phaedo*-Platonism. Unfortunately for him, however, he has no use for purification; he wallows in his pleasures and pains and thereby fetters himself with bonds of corporeality. Morbidly angry as he is, Ahab lusts to effect a violent jailbreak: "How," he asks, "can the prisoner reach outside except by thrusting through the wall?" But such wild passions as motivate his desire to force his way through the prison's walls serve only to reinforce them. He frames his inquiries into the way to reach the metaphysical essence of physical things in the wrong terms. Socrates was offered the opportunity to escape from jail, but he resisted in the name of justice, and as we learn in the *Phaedo*, his dedication to the virtue of the soul over the pleasures of the body is the true route to freedom, leading through purification to the soul's release into the presence of the divine.

Ahab's distorted Platonism, his recognition that he is imprisoned coupled with his ignorance of the proper method of liberation, is a symptom of the physical obsessions that manifest in his confused ontology. He claims that the white whale is the wall of his prison, but he admits to suspecting occasionally that "there's naught beyond." But if this is so, there can be no hope of escape. The universe itself must be a prison of infinite extent, in which case there is no place of sanctuary beyond, nor any reasoning thing behind this physical realm. Visible objects must be, not masks, but naked reality itself.

Ahab's ontological confusions explain his uncertainty whether Moby Dick is "agent" or "principal," which is to say whether he is a surface manifestation of a more fundamental metaphysical reality, or in his physicality he is all there is. Ahab somehow is simultaneously an idealist and a materialist, and this intellectual-spiritual contradiction is the reason he will neither defeat his enemy nor escape the confrontation alive. But Ahab cannot acknowledge his confusion, nor does he seem particularly keen to know himself in this regard. He wants only to vent his anger: he will "wreak [his] hate upon" the whale whatever he may be. But of course he will not accomplish this, and all but one of the men who have wedded themselves to his reckless pursuit will perish from his false philosophy. Ahab is a formidable orator; he has managed to enlist his men as "parties to this indissoluble league." But though he speaks persuasively, his anxieties and confusions prevent him from speaking *well*. And as Plato notes in the *Phaedo*, "not speaking well is not only discordant in itself, but it also does some harm to souls."

Chapter 37: Sunset

In the previous chapter Ishmael says that in winning the three mates over to his cause Ahab "shocked them into the same fiery emotion accumulated within the Leyden jar of his own magnetic life." Judged according to his attitude and actions in that and the two following chapters, Ahab resembles Alcibiades, the great but reckless Athenian general and naval commander whose wild life was a marvel to all of Greece until it came to a violent end through his own self-destructive ways. This younger friend and wavering follower of Socrates makes a brilliant appearance in Plato's *Symposium* as a drunken admirer of the philosopher confessing his intellectual and moral weaknesses to the gathered guests.

When Alcibiades bursts into the party portrayed in the *Symposium*, the guests have all delivered encomia of the god of erotic love, Eros. They had agreed to engage in this oratorical pastime at the beginning of the evening in part as a way to refrain from drinking excessively. But as Ahab in the previous chapter has the steward fill and refill a flagon of alcohol to send round among the crew, so Alcibiades bids a slave to pour wine for the guests to drink in turn. He does not approve of their sobriety, and he intends to have them "drink sufficiently," just as Ahab intends his drinks to "spiralize" in his men, whipping them up into his own frenzied state.

The wine having been passed round, Alcibiades launches into an account of his troubled relationship with Socrates, here representing his vacillating commitment to the philosophical life. It seems that whenever he is around the philosopher, he strives to live virtuously and philosophically; but when left to his own devices, the pull of his bodily appetites and material aspirations overwhelms him. He has, he says, been struck and stung by philosophy, which clings to gifted young souls more savagely than a snake. Nevertheless, the lure of competing interests is forever tempting him to struggle free. Plato describes this sort of situation in the *Republic* by way of Socrates' account of the corruption of potential philosophers. Men who possess the traits that dispose one toward philosophy, in particular a drive to know metaphysical Being rather than to wallow in opinions about the physical realm of Becoming, men who are also intelligent, courageous, and possessed of spiritual grandeur or magnificence—such men naturally attract the attention of inferior individuals eager to use them for their own selfish ends, especially if these gifted souls happen also to be handsome, wealthy, physically robust, and born into a noble family. Alcibiades was precisely this sort of man, though his concern for Being—the indispensable qualification for entry into the philosophical life—was vacillating at best. But despite his evident intellectual potential, he succumbed to the flattery and fawning of those who befriended him for their own purposes, seducing him to their interests with promises of power and glory. A naturally gifted man corrupted in this way is capable of wreaking as much harm on the world around him as he would have been of effecting good had his attention not been distracted and diverted toward material interests.

It seems to me that Ahab's situation is loosely parallel to Alcibiades'. The Captain may not have descended from a noble family, but he possesses the more directly relevant qualifications: he is intelligent and naturally desirous of metaphysical truth. Alcibiades was an impulsive man; Ahab is a pondering man. Yet Ahab was as forcibly diverted from the genuine pursuit of wisdom by his rage against his pain as Alcibiades was seduced away by his lust for pleasure and glory.

In the *Nicomachean Ethics* Aristotle identifies excessive anger as a vice. The excess may proceed from anger directed at the wrong people, for the wrong reasons, to a greater extent, or more quickly, or for a longer time than necessary. But, says Aristotle, it is impossible for all this manner of excess to exist in one man at the same time, for badness (*kakon*) destroys itself, and if it is unmitigated, it is unendurable. But this complete anger is precisely Ahab's problem. Nevertheless, we need not say that Aristotle was utterly mistaken on this point, for if he was wrong to claim that one man cannot suffer from every possible manifestation of excessive anger, he was right to suggest that the condition would destroy him. Later in this same section Aristotle labels harsh or cruel the man who is enraged by the wrong things, and angry more and for a longer time than he should be. Such a man will not be reconciled without exacting vengeance or inflicting punishment. Thus Ahab insists that he would "strike the sun if it insulted me," and thus Starbuck cannot comprehend the Captain's lust for "vengeance on a dumb brute."

In this chapter Ahab says that the "path to my fixed purpose is laid with iron rails, whereon my soul is grooved to run." But these rails were fabricated and put in place by his tormented anger at Moby Dick. As fixed as they are, they lead him in the wrong direction; they lead him away from the wisdom that might have been his had he not so raged at his physical plight that he would not or could not transcend his hardships into a superior state from which he might bear his heavy life lightly, might play with the accursed questions, which is not to fail to take them seriously but rather to rise above the suffering they produce in lesser men. "All loveliness is anguish to me," Ahab says, "since I can ne'er enjoy." Though he is "gifted with the high perception," he is "damned, most subtly and most malignantly." Indeed he is, and precisely this is the condition of the man eternally exiled from wisdom, left to wander unto death in the antechamber to wisdom that is philosophy.

Chapter 38: Dusk

In the previous chapter Ahab remarks regarding his seduction of the crew to his wild cause that his "one cogged circle fits into all their various wheels, and they revolve." He is, he says, "demoniac," "madness maddened." Alcibiades' own mad appeal is perhaps best displayed through his role in convincing the Athenians to undertake the disastrous naval expedition against Sicily in 415 BCE during what was meant to be an interval of peace in the midst of the Peloponnesian War. But I shall come to this event in the course of a general rehearsal of Alcibiades' life and career.

Through his mother Alcibiades belonged to one of the most powerful families in Athens, the Alcmaionidai. In the long course of their active role in Athenian social and political life, the Alcmaionidai also became one of the city's most notorious families, beginning perhaps with Megacles' killing of the men who supported the Olympic victor Cylon in his bid to take over Athens as tyrant in 632. These men had taken refuge in Athena's temple on the Acropolis (not the Parthenon, which was built much later), and when finally they were persuaded to come out to stand trial they tied a rope to the temple to preserve their connection to the place of sanctuary, but the rope broke. Megalces and his men then stoned them all. For this his family was cursed and exiled from the city, and although they eventually returned, their political enemies recalled the curse time and again over the years to have the family exiled more than once after this affair.

Alcibiades' father died in battle when his son was still a child, as a result of which the boy was taken in by Pericles, himself a member of the Alcmaionidai and the man whom the historian Thucydides identified as the sole ruler of Athens' nominal democracy. Pericles was largely responsible for the "Golden Age" of Athenian culture, and Alcibiades grew up pampered and popular under his roof. Besides his impressive family connections, from his youth Alcibiades was recognized as handsome, intelligent, bold, and independent. So influential was he among his peers that, for example, everyone found his speech impediment (pronouncing "r" as "l") charming, and the young men of the city imitated it. When Alcibiades refused to play the woodwind aulos because it distorted his cheeks in an unflattering way, the instrument fell out of favor.

As a young man Alcibiades fought in the battle of Potidaea, and while on this campaign he shared a tent with Socrates. The philosopher even saved his life when he was wounded and collapsed in battle. The Athenian assault on Potidaea was one of the events that occasioned the Peloponnesian War, in the course of which Alcibiades made himself into an influential and notorious figure. During the so-called "Peace of Nicias" he arranged an alliance between Athens and the Peloponnesian cities of Argos, Elis, and Mantinea, with the intention of hemming the Spartans in to their isolated region of Laconia in the southern Peloponnese. It was a brilliant idea, but the Spartans defeated the collected armies of the alliance at the Battle of Mantinea in 418.

Not long after this, in 415, Alcibiades began to agitate for an Athenian expedition against Sicily. He convinced the Athenians that they could defeat the powerful polis of Syracuse, extend their rule over the whole island, and accumulate a mass of wealth such as they had acquired after the Greek defeat of the Persians in 479. With his notable oratorical skill and a bit of luck (involving Nicias's opposing the expedition in a speech that only increased the Athenians' enthusiasm for the undertaking), Alcibiades generated an atmosphere in which, to quote Thucydides, "a passionate desire (*erôs*) to sail out fell upon everyone alike." Such was the "excessive desire of the majority" for the expedition that those few who opposed it refrained from actively resisting it.

Thrilling with excitement and swollen with confidence, the Athenians gathered a huge force to sail against Sicily. But one morning not long before the fleet was scheduled to depart, the Athenians awoke to find many of the city's herms (uncarved stone pillars decorated with the head of Hermes and a phallus) defaced and destroyed. As Hermes was the god of travelers, many took this as a sign that the expedition would fail. Alcibiades was implicated in the mutilation of the herms (probably falsely), and not long after this he was accused of staging a mock ceremony parodying the initiation rites of the Eleusinian Mysteries. The ancient and influential cult of Demeter and Persephone, located in Eleusis just north-west of Athens proper, centered on the fate of the soul in the afterlife: initiates into the Mysteries secured for themselves a good life after death. The Eleusinian ceremonies were extravagant public affairs, but the details of the final stages of initiation were kept secret. To this day no one knows what transpired within the inner sanctum of the temple. In any case, Alcibiades and his friends apparently held a mock initiation ceremony during a drunken party, with Alcibiades himself playing the role of High Priest. The Athenians were shocked at the blasphemy, and his enemies took the opportunity to indict him for "wronging the goddesses Demeter and Korê."

Alcibiades sailed out with the fleet, but learning that he was to be tried *in absentia*, he jumped ship and defected to the enemy, Sparta. The information he provided the Spartans regarding Athenian tactics grievously harmed his homeland. But when a rumor spread that he had slept with the wife of one of the two Spartan kings, he fled to Persia where he schemed against the Peloponnesians. Alcibiades was eventually reconciled with the generals in charge of the Athenian navy based on the island of Samos, and with his own contingent of ships he won major victories over the Spartans at sea. In the wake of these successes he returned to Athens in glory to be elected *stratêgos autokratôr*, general with independent and unlimited authority. Not long after returning to sea, however, Alcibiades left an underling in charge of his fleet while he went off to attend to other business. Though he instructed the man not to engage the enemy, the overeager subordinate provoked Lysander, the brilliant Spartan naval commander, who attacked the Athenian forces, routing and eventually destroying them. Alcibiades was blamed for the incident, and as punishment he was stripped of his command. He then withdrew to a property he owned in northeastern Greece, but while there he was attacked and killed, probably by agents of Sparta.

Plato was roughly twenty years younger than Alcibiades, and he seems to have been fascinated with the man. No doubt he watched in awe with the rest of the city as Alcibiades sailed out of Peiraias in command of the magnificent Athenian armada bound for Sicily, and like everyone else he surely followed with interest the wildly variable course of his subsequent career. He knew well that Alcibiades had been attached to his own mentor, Socrates; and he must have wondered how a man with such natural gifts and acquired culture could stray so far from the virtuous life. I have noted Alcibiades' unnamed appearance in the *Republic*, in which he serves as an example of the potential philosopher corrupted by the very qualities that should have made him great. I have mentioned as well his explicit appearance in the *Symposium* as a drunk and debauched ambivalent admirer of Socrates. There is also a dialogue called *Alcibiades*, in which Socrates meets the young Alcibiades and attempts to convince him that although he has been graced by nature with many advantages, he will go wrong in life unless he strives to know himself, in particular that part of his soul that is the seat of wisdom. That Alcibiades failed even to try to know himself with any serious dedication must have been endlessly troubling to Plato. What sort of man could so willfully spurn the promise of wisdom for the sake of mundane affairs?

Captain Ahab is such a man. Endowed with many natural virtues, including a profound intellect, he deliberately pursues what Starbuck has called a "dumb brute" with a fervor that perverts his mind and ultimately destroys him utterly. Near the end of Alcibiades' life, Aristophanes described the Athenians' ambivalent feelings about him in his comedy the *Frogs*: the city, he wrote, "longs for him, hates him, and wants to have him." I hear an echo of this in the present chapter in Starbuck's reflections on his own relation to Ahab: his "miserable office," he says, is "to obey, rebelling; and worse yet, to hate with touch of pity!" Melville seems to have been as fascinated and troubled by his mad Ahab as Plato was by the dazzlingly doomed Alcibiades.

Chapter 39: First Night-Watch

Thales the Milesian is traditionally identified as the first philosopher. It was said by the ancients that he predicted a solar eclipse, though some today doubt that this is so and suggest instead that he proposed a natural explanation for the event, which would be noteworthy in itself for the time. In any case, scholars date the eclipse in question to 585 BCE, and this is used to date

Thales himself. The Greeks tended to place a great man's first remarkable deed in his fortieth year, but we need not be so programmatically precise ourselves. We need only believe that Thales was in his maturity at the time of the eclipse, which would place his birth sometime in the mid to late seventh century. But if the first philosopher was born at this time, what can we say of the Greek mind during the first half of the seventh century and before?

The standard story has it that philosophy developed in contrast to, and reaction against, the supernaturalist-religious view of the world. The early Greeks believed in the Olympian gods, as we learn from Homer, who was active probably at the end of the eighth century. Hesiod, who composed his poems around this same time, imagined divine or semi-divine beings as originary elements of the universe. The Greek people sacrificed and prayed to the gods, and they held regular festivals in their honor. Greek philosophy, it is often claimed, appeared as a light of understanding in the midst of this dark ignorance.

There is of course some truth to this story, but there are also exaggerations and inaccuracies. We have no idea what a man like Homer really thought about the divine, and the early Greek philosophers (the so-called Presocratics) were by no means exclusively naturalists. The atomists, Leucippus and Democritus, may have come as close as anyone at the time to naturalism, but they were the exception in this regard among the early philosophers. References and allusions to gods and divine beings or entities turn up throughout the entire history of Greek philosophy, from the first Presocratics (Thales himself apparently wrote that "all things are full of gods") to the last of the Neoplatonists.

Among the ancients, Thales was often identified as one of the Seven Sages. These were men renowned for their wisdom who passed around among themselves a tripod found by a fisherman off the coast of Miletus (Thales' hometown) which Apollo through his oracle at Delphi decreed be given to the wisest of all men. The Milesians bestowed the tripod on Thales, but he passed it off to another whom he judged wiser than himself, and this man sent it to another in turn, and so it went the rounds until it wound up with Solon in Athens. The Greeks told different versions of this story, including even different names of the wise men among the Seven. Solon the Athenian is one of the few to appear on every extant list.

Solon was born to a noble Athenian family in the second half of the seventh century; he was most likely an older contemporary of Thales. But despite his reputation for wisdom, he is never taken for one of the early philosophers. Thales straddles the line dividing the early archaic sages from the late archaic philosophers, but Solon stands exclusively on the side of wisdom. This classification is due in part to convention, of course; but it is not without its rationale. Solon is best known for reforming the Athenian constitution at a time of radical civil unrest, and the only contemporary source of information about these events are the poems he wrote to explain and justify his actions. Solon travelled throughout Greece, Egypt, and the coastal cities of Anatolia, and he was respected for the experience and insight into life he acquired in the course of his long and varied career. He was not known for any naturalist or proto-naturalist cosmological speculations. Solon was a poet and a law-giver.

I introduce Solon and the Seven Sages at this point to suggest that we think of the period preceding the development of philosophy in Greece as an age of wisdom rather than an age of religion. Wise men write poems and promulgate laws, sometimes quite literally so. But sometimes their poems manifest as prose—the best works of Plato, Melville, and Nietzsche are far more poetically rich than the treatises or stories of typical philosophers or writers of fiction—and their laws are less legal decrees than creations of values in Nietzsche's sense of this expression. Sages shape our view of man and thereby influence the direction of history. But with Solon in mind we must wonder what to make of a wisdom that is not acquired through philosophy. We must ask: Who were these pre-philosophical, pre-Presocratic sages? Intellectually and spiritually—*what* were they?

For now I leave this question unanswered, in which form it might well do most good. The question arises ultimately from the present chapter of *Moby-Dick*, in which once again we encounter the second mate Stubb as "*wise* Stubb." In what does Stubb's wisdom consist? In this chapter it is summed up in his remark that "I know not all that may be coming, but be it what it will, I'll go to it laughing." In a previous chapter I referred to Stubb as an example of a non-philosophical man, and I have denied that one can acquire wisdom through physical contact with a sage, much less by way of contact with the dream-image of a man who is not actually wise. I have also wondered suspiciously whether we can accept the authority of an imaginary merman's proclamation of an individual's wisdom. Nevertheless, I have not denied Stubb his wisdom. But this is not to say that I take his claims to wisdom seriously. The only point I intend to make is that if Stubb is indeed wise, it is a pre-philosophical sort of wisdom, which may or may not be superior to wisdom acquired through philosophy. If philosophy arises only after the passing of an age of wisdom, then philosophy would seem the result of decline, in which case in this later age even the sage would appear a questionable figure. On the other hand, it might be that reaching the summit of wisdom from out of the depths of philosophy enriches the sage with insights inaccessible to the pre-philosophical wise man. If this is so, then even if we accept Solon (or Stubb) as our original model, we must acknowledge Ishmael as the superior type.

Chapter 40: Midnight, Forecastle

In a previous chapter I introduced Aristotle's account of wisdom as knowledge of necessary principles. Wisdom for Aristotle is a virtue, an intellectual virtue, dependent to some degree even on the virtues of character, for no intemperate or irascible man can attain wisdom. Yet the content of this virtue is a cognitive state; it is the perfection of the highest power of our rational capacity, which manifests as indubitable knowledge of the highest truths. Plato's Socrates in the *Republic* makes knowledge central to his own definition of wisdom. In a polis, he says, wisdom manifests as the rulers' knowledge of what is good for each of the city's three classes—the laborers, the warriors, and the rulers—taken together as a whole. Similarly, wisdom in an individual is reason's knowledge of what is good for the whole soul, which is to say for each of the three parts or powers of the soul—the appetitive, the spirited, and the rational parts—both in themselves and together as an aggregate whole. The philosopher acquires this knowledge by ascending in thought from the cave of material particulars to cognize the metaphysical Forms, and he accomplishes this through a mode of rational investigation known as dialectic. As with Aristotle, wisdom in the *Republic* is a virtue, and it is a virtue whose content is a species of knowledge.

In the *Apology* Socrates insists that because poets are unable to explain the meaning of their poems, they do not compose by wisdom, but rather by nature or under the influence of divine inspiration. But why does he assume that wisdom must be expressed exclusively through the rational analysis of a tragedy or lyric rather than through its composition? The assumption depends on taking wisdom to be a type of knowledge. Indeed, in Socrates' mouth the word *sophia* is usually a synonym of "knowledge" or "skill," as in *know-how*. But the identification of wisdom with knowledge fails to account for the archaic sages. I do not mean to imply that Solon was ignorant; his wisdom must have included some element of knowledge. Nevertheless, he was in fact oblivious of much that we know (or think that we know) today, and in any case his wisdom was not typically characterized primarily as a form of knowledge. Nor were the other archaic sages "men of knowledge." Socrates' epistemic obsession was not theirs, and if he is responsible for the reductive account of wisdom as knowledge, we need not follow him in this. It does not appear that Plato always adhered to the Socratic account. In the *Phaedrus*, for example, the philosopher—which is to say the *lover of wisdom*—is related to the lover of *beauty*. In the *Symposium* too, the man who practices philosophy properly ascends to the Forms impelled by a love of the beautiful, and his goal is not knowledge but communion.

If we can infer anything about Plato the man from the dialogues he created, I conclude that he took the love of wisdom to involve aesthetic qualities as much as cognitive insight. Socrates—the actual man as well as the character who appears in the early dialogues—Socrates may have been more concerned with knowledge than beauty, which would explain his practice of engaging in dialectical conversations with men renowned for possessing some species or other of knowledge; but Plato passed his time composing the dialogues, the best of which transcend the mere representation of dialectical exchanges and are fully realized works of art. Diogenes Laertius reports that Plato dedicated a shrine to the Muses on the grounds of the Academy. I take this to indicate more than that Plato regarded philosophy as the highest form of *mousikê*, as his Socrates puts it in the *Phaedo*. I take it to indicate that his conception of philosophy was infused with his appreciation of beauty. Aristotle's writings are difficult to understand in the way that a dense logical argument is difficult. But Plato's dialogues are difficult as great art is difficult. His works have as much in common with the tragedians as they do with Socrates or Aristotle. Was he then as ignorant as the poets? No, he was as *wise*.

The difference between Plato and the poets and archaic sages is that he chose not to express his wisdom directly. He conceals it behind the mask of philosophy, buries it in the labyrinths of his dialogues. In the *Symposium* Alcibiades compares Socrates to a figurine of Silenus that opens along a central hinge to reveal images of the gods inside. The analogy suits Plato's dialogues: philosophy is their external form; inside the philosophy is wisdom, enthroned like a secret god.

In the present chapter of *Moby-Dick* the sailors congregate on the forecastle and sing in chorus. Their particular song may not be an expression of wisdom, but the songs of the greatest poets sometimes are. Indeed, on the surface of a simple song a man may encounter depths of wisdom that can otherwise be found only by exploring the entirety of a philosopher's collected works.

Chapter 41: Moby Dick

In this chapter Moby Dick finally appears, but only as an ambiguous concept. We do not yet see the white whale himself, but we do learn something about him as filtered through the perspectives and imaginations of men, Ahab in particular. In some ways the experience serves only to obscure our image of the beast, but since he may well be equivocal in himself, this obscurity might actually bring us close to the truth, "indefinite as God."

The descriptions of Moby Dick in this chapter are pervaded with theological language. The whale acts with "supernatural agencies," and although this thought may be little more than the fantasy of sailors' "supernatural surmisings," Ahab himself seems to take it seriously. He is preparing for his enemy a "supernatural revenge." Like God, Moby Dick is thought by some to be omnipresent, or "ubiquitous," for eye-witness reports have placed him in different oceans at one and the same time. Some have claimed that he is "immortal," being either immune to the otherwise deadly barbs of harpoons and spears, or possessed of a miraculous power of regeneration from wounds. Moby Dick is not here labelled omniscient or omnipotent, but that he is unnaturally intelligent, and frighteningly powerful, is certain. In his many deadly attacks he has exhibited an "unexampled, intelligent malignity" and a "direful wrath."

Divine as he may appear, however, Moby Dick has about him traces of the diabolical. His intelligence strikes some as an "infernal aforethought." To some he seems "the great gliding demon of the seas of life." He is, moreover, somehow capable of transmitting his malevolence to others, as if possessing them. He has made of his chief pursuer, Ahab, an "ungodly ... man," and the

Captain's crew would seem to have been collected for the hunt by an "infernal agency."

Is Moby Dick then god or devil? Is he an altogether different species of being? Or might he be somehow the physical embodiment of the absence of being, the menace of nothingness enveloping our reality in a dark death-shroud? Probably the whale is all these things and more; or all these and none simultaneously, a Heraclitean strife of opposites manifesting as a unified thing, congealing and rising from the sea of Becoming to dissolve and reconstitute again and again, eternally. D. H. Lawrence speculated that Melville himself did not know the nature of his creation. But this, he said, is "the best part of it." Indeed it is. Moby Dick is a kaleidoscope—not a stable substance viewed through shifting lenses; in himself he is the shifting.

Moby Dick is as ungraspable in his physicality as he is in concept. He is present but unobtainable. This tension is unbearable to Ahab, who wants not ambiguity but clarity, resolution, finality. But the Captain is ambiguous himself. The Platonic diagnosis that I have advanced in previous chapters, namely that Ahab's soul has been infected by his body, is confirmed in the present chapter. We learn that on his journey home from the voyage during which he lost his leg to Moby Dick, Ahab's "torn body and gashed soul bled into one another." In the *Phaedo* Socrates claims that souls that have been interfused with corporeal elements are "weighed down and dragged back into the visible realm from fear of the invisible and of Hades." These are the "shadowy images of souls" that are said to hover around monuments and graves, trapped in the physical realm because they have not been "purely released." Ahab too is impure, or, as Ishmael says in this connection, he is "mad." I have said that this condition of madness or impurity prevents Ahab from facing the accursed questions with the tranquility and good humor of a sage; he suffers from them as the perpetual philosopher. Heavy as he is, bound to earth by "the infixed, unrelenting fangs of [his] incurable idea," he cannot ascend to wisdom. So Ishmael informs us that Ahab identified Moby Dick with "all his intellectual and spiritual exasperations." The wise man is not exasperated; he is at peace. He does not pursue "the subtle demonisms of life and thought" into the very void of death; he takes them seriously but sports with them. He does not brood and finally perish like Ahab; he lives and sings like Ishmael.

Ahab suffers in part because he is as ambiguous as the object of his hunt, in part because he does not know this, or cannot bring himself to admit it.

Thus he is forever seeking clarity through the medium of befogged lenses. Ishmael suggests that Ahab does not know himself because his "awful essence" resides "far beneath" the ground-level of his conscious self, as below the Hotel De Cluny in Paris and the Baths of Caracalla in Rome there are winding substructures intricate and ominously silent as the Minoan labyrinth. But does a Minotaur stalk within? Ishmael suggests that "the old State-secret" is guarded by the buried essence of the self. But we must remember the possibility, as expressed by Melville in a letter to Hawthorne, that "there is *no* secret." Perhaps our essence is not buried, but is absent. Nietzsche suspected as much. Indeed, he was inclined to "maintain the phenomenality of the inner world," by which he meant that "everything of which we become conscious is arranged, simplified, schematized, interpreted through and through—the actual process of inner 'perception,' the causal connection between thoughts, feelings, desires, between subject and object, are absolutely hidden from us—and are perhaps purely imaginary." If this is so, then every one of us is necessarily as ambiguous as Ahab and Moby Dick. We cannot obey Apollo's command to know ourselves because there is no self to know. But who can say what lies beneath the foundations of the human psyche? Or, in Ishmael's words: "The subterranean miner that works in us all, how can one tell whither leads his shaft by the ever shifting, muffled sound of his pick?"

Chapter 42: The Whiteness of the Whale

The color white has symbolized divinity for many thousands of years, perhaps more—*probably* more, but the tracks of traceable history eventually fade from view. Comparative linguistics and comparative mythology provide information about periods far more ancient than any for which we possess written records. For example, not long before Melville was born, scholars began to notice similarities between Sanskrit and Greek and Latin, the latter two of which languages they already knew to share commonalities of grammar and vocabulary. To take just one example, consider that the Latin name Jupiter (*Ju Piter*) is related to the Greek *Zeus Patêr*, which is itself etymologically equivalent to the Sanskrit *Dyauṣ Pitrâ*, all of which mean "sky father." Such discoveries eventually led to the recognition of a new language family. This group includes not only Sanskrit, Greek, and Latin, but also the ancient Iranian languages, and Anatolian, Armenian, Slavic, Celtic, and the Germanic languages, including English. These and other languages and language groups are related in the same way that Italian, French, Spanish, Portuguese, and Romanian are related, which is to say they share a common ancestor. The five Romance languages descend from Latin. The broader grouping, of which Latin itself is only one among many branches, descends from a language that no longer exists in either spoken or written form, but which scholars reconstruct as Proto-Indo-European. The reconstructed original of "sky father," for example, is *dyêus phatêr*. The recognition of the existence of an ancestral language naturally generates speculation about the ancestors themselves, whom scholars today designate Proto-Indo-Europeans, or PIE speakers. Ignoring for now the widespread scholarly disputes concerning particular details, we may picture these people living somewhere north-east of the Black Sea from at least as far back as 4,000 BCE. Over the course of centuries various groups of Proto-Indo-European speakers emigrated from their homeland into India and Iran to the southeast, the Balkan and Italian peninsulas to the southwest, Russia to the north, and Europe to the northwest. They brought with them not only their language but also their culture, including their social arrangements and mythologies.

In the twentieth century the French philologist and comparative mythographer Georges Dumézil identified several striking cultural-conceptual correspondences among various ancient Indo-European peoples, among them a tripartite division of society into a laboring-agricultural class, a military class, and a priestly class. We see this, for example, in the three Hindu castes of Brahmin, Kshatriya, and Vaishya. The fourth and lowest class of "untouchable" Shudra may originally have been composed of native Indic peoples whom the invading Indo-Europeans excluded from their own three-tiered social structure. Earlier I noted the three classes in Plato's *Republic*, the laborers, warriors, and rulers, the latter group comprising the so-called "Philosopher-Kings." Here we see even supposedly rational philosophical cogitations subtly guided by deeply rooted psychic tendencies. Nietzsche recognized the philosophical implications of this connection between linguistic commonalities and cultural-intellectual similarities, noting that because of "the innate systematic structure and relationship of their concepts," the thinking of even "the most diverse philosophers" is "far less a discovery than a recognition, a remembering, a return and a homecoming to a remote, primordial, and inclusive household of the soul, out of which those concepts grew originally: philosophizing is to this extent a kind of atavism of the highest order." From this he concluded that the "strange family resemblance of all Indian, Greek, and Germanic philosophizing is explained easily enough."

But to return to the subject of Indo-European social classes, Dumézil noted that specific colors typically correspond to the three different groups, black (or blue or green) designating the laboring class, red designating the warriors, and white designating the sacred priests. This fact is at the root of Ishmael's observation that "in the higher mysteries of the most august religions [white] has been made the symbol of the divine spotlessness and power." The color white, in sum, is commonly associated with "whatever is sweet, and honorable, and sublime." Yet in this chapter Ishmael retails the many ways in which white terrifies and "strikes ... panic to the soul." But how can this be? How can a symbol of the divine and its earthly representatives appear so diabolical as Ishmael demonstrates it to be?

Ishmael prefaces his dissertation on the frightfulness of the color white by remarking that he intends to relate "what, at times," Moby Dick was to him. Not always; only "at times." And in this case the time evidently is the period when, as he says at the beginning of the previous chapter, he was "one of that crew" that swore an oath to join with Ahab in his mad pursuit of the white whale, which he did all the more fervently from "the dread in [his] soul." He abandoned himself to the dark mood of the moment, even took some element of ungodly Ahab's rebellion into himself. In short, Ishmael was a willing participant in Ahab's spiritual revolt. And might not the most divine of colors appear dreadful to a spiritually rebellious man?

But Ishmael was never as furiously consumed as Ahab. Although he joined in the hunt, he knew enough to anticipate "the deadliest ill." He preserved the insight and power that Ahab lacked or had lost, the insight into the need for ascent and the power to raise himself up. But now we are considering Ishmael's darker self, that aspect of his self that is temporarily entangled with Ahab. This Ishmael resembles the New England colt described near the end of the present chapter, the young horse terrified by the scent of buffalo even though he has no experience of the species. Some deep instinct is at work in the colt, namely the "instinct of the knowledge of the demonism in the world." So Ishmael sometimes is horrified by the whiteness of roiling water, mountain frost, or snow-covered prairies. On such occasions he suspects that "the invisible spheres were formed in fright," alluding presumably to the transparent spheres that according to Aristotle carry the visible planets along their orbits around the earth. They are composed of aether, a fifth element beside the earth, water, air, and fire that make up the sub-lunar or terrestrial region. The celestial spheres move eternally in perfect circular motions, and their motion is caused by the "Prime Mover," an incorporeal unmoving entity that acts on the spheres as a final cause, imparting motion to things as an object of desire causes a desiring agent to move while remaining motionless itself. Aristotle identifies the Prime Mover with God: it is a living, thinking being that lives the fullest possible life and thinks about the highest possible object, namely itself. Thus Aristotle's famous definition of the divine as "thought thinking of thought," or "intellect intellecting intellect."

Aristotle's account of the Prime Mover was taken up and modified by Christianity, appearing for example in Thomas Aquinas's "Five Ways," five brief summaries of arguments for the existence of God. But early modern philosophers rejected Aristotle's ancient cosmology. Galileo's telescopic observations of the moon and other planets were particularly damaging, for they not only revealed no spheres, they supplied reasons to reject them, for example the moons of Jupiter, which in order to orbit the planet would have to crash through any sphere in which it was embedded. The modern rejection of Aristotelean cosmology amounted to a rejection of Catholic theological cosmology to the extent that Catholicism had absorbed Aristotle's system. And this was followed, though much more gradually, by doubts about Christian theology itself, which eventually culminated in Nietzsche's proclamation that God is dead. Thus after reflecting on the invisible spheres Ishmael speculates that since "in essence whiteness is not so much a color as the visible absence of color," it disturbs by representing the "colorless, all-color of atheism."

Ishmael's suffering from his rebellion, as expressed in his reflections on the fearfulness of Moby Dick's divine whiteness, is a symptom of his infection with Ahab's dis-ease. But his will be only a temporary illness. He will come close to death, even die symbolically. But this experience will give him new life, reinvigorated health and well-being. It will make of him a type resembling a Zarathustran sage.

Chapter 43: Hark!

I concluded the chapter entitled "Moby Dick" with reference to Melville's reflections on the self. Beneath the foundations of our conscious mind, does a hidden essence of the self reside enthroned, the royal guardian of our personal "State-secret"? Or might there be nothing of particular interest below, our psychic foundations grounded on unremarkable dirt and stone? Or if we penetrate far enough in pursuit of our subterranean miner, might we finally break through to—void? And would we not then be grounded on nothing, an illusion hallucinating itself, or at best a psychic infinite regress, layer beneath layer supporting and supported with no final bedrock, and so just another kind of illusion?

Melville brooded on the nature of the self throughout his life, and his reflections surface often in his works. For example, four years after *Moby-Dick* he wrote a short story entitled "I and My Chimney" about a man whose wife would have him reduce or altogether remove the large central chimney of their house. The woman hires a "master-mason" to inspect the structure, and this man eventually reports his suspicion that the wide foundation of the chimney below the house in the cellar conceals "a reserved space, hermetically closed, in short, a secret chamber" that might contain "some extraordinary object" or "treasure." On learning of this possibility the wife is eager for a treasure hunt, but the husband manages to bribe the mason to draw up a certificate stating officially that the chimney is perfectly sound and exhibits no sign of containing any such "secret closet."

Melville wrote this story on the farm he called Arrowhead in Pittsfield, Massachusetts, where he composed much of *Moby-Dick*. The house at Arrowhead was built around precisely such a chimney, a massive structure in the very heart of the place. Commenting on the story in later years, Melville's wife Elizabeth stated that no one had ever proposed removing this actual chimney. But there may yet be some deeper truth to the tale. In an insightful essay on Melville's story, Merton Sealts proposed that the chimney is a representation of Melville himself, its foundation a symbol of his soul. The narrator of the story frequently compares his chimney to a pyramid, which prompts Sealts to quote the following line from *Pierre*, the novel Melville wrote immediately after concluding *Moby-Dick*: "By vast pains we mine into the pyramid; by horrible gropings we come to the central room; with joy we espy the sarcophagus; but we lift the lid—and no body is there—appallingly vacant as vast is the soul of man!"

We might compare this view of the absent self to David Hume's vain search for a unitary source of personal identity. Expressing his disagreement with philosophers who claim that "we are every moment intimately conscious of what we call our self," Hume denies that there is "any single power of the soul, which remains unalterably the same, perhaps for one moment." On his view, the mind "is a kind of theatre, where several perceptions successively make their appearance; pass, re-pass, glide away, and mingle in an infinite variety of postures and situations. There is properly no *simplicity* in it at one time, nor *identity* in different [times], whatever natural propension we may have to imagine that simplicity and identity." And, finally, in order that the theater analogy not encourage us to imagine the self as the auditorium in which the flux of perceptions is projected, he concludes by noting that "they are the successive perceptions only, that constitute the mind; nor have we the most distant notion of the place, where these scenes are represented, or of the materials, of which it is compos'd."

Hume's view is similar to Nietzsche's, though Nietzsche radicalizes Hume's insights, as he radicalizes so much else. For Nietzsche the self is an illusion generated by "the prejudice of reason" in favor of Being that induces us to posit islands of stable substance within the ever-rushing river of Becoming. Thus everything from God and souls to physical objects and atoms are constructs of that part of our mind that projects its belief in Being onto and into the universal flux. Melville himself was less dogmatic than either Hume or Nietzsche on the self, as is indicated by another line from *Pierre*: "Deep, deep, and still deep and deeper must we go, if we would find out the heart of a man; descending into which is as descending a spiral stair in a shaft, without any end, and where that endlessness is only concealed by the spiralness of the stair, and the blackness of the shaft."

The present chapter of *Moby-Dick* is very short, consisting only of a sailor's suspecting that he hears a noise below, a noise from which he infers that "there is somebody down in the after-hold that has not yet been seen on deck." His friend dismisses the idea, but he shouldn't. For if we may for the moment take the *Pequod* for a soul, we can say that it does conceal a thing below—if not a secret essential self, then at least a few as yet unarticulated thoughts.

Chapter 44: The Chart

This chapter, in which we encounter Ahab below in his cabin pouring over his charts, plotting and re-plotting the course he hopes will lead him to Moby Dick, concludes with a bizarre scene. Ishmael describes Ahab's behavior when in his "spiritual throes," as apparently he often was, in such terms as to suggest a state that we might conceive as the converse of a mystical experience. On these occasions Ahab's mind dissociates from his soul and thereby temporarily ceases to exist. But yielding its "thoughts and fancies" to the Captain's "one supreme purpose," the mind leaves in charge of the man this very purpose itself, which through its "sheer inveteracy of will" becomes "a kind of self-assumed, independent being." Ahab abides as agent, but driven as he is by neither mind nor soul, but rather by willful purpose alone, he functions as an animated corpse, "a vacated thing, a formless somnambulistic being … a blankness."

During these episodes Ahab is somehow separated from his vital, spiritual elements; he becomes almost exclusively his body, his nerve stimulations, muscular contractions, and skeletal movements. He recalls the image of man that Socrates rejects in the *Phaedo*, man as a being whose actions are guided not by reason but by physical causes alone. Socrates cannot imagine such a thing. It is, he says, as if someone were to ask him why he is sitting in prison, and he replied that he sits there because his body is made of bones and sinews, and because the bones are hard and divided by joints covered by sinews that contract and relax which are themselves covered by flesh, and as the sinews are contracting and relaxing in such a way as to cause his bones, and thereby his limbs, to bend, this is why he sits as he does. The explanation is of course preposterous; it certainly is not the answer anyone inquiring into Socrates' predicament would anticipate or accept. It is true that without bones and sinews he could neither sit nor act in any other way, but the physical condition of his body does not by itself suffice to explain his actions. According to Socrates, the reason he is sitting in prison is that after the Athenians thought it best to condemn him, he thought it best to sit there and await the penalty they decided to impose on him. In short, the proper explanation involves mind, or intellect (*nous*), which always acts in accordance with the course it determines to be the best.

If we evaluate Ahab's crazed actions with reference to this account, we must conclude that they are not motivated by recognition of the good. Ahab has not properly deliberated about the ends, the final goals, of his actions. He formulated his monomaniacal aim under the influence of shock and delirium at the loss of his leg, and now he pursues the means to that end through will unaided by consideration. Blind purpose drives him on, unknowing and uncaring for the best course of action.

I have described Ahab when dissociated from his mind and soul as a man undergoing something like an anti-mystical experience. Rather than being taken up into his spirit, so thoroughly absorbed by his higher soul as to lose his identity in communion with the divine of which his soul is only conceptually distinct, but not actually independent—instead of this, Ahab is thrust into the physical realm completely, his body severed from the divinity indwelling his soul, as a result of which he becomes a blind material force, a thing simultaneously nothing but a personal identity—for this raging man most definitely is Captain Ahab—and also a featureless nothing utterly void of identity—for he possesses neither the unified soul nor the unity of mental states that would serve as the core of an undivided and continuous individuality.

According to *Phaedo*-Platonism, a man is his soul, not his body. When the two are finally separated, the man himself will live on as a soul while the body with which he had been associated will be nothing more than a corpse. Thus Socrates assures his friend Crito that after he drinks the poison and dies, he will be gone. Therefore Crito should not worry during the funeral that he is "burying Socrates," for at that time there will be no Socrates. There will be only a body, a man-shaped agglomeration of matter; and as Heraclitus wrote, "corpses are more to be thrown out than dung."

Would Ahab agree? In his sane moments, perhaps. But Ahab is rarely in his right mind, and even when he is, the fiery river of his insanity runs broiling beneath the surface of his thoughts, waiting there to draw him down into its "forked flames and lightnings," among the "accursed fiends" below. Submerged in these waters, or even when merely bathed in the steam rising up from them, Ahab could never accept the account of the relations between body and soul as presented in the *Phaedo*. Here, then, we have another sense in which *Moby-Dick* expresses an inverted-Platonism.

Chapter 45: The Affidavit

Ishmael would have his readers believe his story, to which end he records several accounts of similar events at sea. The most famous of these is the sinking of the whaleship *Essex* by a sperm whale in the Pacific in 1820. Ishmael claims to have spoken with the son of the first mate of the *Essex*, and to have received from him a copy of his father's narrative of the event, and "all this within a few miles of the scene of the catastrophe." Ishmael here gives voice directly to Melville himself. Owen Chase wrote the factual *Narrative of the Most Extraordinary and Distressing Shipwreck of the Whale-Ship Essex*, and Melville did indeed meet and receive from his son a copy of the book not far from the site of the disaster. He read the work while sailing on the whaleship *Acushnet*, and the story served as one of the inspirations for *Moby-Dick*.

Reliable as Ishmael's reporting of other attacks on whaleships may be, we know that he himself is a character in a novel conceived and composed by Herman Melville. We know too that the central storyline of this novel is untrue. There were no more an Ahab and a Moby Dick than there was an Ishmael, and the mad pursuit of the white whale and his sinking of the *Pequod* never happened. At the same time, however, we understand that the story is based at least to some extent on actual facts, and also that it communicates a type of truth. There did at one time live and breathe a large, indomitable albino whale whom sailors called Mocha Dick, and Ahab and Ishmael represent aspects of Melville's own psyche. As often, there is some truth in this fiction.

Ishmael's attempts to convince us of the reliability of his story reminds one of similar assurances offered by characters in Plato's dialogues. The first word of the *Phaedo* is *autos*, which in this instance is the "yourself" in the initial question put to Phaedo by a friend, "Were you yourself present with Socrates on that day he drank the poison in prison, or did you hear about it from someone else?" To which Phaedo responds, *autos*—he was there himself. The repetitive stress on the *autos* assures the reader that he can trust Phaedo's narrative of the events, and more particularly the conversation, that transpired that day. He was an eye-witness. There was a real Phaedo, and this man did indeed know Socrates. He may very well have been with him in prison when he died. But as readers of Plato's dialogue, we know that this Phaedo, this *autos*, is a character in a creative work. However much faith the character speaking with Phaedo within the frame of the dialogue may have in his words, can we readers external to the work believe him? Phaedo states explicitly that Plato was not there to hear or participate in the discussion himself, and even though he notes that it pleases him to talk about Socrates, he does not say that he reported the details of Socrates' last conversation to Plato. I have noted in a previous chapter that the relation between Phaedo as character and Plato as author raises puzzling questions about the facts as presented in the dialogue: Phaedo implies that we can trust his account because he was there. But according to his account the man who composed his account was *not* there. Therefore, what? We can *not* trust Phaedo's account? Including his claim that Plato was not there? But if Plato was present after all, can we then trust Phaedo's account as Plato wrote it? But if so, we are back to trusting his statement that Plato was not there!

Ishmael worries that his readers will mistake his tale of Moby Dick for "a hideous and intolerable allegory." In this he is one with Melville, who claimed in a letter to Sophia Hawthorne that while writing his novel he had only "some vague idea" that it was "susceptible of an allegorical construction." He did not notice "the part-&-parcel allegoricalness of the whole" until Nathaniel Hawthorne pointed it out to him. One wonders whether this can possibly be true. Might it be that Melville was loathe to explain or interpret the work for his audience? Poets and artists are like this. And here I am reminded of another parallel with Plato. In his *Timaeus* Plato writes of the "Demiurge," a sort of deity that composed the universe out of the initial material of eternally existing triangles. No need to explore the cosmological geometry here—suffice it to say that some among the ancients took the Demiurge's step-by-step construction of the universe for Plato's fanciful method of exhibiting clearly the various elements of reality and their interrelations, while others took the construction process literally, as if Plato intended to assert that the universe had come together from component elements in time. Aristotle took this part of the *Timaeus* literally. Xenocrates, the third head of the Academy, took it figuratively. Now what fascinates me about all this is that both these men knew Plato well. So I wonder: could they not simply ask Plato what he meant? If not, why not? Or did they ask him but receive different answers? Or did he refuse to explain himself, as poets and artists are wont to do?

Plato's ambiguous relation to his dialogues motivates me to impute to him characteristics we are accustomed to finding in artists. Usually we overlook

Plato's artistry because we overlook Plato altogether. We are so distracted by the Socrates who appears in the dialogues that we fail to see the man who in writing the dialogues rendered him so distractingly. As common as it is to attend to the dramatic elements of the dialogues and praise their artistry, it is rare that anyone attempts to think through what Plato must have been like as a philosopher infused with the artistic drive, and what his conception of philosophy must have been given his self-conception as, at least in part, an artist. Here it is worth emphasizing a claim I have made previously: Plato was a sage whose artistic expression of his wisdom manifests as what we call philosophy. Similarly, Herman Melville was a sage whose philosophical expression of his wisdom manifests as what we call art.

Chapter 46: Surmises

A thirteenth century drawing by Matthew Paris shows Socrates sitting at a writing desk, a pen in each hand. Plato stands behind him touching his back with one hand and with the other raising his index finger in a gesture of direction or command. The image is unusual in seeming to portray Plato as the more authoritative figure, whereas today we tend to privilege Socrates. Of course we understand that most of what we think we know about Socrates, his attitudes and ideas, derive from Plato's dialogues; yet when discussing these matters we constantly focus on Socrates rather than Plato. Listen to a group of academics talking about Plato: you will hear Socrates' name almost exclusively. We do this even when considering ideas that if pressed we would admit Socrates never dreamt of, ideas that were Plato's own which he communicated through the character Socrates as through a semiopaque medium.

In fact, however, Plato as author dominates the character Socrates' will every bit as much as we learn in the present chapter that Ahab dominates Starbuck. Even more, for the Socrates at issue here is a fiction of Plato's own invention. Of course he based his character on an actual man of extraordinary charisma and influence. The historical Socrates must saturate Plato's depiction, at least in the so-called "early" dialogues. But even so, Plato is in control of every aspect of his character, from the subject and setting of his conversations to the very words he speaks. Ahab coerces Starbuck's body and intellect, but not his soul. But Plato, as in Paris's drawing—and to adapt

Ishmael's characterization of Ahab's power over Starbuck—Plato employs "his own predominating brain, heart, and hand, backed by a heedful, closely calculating attention to every minute atmospheric influence which it was possible for his [Socrates] to be subjected to," and thereby he acquires an "ascendency" over Socrates that "cover[s] the complete spiritual man." When reading the dialogues we must try to keep in mind that Socrates is really always Plato's Socrates, and thus in a way always primarily Plato.

This is not to say that the character Socrates always speaks for Plato the philosopher in any straightforward sense. I have mentioned the early dialogues. If in any dialogue Plato attempts to communicate faithfully the ideas and personality of his friend and mentor, that dialogue is the *Apology*, which purports to record the speech that Socrates delivered to the jury during his trial. In this work Socrates insists that he does not claim to know what he does not know, which, he says, distinguishes him from the many reputedly wise men who think they know many things of which they are in fact ignorant. Since these men think they know the truth, they do not seek it; since they do not seek it, they do not find it; and so they pass their days in the darkest night of unrelieved ignorance. Socrates is different, for since he is aware of his own ignorance, he seeks knowledge. He may not find it, but still he seeks. His search for knowledge is his love of wisdom; his pursuit is the enactment of his philosophical life.

This ceaselessly seeking Socrates has become for us the paradigm of the philosopher. If we would be philosophers, we too must confess our ignorance and search for knowledge. We must emulate Socrates. Or so it is said. But what about Plato? His love of wisdom did not manifest as a Socratic dialectical seeking. As a philosopher, Plato was not a garrulous critical interrogator; he was a solitary creative writer. The difference is on display in and through every one of the dialogues, but we overlook it because the character Socrates draws us so thoroughly into the conversation that we neglect to look behind the words at their author, Plato.

In the *Symposium* Socrates defines love in terms of desire (*erôs*) and desire as the pursuit of that which one lacks. But if to love wisdom the philosopher must lack it, then the philosopher must by definition be a perpetual philosopher. And who would define himself—his life and his life's goal—in such a way as literally to necessitate that he never becomes who he is? No one in his right mind. But there is another account of desire in the *Symposium*, an account mentioned only in passing, of desiring to maintain that which one already possesses, as a rich man may desire his wealth or a healthy man his health. In such cases one desires that "things present now be present even in the future." According to this interpretation of the lover of wisdom's love, the philosopher may be wise. This sort of philosopher does not seek a wisdom he does not possess, but cherishes the wisdom he has. We call him a philosopher rather than a sage by way of admitting that since we do not know the future, we don't know to a certainty that he will maintain his wisdom; therefore we must regard his future condition as a lack he seeks to fill. But this is a consequence of our temporally-constricted knowledge, which in actuality reveals our own lack rather than the philosopher's. For all we know, some lovers of wisdom, some few rare philosophers, might well be wise *sub specie aeternitatis*. I don't know about Socrates, but I believe that Plato was one of the few examples of this type in western intellectual history—the sage who operates from behind the mask of philosophy.

In some sense, then, in some vital, substantial sense, Plato was closer to Melville and Nietzsche than to Socrates. Socrates loved wisdom by chasing after it, like Ahab after his white whale, but without the insanity—though Nietzsche did like to suggest that Socrates was mentally unsound by characterizing the messages he claimed to receive from his *daimonion* as "auditory hallucinations." But be this as it may, Plato, Melville, and Nietzsche did not so much seek knowledge through their works as play with ideas (which play may occasionally include the search for knowledge). And considering the amount of time they dedicated to producing their works, I conclude that this playing with ideas was their primary love. They loved wisdom not by seeking to supply for themselves a thing they lacked, but by cherishing their most prized possession. Their philosophy therefore is not of that species we associate with Socrates, and that I have in this book associated with Ahab as a tortured seeking. Their philosophy is a creative celebration, a joyful wisdom.

Chapter 47: The Mat-Maker

This chapter, to my mind one of the best in the whole of *Moby-Dick*, contains the creative-intellectual harvest of Melville's long, slow ruminations on "Fixed Fate, Free-will, and foreknowledge absolute." While working with Queequeg to weave a so-called "sword-mat" for their boat, Ishmael imagines them standing over a "Loom of Time" that combines the influences of fate, free will, and chance. The "fixed threads of the warp" represent the element of necessity in the events of the world; Ishmael's moving of the shuttle in and out among these threads represents his acting according to his free deliberations within the parameters set by necessity; and Queequeg's idle, indifferent use of a wooden sword to compact the yarns of the woof "slantingly, or crookedly, or strongly, or weakly, as the case might be," represents the influence of chance. Each element plays a role in shaping the course of a man's life: "aye, chance, free will, and necessity ... all interweavingly working together."

Notice that Melville has written of fate or necessity rather than Providence. There is no suggestion in his image of the Loom that a divine intellect is at work in the world or behind the scenes, directing cosmic history in accord with its intentions. It was as common in Melville's day as it is in ours for believers to speak of God's plans, to interpret the trials and triumphs of their lives as the various results of God's working out of his purposes, and to think of God not just as their inspiration but even as their guide, closing some doors and opening others. As a Calvinist, Melville was raised to believe that God from eternity has predestined "whatsoever comes to pass," not only one's ultimate glorification or damnation, but even "all the means thereunto," while somehow preserving "the liberty or contingency of second causes." *Moby-Dick* is informed throughout by ideas one can trace back to this heritage, but the backward path is winding and the ideas themselves equivocal. Despite the many references and allusions to supernatural agencies in *Moby-Dick*, the God of Melville's parents was dead for the son.

When he wrote *Moby-Dick* Melville was not yet familiar with the work of Arthur Schopenhauer, whom Nietzsche called "as a philosopher ... the *first* admitted and inexorable atheist among us Germans." Later in life he would read and admire Schopenhauer; but in 1851, the year his *Moby-Dick* appeared, he had no idea that Schopenhauer had that same year published a collection of essays entitled *Parerga und Paralipomena* that included a piece addressing the very theme he explored in "The Mat-Maker." This essay, to which Schopenhauer affixed the stupendous title, "Transcendent Speculation on the Apparent Deliberateness in the Fate of the Individual," is the philosopher's attempt to explain the mysterious mechanisms behind the widespread belief in "a supernatural guidance of the events in an individual's life." Schopenhauer believed that fatalism could be demonstrated, indeed that he had demonstrated it himself in his magnum opus, *The World as Will and Representation*. According to this account, every event in the phenomenal world is the effect of a previous cause, which is itself the effect of a still earlier cause, and so on and on into the past *ad infinitum*. There is no break in the causal chain, and therefore every event without exception is entirely determined. And because the world is characterized by space, there are many such causal chains "side by side," the totality of them generating at any given moment countless simultaneous effects. These effects are independent of one another, but "the simultaneity itself ... is necessary since what is now simultaneous was *as such* already determined by causes in the remotest past." Therefore "the accidental coincidence of all the conditions of an event" is "necessary in a higher sense." For example, if I round a bend to see a friend trip on a stone, and while walking over to assist him I am struck by an apple falling from a tree, there is only an accidental relation between my friend's tripping, my being in a position to see this, and the apple's falling when it does; yet each of these events is necessitated in itself as the latest effect of a chain of causes and effects stretching back into the mists of time. If as a result of being hit on the head I formulate, say, the theory of gravity, it might seem as if a superior intelligence had conspired to coordinate all these events in order that the insight would come to me at precisely that moment; but this would be an illusion. And we may say the same of all those coordinated events that make up the course of each and every one of our lives. As Schopenhauer puts it, in virtue of the unity of "the accidental and the necessary..., the inner necessity showing itself as a kind of instinctive impulse, then rational deliberation, and finally the external operation of circumstances had to assist one another in the course of a man's life in such a way that, at the end thereof when it had been run through, they made it appear like a well-finished and perfect work of art."

Schopenhauer believed in free will only as a metaphysical phenomenon. According to his version of Kant's "transcendental freedom," each of us is responsible for his essence, which in itself is independent of empirical causal connections. But this essence having been freely adopted, "neither our *action* nor our *course of life* is our work," for given our essence in association with the causally necessitated events of the empirical realm in which our lives play out, "at his birth the whole course of a man's life is already determined irrevocably down to its details." So Melville and Schopenhauer might have disagreed on this point. But, really, Melville never was committed to a belief in free will. He did not know; he wavered. Schopenhauer's rejection of "empirical freedom" was final, but I suspect that Melville would not often have summoned the passion of confidence to dispute the matter with him.

Neither Melville nor Schopenhauer believed in God in any traditional sense, but Schopenhauer thought—and thought that he had proved—that a metaphysical Will is operative at the core of all things, and Melville as often suspected as doubted inscrutable forces moving beneath the surface features of the world. And both men at least entertained the possibility of human foreknowledge, for if at bottom all events are causally necessitated, then the future must have a determinacy that is foreseeable at least in theory. Thus Schopenhauer writes that "that which in an event is natural and can be causally demonstrated as necessary, does not by any means do away with the ominous element therein," and Ishmael says of the crewman who sights the first whale from a mast-head above the *Pequod* that "you would have thought him some prophet or seer beholding the shadows of Fate." The fate in question includes among other events Ishmael's dying before he dies, as we shall see in the next two chapters.

Chapter 48: The First Lowering

The mast-head prophet has alerted the crew to the presence of whales. This is the reason the men have signed on to the voyage, most all of them anyway but Ahab. Therefore they hurry to their stations and their chores, particularly the rowers and harpooners who will man the whaleboats. These boats are lowered to the sea, and the men rush down the side of the ship behind them. Everywhere excitement hums as the mates urge their crews to row, the crewmen strain to pull the oars through churning water, and the harpooners prepare to hurl their weapons of death. Whenever a sailor sings out for whales, he is chanting a prophecy of death; and for all anyone knows, it might as well be a man's death as a whale's.

Ishmael is on a boat with Queequeg and the first mate Starbuck. Beneath the clouds of an approaching storm they have rowed right up to the side of a whale. Queequeg stands and lets loose his iron, but he only grazes his prey. Yet even this suffices to startle or enrage the whale, with the result that before swimming away he tumbles and rolls beneath the boat. So violent is the whale's commotion that the men fall overboard. With effort they manage to right the boat and climb back inside, but the little vessel is swamped and, what's worse, the storm rages, dusk descends ominously, and the *Pequod* is nowhere to be seen. The men then pass a nervous night adrift on the blank sea, Queequeg thrusting a makeshift lantern into the abyss to no purpose. He is a "symbol of a man without faith, hopelessly holding up hope in the midst of despair."

In the morning as the mist burns off the water, suddenly the *Pequod* appears. But rather than a promise of salvation, the ship bears down on the men like an engine of doom. Leaping frantically into the waves, they escape before the ship plows over their boat, destroying it utterly. A harrowing episode, but finally they are rescued, to the relief of everyone involved. The crew on the ship had given up finding their lost crewmates alive, and Ishmael reports that they came on them while searching for "some token of our perishing." He and his mates had been in peril, to be sure; fortunately, they had fallen into the ocean's "jaws of death" as if they were "immortal."

Ishmael takes this last formulation seriously. In the next chapter he reflects that "all the days I should now live would be as good as the days Lazarus lived after his resurrection." He had died before his death. "I survived myself," he says, "my death and burial were locked up in my chest."

I have said that philosophy as training for death is a central theme of Plato's *Phaedo*. The man who truly lives the philosophical life dies before his death by separating his soul from his body through a process of spiritual-intellectual purification. This separation or release (*lusis*) is introduced early in the dialogue, and the work concludes with Socrates' actual biological death. In the final scene the philosopher drinks a small cup of poison, paces the room, then finally lies down to await the end. His feet and legs are numb; his body is growing cold and stiff; and the official who gave him the poison says that when the cold reaches his heart, he will be gone. But when the chill begins to affect his abdomen, Socrates speaks, addressing his old friend Crito. His last words are notoriously enigmatic. Nietzsche makes much of them, as we shall see. But for now I focus on something other than Socrates' last *words*, on a detail that no one previously has considered particularly significant but which seems to me vital. I refer to Socrates' last *act*.

Plato informs us that Socrates uncovers himself before speaking to Crito, for, he adds, he had covered himself. The implication of course is that at some point after lying down Socrates covered himself with a cloak or shroud and, presumably, remained motionless as if he were dead. Certainly the men standing around would have taken him for dead, for it was as unusual in their day as in ours to cover a living man with his death shroud. One covers a corpse, not an animate man. Plato does not portray the scene this way, but I can only imagine that when Socrates lifted the shroud his friends were shocked. Had he come back to life? He had spoken at length of the soul's coming back to life after death, and formulated an argument to prove that this happens. He had even referred to "resurrecting" an argument. But if a *logos* can be brought back from the dead, then surely a philosopher whose life has been a training for death can too.

But whatever reaction his friends may have had to Socrates' surprising act, I am more interested in Plato's intentions in presenting the scene as he did. I believe he intended the uncovering to signify something beyond itself, for he embedded the gesture in a broader cycle of acts of covering and uncovering surrounding Socrates' death. Immediately after Socrates drinks the poison, Phaedo *covers* his eyes. Next we are told that Socrates *uncovered* himself, for, Phaedo says, he had previously *covered* himself. Finally, Phaedo notes that the prison official *uncovered* Socrates to inspect his condition. Plato employs the same Greek word in each of these instances, and taken together they form an ordered series of covering, uncovering, covering, and uncovering. And this is without even mentioning the other acts of covering and uncovering that must have occurred along the way. Surely Phaedo *uncovered* his eyes after covering them, for he provides the eyewitness report of Socrates' death. And just as surely Socrates *covered* himself after uttering his final words, for the guard had later to uncover him to verify that he was dead; and naturally he *covered* Socrates again after doing so. Now consider these acts as a series: covering, uncovering, covering, uncovering, covering, uncovering, covering. The interplay of opposites is reminiscent of Socrates' argument that since all things that have opposites come to be from their opposites, then just as sleeping comes from waking and waking from sleeping, and even as death comes from life, so life must come to be from death. The process by which this happens is called "coming back to life," and this is the conclusion of the very argument I mentioned above as proving that souls may live again after death.

In short, then, Socrates' final act is a symbolic representation of the recurring cycle of death-from-life and life-from-death that is the fate of the human soul until it has purified itself by philosophy and thereby escaped the cycle to live in the future without a body. That Socrates' soul has attained to this condition may well be indicated by the fact that the series of covering-uncovering oppositions concludes with the covering of his body. The cycle is closed by death, a corporeal death signifying the end of all physical rebirths. Socrates' soul has been released from its prison, never to return; forever now he is free.

Neither Melville nor Ishmael was a faithful adherent of *Phaedo*-Platonism, so the latter's dying before he dies does not liberate his soul from the bonds of his body literally unto eternity. The episode affects Ishmael through an existential rather than a metaphysical transformation, and the philosophy he develops in the wake of his death-and-resurrection experience sets him on his way to becoming a sage.

Chapter 49: The Hyena

I have referred to Ishmael's Zarathustran wisdom, the *gaya scienza* through which he contemplates the accursed questions without regarding them *as* accursed, which is to say without suffering from them. I have, in short, branded Ishmael a sage. I am speaking here of Ishmael as narrator, who addresses his audience many years after the events related in his story. Recall that when he went to sea it was a "damp, drizzly November in my soul." Depressed, he had been brooding in front of mortuaries, trailing funeral processions, contemplating suicide. He overcame his morbid longing for death through his physical, emotional, psychological, spiritual, and intellectual experiences aboard the *Pequod* in pursuit of the white whale. These experiences eventually forged him into the sort of man who says Yes— who *has the right* to say Yes—to the tragedy and the comedy of life through a Dionysian song of affirmation.

Ishmael's Bacchic lyricism is interspersed with verses of denial and destruction, to be sure; but overall he sings the songs of a Nietzschean *Ja-sager*. By saying No to the lazy comforts of convention he says Yes to all that is new, strange, and unsettling. Nietzsche once wondered "how he that says No and *does* No to an unheard of degree, to everything to which one has so far said Yes, can nevertheless be the opposite of a No-saying spirit; how the spirit who bears the heaviest fate, a fatality of a task, can nevertheless be the lightest and most transcendent." The question is his formulation of "the psychological problem in the type of Zarathustra" in association with "the concept of Dionysus." It is, in short, the problem of the affirmative No-sayer. Nietzsche's problem recalls Melville's formulation of the "Problem" in the type of Hawthorne, as he once expressed it in a letter to the subject in question. Hawthorne "says NO! in thunder," and even "the Devil himself cannot make him say *yes*." Yet Melville takes this for a form of affirmation. The objects of Hawthorne's stern denials are all those little cowardices and conventionalities that confine the average man within the borders of his comfortable, prefabricated world. The adventurous spirit who says No! to these things says Yes! to all that contradicts and leads away from them, enabling him to transcend his surroundings and to declare himself "a sovereign nature (in himself) amid the powers of heaven, hell, and earth."

As often when he writes about Hawthorne, Melville is writing also about himself. Here he reckons himself among these audaciously affirmative No-sayers, and his characterization of the type is reminiscent of Nietzsche's light and transcendent spirit. Those who deny and cast off convention are "in the happy condition of judicious, unincumbered travelers in Europe; they cross the frontiers into Eternity with nothing but a carpet-bag." Like the lion in Zarathustra's speech "On the Three Metamorphoses," they create freedom for themselves through "a sacred 'No' even to duty." The facile Yes-sayers, on the other hand, "never get through the Custom House" because "they travel with heaps of baggage." In this they are reminiscent of the camel in Zarathustra's speech, weighed down by inherited reverences, dominated by conventional pieties.

Ishmael as narrator, Ishmael as sage, is a reflection of Melville himself, sometimes literally, sometimes symbolically. Both men attain their condition through familiarity with foreign perspectives, skeptical reflections on the religious assumptions of childhood, thoughtful encounters with nature's mysterious and ominous undercurrents, and finally the transformative experience of death and rebirth, all these things tending to an expansion of the psyche, an expansion of the breadth and depths of thought and emotion. Ishmael refers to the intellectual-spiritual condition he has attained as a "free and easy sort of genial, desperado philosophy." In this chapter he articulates this philosophy, and it is worth quoting the relevant passage in full. Consider, then, Ishmael's reflections immediately after falling into, and escaping from, "death's jaws":

There are certain queer times and occasions in this strange mixed affair we call life when a man takes this whole universe for a vast practical joke, though the wit thereof he but dimly discerns, and more than suspects that the joke is at nobody's expense but his own. However, nothing dispirits, and nothing seems worth while disputing. He bolts down all events, all creeds, and beliefs, and persuasions, all hard things visible and invisible, never mind how knobby; as an ostrich of potent digestion gobbles down bullets and gun flints. And as for small difficulties and worryings, prospects of sudden disaster, peril of life and limb; all these, and death itself, seem to him only sly, good-natured hits, and jolly punches in the side bestowed by the unseen and unaccountable old joker. That odd sort of wayward mood I am speaking of, comes over a man only in some time of extreme tribulation; it comes in the very midst of his earnestness, so that what just before might have seemed to him a thing most momentous, now seems but a part of the general joke.

The tone of the writing is more light-hearted than we are used to from Nietzsche, even in his playful moods; but it is not incompatible with his description of *The Gay Science* as a book in whose every sentence "profundity and high spirits go tenderly hand in hand." And when Nietzsche writes of "the Provençal concept of gaya scienza—that unity of *singer*, *knight*, and *free spirit* which distinguishes the wonderful early culture of the Provençals from all equivocal cultures," one is reminded of Melville on his thirty-second birthday, only recently having completed his masterpiece, riding over to visit Hawthorne, who later recalled that "a cavalier on horseback came along the road, and greeted me in Spanish." Finally recognizing the cavalier as Melville, Hawthorne brought him inside where the two friends talked at length about "time and eternity, things of this world and of the next ... and of all possible and impossible matters." Here one thinks of Zarathustra "whispering of eternal things" with the personified spirit of gravity. And Ishmael's desperado philosophy is compatible too with Nietzsche's account of the Zarathustra type in the fifth book of *The Gay Science* as:

the ideal of a spirit who plays naively—that is, not deliberately but from overflowing power and abundance—with all that was hitherto called holy, good, untouchable, divine; for whom those supreme things that the people naturally accept as their value standards, signify danger, decay, debasement, or at least recreation, blindness, and temporary self-oblivion; the ideal of a human, superhuman well-being and benevolence that will often appear *inhuman*—for example, when it confronts all earthly seriousness so far, all solemnity in gesture, word, tone, eye, morality, and task so far, as if it were their most incarnate and involuntary parody—and in spite of all of this, it is perhaps only with him that *great seriousness* really begins.

Ishmael was "the last man" plucked from the sea and lifted onto the *Pequod*. He was frantic; he even decided to write out a will. Such are "the perils of whaling." Yet when his encounter with death settled over him, his condition improved; he mellowed. He regarded the world around him "tranquilly and contentedly." Here we have an indication of Ishmael's *ataraxia*, his freedom from psychic disturbance. Whereas previously he saw nothing in the whale "but the deadliest ill," now he regards "this whole voyage of the Pequod, and the great White Whale its object," through the affirmative perspective of his desperado philosophy.

Still, it would be a mistake to think of Ishmael at this point in the story as having acquired a firm and lasting grip on wisdom. As we have seen, it is no simple matter to know whether a man is on his way to wisdom, is wise but only tenuously so, or is fully and finally a sage. Ishmael's first encounter with death was profoundly affecting. But he will confront the abyss a second time, a more absorbing and darker confrontation than he can imagine possible even after this harrowing episode. In the end he will attain a joyful wisdom, and he is inexorably on his way to it now, but still at this point he is only on his way.

Chapter 50: Ahab's Boat and Crew • Fedallah

When I discussed the first lowering of the *Pequod*'s whaleboats in chapter forty-eight, I omitted one significant element of the scene. Here and there throughout the book there have been indications of other men on board the ship than those we have met so far, beginning with Ishmael's sighting of several shadowy figures moving near the *Pequod* on the morning he and Queequeg boarded her, and most recently one sailor's hearing noises below deck that he took to signify the presence of men. He was right: there are other men on board, or anyway entities "looking like men," to quote from Elijah's earlier exchange with Ishmael. They showed themselves at last to join in the hunt during which Ishmael fell "immortal in [the] jaws of death."

Ahab has smuggled on board the *Pequod* an entire whaleboat's crew, four rowers and one harpooner. He secreted this crew below deck, and there the men have remained until, upon the mast-head prophet's cry of "There she blows!" they manifested at last, appearing like "five dusky phantoms ... fresh formed out of air." Ishmael's description of this apparitional crew is portentous: the rowers exhibit features of a race "notorious for a certain diabolism of subtlety" and supposed by some to be emissaries of the devil himself. The crew's leader, the harpooner, displays a crooked, evil tooth, wears a dark funereal jacket, and speaks with a hiss. This man's name is Fedallah, and as we learn in the present chapter, he has "some sort of half-hinted influence" over Ahab.

Later we learn that Fedallah is a Parsee, which is to say a descendent of those Persians who fled Iran for India during the Muslim invasions of the eighth to tenth centuries to preserve their Zoroastrian faith. Zoroastrianism was founded in Persia by a figure named Zoroaster, called Zarathustra by the ancient Greeks. Zoroastrians believe that the universe is controlled by a pair of opposed forces personified by a beneficent deity called Ahura Mazda and a malevolent deity called Angra Mainyu. Fedallah seems particularly dedicated to the latter.

Despite Fedallah's apparent devotion to infernal influences, his religion is known for stressing both the good and the evil at work in the world. Best to live in accord with the good, but evil is a real and fundamental element of things. This objectivist dualism, this belief that good and evil are not just matters of perception or judgment but properties of reality existing independently of the human mind, immaterial but as actual as air or light—this view attracted Nietzsche's attention, and more particularly his hostility. Nietzsche entitled one of his books *Beyond Good and Evil*, and in a later work he stated his "demand upon the philosopher" that he "take his stand *beyond* good and evil and leave the illusion of moral judgment *beneath* himself." To his mind this is the only honest position, for "*there are altogether no moral facts.*" This same theme informs his *Thus Spoke Zarathustra*.

But if Nietzsche advocates a position *beyond* good and evil, why did he name the book he considered his greatest and most important work for a figure who advocated precisely the opposite position? Nietzsche himself has answered this question in his *Ecce Homo*. Near the end of this book he remarks that "Zarathustra was the first to consider the fight of good and evil the very wheel in the machinery of things: the transposition of morality into the metaphysical realm, as a force, cause, and end in itself, is *his* work." Whether or not the Persian Zoroaster really was the world's first moral objectivist, he is certainly among the first of such men who lived and taught during an era whose ideas have come down to us. In any case, given Zoroaster's antiquity, Nietzsche judges imaginatively that he has had much time to rethink his moral objectivism, and since "he created this most calamitous error, morality," he concludes that "he must also be the first to recognize it." Nietzsche does not portray his Zarathustra as identically the same man as the ancient Zoroaster: his work is set in a different time and place, and his protagonist is his own man. But he does intentionally associate the two by way of a symbolic sympathy representative of spiritual antagonism, re-forming and re-framing the moralist Zoroaster to use for his own purposes as Zarathustra, the great immoralist.

I have mentioned the reading of *Moby-Dick* as expressive of an "inverted Platonism," and I have noted as well that Nietzsche once characterized his own philosophy in precisely these terms. We are not done encountering Platonic elements in the story, as we shall see in the next chapter, but gradually now we begin to approach more strictly Nietzschean themes.

Chapter 51: The Spirit-Spout

The appearance of a mysterious "silvery jet" of spray, as from a whale, enchants the crew. Far in advance of the *Pequod*, it seems almost a "god uprising from the sea." Night after night the men spot the jet in the distance, and though it allures them, it constantly withdraws and disappears. Some of the men are sure this is Moby Dick himself, others are simply afraid. The divine apparition remains in their van even after the ship turns eastward toward the Cape of Good Hope.

Formerly this place had been known as "Cape Tormentoso," Ishmael says. The "stormy cape," a fitting appellation, for the surrounding waters are treacherous, tormented indeed. The sea heaves "as if its vast tides were a conscience; and the great mundane soul were in anguish and remorse for the long sin and suffering it had bred." Even the animals are affected by the atmosphere, the fish and the birds seeming reincarnations of "guilty beings ... condemned to swim on everlastingly without any haven in store, or beat that black air without any horizon." The *Pequod* now has sailed into something like an antechamber of hell.

Ishmael associates the sea with the "mundane soul," as previously he associated it with the "bottomless soul, pervading mankind and nature." This is the Platonic World Soul, as I have said; it is the animating principle that infuses all things with the powers of motion and life. The stars fly, the earth revolves, the tides flow, whales swim, and men walk and see and think, all by way of the World Soul as their active source. The orthodox Platonist would never attribute an anguished conscience to this principle, for it is an offspring of God, or the Good, the divine One, and therefore in no way responsible for evil. Matter, particularly as manifest in human bodies, is the principle of sin and suffering. We are told in the *Phaedo* that philosophers understand that a fundamental problem with humans is that the soul is bound up with the body, which is base or vicious (*kakon*); it is also the source of strife and other such distractions from philosophy. Ahab, whose material element dominates in his person, and who at times dissociates from his mind and soul altogether to become solely his body and his body's purposeful willing—Ahab is the immediate source of all that is bad on and about the *Pequod*. But at this point Ahab looms so large in Ishmael's mind that he seems somehow to contaminate even his conception of the world's soul with the Captain's personal demonism.

Ishmael's imagining the fish and birds as guilty beings is somewhat more traditionally Platonic. In the *Phaedo* it is said that the souls of vicious men will be reborn into the bodies of that species of animal that corresponds to their character-types. Those who love injustice, for example, will be reborn as birds of prey. Only the philosopher, complete in his purity, will be permitted after death to escape forever the prison-house of the body and transition finally to live among the gods. Plato writes about the transmigration of souls in several places, but the stress in the *Phaedo* on men becoming non-human animals in connection with a soul's involvement with the body is somewhat unusual. Like so much else in *Phaedo*-Platonism, it is an extreme formulation of a Platonic doctrine expressed less radically elsewhere. It may be that the

finality of death, the immediacy of the underworld, in the context of which
the *Phaedo* is set, demands precisely this urgency of expression. If so, it has
since been applied beyond its proper context, for *Phaedo*-Platonism is the
version of Platonism that has had the greatest impact on western theological
and philosophical thought, to the dismay of Nietzsche, the perplexity of
Melville, and if he could have known, probably to the consternation of Plato
himself.

The *Pequod* never does overtake the "celestial" silvery jet. It shines before
them in the moonlight almost as a ghost, drawing them on. But toward what
end? If it were an angel or a god, a manifestation of the World Soul erupting
into visible form, then it might signify the hope of life. But the *Pequod* is
bound for hell, and although Ishmael has died before his death, and benefitted
from the experience, he has not yet fully returned from his descent to the
underworld to stand in the light of a gift-giving sun.

Chapter 52: The Albatross

This chapter, in which the *Pequod* meets another whaleship for the first time
since leaving Nantucket, concludes with an expression of Melville's
epistemological pessimism. Although in the previous chapter the spirit-spout
swam dreamily ahead of the ship as if it were leading the crew toward a goal,
a final destination hellish or divine, now Ishmael reflects on the utter lack of
attainable goals in life. To circumnavigate the globe seems a great adventure,
and it would be if there were hope of attaining the object of one's desire. "But
in pursuit of those far mysteries we dream of," Ishmael says, "or in tormented
chase of that demon phantom that, some time or other, swims before all
human hearts; while chasing such over this round globe, they either lead us on
in barren mazes or midway leave us whelmed."

The demon phantom at issue here could be the "ungraspable phantom of
life" that Ishmael in the first chapter called "the key to it all." It certainly is a
key of some sort, by which I mean an answer, a solution, a healing. We have
seen that according to *Phaedo*-Platonism the primary answers reside in the
Forms, the metaphysical essences of natural kinds of being. With the right
education and training we can come to know the Forms, can know Justice or
Beauty or Equality or Triangularity. In fact we already do know these things;
we need only turn our mind toward the Forms by dissociating from bodily

distractions. This is the Platonic doctrine that "learning is recollection." In the *Phaedo* Socrates explains that before our immortal souls are incarnated in a physical body, we somehow acquire knowledge of the Forms. In another dialogue, the *Phaedrus*, it is claimed that our disembodied souls approach the rotating rim of heaven and look out beyond the divide toward "the plain of truth" where the Forms reside. The more like God a soul is, the more it sees of reality, truth, the Forms. But, to return to the *Phaedo*, when our souls are born into physical bodies, from the moment of birth they are flooded with sensory input, information pertaining to the physical world. This causes us to forget our prenatal knowledge of metaphysical truth, which we can recover only by way of the proper practice of philosophy, which we may sum up in the word "purification." The "key to it all," then, according to *Phaedo*-Platonism, is knowledge of the Forms. The man who acquires this key unlocks the gates of the prison that is his body, from which he lives as separately as possible while alive, with the good hope that after death he may never again be condemned to inhabit another.

I have called "the key" not only an answer but a healing. And, indeed, Socrates in the *Phaedo* equates purification, which prepares the mind to acquire knowledge of the Forms, with health. Purification is a sort of spiritual cleansing productive of knowledge and virtue. And a pure, virtuous, and knowing soul is a happy soul. This is precisely the element of *Phaedo*-Platonism that most irritated Nietzsche, who identified Socrates as its principle source. In his late work *Twilight of the Idols* Nietzsche attributes to Socrates the "bizarre equation" reason = virtue = happiness. If we know the good, we will be good, and thereby we will be happy. Nietzsche's account of this equation is a restatement of his objection in *The Birth of Tragedy* to "the Socratic love of knowledge and the delusion of being able thereby to heal the eternal wound of existence." In short, the idea that knowledge is a cure for what ails us is a pernicious fiction. Knowledge of the sort Socrates sought is illusory, nor is there anywhere a salve for the physical and spiritual pains of existence, which cannot be healed but must be endured.

Melville was closer to Nietzsche with respect to these matters than to *Phaedo*-Platonism. He was perhaps less certain than Nietzsche of the absence of eternal objects of knowledge, but he was definitely less certain than his contemporaries—Christians and Transcendentalists in particular—of their presence. It would not be accurate to label Melville during his *Moby-Dick* period a nihilist, but he was something of a pessimist, particularly, as I have said, with respect to epistemology. I have associated Melville with Pyrrhonian skepticism, with, that is, the position that since any argument can be met with an equally persuasive counter-argument, we should withhold judgment about all non-evident matters. This sort of skepticism may in some men amount to an expression of weariness and weakness, and a question like Ishmael's self-reflective "whereto does all that circumnavigation conduct?" may be little more than an articulated sigh of resignation. This would be the sort of skepticism that Nietzsche condemns as "the most spiritual expression of a certain complex physiological condition that in ordinary language is called nervous exhaustion and sickliness." But Ishmael is as physiologically sound as Melville was himself when he created his literary alter-ego. His is "another and stronger type of skepticism," a type that "does not believe but does not lose itself in the process; it gives the spirit dangerous freedom, but it is severe on the heart."

Melville understood that at the root of the doctrine of original sin there is something real and true. Probably it is not the case that a pair of primal humans partook of forbidden fruit, but something in the universe is out of joint, even if it is only that the real as we experience it fails to meet our expectations. This would be less a problem with the universe than with ourselves, but as we are a part of the universe, perhaps the whole is at fault after all. This would be true even if there were no solution to the problem, and even if there were no problem at all—for our suffering from and seeking a solution to a non-existent problem would then itself be the problem. In any case, Melville carried these puzzles in his bones, felt the wound of existence—real or imaginary, the pain is the same—and knew that there is no cure. This is his pessimism. But that in the face of all this he affirmed the world and his life nonetheless, this is his "pessimism of strength," which expression Nietzsche employs to designate the "intellectual predilection for the hard, gruesome, evil, problematic aspect of existence, prompted by well-being, by overflowing health, by the *fullness* of existence." Melville was overfull, and he poured his excess into Ishmael, who as a result is the literary personification of a joyful sage.

Chapter 53: The Gam

Herman Melville was not a garrulous man, but in the right company he could be a scintillating conversationalist. For a time early in his career he attended various literary salons, particularly those hosted by his friend Evert Duyckinck. A frequent guest at one such gathering later wrote that Melville was "taciturn, but genial, and, when warmed-up, capitally racy and pungent." Similarly, Maunsell B. Field recalled in a memoir that he "had always known [Melville] as the most silent man of my acquaintance." Yet one day, probably in 1854, he and a friend paid a visit to the author, and the three men eventually rode over to the estate of Oliver Wendell Holmes. There, according to Field, "the conversation drifted to East India religions and mythologies, and soon there arose a discussion between Holmes and Melville, which was conducted with the most amazing skill and brilliancy on both sides. It lasted for hours… I never chanced to hear better talking in my life." So Melville could speak with verve when he was in the mood, but one has the impression that even considering his deep-diving conversations with Hawthorne, his favorite interlocutor was himself, as himself and as his characters.

Melville loved to write conversations into his books, especially philosophical discourses. Beginning with his third novel, *Mardi*, and up through his last prose work, *The Confidence-Man*, and including also his long narrative poem *Clarel*, his books read at times like Platonic dialogues. *Mardi* is a maritime romance-adventure shading over into metaphysical speculation and an account of the philosophical pursuit of an ever-retreating ideal. The protagonist Taji spends much of the story in the company of a king, a historian, a philosopher, and a poet visiting numerous islands representative of various aspects of Melville's contemporary world, and all through their wanderings the men talk, talk, talk. For a taste of the contents of this wild work, consider this from the philosopher Babbalanja: "I am intent upon the essence of things; the mystery that lieth beyond … that which is beneath the seeming … I probe the circle's center; I seek to evolve the inscrutable." Melville wrote *Mardi* in 1847-48, not long after his first serious encounter with Platonic philosophy, which has at its core the search for the real "beneath the seeming." *The Confidence-Man* comes much later, in 1857. The story is set aboard a Mississippi steamboat on which a shifting variety of characters meet and enter into conversations, many of them having some philosophical import, from the ethical to the metaphysical. The work includes a chapter entitled "In the Polite Spirit of the Tuscular Disputations," a reference to Cicero's collection of philosophical essays, and scholars have detected representations of philosophers from Socrates to Emerson involved in the shipboard discussions. One critic was so dismayed by the book's resemblance to "the Dialogues of Plato" that he pronounced it "undoubted Greek to ordinary men." *Clarel* is the story of a young student of theology travelling through the Holy Land in the company of several philosophically inclined men who discuss and debate the accursed questions throughout the length of their journey. There are representatives present of most every relevant perspective, from the orthodox religious through the seeking agnostic to the atheistic positivist, and each man not only articulates his own worldview but engages critically with the ideas of each of the others. The result is a work of philosophical reflection in nearly 18,000 lines of verse.

All this is to say that in his most interesting books Melville writes at times as if he were composing philosophical dialogues in the manner of Plato. Plato's works center on conversations taking the form of "dialectic," which is the English translation of the Greek *dialektos*, a noun deriving from the verb-form *dialegesthai*. The word itself means simply "to converse" or "to discuss," but in Socratic and Platonic philosophy it has the more technical meaning of an exchange in which one of two dialectical partners poses a question, the other provides an answer, the first then criticizes the answer, the second formulates a new answer in response to the criticism, and so on, with the interlocutors rejecting or revising flawed answers until they arrive at a mutually acceptable account. In the ideal circumstances through this procedure men may identify and discard false ideas and so make their way to the truth. Very few of Plato's dialogues adhere strictly to this method for any significant length of time, much less to more abstruse modes of dialectic. More common is a less technical conversational question-and-answer format, and sometimes the exchanges are so perfunctory that the questions amount to statements and the answers serve only to break up what would otherwise be a lengthy continuous discourse. At their best, Plato's dialogues are less like logical-dialectical treatises than discussions "conducted with the most amazing skill and brilliancy," discussions from which one departs thinking, "I never chanced to hear better talking in my life."

I write about conversations here because in the present chapter of *Moby-Dick* Ishmael explains the meaning of the word "gam," unfamiliar to all but whalemen, as signifying a meeting of two whaleships at sea, during which the crews visit one another for social interaction. One imagines that on such occasions the conversation hardly rises to the level of a Platonic dialogue, but I suppose that depends on the sailors. With a Melville or Ishmael aboard, and in an expansive mood, the talk may well be profound.

Chapter 54: The Town-Ho's Story

This chapter has a subtitle: "As told at the Golden Inn." This is so because, as Ishmael explains before telling his story of the whaleship Town-Ho, he intends to "preserve the style in which [he] once narrated it at Lima" to a group of his Spanish friends on the piazza of the inn. This accounts for the fact that his narrative on occasion is interrupted with questions from those who were present, and his own replies thereto. From my various descriptions above of Plato's style, this story within a story (or *mythos* within a *mythos*), which is a retelling of a tale received from another who received it himself from someone else, and not just a retelling but a second retelling modeled on an earlier version so closely as even to retain remarks from the earlier audience, and which also communicates an insight bearing on the larger *mythos* of which it is a part—these elements of Ishmael's story must remind one of a Platonic dialogue.

Plato's *Phaedo* concludes with a *mythos* of which Socrates says someone has persuaded him. And since Phaedo is the narrator, Phaedo is telling a story that Socrates told after receiving it from another. I do not intend to suggest that Ishmael's Town-Ho story is modelled strictly on the myth at the end of the *Phaedo*, but there are sufficient similarities to justify my recounting the myth in order to add to the account of *Phaedo*-Platonism that I have been developing throughout the book so far.

Socrates' *mythos* relates what we might call an eschatological metaphysical cosmology, or in other words, a description of the universe, the earth in particular, as the setting in which the fates of souls play out. The earth in this scheme is three-tiered, the lowest level being the underworld, including Tartarus, and its fiery and foul rivers; the next tier is the level familiar to us, which we take to be the surface of the earth but which is really one of many hollows and pits marking the surface of the true earth; and finally there is the earth's true surface, which is pure and surrounded by pure aether. Souls make their way in and out of the underworld to be purified of their wrongdoings by way of various rivers. The worst among these souls are cast into Tartarus forever; the others eventually make their way out by the river appropriate to their specific circumstances. These souls are then reborn into our world in the hollows of the earth, a world of corruption and pollution populated by imperfect flora and fauna. But as we in the hollows pass away, "those who are judged to have lived exceptionally piously" are released from our region as from a prison and ascend to the high and pure habitation. There, on the true surface of the earth, our air is like a sea, which is to say that the element above us is beneath them; and above them there is not air but aether. In their temples the gods actually live, speaking with them face to face. In short, they dwell above us in a wondrous region to which we have no physical access. Only those who have thoroughly purified themselves by philosophy are released from the earth and earthly embodiment to live as pure incorporeal souls.

Ishmael's descriptions of the Great Lakes as containing "round archipelagoes of romantic isles" with "territorial colonies ... dotted all round their banks" reminds one of Socrates' description of the hollows in the earth as containing seas and lakes around which people live like ants or frogs around a marsh. And his description of the Erie Canal flowing through cities and swamps, past bars and churches, in forests and fields, as "one continual stream of Venetianly corrupt and often lawless life," recalls Socrates' account of the winding rivers that carry the souls of corrupt men and women to Tartarus. But most of all, the central point of Ishmael's story, namely the justice visited apparently by fate on the brutal first mate Radney for his mistreatment of the Cannaler Steelkilt, recalls the judgment of souls at the center of Socrates' *mythos*. Though Steelkilt intends to murder Radney for flogging him, "the fool [Radney] had been branded for the slaughter by the gods." Moby Dick affects their purpose, catching "the predestinated mate" in his jaws and bearing him beneath the sea as later he will drag the doomed Ahab to his death in the deep.

Melville's manner of relating Ishmael's story is intentional. He calls our attention to the story *as a story*, and as a story with a specific narrator aware of his narrative activity and also of his audience's reception of his words. This is not to say that we must take it for nothing more than a story. Ishmael swears to its veracity. Still, by calling our attention to Ishmael's story as a story, Melville compels us to attend to the related fact that Ishmael himself is a character in a story. His affirming that his story "is in substance and its great items, true" recalls another story-telling character in another story, who concludes his tale like Ishmael by admitting that no one need believe every detail as he has related it, but insisting nonetheless that some such account is true. I refer to Socrates and his underworld *mythos* at the end of the *Phaedo*. Is there really a three-tiered earth, and do the souls of the dead really flow down rivers to receive their judgment? Did Moby Dick really kill Radney as a function of divine retribution? Maybe not. But that good men fare well and bad men suffer—this at least is a belief worth committing to, if not for the sage or the philosopher himself, then for those of his acquaintance who require such reassurances when caught in the teeth of life's accursed questions.

Chapter 55: Of the Monstrous Pictures of Whales

This chapter includes references to various time periods, from ancient to modern, and various regions, from East to West. By way of objecting to inaccurate depictions of whales, Ishmael as cultural guide leads his readers on a tour extending from Hindu avatars to Jeremy Bentham's skeleton. But for now I keep to the ancient side of the divide between tradition and modernity; modern philosophy and modern thought more generally will concern us soon enough.

Melville's mention of "Hindoo" Brahmins and the deity Vishnu is perhaps somewhat surprising, for in his day there was little reliable information available concerning Eastern philosophies and religions. But it is not out of place, particularly as the most prominent themes in the *Phaedo* resonate not only with *Moby-Dick* but with philosophical elaborations of ancient Hinduism as well. A Brahmin is a member of the highest of the four Hindu castes, the caste to which priests and wise men belong. These caste-divisions and the roles associated with each of the four groups go back to the ancient Indo-European invaders of north-western India, as I have noted previously. The ancient Brahmin were spiritual leaders and teachers; it was their business to understand and to guide others to a realization of Brahman, the unified, unchanging, and immaterial source of the plurality of mutable material objects that constitute the world around us. In Platonic terms, Brahman is the Being behind Becoming, the One behind the Many. A complex philosophical account of Brahman was elaborated in the *Upanishads*, a collection of texts of philosophical reflections on the Vedic religion as expressed in the Vedas, which are the Sanskrit scriptures on which the most ancient layers of Hinduism are grounded. Schopenhauer, who acknowledged Plato as one of his two primary philosophical influences (Kant being the other), was a great admirer of the *Upanishads* by way of the *Oupnekhat*, a Latin translation of a Persian version of the original text. He judged this work "the most profitable and sublime reading that is possible in the world," and he affirmed that "it has been the consolation of my life and will be that of my death." Schopenhauer's philosophy centered on a unified source of physical plurality, which he called Will, from which all beings arise and into which they all return at death. In this it is similar to the Hindu Brahman.

Brahman as the unified source of all things manifests as the *Trimûrti*, or the "three forms." This is the Hindu trinity of deities responsible for the creation (Brahma), preservation (Vishnu), and destruction (Shiva) of the universe. Thus Ishmael's Vishnu is a divine expression of Brahman, or ultimate reality, and as this god has incarnated "in the form of leviathan," we may consider the whale as having some special relation to the divine. This is not to say that Moby Dick himself is divine, for Ishmael does not explicitly state that all whales are incarnations of Vishnu. But the association adds to the shifting layers of meaning that hint at the significance of the white whale while simultaneously obscuring him from our view.

Vishnu is an immaterial being that occupies an immaterial realm beyond the physical cosmos. This realm, called *Vaikuntha* or *Paramdhama*, is the habitation of those souls that have been released from the cycle of physical embodiment. The spiritual inhabitants of this realm enjoy eternal bliss. On a more abstract, and perhaps more literally accurate, account, a soul's being liberated into Vaikuntha may be taken for the Atman, which is Brahman as expressed within an individual, attaining moksha, or liberation from samsara, the cycle of rebirth, and dissolving into Brahman. In short, bliss in heaven is really absorption into the One. As Schopenhauer liked to point out, religious language is an expression of philosophical truth in terms that non-philosophers can comprehend.

The parallels between these aspects of Hinduism and *Phaedo*-Platonism should be apparent. We have seen that according to the *Phaedo* the goal of the philosopher is to separate his soul from his body through purification, and thereby to transcend our earthly prison and live on the true surface of the earth among the gods, or better, to live eternally without a body in "dwellings still more beautiful than these, which are not easy to describe." The account of the true earth we may take as parallel to the Hindu Vaikuntha, as an expression in mythological terms of the literal dissolution of the individual into the one true reality that is beyond all distinction and identity.

But to return to Greece from India, I note that in this chapter Ishmael mentions the hero Perseus again. Recall that earlier he compared Ahab to Cellini's sculpture of Perseus standing on the decapitated corpse of Medusa. Now he refers to another of Perseus's adventures, namely "his rescuing Andromeda from the sea-monster or whale." This monster is referred to as the *kêtos* from the period of our earliest evidence of the story, a Corinthian black-figure amphora from around the first half of the sixth century BCE, on which are depicted all three principal figures of the drama, Andromeda, Perseus, and the monster, helpfully labelled "*kêtos*." The monster on this vase (only his head is shown) resembles a dragon or triceratops more than a whale, but though the Greeks called mythical as well as actual enormous sea-beasts "*kêtos*," they employed the word primarily in reference to whales. Ishmael includes the term in his "Etymology" prior to the commencement of his tale, a term from which the title of his notorious "Cetology" chapter derives. In any case, Perseus managed to slay the monster and win the hand of Andromeda. Together they bore numerous children and founded the great Bronze Age city of Mycenae. Ahab will not be so fortunate: he will neither kill Moby Dick nor return home to relieve the loneliness of his pining wife and child.

Chapter 56: Of the Less Erroneous Pictures of Whales, and the True Pictures of Whaling Scenes

I have concentrated on the ancient material from the previous chapter, but in that chapter, as well as in this one, for the first time in the book Ishmael references several modern thinkers. Particularly noteworthy is his mention of Francis Bacon (1561-1626), who is often regarded as the founder of modern empirical science. He certainly intended to diminish the influence of those of Aristotle's logical and scientific works that since antiquity had passed together under the title of the *Organon*, which is evident from the fact that he called his own treatise on scientific method the *New Organon*. In this work Bacon stresses the importance of induction, whereby observational information is collected, hypotheses are formulated to account for the observed facts, and these hypotheses are tested by further observation. In this process one must avoid the errors arising from those pernicious intellectual propensities that Bacon designates the four "idols of the mind," namely the "idols of the tribe," whereby one's reasoning is distorted by the natural flaws of human understanding; the "idols of the cave," whereby one's own preconceptions and preferences unduly influence one's reasoning; the "idols of the marketplace," which involve the inexact and misleading use of language; and the "idols of the theatre," whereby one substitutes traditional dogma for one's own efforts and observations. This last idol was especially worrisome to early modern thinkers, who objected to the oppressive influence of Aristotle's works, particularly in the universities. A young student of the period was expected to learn about the world not by studying it for himself, but rather by studying Aristotle's treatises, which themselves advocate a deductive approach to the acquisition of knowledge, relying more on syllogistic reasoning—the derivation of indubitable conclusions from certain premises—than on careful, trial-and-error working with one's hands in the dirt. Now in fact Aristotle had personally engaged in the meticulous observation of nature, and he documented his findings at length in his works on animal- and plant-life in particular. But when formulating his ideas about the proper method for arriving at knowledge, he prioritized the certainties of logic over the fallibility of empirical observation. The early moderns wanted to read the "book of nature" for themselves, so they welcomed with enthusiasm Bacon's call for observation and the systematic gathering of facts.

Melville had little use for Francis Bacon. He did admire his *Wisdom of the Ancients*, from which he acquired insight into the symbolic interpretation of Greek mythology; but by and large he rejected Bacon's philosophy. In *Pierre*, which he wrote immediately after *Moby-Dick*, he includes a treatise composed by a philosopher who calls himself Plotinus, in which it is said that "Bacon's brains were mere watch-maker's brains." The eponymous protagonist of the novel invidiously contrasts the modern to the ancient world by speaking of "old Greek times, before man's brain went into doting bondage, and bleached and beaten in Baconian fulling-mills, his four limbs lost their barbaric tan and beauty." In *The Confidence-Man*, the last of Melville's prose novels, Bacon is associated with the materialism of stock-trading and "those philosophies which come home to [one's] business and bosom." In the same work it is claimed that Bacon's philosophy of knowledge is "vain" and such as to "betray him who seeks to steer soul and body by it, like a false religion." Bacon's reflections on knowledge are taken up again in *Clarel*, the long narrative poem published almost twenty years after *The Confidence-Man*, in which one of the characters remarks, "*Knowledge is power*: tell that to knaves / 'Tis knavish knowledge."

I have said that Melville was not a Platonist. He could not abide the idealism of the Good, which seemed to him to imply a rosier view of the world than he could square with his own experience. Yet he did admire the grandeur of Platonism, which a thoughtful man might take on occasion to embody a "reckless sky-assaulting mood," to borrow an expression from *Pierre*. As is clear from *Moby-Dick*, Melville's mind tended toward the gigantic, the cosmic, the universal; the mysteries that most concerned him were existential in the deepest sense, for the human psyche may be taken for a universe within, and the question whether one's soul is a cosmos or a chaos is pressing. By comparison, to worry over the technological uses to which we might put nature by subduing her through science seemed to Melville a waste of time. For his thoughts concerning the relative significance of internal versus external investigation, consider the following passage from *Pierre*:

But, as to the resolute traveler in Switzerland, the Alps do never in one wide and comprehensive sweep, instantaneously reveal their full awfulness of amplitude—their overawing extent of peak crowded on peak, and spur sloping on spur, and chain jammed behind chain, and all their wonderful battalionings of might; so hath heaven wisely ordained, that on first entering into the Switzerland of his soul, man shall not at once perceive its tremendous immensity; lest illy prepared for such an encounter, his spirit should sink and perish in the lowermost snows. Only by judicious degrees, appointed of God, does man come at last to gain his Mont Blanc and take an overtopping view of these Alps; and even then, the tithe is not shown; and far over the invisible Atlantic, the Rocky Mountains and the Andes are yet unbeheld. Appalling is the soul of a man! Better might one be pushed off into the material spaces beyond the uttermost orbit of our sun, than once feel himself fairly afloat in himself!

Even if there were such a thing as *the* scientific method (there isn't), and even if Bacon had articulated it unproblematically (he didn't), it would be of little interest and less use to an explorer of the soul in Melville's lineage. This sort of adventurer treks the internal way, and he navigates by creative association and poetic correspondence every bit as much as the treasure-hunter steers by maps and the stars.

The great Michelangelo Buonarroti lived from 1475 to 1564. In the very month of his death, only three days prior in fact, Galileo Galilei was born. The coincidence has long struck me as significant of the final demise of the ancient ideal and the birth of the modern mind. Galileo's telescopic observations of the moon and the planets undermined the authority of Aristotle's cosmology, as I have noted previously. This may have been an advance in empirical knowledge, but it simultaneously instigated the collapse of a thought-world that animated artists like Michelangelo, and Dante too, whose view of the cosmos as recorded in his *Divina Commedia* was informed by Aristotle by way of Aquinas. The distinction mattered to Melville, for like Nietzsche he was often less concerned with truth than with beauty and greatness. As overshadowed by falsehood as the ancient world may have been, it seemed to Melville to express a magnificence beside which the modern world appears paltry and sordid. In *Clarel* Melville writes of "Those legends which, be it confessed / Did nearer bring to them the sky— / Did nearer woo it in their hope / Of all that seers and saints avow— / Than Galileo's telescope / Can bid it unto prosing Science now." Science is prosaic, and the scientific mind would restrict human aspiration to the mundane. Of course the scientist will insist that this is as it should be, for the earth is our home, and to aspire beyond the earthly is to entangle oneself in webs of fantasy and illusion. Melville was too poetic a soul to agree. He simply could not submit to the restrictive imposition of boundaries on the wild wandering of his mind. Galileo's *Starry Messenger* be damned: Melville would have his *Moby-Dick*.

Chapter 57: Of Whales in Paint; in Teeth; in Wood; in Sheet-Iron; in Stone; in Mountains; in Stars

Melville's distaste for the modern world comes out clearly in this chapter by way of Ishmael's obvious esteem for the pre-modern. Contrasting Christian civilization with "what is called savagery," he expresses a preference for the latter by equating it with man's original state, the "condition in which God placed him." Ishmael is evidently a well-read and thoughtful young man, as was Melville when he went to sea, but presumably like Melville he was a raw youth, an autodidact and something of a free-spirited wandering, roaming rustic. We might think of him as a semi-cultivated noble savage.

Ishmael's cultivation distinguishes him from the unadorned noble savage, Rousseau's man in the pre-civilizational state of nature. Melville had some experience with men in this condition, or anyway not too distant from it, through his brief residence among the Marquesan Typee natives. Although initially he admired their freedom from the oppressive punctilios of thought and action to which he was accustomed as a child of Christendom, he soon realized that they suffered from their own vices, indolence and intellectually constricting ritualized superstitions among them. The noble savage of Rousseau's construction was perhaps too primitive for Melville's taste: Melville lived a life of the mind, and he could as little bear the mental darkness of a genuinely aboriginal man as he could accept the small-mindedness of the cultured Christians of his acquaintance. Rousseau admired the ancient Spartans for abolishing the arts and sciences from their city; but Melville's sympathy was with Athens, the artistic and cultural capital of ancient Greece. When in his poem "The Parthenon" Aspasia remarks to Pericles that the completed temple is "Art's meridian," Melville invokes the "Golden Age" of Greek civilization and three representatives of the pinnacle of its cultural life.

In the present chapter Ishmael declares himself a savage who owes allegiance only to "the King of the Cannibals," but this of course is hyperbole. I have said that Melville while staying with the Typee natives came to suspect them for cannibals and was horrified. So here he boasts of the elemental influences of his untamed life at sea on his body and mind, and in doing so he communicates a truth distinguishing him from the majority of provincial Americans of his generation. We may acknowledge the exaggeration without denying the distinction.

Ishmael's invocation of Achilles as a "Greek savage" gives some indication of the state of savagery he means to commend. Homer's Greeks are no cannibals: Achilles in anger wishes that he could carve the flesh from Hector's bones and consume it raw, but he cannot. Indeed he *would* not, and his wish is a graphic expression of his fury, not a genuine desire. He will vent his rage on Hector's corpse brutally, dragging the body through the dirt by straps strung through pierced ankles and tied to the back of a chariot, but he will not cannibalize the man. And when the gods command that he return the body to king Priam, Hector's father, he obeys. Achilles is a lethal warrior, and when enraged by the death of his friend Patroclus he descends into a frenzy of cruelty and violence; yet taken all in all he is a cultivated man: he appreciates beauty; he plays the lyre and sings; he expresses genuine love for friends and family. He is no more Melville's ideal than he was Plato's, but both men could recognize his nobility.

Ishmael mentions Achilles in connection with the armor made for him by the god Hephaestus, specifically the famous shield described in Book 18 of the *Iliad*. This shield, "close packed in … maziness of design," as Ishmael puts it, is adorned with images of constellations of stars, the moon and the sun, and the earth itself on which are depicted "two beautiful cities of mortal men," one at peace and one at war. We see a wedding, a trial, and a battle; there are fields under the plow and grapevines harvested; lions stalk and prey on cattle; young men and pretty girls dance on a choral ground; and around the whole the stream of Ocean flows. The shield is at once a work of beauty and an implement of war: in this it is like Achilles himself, terrible and grand.

The Greek heroes as Homer portrays them are larger than life. They have special relationships with the gods; some are children or descendants of deities. Occasionally they even engage the gods in combat. Achilles himself, son of the divine Thetis, fights a river, and according to later traditions, after his death he is transferred to the Isles of the Blessed. So Ishmael, when imagining himself a savage, seems a heaven-storming over-human riding a whale bareback, launching into and beyond the sky in search of the metaphysical afterworld. He would, he says, "see whether the fabled heavens with all their countless tents really lie encamped beyond my mortal sight!" And if we call to mind the three-tiered earth in the *Phaedo*, we might picture Ishmael leaping from the sea at the bottom of one of our earthly hollows and rising through the air into the aether, there to behold pure souls living with the gods on the true surface of the earth. As implausible as Achilles inhabiting the Blessed Isles eternally, no doubt; but like the ancients who moved them, Melville and Ishmael did not confine their vision to those material things the moderns mistake for the only possible sights.

Chapter 58: Brit

If knowledge is power, then so is ignorance, and mightier still is the absence of mind altogether, nature devoid of intellect. We lift the veil from nature's face slowly, century by century, inch by inch; and with every minute section exposed we "progress": we harness electricity, explore the planets, heal the sick and eradicate disease. But still we suffer, psychologically, spiritually, physically. Still we die. Advance as we will, the world in the end has its way.

Ishmael says that "however baby man may brag of his science and skill, and however much, in a flattering future, that science and skill may augment; yet for ever and for ever, to the crack of doom, the sea will insult and murder him, and pulverize the stateliest, stiffest frigate he can make." Notice that Ishmael associates science with skill, understanding with productivity. Doubtless he still has Bacon in mind, and he means to indicate the pettiness of the power deriving from our knowledge by suggesting that even the maturest man is but an infant beside the hoary cosmos. Water is only one of the world's many elements, yet we are helpless when it rages against us.

Ishmael is right of course, as right as the other serious souls who time and again have expressed the same or a similar opinion. Well over two thousand years ago Heraclitus stated bluntly that "much learning does not teach understanding." Learning is just so much easier than understanding, skill so much more immediately and obviously fruitful than insight. Very few listen, even today. Instead they idolize the scientist, fetishize technology, make obeisance before the technocrat.

Like Heraclitus long before him, Melville through his Ishmael plays on the difference between wisdom and knowledge. If the distinction between the sage and the philosopher is significant, the distinction between the philosopher and the scientist is even more remarkable, for the division here marks a difference between ultimate objects of concern. The wise man and the philosopher cherish *sophia*. The scientist chases knowledge, and not knowledge as *epistêmê*, the Greek word the Romans generally correlated with *scientia*, meaning demonstrated or certain knowledge, but rather "knowledge" as a fallible but conditionally accepted *belief*. So even modern "science" is a decline from the ancient understanding of the concept. The modern conception may represent a more practicable undertaking, but the gains in productivity come by way of the loss of lasting consequence. Hence the easy slide from knowledge to information, and what began with the sage winds up with the intellectual, or worse, the journalist.

The world is not only broad: it is deep. But Melvillean divers are a rare breed, and even those with potential to sound the depths are distracted early by the splashing surfaces of life. Ishmael remarks that "as this appalling ocean surrounds the verdant land, so in the soul of man there lies one insular Tahiti, full of peace and joy, but encompassed by all the horrors of the half known life." He then warns his readers against abandoning the land for the sea, for, he says, "thou canst never return!" But really he need not worry himself, for men in the mass are far more enchanted by the superficial sparklings of safety and pleasure than they are lured by the perils of the deep. It is true, as Ishmael says, that Noah's flood still covers two-thirds of the globe, but today the waters encircling French Polynesia are less symbols of man's obscure unconscious than tourist attractions with cocktails and snorkels to distract us from anything in life not intoxicating, bubbling, and bright.

Chapter 59: Squid

Nietzsche was as ambivalent about modern philosophy and science as Melville. Ambivalent, which is not to say that he reckoned the ancient and modern conceptions and practices of philosophy equally legitimate. To his mind the balance of the *negative* weight was on the side of modernity. In *Beyond Good and Evil*, which Nietzsche wrote to a friend had flowed from his pen very black, like ink from a squid, he laments the modern turn away from philosophy toward science. By "science" (*Wissenschaft*) he means the methodologically systematic disciplines in general, including for example history and philology (the latter being his own discipline by training), but that he also has science in a strict sense explicitly in mind is evident from his mention of "*Naturforscher*," naturalists or natural scientists.

Beyond Good and Evil is the one book in which Nietzsche is consistently (if not unreservedly) favorable to Plato. In one section he calls "the Platonic way of thinking" a "*noble* way of thinking" specifically in contrast to physics; in another he says that Plato possessed "the greatest strength any philosopher so far has had at his disposal"; and reflecting on the relative merits of ancient philosophy and modern philosophy and science, he groups Plato together with Heraclitus and Empedocles as "royal and magnificent hermits of the spirit" and complains of the absence of such figures from the modern intellectual scene.

In Nietzsche's day the university specialist, the scientific man broadly construed (the *wissenschaftlicher Mensch*), was regarded with the highest admiration, to the exclusion of the philosopher on the ancient model. Today of course the scope of our esteem has narrowed even further: not only do we not take philosophers seriously, academics in general are widely distrusted as mongers of abstruse, sophistical, or pernicious theory. For us the scientist is the source of all truth, and anyone who aspires to a position of public respect and influence conforms his ideas, or at least his rhetoric, to the scientific paradigm. Thus we have our own fresh examples of the type Nietzsche refers to contemptuously as "philosophers of reality" and "positivists." In our contemporary nomenclature, these are the adherents of physicalism and scientism who believe that science alone provides knowledge of the world, and that only that which science can know is real. You will recall that Plato long ago was acquainted with such men, and that he condemned them as anti-philosophical despisers of reason (*misologists*) infected with the basest of intellectual-spiritual diseases.

Nietzsche was no Platonist, needless to say. But he was as hostile to a simple-minded materialism as any metaphysical idealist. He rejected the Platonic and Christian conceptions of the soul as an immaterial and eternal substance, but he rejected as vehemently the materialists' conception of the atom as substance. The one is as illegitimate an insertion of Being into the river of Becoming as the other, and each represents in its way a belief in the God that Nietzsche judged to be dead. I shall have more to say about these matters later, but it is worth keeping in mind that we can no more situate Nietzsche on one side of our contemporary debates between science and religion, or materialism and spirituality, than we can Melville. Our formulations of such disagreements—the assumptions and consequences at issue—are usually too shallow to accommodate the perspectives of deep thinkers.

I have written of Melville's aversion to Francis Bacon's watchmaker mentality, the typically modern perspective that estimates the value of knowledge by its practical functionality. Nietzsche too disdains "the utility man" who has no use for philosophy because it produces no obvious and immediate material benefits. If Melville and Nietzsche could have discussed these matters, they would have agreed that this modern view is a symptom of a profound misunderstanding of the spirit of philosophy. The philosopher is not meant to be a utilitarian technician, nor even an unbiased seeker of "knowledge for its own sake." The philosopher—Melville likely would have stressed *the artist* here, but for Nietzsche the philosopher is himself an artist in this regard—the philosopher creates a worldview, or what I have called a thought-world, that by inhabiting the minds of men shapes the world they inhabit. This is the sense in which according to Nietzsche the philosopher is a legislator of values. But modern men no longer believe in this "masterly task and masterfulness of philosophy," for they take for granted the image of the world they have inherited from science or their religion. They can no more conceive of a new perspective on reality than of the possibility that reality is in itself perspectival. But Melville and Nietzsche thought through these matters at length and in detail, and in their different but allied fields—the one man being an artist-philosopher the other a philosopher-artist—they intended to fashion a world from their own fecund internal resources, which is to say from the depths of their own fertile minds.

While on the subject of modern philosophy, and writing in a chapter concerning the squid, which Ishmael reports some naturalists include "among the class of cuttle-fish," I should recall Nietzsche's distinction between healthy and exhausted skepticism. Under the influence of Descartes in particular, the moderns tended to identify philosophy with epistemology, or the study of the nature, sources, and possibility of knowledge; and according to Nietzsche this is an objectionable reduction of the scope of philosophy amounting to "a timid epochism and doctrine of abstinence—a philosophy that never gets beyond the threshold and takes pains to *deny* itself the right to enter." By "epochism" Nietzsche means an obsession with *epochê*, the suspension of judgment introduced into philosophy by the ancient skeptics. The first systematic and lasting skeptical movement in philosophy sprang up, of all places, in Plato's Academy. The seventh scholarch of that institution was Arcesilaus, and with him there began (around 270 BCE) what is sometimes known as the "New Academy," a tradition lasting nearly two centuries of so-called Academic Skepticism. Arcesilaus was said to have advocated *epochê* as the proper response to the fact that arguments in favor of any position may be met with equally persuasive counter-arguments. The two sides in the controversy being equipollent, the thoughtful man will suspend judgment between them. There was, however, some controversy among the ancients concerning the extent to which Arcesilaus was genuinely committed to the suspension of judgment, and at least one source charged him with advocating *epochê* as a defense against the exposure and refutation of his actual commitments. This source, Numenius, claimed that Arcesilaus "projected suspension of judgment in front of himself, like the ink of the cuttlefish."

Contemporary scholars find it difficult to settle on a stable account of what the early Academic skeptics really believed about the matters they addressed. This is so in part because some of them, Arcesilaus included, declined to commit their views to writing. Nietzsche would add that part of the problem is that the typical skeptic is too "delicate [a] creature" to commit to an identifiable position, for he lacks "balance, a center of gravity, and perpendicular poise ... in body and soul." And considering Nietzsche's language here, I imagine he would happily apply to the skeptic Melville's description of the squid as having "no perceptible face or front ... no conceivable token of either sensation or instinct ... an unearthly, formless, chance-like apparition of life." I have noted previously that Nietzsche does not object to every manifestation of skepticism, and that he admires the type that "despises but nevertheless seizes" and "gives the spirit dangerous freedom." But this is a variety of the species rarely encountered, and the skepticism typical of modern philosophy is so squid-like in its spineless squishiness that when confronted with the beast one can only wonder, with Nietzsche: "How could such a philosophy—*dominate*!"

Chapter 60: The Line

Late in his life Leo Tolstoy is reported to have said to Maksim Gorky, "If a man has learned to think, no matter what he may think about, he is always thinking of his own death. All philosophers were like that." It is not clear to me that all philosophers *were* like that, but Melville certainly was. *Moby-Dick* is about death, not exclusively, but very much so. In the present chapter, for example, Ishmael meticulously explains the material, arrangement, and function of the "magical, sometimes horrible" lines secured to the harpooners' weapons in order to keep the whaleboats fast to struck and fleeing whales. But he is particularly interested in the dangers attending the lines' use, for when they whiz from a boat from back to front behind a speeding whale, they may catch a sailor up and drag him to his doom. In this phenomenon Ishmael observes an analogy with every man's life: "All are born with halters round their necks," he says, "but it is only when caught in the swift, sudden turn of death, that mortals realize the silent, subtle, ever-present perils of life." But here he is speaking of ordinary, unreflective mortals, for he adds that "if you be a philosopher," you would be no more terrified when sitting in a whaleboat at sea than when lounging comfortably in a chair beside your fire at home. Death shadows all of us down every alleyway of life, and pondering men like Tolstoy and Melville are always aware, at one level or another of consciousness, of being pursued.

I have expressed a doubt about Tolstoy's claim that all philosophers always think of death, for I have long been struck by the lack of similar reflections in the works of Plato and Aristotle. The Romantics and (especially) the Existentialists have accustomed us to brood at length on the bearing of the fact of death on our lives. Kierkegaard stressed the limitations of a purely "aesthetic" or hedonistic life by observing that "no one comes back from the dead; no one has come into the world without weeping. No one asks when one wants to come in; no one asks when one wants to go out." If we live only for pleasure, then the fact that our experience of pleasure must end threatens to render our lives meaningless. We must, therefore, aim for something more than pleasure, something higher. Heidegger conceptualizes humans in terms of "being-toward-death": we are mortal, our time is finite, and we may live authentically only by realizing that our human being at its core is oriented toward non-being, toward death. To confront the inevitability of dying is to realize the possibilities of life and to open oneself to living affirmatively. Camus regarded death, and the meaninglessness of death, as an element of life's absurdity. The existentialist hero confronts this absurdity and affirms life nonetheless.

We have seen that Plato is concerned with death, and that according to *Phaedo*-Platonism philosophy is training for death. Yet Plato writes of death in connection with the judgment of souls in the afterlife, and he writes of judgment in order to stress the importance of virtue. For Plato, in short, the fact of death has ethical implications. Nowhere does he address what we today think of as the existential implications of death, the threat of the meaninglessness of life, or the possibility of the affirmation of life, in the face of death. Tolstoy concludes the lines I have quoted above with the following melancholy question: "And what truth can there be, if there is death?" Plato (or anyway Plato as reflected in the tradition of *Phaedo*-Platonism) not only did not regard death as undermining the possibility or value of truth, but in the *Phaedo* Socrates suggests that pure knowledge of truth is possible only after death, when the soul is literally and completely separated from the body.

I have characterized Tolstoy's question about death and truth as melancholy. Melancholia is characteristic of the thought of the Romantics, who influenced Melville and Nietzsche, and also of the Existentialists, whom Nietzsche influenced, though men like Sartre would prefer to see themselves as manfully resisting the human tendency toward brooding sorrowfulness. But what about the ancients? Aristotle in his *Problems* discusses melancholy, and he associates the condition in particular with thinkers and artists, as we are inclined to do ourselves. Melancholia, he says, may manifest as a general despondency, as when we suffer but cannot say why. Some men may even be driven by melancholy despair to suicide by hanging, the young in particular. All this sounds familiar: melancholy and depression are all too common today; and it is evident from Aristotle's work that such psychological-spiritual disorders were not unknown to the ancients. Yet, like Plato, Aristotle exhibits a far greater interest in showing men the way to virtue than in helping them overcome melancholy. Why is this? Did the ancients on the whole suffer less from existential malaise than we moderns do? Were they more in need of ethical guidance? I find this hard to believe. It seems to me that even the moderately well-educated man upon maturity recognizes the importance of virtue, and is capable of resisting the temptations of vicious pleasures. But we have no idea how to deal with melancholy—hence the widespread need for medical care in the form of therapy or prescribed pharmaceuticals. Melville and Nietzsche suffered in this way, as I shall later detail, and according to Aristotle Socrates and Plato did too. In the *Laws* Plato writes that although we humans have been fashioned by the gods, we have no idea whether they made us to be their playthings or for some serious purpose. This is a melancholy idea, reminiscent of the moral of many tragedies. And, indeed, Plato was said to have aspired to be a tragedian himself when young, but supposedly he burned his early works when he met Socrates. Is Nietzsche right, then, when he blames Socrates for the death of the tragic worldview? Certainly the absence of tragic insight among the classical Greek philosophers, their apparent lack of sustained interest in melancholy as an existential problem, is striking.

Having just mentioned Nietzsche in connection with these matters, I conclude this chapter with a reference to a late poem included in his

Dithyrambs of Dionysus that bears on both Aristotle's account of suicidal melancholiacs hanging themselves and Melville's idea that men are born with nooses around their necks. In "Between Birds of Prey" Nietzsche identifies the search for knowledge of the self with suicide by hanging. Strangled by the rope of his wisdom, the self-knower is a self-executioner. Nietzsche composed this poem in the form of an address to "the *wise* Zarathustra," but we may take it as relevant to anyone who dares to plunge into the abyss of the self. Such a man is at risk of sinking, never to surface again, every bit as much as a sailor in a whaleboat tangled in the horrible running line.

Chapter 61: Stubb Kills a Whale

This chapter begins with Ishmael taking his turn looking for whales from high up on the mast-head, and as in the earlier chapter in which he describes the mast-head and its history, the gently rolling ocean lulls him into a sort of waking dream-state. "No resolution could withstand it," he says, and "in that dreamy mood losing all consciousness, at last my soul went out of my body." This is precisely the condition he warns against in the earlier chapter, for lost like this inside his own distracted mind, a sailor is in danger of slipping and falling into the sea through "Descartian vortices." Now since I have begun sporadically to introduce some elements of modern philosophy, and since modern intellectual developments contributed to the shaping of Nietzsche's philosophy, it will be helpful if when covering the next few chapters of *Moby-Dick*, which contain little of philosophical interest in themselves, I explain a few relevant features of Descartes' philosophy. After this I will discuss those other modern philosophers who influenced, directly or indirectly, either Melville or Nietzsche, or both.

Since Melville refers to Descartes' theory of vortices, we may begin with Cartesian physics. René Descartes (1596-1650) is often dubbed the father of modern philosophy, and this may well be correct, even though Francis Bacon and Thomas Hobbes wrote before or contemporarily with him. But like other early modern philosophers, Descartes contributed to the development of modern science as well. He formulated his theory of vortices to explain the motions of the heavenly bodies, and he believed that the vortices were responsible for terrestrial gravity too. But the theory relates also to his "corpuscularianism," which is the subject on which I intend to concentrate here.

Descartes believed that the universe is completely full of matter, with no empty or void space whatever. The universe, in short, is a "plenum." The matter in question Descartes refers to as corpuscles, by which he means tiny particles infinitely divisible at least in theory. These corpuscles move in great interconnecting bands of circular motions—the vortices—throughout the universe, their motions having been initially imparted to matter by God. Descartes developed this theory in contrast to early modern atomism, for which Pierre Gassendi (1592-1655) is primarily responsible. This is not to say that Gassendi was the first man to postulate the existence of atoms, for he was in fact reverting to the ancient theory of Democritus, a contemporary of Socrates from Abdera in northern Greece. Democritus theorized that the universe is composed of particles of matter situated in void space. Reasoning that these particles cannot be infinitely divisible, he concluded that they must be sufficiently small to escape detection by human sight, but not infinitely small. At some minute level of magnitude these particles cannot be divided into further subsections, and this supposed fact accounts for their name: the Greek word *atomos* means "indivisible" or, more literally, "uncutable." Democritus's idea was taken up by Epicurus (341-270 BCE), founder of the materialist-hedonist philosophy known as Epicureanism, and it was further systematized and elaborated in the great epic poem *De rerum natura*, or *On the Nature of Things*, composed by the Roman Epicurean philosopher-poet Lucretius (first century BCE). Gassendi inherited his atomism by way of the Epicurean tradition, and it was against this philosophy of "atoms and void" that Descartes developed his corpuscularianism.

Gassendi's atomism is an example of early modern "mechanical philosophy," which is to say the philosophical explanation of reality based solely on matter in motion without reference to Aristotelian formal or final causality, which was supposed to act independent of direct physical contact. Atomic theory was not thoroughly materialist, however, for Gassendi was a faithful (if not quite orthodox) believer in the Christian God. He was, in fact, a priest. The ancient atomists also believed in God, or the gods, though in their view the gods were themselves material beings (albeit immortal) who have no interest in human affairs. They held that the human soul is material too, and that the atoms that compose it disperse at death. Thus the Epicureans in particular insisted that we should fear neither death nor the gods, for nothing bad can come to us through death, since when we die we quite literally *are not*, and therefore also the gods could not punish us postmortem if they wanted to, which they don't because they pay us no mind anyway. Atomistic materialism seems to have been particularly distasteful to Plato, who never mentions Democritus in the dialogues. There was even a story, which Nietzsche liked to cite, that Plato wanted to collect and burn all of Democritus's writings.

Descartes' corpuscularianism differs from atomism by insisting that matter is infinitely divisible (for God may so divide it), denying void space (the universe, recall, is a plenum), and denying also that weight or gravity is an intrinsic property of matter (the rotating vortices explain the downward movement of matter). Descartes' theory is similar to atomism in that it is a physical system with no place for immaterial or teleological principles such as Platonic Forms or Aristotelian final causes. It is similar also in distinguishing between so-called primary and secondary qualities or properties, which distinction plays a significant role in shaping the modern conception of reality. Stated briefly, this is the distinction between those properties that are supposed to be objectively real features of matter, such as shape, size, and motion—these are the "primary" qualities—and those properties supposed to exist only in the subjective experience of properly mental beings, properties such as color, odor, taste, sound, and feel—the "secondary" qualities. Democritus himself formulated our earliest version of this distinction, which comes down to us in the following words: "By convention sweet, by convention bitter, by convention hot, by convention cold, by convention color, but in reality atoms and void." The idea that the world is not as it appears to be was radicalized by later thinkers like George Berkeley and Immanuel Kant, and their distinct but roughly related views were radicalized even further by Nietzsche. But Descartes' philosophy wreaked havoc with the traditional conception of reality in other ways too, so in the next chapter I discuss his surprising view of the relation between body and mind.

Chapter 62: The Dart

Let us take the distinction Ishmael draws in this chapter between the physical strength required of the harpooner and the directive authority invested in the "headsman" of the whaleboat for a distinction between body and mind. By doing so we may introduce Descartes' famous division of reality into two types of substance, physical and mental. By "substance" in this context I mean the kind or type of being that is most fundamentally real and whose existence, therefore, does not depend on any other being (apart perhaps from God). To state the matter briefly, we may say that substances are ontologically primary. Descartes is a substance dualist, for, as I have said, the world in his view is composed of both physical substance and mental substance, otherwise known as body and mind. In his *Meditations on First Philosophy* he distinguishes his mind, with which he identifies himself (or his self), from his body by arguing that because his mind is in essence a non-spatial thinking thing and his body essentially a non-thinking spatially-extended thing, his mind and body are distinct types of substance. He conceives moreover that his mind can exist independently of his body. This may or may not be a surprising thought, but it does generate at least one vexing problem, namely the practicability of mind-body interaction. As Descartes is working in the context of the early modern "mechanical philosophy," which explains causal interactions by way of matter in motion and physical contact between material objects, one wonders how an incorporeal substance like a mind can effect changes in a corporeal substance like a body, and vice versa. It seems obvious to common sense that if, for example, one's body is pricked by a pin, this causes one's mind to experience pain, or that one's mind desiring a thing causes one's body to reach out for it. But Cartesian dualism makes this sort of interaction difficult, some would say impossible, to explain. Bodies act on other bodies through direct impact, but the mind, not being physical, cannot enter into any such physical relations. It is as if an immaterial ghost were to try to lift a solid material object: it seems that it would not only not be able to lift it, but that it would not even be able to grasp it; its ghostly hand would pass right through it. Thus we imagine ghosts walking through walls: the solid wall does not impede their progress because the material cannot interact with the immaterial. How, then, can an immaterial mind interact with the material body?

The Cartesian problem of mind-body interaction was so urgent that modern philosophers performed what many have since regarded as outrageous intellectual acrobatics to resolve it. Leibniz (1646-1716), for example, formulated the doctrine of "Pre-established Harmony," according to which the mind and body do not (because they cannot) affect one another, but

God has so arranged the world that when my body is pricked by a pin, my mind suffers the pain of a pin-prick, and when my mind intends an act, my body performs the deed. The pricking does not cause the pain, nor does the intention cause the deed, for causality does not and cannot operate between the mental and the physical; but God has harmonized the mental and physical tracks of reality in such a way that the two sync up precisely as if such causality were in effect. Appealing to a similar but distinct explanation of apparent causality, the so-called Occasionalists believed that God is the one and only true cause of things, not just as between different types of substance (body and mind) but even within one and the same type of substance (body and body or mind and mind). Events that we think of as causes are really just occasions for God to intervene causally in the world. So, for example, my kicking a stone does not cause the stone to move; rather, my kicking is the occasion for God to move it. Similarly, my thinking of my father does not cause me to recall the sound of his voice, but God causes that recollection on the occasion of the thought.

This is all very unusual, no doubt. But these are the sorts of problems that occupied modern philosophers under the influence of Descartes' formulation of the relevant themes in physics and metaphysics. His account of the nature of mind as exclusively a thinking thing was informed by his famous "Cogito, ergo sum." But as this is related also to his attempt to refute skepticism, and as skepticism itself is a major theme in modern philosophy, I reserve these matters for independent consideration in the following chapter.

Chapter 63: The Crotch

Ishmael begins this short chapter by remarking that as twigs grow from branches, and branches from the trunk, so "in productive subjects, grow the chapters." Following this principle, then, and as there is nothing of philosophical interest to concern us in Ishmael's account of the "notched stick" against which the harpoons on a whaleboat rest, I continue my treatment of Descartes' philosophy, and more specifically his attempted refutation of skepticism.

The founders of the two schools of ancient skepticism—Pyrrho the founder of, or at least the inspiration for, Pyrrhonism, and Arcesilaus the founder of Academic Skepticism—wrote nothing. Several other skeptics followed their example. Yet some did write, and prolifically too. Most of these writings, however, did not survive the collapse of the ancient world. To this day our best source of information about the Academics is Cicero's *Academica*, which itself is only partially preserved. A late Pyrrhonian skeptic, a medical doctor called Sextus Empiricus (second or third century CE), wrote about Pyrrhonism extensively in Greek, including in a kind of compendium of principles usually referred to as the *Outlines of Pyrrhonism*. Yet Sextus's works were lost to Western Europe through the chaos attending the end of the ancient period, and they did not reenter the tradition until the Renaissance, and then only indirectly. But by the sixteenth and, certainly, the seventeenth centuries Sextus's works were well known by way of Latin translations. Most immediately, and famously, they influenced the work of the French essayist Michel de Montaigne (1533-1592), who was so taken with skepticism that he commissioned a medal inscribed with the word ΕΠΕΧΩ, the first person verb-form of the noun *epochê*. We may translate the inscription as "I withhold judgment."

Many early modern philosophers were concerned to refute skepticism, some in order to defend the epistemological credentials of Christianity, others in defense of nascent modern science. Descartes may have been sympathetic to both projects, but he seems to have been particularly interested in the latter. If the skeptics are right, then we can be sure of neither philosophical nor scientific claims to knowledge and must, therefore, withhold judgment respecting them. But this attitude threatens to undermine every impulse to engage in scientific activity. In order to secure the ground for science, then, skepticism must be refuted. This is one of the projects undertaken by Descartes in his *Meditations*.

In the First Meditation Descartes marshals what he takes to be the most powerful arguments in favor of skepticism. He argues against the reliability of the senses by, first, noting that his senses sometimes deceive him about small or distant objects, and then appealing to the principle that one must not trust that which has misled one in the past. He then radicalizes this principle by observing that he has often had dreams in which he seemed to be awake and sensing his surroundings with minute and perfect accuracy, dreams from which he later awoke to realize that his impressions had all along been false. From this he concludes that he cannot be sure at any particular moment that he is not dreaming, and that therefore he must withhold judgment concerning the reliability of his sense impressions even when they seem to reveal the most evident objects up close. Regarding truths he seems to know independently of his senses, for example the truths of mathematics and logic, he says that since he cannot rule out the possibility that a powerful evil spirit is deceiving him, he must withhold judgment about these matters as well. Finally, because he believes that God himself in his omnipotence could easily cause him to be misled in his every perception and belief, and since for all he knows or is able to prove God is in fact doing just this, he must withhold judgment about literally all matters of perception or belief.

I should note here that Descartes does not mean to claim that anyone should take seriously in his practical life and daily activities the possibility that at every moment he is dreaming or that God is deceiving him. Rather, he is urging a theoretical claim within the context of epistemology. But I should note as well that "theoretical" here does not imply "pointless" or "unimportant." The point is that unless we can rule out every possibility of error, we cannot claim to possess certain knowledge. That this is not unimportant we may recognize by reflecting, for example, on the impact of debates between conflicting religious claims, or between religious and scientific claims: if we can have no certain knowledge, then we cannot know for sure whether our wills are free, or indeed whether we possess any such things as wills to begin with; the atheist cannot know that those religious doctrines that conflict with the findings of science must be false, for he cannot know that scientific findings are in fact true; the Christian cannot know that the Hindu is mistaken about the nature of the divine, for he cannot know anything himself about the matter. Some—indeed many—possibilities of error we may perfectly well ignore in our daily practical lives; but we must proceed more methodically when searching for knowledge. Every ineliminable potential for error renders a claim to knowledge correspondingly uncertain.

Having presented the arguments in favor of skepticism in his First Meditation, Descartes attempts to refute them in the Second. And here we come back to his famous assertion, "Cogito, ergo sum," or "I think, therefore I am." The significance of this statement is that it expresses a proposition that Descartes claims to be indubitably true. Let God deceive him as thoroughly as he will, this only serves to reinforce the fact that Descartes is thinking—for to be deceived is to be engaged in an intellectual activity—and if he is thinking, he must also exist. That he is thinking and that he exists, then, are truths that even the most powerful skeptical arguments cannot call into question. To the contrary, they confirm them. "I think." "I exist." "I think, therefore I exist": we know these truths, without any possibility of error, and so without any call for doubt. There are, then, at least some propositions about which we need not withhold judgment. Descartes has refuted universal skepticism.

Or so Descartes himself believed. We shall see that Nietzsche, for one, was not convinced. We'll see also that Melville did not take the skeptical challenge as seriously as Descartes. Skepticism is but a phase of a pondering man's intellectual development, a phase to be arrived at, passed through, and returned to again and again. Do not misunderstand: skepticism is serious, but it is one among several serious intellectual conditions. But for Melville it was not the all-consuming abyss, to be back-filled before any other work may proceed, that it once seemed to be to so many modern philosophers. Once, I say, not because Descartes' refutation of skepticism met with universal, or even widespread, acceptance (it did not), nor because anyone else has since managed to refute it (no one has); but rather because the majority of intellectuals of recent vintage have chosen to ignore skepticism in order to cling without scruple to their most cherished pet beliefs, their religion or their science in particular. Melville and Nietzsche were not skeptics, but for different, and deeper, reasons, as we shall see. But for now: for now we are not yet done exploring those modern intellectual and spiritual developments that made such minds as Melville's and Nietzsche's possible in the first place.

Chapter 64: Stubb's Supper

Giordano Bruno was burned at the stake by the Roman Inquisition in 1600, just four years after Descartes' birth. Galileo fell afoul of the Inquisition in 1616, and beginning in the 1630s he was forced to live under house arrest at his home near Florence. Descartes was of course well aware of these facts, and he was forever concerned not to offend the religious authorities. He withheld his book *Le Monde* (*The World*) from publication, for in it he defends an anti-Aristotelian, heliocentric view of the universe—including (at least by implication) the proposition that the earth moves, as he admitted in a letter to Marin Mersenne—of the sort that caused Galileo's troubles. He affixed to his *Meditations* a letter of dedication to the Sacred Faculty of Theology in Paris in which he not only affirms his belief in the immortality of the soul and the existence of God, but claims to have demonstrated these truths in his work. Despite his assurances, however, some have suspected that Descartes was an atheist, including some among his contemporaries. Their chief, or at least their most immediate, reason seems to be that Descartes' proof of God's existence in the *Meditations* appears to be radically problematic. I shall not here attempt to discern whether Descartes' argument is fallacious in fact, much less whether he knew and perhaps even intended it to be, as has been claimed; but it is worth addressing the matter, if only briefly, since it has its place in the history of the modern decline of belief in God that culminated in Nietzsche's pronouncing the deity dead.

Having demonstrated to his satisfaction the indubitable truth of his own existence, Descartes argues that because his certainty in this case is guaranteed by the "clarity and distinctness" of his perception of the "Cogito," he may likewise take as certain all those other propositions that he perceives clearly and distinctly. To make this case he composes an argument for God's existence based solely on propositions that he judges to be clear and distinct, for example that since his conception of God is of an infinite being, and since he himself as a finite being could not have generated this conception, an actual infinite being—God—must have done so. Therefore, God must exist. Relating more directly to the problem of radical skepticism, Descartes claims to perceive clearly and distinctly that God is good, and that being good, he is not a deceiver. And since a good God created humans and our cognitive faculties, we can trust that our intellect will not be deceived whenever we employ it properly, taking due caution to avoid error, which we my do by limiting our intellectual assent to clear and distinct propositions.

This is the argument that some have found, as I have put it just above, radically problematic. It seems in fact to be viciously circular, for consider: Descartes employs clear and distinct propositions to prove that a good, non-deceptive God exists; but the existence of a good, non-deceptive God is required to guarantee the truth of clear and distinct propositions. So we cannot know that the argument's conclusion is true unless we can trust that the premises are true; but the truth of the premises depends exclusively on the truth of the conclusion. Stated this way, the argument certainly seems to be an example of fallaciously circular reasoning, for if there is no other way to establish the conclusion than by the premises, and no way to establish the premises but by the conclusion, we must have a vicious circle.

Now it may well be that this critical reading of the argument is an oversimplification, even if Descartes' own formulation lends itself to this interpretation. The argument has defenders who insist that if we understand the reasoning in all its subtlety of complexity, we will realize that it is not after all viciously circular. But I am not here concerned to analyze the logic of Descartes' argument for its own sake; I intend only to indicate something of the status of belief in God in early modern philosophy. The transition from medieval belief to nineteenth-century atheism is, judged on a world-historical time-scale, rapid and stark. Nietzsche's atheism did not come out of nowhere; as a philosopher, he has his precursors. This is not to say that his ideas are the simple and obvious consequences of previous intellectual history. Far from it. But it is nonetheless worth contextualizing his philosophy as thoroughly as we can. And Melville too: his philosophical and theological views were radical for his time and place. In his early works he derides certain Christian practices (especially the behavior of those missionaries he experienced first-hand on the Pacific islands), and he even subjects some elements of Christian doctrine to playfully ironic examinations. In the present chapter of *Moby-Dick*, for example, the second mate Stubb toys with the old cook and mocks his simple piety, though the man expresses no belief that most of Melville's contemporaries would not have shared. But Melville goes further than derision or irony: in both *Moby-Dick* and his later works he gives voice to outright atheism and at times to a position very much like nihilism. He was moved, troubled, and stimulated by those deep puzzles that Ishmael in the present chapter sums up as "the universal problem of all things." And though Ishmael is thinking here of the behavior of sharks feeding on a dead whale, he knows that this is only "a part" of the universal problem. We have already encountered other, and darker, parts of this problem, for example the nature of truth, the fact of death, and questions concerning God's essence and even his—or its—existence. If the diabolical behavior of sharks is sufficient to motivate one to consider seriously "the expediency of conciliating the devil," then the behavior of the universe at large is often enough to arouse doubts about the existence of every sort of supernatural being, good or evil.

Chapter 65: The Whale as a Dish

The present chapter consists of a short series of reflections on "the history and philosophy of" the whale-hunter's eating of whales. Whale meat, and even whales' brains, are considered by some an "epicurean" delicacy, as we learn in this as well as in the previous chapter, and to employ a philosophical term that even before Melville's day survived popularly only in its shallowest signification. Then as now an oenophile or foodie, as ignorant of Epicurus's philosophy as a schoolchild is of *Moby-Dick*, will refer to himself as an "epicure." Such is the fate of all high things in low times.

Melville was no vegetarian, nor is his Ishmael, but in this chapter there is some acknowledgement of the moral problem involved in "live bipeds" purchasing and consuming "dead quadrupeds." It is a sort of cannibalism, or so it seems to Ishmael, but he wonders too "who is not a cannibal?" I have noted, in the chapter on Queequeg's "Ramadan," Ishmael's reflections on the relation between digestive health and a sound intellect, and I associated there his opinion with Nietzsche's account of the so-called "ascetic ideal." By way of a reminder, I quote a representative passage that I omitted previously: "fasting makes the body cave in; hence the spirit caves in; and all thoughts born of a fast must necessarily be half-starved. This is the reason why most dyspeptic religionists cherish such melancholy notions about their hereafters." Nietzsche flirted with vegetarianism for a time when young, but he was argued or ridiculed out of it by Wagner, who later embraced the practice himself. Nietzsche was eventually a hearty eater of beef, and of fruits and vegetables too. He required the nourishment for his long walks and hikes, believing, as he did, that the best thoughts "are born outdoors while one move[s] about freely" and "the muscles are … celebrating a feast, too." So as for fasting, Nietzsche agreed with Ishmael's critical assessment, as we may read in a passage from *On the Genealogy of Morals* relating directly to the ascetic ideal: reflecting on the "morbidity" of the cures that priests prescribe for the "brooding and emotional explosions" that they themselves incite in their flocks, Nietzsche writes that "mankind itself is still ill with the effects of this priestly naïveté in medicine! Think, for example, of certain forms of diet (abstinence from meat), of fasting." Such dietary practices derive from the priestly obsession with purity, which in the ancient period, Nietzsche says, was understood coarsely, externally, unsymbolically.

We have seen that Plato, though an ancient, advocated an internal and symbolic notion of purity. And the truth is that Nietzsche lived by his own version of similar practices, though preoccupied as he was with physiological concerns, he externalized purity every bit as much as a coarse ancient priest, but (to be fair) from different motivations and with different intentions. In his autobiographical *Ecce Homo* Nietzsche ascribes the smooth functioning of his intellect to prudent choices regarding recreation, climate, and (most relevant to our present concern) nutrition. He even insists that the "salvation of humanity" depends more on "the question of *nutrition*" than on "any theologians' curio." Nietzsche spent most of his adult life travelling throughout Western Europe, and in *Ecce Homo* he invidiously compares German and French cuisine to that of the Piedmont region of Italy, which to his mind excelled all others. Worst of all, he says, is English food: like Ishmael thinking of the meat-market, he condemns it as a form of "cannibalism." The English diet, Nietzsche complains, "gives the spirit *heavy feet.*" Nietzsche ate to walk, and he walked to think; therefore he demanded that his body and spirit both move lightly, like a dancer.

Nietzsche recalls that as a schoolboy he abstained from drinking and smoking, much like Melville's semi-autobiographical Wellingborough Redburn, but he adds that later in life, and respecting "*strong* doses" of alcohol, he became "almost a sailor," like Melville himself if we factor in Nietzsche's exaggeration. Nietzsche drank occasionally, probably less often than Melville, for his health was much more fragile than Melville's. He was probably not stretching the truth too far when he claimed that even one glass of alcohol could violently disrupt his system. It was from personal experience, then, that he advises "all *more spiritual* natures ... to abstain entirely from alcohol. *Water*," he assures us, "is sufficient."

But to return to vegetarianism: Nietzsche seems to have regarded a vegetarian diet as a symptom of decadence. In *The Case of Wagner* he claims that vegetarians are "*attracted* by what is harmful," and in *The Antichrist* he writes that "an animal, a species, or an individual" is decadent "when it chooses, when it prefers, what is disadvantageous for it." As I say, Nietzsche believed that good thoughts depend on good walks, and good walks require hearty meals. Of course recent advances in our understanding of diet and nutrition have made it possible to live well as a vegetarian, without sacrificing the protein necessary for a robust constitution. But even as late as 1840 Schopenhauer worried that without meat we humans could not survive in cold northern climates, and Schopenhauer was an early advocate of compassion for all animal life. Indeed, in his work *On the Basis of Morality* he condemns the view that animals have no rights, and that our behavior toward animals has no moral significance, as "revoltingly crude" and a "barbarism." This barbarism he attributes to the belief that there is "a total difference between man and animal," which idea, he says, "was expressed most definitely and

strikingly by Descartes as a necessary consequence of his errors."
Schopenhauer is alluding to Descartes' infamous belief that animals have no
intellectual capacities because they have no minds or souls. They act not from
reason but from reflex. Deploying the principles of his mechanical
philosophy, Descartes declared animals to be nature's automata; and many
have taken his stated position that animals do not think to imply that he must
also have denied that they have feelings. Whether he himself drew this last
conclusion is not uncontroversially clear, but he certainly did hold that we
may kill and consume animals, and even perform vivisections on them,
without moral compunction or guilt.

As a consequence of Descartes' errors: Schopenhauer rejected the
ontological and epistemological assumptions of the bulk of modern
philosophy prior to Kant, not only as represented by Descartes' form of
rationalism, but also as expressed in the materialistically-inclined versions of
British empiricism. Melville and Nietzsche were both influenced by the
Kantian Transcendental Idealism that informed Schopenhauer's philosophy,
and though neither man was himself a Kantian or a Schopenhauerian (though
Nietzsche was a devoted acolyte of Schopenhauer for a time in his youth),
they too rejected a great many modern philosophical assumptions, as we shall
see.

Chapter 66: The Shark Massacre

Observing the gruesome display of sharks at their whale-feast, Queequeg is
struck by the divergent natures of the gods that various peoples believe in.
The Fejee and the Nantucketer worship different deities, the former
presumably conceived as more violent or cruel than the latter, and the "dam
Ingin" god, who created sharks, is the most malicious of all. But even within
a single faith there may well exist profound differences of opinion concerning
the nature of the divine. Consider the history of Christianity, marked as it is
with traces of bitter disputes from its inception, some of these disagreements
having their origins in controversies present in the pre-Christian ancient
world.

Plato's *Euthyphro* exposes some of these ancient controversies. The
dialogue is set in the Stoa Basileus, or the Royal Stoa, a government building
in the Athenian agora to which Socrates was summoned to receive the

charges lodged against him that eventually led to his execution. There Socrates meets Euthyphro, who fancies himself a religious authority gifted with special insight into the nature, activities, and opinions of the gods. Striking up a conversation, Socrates asks Euthyphro to define for him the essence of piety, and when Euthyphro replies that a pious act is a deed that all the gods love, Socrates poses a question that has reverberated ever since through the history of theology in the West. Is a pious act pious because all the gods love it, Socrates wonders, or do all the gods love it because it is pious? This is the so-called "Euthyphro dilemma." The first horn of the dilemma implies that the gods' love is a cause that produces the effect of the property of piety: the fact that the gods approve of an act is the sole reason the act is pious. The second horn suggests that an act is pious independently of the gods' approval: the fact that it is pious motivates the gods' to love it. Socrates is interested in the question in this context because if the pious is pious independently of the gods' love, then the fact that the gods love it does not provide insight into its essence; it informs us only of an extrinsic fact about the deed, namely that the gods love it, but it does not explain the feature or features that make it pious, which is what Socrates is eager to learn. The two men never do settle on a satisfactory account of piety, and in fact Euthyphro hurries off before Socrates is done interrogating him. Concluding as it does without resolution, the *Euthyphro* is generally classified as one of Plato's early, "aporetic" dialogues.

But quite apart from its role in this inquiry into the essence of piety, there is another aspect of the Euthyphro dilemma that Socrates does not explore, but that has been particularly worrisome to more than a few Christian philosophers and theologians. The Christian deity has traditionally been conceptualized as omniscient, omnipotent, and omnibenevolent. But what exactly is his relation to morality, to the fact of an act's being either good or evil? Is a deed good because God enjoins us to perform it, another deed evil because he forbids it? Or are some deeds good and others evil in and of themselves, and God's recognition of their good or evil motivates him to enjoin or forbid them? Either horn of this dilemma poses a problem for our traditional conception of God. If a deed is good or evil for no reason other than God's approval or disapproval, then his approval and disapproval must be unmotivated, groundless, arbitrary. He enjoins us to love our neighbors as ourselves, and he forbids murder; but he might just as well have commanded us to murder our neighbors and condemned our loving them. Since nothing about the acts themselves makes them either good or evil, but only divine approval or disapproval, God could even change his mind on a whim tomorrow, reassigning good and evil according to a radically different—a totally opposite—plan from the arrangement presently in place. Does it seem odd to imagine God's acting on a whim? Maybe. But if in the beginning there was nothing about the inherent nature of any act that motivated God's approval or disapproval, then God acted on a whim when he designated some acts good and others evil from the beginning. The belief that good and evil depend solely on God's will, then, seems to suggest that God is irrational.

We may restore our faith in God's rationality by grasping the other horn of the dilemma and pronouncing morality independent of God: some acts are inherently good and others inherently evil, and God's knowledge of their natures motivates him to approve the former and disapprove the latter. According to this account, God's knowledge moves his will, which is a rational procedure. Yet although this resolves the matter of divine rationality, it generates a problem for divine omnipotence. We tend to believe that God's being all-powerful means that he created all things, and that he can annihilate or alter anything too as he sees fit. But if the moral properties of deeds are independent of God's will, then he neither created them nor can he change them, which certainly appears to imply a limit to his power.

This, then, is the Christian version of the Euthyphro dilemma: God is either omnipotent but irrational, or rational but of limited power. Neither option is satisfying, and the various attempts to address the problem, and related issues, have produced different accounts of the Christian deity. Some stress God's power and will, others emphasize divine rationality. The debate was prevalent among medieval theologians, as one can imagine; but it also influenced the development of early modern philosophy, and not only those aspects of philosophy dealing directly with the divine. Ontology and epistemology in general were affected by these controversies concerning God's nature, as I illustrate in the next chapter with reference to the rationalism and empiricism that I mentioned in the final paragraph of the previous one.

Chapter 67: Cutting In

Modern rationalism is the position that at least some knowledge is *a priori*, which is to say that some propositions may be known to be true prior to, or independently of, experience. Empiricism is the position that all knowledge is *a posteriori*, which is to say that knowledge comes only after, or by way of, experience. The historian of science Margaret J. Osler has argued that these two positions, particularly as articulated by Descartes and Gassendi respectively, were shaped by assumptions about the nature of God inherited from medieval theology. These assumptions are not identical to the two horns of the Euthyphro dilemma, but the similarities will be apparent.

Recall that one horn of the dilemma stresses God's rationality while the other stresses his omnipotence. God either employs his intellect to identify moral properties that are as they are independently of his creative activity, or he exercises his power to create moral properties according to the whim of his unmotivated will. Medieval theologians carried the debate concerning the interplay between God's reason and power well beyond the point to which the ancients had brought it. For present purposes we may distinguish two schools of thought regarding these matters, first the so-called "intellectualists," who stressed God's rationality. One group of intellectualist theologians believed that some elements of creation exist independently of God, while another believed that although God has created everything that exists, he included in his creation some universal and absolutely binding principles, laws, or relations. In either case, whether some elements of creation are as they are independently of God, or whether they have been created by God to be unalterably as they are, they limit the scope of God's power to the extent that he can do nothing to change them. One implication of this view is that *a priori*, demonstrative, and therefore certain, knowledge of the world is possible. According to the "voluntarists," on the other hand, God is perfectly free to exercise his will however and whenever he pleases. He may alter any element of his creation at any time, including even the laws of logic. This implies that we can know only what we observe, or that knowledge is *a posteriori*, and consequently that no proposition expressive of anything beyond an immediate individual fact may ever be known with certainty.

These competing views of God and his creation resurface in rationalist and empiricist views of nature and our cognitive access to truth. A rationalist like Descartes thinks of God as a sort of divine geometer: God created the world with mathematical precision according to necessary principles. And here I employ the word "necessary" in the strict sense: that which is necessary cannot be otherwise than it is. A necessary truth is true at all times and everywhere. Therefore, if I know such a truth—for example, that every point on the circumference of a circle is equidistant to the center—I need not worry that it ever was or will be false; I may be certain of it. An empiricist like Gassendi, on the other hand, thinks of God as a sort of experimentalist or, better, an inventor of utterly contingent individuals. And by contingent I mean that which may be otherwise than it is because its being, and its being as it is, is not the expression of an inalienable essence but depends on something other than itself. That which is contingently true at present may or may not have been true in the past, and it may or may not be true in the future. Therefore, if I know such a truth—for example that the moon orbits the earth once every twenty-eight days—I cannot be certain that it always was or will be true.

These ontological and epistemological differences imply equally significant methodological differences. If the world is structured mathematically, then we need not always depend on observation to acquire knowledge of nature, just as we need not examine all triangles to know that each one has three angles measuring 180 degrees. Some truths we may simply deduce from other truths. Thus the rationalist contends, as I put it in the opening paragraph of this chapter, that some knowledge may be had independently of experience. If, on the other hand, the world is radically contingent, then we must observe and investigate in order to acquire knowledge of nature, as we must measure the distance between New York and Rome to know that it is roughly 4,280 miles, and just as anyone who may want to know the distance between these same two cities a millennium from now will need to measure again, for as the earth's crust is moving, the distance will have changed by then. Only those claims verified by observation may qualify as truths. Thus the empiricist believes that all knowledge ultimately derives from experience.

To sum these matters up, I quote from Osler: "the differences between Gassendi's and Descartes' versions of the mechanical philosophy directly reflected the differences in their theological presuppositions. Gassendi described a world utterly contingent on divine will. This contingency expressed itself in his conviction that empirical methods are the only way to acquire knowledge about the natural world... Descartes, on the contrary, described a world in which God had embedded necessary relations, some of which enable us to have a priori knowledge of substantial parts of the natural world." Gassendi and Descartes are convenient representatives of the empiricist and rationalist traditions, but there were other influential members of these two schools. The three canonical empiricists are John Locke, George Berkeley, and David Hume. The most important rationalists, after Descartes himself, are Baruch Spinoza and Gottfried Leibniz. These two philosophical approaches dominated modern philosophy, and the various debates within and between each school set the agenda for thinking about ontology, epistemology, and philosophical and scientific methodology until Kant intervened and upset most every traditional philosophical assumption, not just modern but medieval and ancient assumptions as well.

I shall have more to say about some of the pre-Kantian philosophers whom I have just named, but it is important to keep in mind that no single philosopher, or school, or period of philosophy explains the cast of either Melville's or Nietzsche's mind. These men lived and thought as they did as a result of engaging their natural intellectual tendencies with the entire history of philosophy conceived as a singly unified, ongoing cross-talking argument, or as a grand enduring intellectual-creative experiment. Neither man philosophized in the mode of any previous philosopher, but they did have much in common with one another, despite their differences, because each man combined philosophy with artistry, which they had in common with Plato too. We may see beyond their differences to recognize their commonalities by noting that in Melville the artist takes precedence over the philosopher, whereas in Nietzsche the philosopher dominates the artist. But the two elements are always present, certainly at least in the best of their work.

Chapter 68: The Blanket

Referring just above to Melville's and Nietzsche's engagement with philosophy, I mentioned not only their manner of thinking but their way of living as well. The ancients had thought of philosophy as a way of life, but the moderns conceived of philosophy as more akin to science, as being, or involving, or as potentially leading to the discovery of, a method for the acquisition of knowledge. Modern philosophy, like much of contemporary philosophy, is often systematic to the point of being bloodless, concerned with solving a certain canon of problems to the neglect of thinking about living or, better, experimenting with life. It is true that Melville was puzzled by what he sometimes called "the problem of the universe," as we have seen; but to him this was an existential problem, not susceptible of anything like a scientific solution. Nietzsche was curious about various problems himself, even problems that we might classify as scientific, but he was preeminently a philosopher of life. The philosopher according to Nietzsche's idea "demands of himself a judgment, a Yes or No, not about the sciences but about life and the value of life." This is a task beyond the capacity of the conventional *wissenschaftlicher Mensch*.

In the present chapter of *Moby-Dick* Ishmael expresses his wonder that the whale, a warm-blooded creature, can flourish in "Hyperborean waters." Reflecting on the significance of this marvelous phenomenon, he advises man to "admire and model thyself after the whale! Do thou, too," he says, "remain warm among ice." Ishmael's remarks recall Nietzsche's declaration at the beginning of *The Antichrist* that "we are Hyperboreans; we know very well how far off we live... Beyond the north, ice, and death—*our* life, *our* happiness." Nietzsche characterizes himself as a Hyperborean to keep his distance from modern man and modern philosophy. He even compares modernity to a disease. "Rather live in the ice," therefore, "than among modern virtues." Similarly, Ishmael elaborates his advice that we learn to live well among ice by admonishing us to "live in this world without being of it." Melville and Nietzsche both strove to separate themselves from the world they inhabited, and more urgently from the worldview their contemporaries had thoughtlessly inherited and would have them accept too. Belief was not for them, nor even knowledge conceived as it generally has been since the beginning of the modern period, perhaps even as it has been since the inception of philosophy as an activity distinct from wisdom.

Nietzsche had no interest in the modern project of acquiring knowledge for its own sake, or for the sake of utilitarian "progress" through technology. He believed that philosophy is, or should be, concerned with profundities; and "all profound knowledge flows cold," his Zarathustra says, for "ice cold are the inmost wells of the spirit." Nietzsche reads like Ishmael when he writes in the preface to *Ecce Homo* that "philosophy, as I have so far understood and lived it, means living voluntarily among ice and high mountains." And when he adds that this means "seeking out everything strange and questionable in existence" by way of "wanderings *in what is forbidden*," I am reminded of Ishmael's "everlasting itch for things remote" and his "love to sail forbidden seas, and land on barbarous coasts." These are not sentiments we typically associate with the scientist, or with the philosopher who models himself on the scientist. But Melville and Nietzsche were not typical men.

I have mentioned Nietzsche's objection to the modern tendency to privilege science over philosophy. In the section from *Beyond Good and Evil* that I cited in this connection, Nietzsche complains that in contrast to science, "the level to which modern philosophy has gradually sunk ... invites mistrust and displeasure, if not mockery and pity." I noted that Nietzsche reported that *Beyond Good and Evil* flowed from his pen very black, like ink from a squid; and since I now begin to associate Melville and Nietzsche more closely and at greater length than I have done so far, I should like here to relate Nietzsche's conception of his work to Melville's conception of *Moby-Dick*.

In the letter in which Nietzsche refers to the squid-like blackness of *Beyond Good and Evil*, he calls the book "frightful." These images recall Melville's comparison of *Moby-Dick* to whale blubber that must be cooked to produce oil, and also his warning a friend against reading the book because it "is of the horrible texture of a fabric that should be woven of ships' cables & hawsers. A Polar wind blows through it," he adds, "& birds of prey hover over it." And when he instructs his friend in this same letter to "warn all gentle fastidious people from so much as peeping into the book," I think of Nietzsche's remarking to a friend that one must read *Beyond Good and Evil* "with clinched teeth."

Nietzsche concluded *Beyond Good and Evil* by referring to the contents of the book as the "sudden sparks and wonders of my solitude ... my old beloved—*wicked* thoughts." It is hard to resist juxtaposing this with Melville's observation in a letter to Hawthorne that in writing *Moby-Dick* he had produced "a wicked book." Then there is Melville's reference in an earlier letter to "the hell-fire in which the whole book is broiled," and to "the book's motto (the secret one), – Ego non baptiso te in nomine," the rest of which formula he advises Hawthorne to make out himself. It is in fact the beginning of a passage that Melville had read in an essay on witchcraft that runs, "Ego non baptizo te in nomine Patris et Filii et Spiritus Sancti – sed in nomine Diaboli." I do not baptize you in the name of the Father and the Son and the Holy Spirit—but in the name of the devil.

Nietzsche wrote in *Daybreak*, to which *Beyond Good and Evil* was originally intended as a sequel and expansion, that "we investigators are, like all conquerors, discoverers, seafarers, adventurers, of an audacious morality and must reconcile ourselves to being on the whole considered evil." Melville of course was the authentic seafaring adventurer here, and as for being considered evil, quite apart from the rebukes he received in the press for his ironical-critical treatment of Christianity, he himself once claimed to have summoned *Moby-Dick* with an "evil art."

Chapter 69: The Funeral

The sections of Nietzsche's works from which I have quoted in the previous chapter contain several references to knowledge and truth. Clearly, Nietzsche's conception of himself as an audacious philosopher has something to do with his relation to these matters, or with his own conception of this relation. What he took this relation to be, however, is not easy to discern. Throughout the second half of the twentieth century scholars proposed, debated, and rejected numerous reconstructions of Nietzsche's understanding of knowledge and truth, and the disputes continue to this day. Some claim that Nietzsche denied that humans can ever know truth, even that he dismissed the very idea of truth as conceptually fantastic. Others insist that he not only believed in truth but was confident that we can know it through the methods of science properly applied. I myself have written that Nietzsche was less interested in knowledge than the modern philosophers, whose obsession with epistemology he held responsible for "the wretchedness of the most recent philosophy." I have also associated him with Melville's idea that truth resides in landlessness, which may well be sufficiently eccentric to imply that truth as commonly understood is altogether a fiction. I address these matters here and there throughout the rest of this book; in this chapter I cover material relating to Ishmael's mocking of orthodoxy in the present chapter of *Moby-Dick*.

The corpse of a whale seen from a distance may appear to sailors at sea a shoal or a mass of rocks. If they mark the site on their log as dangerous, and if they spread dire warnings abroad, ships thereafter will warily keep their distance despite there being nothing whatever to fear in the area. The situation reminds Ishmael of the way "silly sheep leap over a vacuum, because their leader originally leaped there when a stick was held." To his mind the phenomenon proves the worthlessness of the "law of precedents ... utility of tradition ... [and] the obstinate survival of old beliefs." Nietzsche also mocks the tendency of men to cling to established principles and dogma, as for example when, in the speech from which I have quoted the image of profound knowledge as ice cold, his Zarathustra dismisses the advocates of orthodoxy as "lukewarm." Those whom the masses have admired as wise, Zarathustra complains, have all too often been timid sponsors of popular prejudices, supporters of the objects of the mob's reverence, "servants" of "the dumb-eyed people." In other words, the famous wise men have been "asses" freighted with the burden of every mistake that through ignorance or cowardice has been established as the mark of the good and pious man. The authentic wise man would be different; he would abandon the comforts of the city, with its masses of thoughtless men, for the harsh solitude of the desert. He would be no beast of burden: he would have a "lion-will."

The imagery here recalls Zarathustra's earlier discourse "On the Three Metamorphoses." In this speech Zarathustra explains the spirit's transition through the stages of reverence for tradition, represented by the camel as a beast of burden; rejection and destruction of traditional value judgments, represented by the lion "in the loneliest desert"; and finally arriving at the inventive activity of the child, who in his playful innocence creates new values, new thought-worlds and ways of life. In his later speech "On the Famous Wise Men" Zarathustra associates authentic wisdom with the free-spirited lion-will of those who "search, seek, and conquer." And in this speech we encounter his notion of truth. "Truthful," he says, "I call him who goes into godless deserts, having broken his revering heart." The aim of the truthful thus conceived is not the identification and collection of all those propositions that can be said to "correspond to the facts." This is the business of the scholar and the scientist. We may if we like refer to the labors of such men as expressing their will to truth, but this proves only that the word "truth" is equivocal. Zarathustra is interested in a deeper conception of truth, a conception that justifies his describing "the will of the truthful" as "fearless and fear-inspiring, great and lonely." No one would say with reference to the man of science, as Zarathustra says with reference to the sage as he conceives the type, that "spirit is the life that itself cuts into life: with its own agony it increases its own knowledge." This conception of truthfulness and wisdom motivates Nietzsche to wonder, in connection with his idea that the philosopher lives among ice and high mountains, "how much truth does a spirit *endure*, how much truth does it *dare*?" This is Nietzsche's "measure of value," and he means to measure the value of the life of a man, and more particularly of a philosopher; he is not especially interested in the truth-value of a theory, for truth and falsity are less valuable in themselves than as marks of a philosopher's courage or cowardice, wild creativity or tame belief.

Nietzsche's stress on fearlessness and resolution recalls Melville's remarks on truth in Shakespeare as articulated in his review-essay "Hawthorne and His Mosses." In this piece, which he composed while writing *Moby-Dick*, Melville praises Shakespeare for "those deep far-away things in him; those occasional flashings-forth of the intuitive Truth in him; those short, quick probings at the very axis of reality." And what does Melville mean by "Truth" in this context? He associates the idea closely with what he calls a "mystical blackness," which, as it manifests also in Hawthorne's work, "derives its force from its appeals to [a] Calvinistic sense of Innate Depravity and Original Sin." Now Shakespeare was no Calvinist, and anyway Melville intends only "something, somehow like Original Sin." He seems to have in mind, then, all that is terrible, all that is frightful and painful in life; those dark experiences that through the ages have induced pondering men to suspect that something has somehow gone awry in the world. The Abrahamic traditions symbolize these things in the story of the Fall and the doctrine of Original Sin, but these are but crude attempts to capture in words and figures an insight into the human condition too deep to be neatly articulated. In the present chapter Ishmael sums up the problem as the "horrible vulturism of earth!" Nietzsche refers to "the eternal wound of existence," the "meaninglessness of suffering," "life ... in its strangest and hardest problems," and these are his own attempts to express the obscure underside of life as he had learned of it through his greatest teachers, from the Greek tragedians to Schopenhauer, and also by way of personal experience.

We might as well call these insights expressions of wisdom as expressions of truth. The philosopher, after all, is a lover of wisdom, and it is at least doubtful whether this love is identical to the love of truth. Ishmael acquired his wisdom on the sea and later by way of reflections on all he experienced there. But I let Zarathustra speak for Ishmael here, and for himself too, of course: "Have you never seen a sail go over the sea, rounded and taut and trembling with the violence of the wind? Like the sail, trembling with the violence of the spirit, my wisdom goes over the sea—my wild wisdom."

Chapter 70: The Sphynx

As extravagantly as Melville praises Shakespeare in "Hawthorne and His Mosses," he does voice one complaint, namely that the bard was "forced by circumstances" to hide his truths behind "the popularizing noise and show of broad farce, and blood-besmeared tragedy." This world being "a world of lies" inhabited by men who thrill to the shiny and smooth facets of life, Shakespeare was careful to reveal the blackness of truth only "covertly, and by snatches." Melville issued the same objection in a letter written the previous year to his friend Evert Duyckinck. Even Shakespeare, he wrote, "was not a frank man to the uttermost." But the main subject of his letter is Ralph Waldo Emerson, who was a particular favorite of Nietzsche; and the words Melville penned with reference to Emerson ring with a Nietzschean tone.

While visiting with the family of his wife in Boston, Melville attended one in the series of Emerson's lectures on "Mind and Manners in the Nineteenth Century." Reporting the event to Duyckinck, Melville pronounces Emerson "a great man." Duyckinck's reply is not preserved, but in it he apparently objects to this characterization, so Melville clarifies his opinion in the letter at issue. Although he does not "oscillate in Emerson's rainbow," he does insist that "Emerson is more than a brilliant fellow." Like Emerson himself, Melville was a resolutely independent man; he would cut his own path rather than follow in the steps of even the most experienced traveler. But he did not stubbornly withhold admiration from genuine explorers: he was not a petty man; he could admit to respecting and receiving inspiration from others. Melville was attracted to depth of thought, and he perceived this in Emerson on the stage in Boston as he had previously encountered it in the writings of Shakespeare and Hawthorne. Emerson stood out in particular for his courageous willingness to explore ideas and to state opinions that ran counter to the intellectual fashions of his day. The spirit of independence, yes; the celebrated Emersonian self-reliance. But not this alone: also the *content* of Emerson's sovereign mind. The masses of men always have been, and presumably always will be, shallow followers—Nietzsche calls them men of the herd. But some strike out own their own, and some few members of this class understand that authentic autonomy demands not just independence but profundity. "I love all men who *dive*," Melville wrote; and whether or not they successfully plumb the profoundest depths, the diving, the daring attempt, is the thing. Melville dared most in *Moby-Dick*, with which work he earned a place among that "corps of thought-divers" he so admired, those rare individuals who "have been diving & coming up again with blood-shot eyes since the world began."

I have referred to Ishmael, and to Melville in his own person too, as wise, and I have characterized their wisdom as positively Zarathustran. In *Ecce Homo* Nietzsche declares that in all the world, and throughout the span of world history, there was "no wisdom … before Zarathustra," by which he means *his* version of Zarathustra. Most impressive to him is Zarathustra's uncanny ability to ascend and descend simultaneously, to contradict and yet say Yes, to plumb the depths of malice while maintaining an exuberant good humor. These qualities are "typical of the type of Zarathustra," yet "none of this has ever before been dreamed of as essential to greatness." So Nietzsche claims; but I would counter that Melville not only dreamed these things but realized them in *Moby-Dick*. Nietzsche notes that in Zarathustra "all opposites are blended into a new unity." I say that Melville's Ishmael similarly blends opposites into one, which is another way of characterizing the perspective through which the healthy man regards the accursed questions without regarding them *as* accursed. Such men somehow plumb the depths without descending from their heights. Consider: all that we know of unhappy Ahab comes to us by way of cheerful Ishmael—and Ishmael is cheerful not from ignorance or superficiality but from the overabundance of strength required of one who would dive into the abyss without drowning. "The ladder on which [Zarathustra] ascends and descends is tremendous," Nietzsche says, and he is right. But it seems to me that we can say the same of Ishmael's hempen rigging.

In the chapter of *Ecce Homo* from which I have taken the above material, Nietzsche quotes the following passage from *Thus Spoke Zarathustra*:

> The soul that has the longest ladder and reaches down deepest—the most comprehensive soul, which can run and stray and roam farthest within itself; the most necessary soul that plunges joyously into chance; the soul that, having being, dives into becoming; the

soul that *has*, but *wants* to want and will; the soul that flees itself and catches up with itself in the widest circles; the wisest soul that folly exhorts most sweetly; the soul that loves itself most, in which all things have their sweep and contersweep and ebb and flood——

This, Nietzsche says, is "the concept of Dionysus." To me it reads also as a faithful description of Ishmael. And when Zarathustra declares, "I love him whose soul is deep," I think of Melville's "thought-divers," Melville himself included.

In the present chapter of *Moby-Dick* Ahab remarks of a whale his crew has recently killed and hauled aboard that "of all divers, thou hast dived the deepest. That head upon which the upper sun now gleams, has moved amid this world's foundations." The fact unsettles the monomaniacal Captain, and as he speaks his brow is overcast by thunder-clouds. But Ishmael reports these words from a superior perspective: years later he has not forgotten that as Ahab thundered, an "intense copper calm, like a universal yellow lotus, was more and more unfolding its noiseless measureless leaves upon the sea." Ahab is agitated; Ishmael is serene. And this, as I have said, is a fundamental difference between the perpetual philosopher and the sage.

Nietzsche admires his Zarathustra as one who "*creates* truth, a *world-governing* spirit." But this to me is precisely the type that Melville created in his Ishmael, and thereby became, at least for a time, in and for himself. Nietzsche once praised Emerson as roving, manifold, subtle, and happy. Emerson, he wrote, "does not know how old he is already and how young he is still going to be." But in his notes he admits that Emerson was "made obscure by German philosophy—frosted glass." If only Nietzsche had known of Melville. Then he would have found a true contemporary, an independent mind, deep but still a dancer, and free from the naive idealism, the "transcendentalisms, myths & oracular gibberish," that Melville could not abide in Emerson, and that Nietzsche had to ignore in order to admire him.

Chapter 71: The Jeroboam's Story

In this chapter Ishmael tells the story of the *Pequod*'s encounter with a ship whose men have fallen under the sway of a sailor suffering from a "deep, settled, fanatic delirium." Not long after the *Jeroboam* had sailed beyond the sight of land, this crazy young man being seized by a "strange, apostolic whim" proclaimed himself the archangel Gabriel descended to earth as "the deliverer of the isles of the sea and vicar-general of all Oceanica." As manifestations of his divine power Gabriel let it be known that he was responsible for an epidemic that had broken out on board, which he termed "the plague"; that he could, and would, condemn his enemies to hell; and that "sacrilegious assailants of his divinity" and all "blasphemers" would suffer condign punishment.

The divinity whose holiness Gabriel claims to defend is none other than Moby Dick, whom he identified early in the voyage as "the Shaker God incarnated." A year or two after this declaration the *Jeroboam* encountered and gave chase to the whale, and the first mate lowering a boat eventually caught up to the beast and harpooned it. Gabriel had warned the captain against the pursuit with a variety of furious imprecations, and with Moby Dick wounded he mounted a mast, gesticulating wildly, and shouted "prophecies of speedy doom" against the mate below in the whaleboat. Then, as the mate prepared to let loose a second harpoon, "a broad white shadow rose from the sea" and struck him full in the chest. He flew from the boat nearly fifty yards before dropping into the water, dead.

Adding to the portentous strangeness of this event was the fact that neither the boat in which the mate had stood, nor any member of the crew so closely surrounding him, was harmed in the slightest. It seemed as if the mate's particular death had been divinely foreordained, and that Gabriel was gifted with special insight into the man's fate. Thus was this strange fanatic "clothed … with added influence." A majority of the "ignorant" sailors aboard the *Jeroboam* began to fear Gabriel; they regarded him as sacred and deferred to him "as to a god." With the assistance of these, his "disciples," Gabriel tyrannized over the ship, to which he had become "a nameless terror." Not even the captain could wholly resist his dread influence.

Looking back on this episode Ishmael remarks that "the history of fanatics" is not "half so striking in respect to the measureless self-deception of the fanatic himself, as his measureless power of deceiving and bedeviling so many others." And with these words he sums up an idea that Nietzsche develops at length in his account of the "ascetic priest" in the Third Essay of *On the Genealogy of Morals*. In the course of the last half-century or so this book has emerged as Nietzsche's most popular and influential work. And since it aligns at least in part with Melville's conception of traditional religion, especially as he hints at it here in the present chapter of *Moby-Dick*, it will be good to provide a brief account of the relevant content of the book.

What is the meaning of ascetic ideals? This is the question with which Nietzsche heads the third and final essay of the *Genealogy*. The essay is by far the most difficult of the three in the book, and considering that in his *Ecce Homo* Nietzsche describes these essays together as "perhaps uncannier than anything else written so far," I think it safe to say that it is among the most demanding of all his writings. I will not therefore attempt to summarize the totality of the essay in this one chapter, but I will address those sections that bear on Ishmael's portrait of the fanatic Gabriel and the influence he wields over the crew of the *Jeroboam*.

By way of a first approximation, we may understand the ascetic ideal as a worldview founded on a vision of man not unlike that familiar from Plato's *Phaedo*: Soul is superior to body; the metaphysical is more real, and more valuable, than the physical; the true home of our true selves is a pure immaterial realm wholly other than this earthly vale accessible to our senses; and truth is our ultimate aspiration. To live well, therefore, one must withdraw from one's body through various forms of self-discipline or self-denial. The word for such practices is *askêsis*, from which we have our word "asceticism." Originally this word was used to indicate straightforward forms of practice or training, as undertaken for example by athletes; but through association with the philosophical-spiritual training for death of *Phaedo*-Platonism, and as it emerged in connection with early Christianity as well, *askêsis* acquired more extreme connotations.

Nietzsche has the Platonic-Christian anti-natural varieties of asceticism in mind when he writes about the "ascetic ideal." Hence he considers it grounded on a reckless and ignorant denial of reality and therefore radically unhealthy, life-denying even. The ascetic way of life is a contradiction, for it represents the power of life turned against life. But who could bear such a paradoxical existence? Who could *advocate* it? Only one whose life-force is self-consuming, self-destructive, which is to say the human as a *sick* animal. And by "sick" Nietzsche means unwell at the deepest possible level—not a passing illness but a fundamental unsoundness or, in Nietzsche's words, a "physiological depression"; a "certain weariness and heaviness grown to epidemic proportions"; a "feeling of physiological inhibition ... not diagnosed as such" that produces a "dominating sense of displeasure." In other places Nietzsche refers to this sort of condition as decadence. The ascetic ideal, then, is an ideal of man promulgated to decadents by men who are decadent themselves, these latter forming a class Nietzsche refers to as the "ascetic priests."

I have called the advocates of the ascetic ideal self-destructive, for Nietzsche employs such terms himself. For example, he labels ascetic man the "*life-inimical* species." Later in the essay, however, he insists that "such a self-contradiction as the ascetic appears to represent, 'life *against* life,' is, physiologically considered and not merely psychologically, a simple absurdity." The ascetic conceived as an existential paradox is, he says, a "provisional formulation." In fact, the ascetic ideal functions to *preserve* life—but only a certain type of life, namely the life of the sick.

The ascetic priest, then, is a "savior" and physician of the decadent. He is decadent himself, as I have said; but he has at least some measure of control over himself, and therefore he is superior to his patients. One manifestation of the sickness the ascetic priest aims to heal is the need of the sick to hold someone responsible for their condition. "For every sufferer instinctively seeks a cause for his suffering," Nietzsche explains, "more exactly, an agent; still more specifically, a *guilty* agent who is susceptible to suffering—in short, some living thing upon which he can, on some pretext or other, vent his affects, actually or in effigy." The priest-physician treats this symptom by convincing the sick that *they themselves* are to blame for their suffering, which diagnosis he arrives at by manipulating preexisting notions of sin, guilt, responsibility, and punishment to produce a "psychological-moral" interpretation of his patients' corrupted condition. Now this is in fact a *mis*interpretation, "owing to [a] lack of physiological knowledge," but it serves the priests' immediate purposes. For under the sway of the priests, the decadents hold themselves responsible for their suffering, and although in reality this prolongs their illness rather than eradicating it, it satisfies them, and so they become manageable, malleable, controllable. In short, they submit to the power of the priest. Suffering man can bear his suffering, Nietzsche says, so long as he believes there is some reason for it, some *meaning* in it. The ascetic priest provides that meaning through his religious-moral interpretation of suffering. And as he positions himself as the supreme earthly religious and moral authority, he acquires power over his flock, precisely as the fanatic Gabriel aboard the *Jeroboam* acquired his own "measureless power of deceiving and bedeviling so many others."

Chapter 72: The Monkey-Rope

According to Nietzsche in *Twilight of the Idols*, "the priests at the head of ancient communities" employed "the psychology of will" to make their fellows dependent on them. In this way they claimed for themselves the highest rank within ancient society. Dependence is an asymmetrical relation, and he on whom all others depend, while not depending on anyone himself, necessarily occupies the supreme seat of power. The psychology of will is relevant here because in their struggle to acquire and maintain power the priests employed as their principal weapon the institution of punishment, and punishment is grounded on assumptions about the human psyche, in particular the assumptions that humans possess an incorporeal will, and that this will is free.

He who successfully arrogates to himself the right to punish others thereby has command of them. In brief, since the punisher has power over the punished, the man invested with the authority to punish has power over everyone else. The ancient priests understood this, and they manipulated the institution of punishment for their own ends. But this is not so straightforward an undertaking as it might at first appear. Punishment is not merely the act of inflicting pain on another, nor even doing so from a position sanctioned for the purpose. Any such sanction might be no more than the making official of a group's peculiar commitment to sado-masochism. No: to distinguish itself and mark its power as legitimate, punishment must be accompanied by certain moral-psychological features, which is to say that the very concept of punishment is founded on other concepts whose collective contents encode assumptions about the human mind and morality. Consider the notion of *guilt* for example. I refer to guilt as a moral and psychological phenomenon, not merely as the bare identification of the specific individual who caused some particular effect. In the latter sense we might say that *this* stone as opposed to *that* one is guilty of causing a man to stumble, but we would never pronounce a stone morally guilty of this or any other event. Thus we might kick a stone out of anger or frustration, but we would not mistake our behavior in this instance for a form of punishment for moral guilt. The institution of punishment, then, assumes the legitimacy of guilt as a psychological-moral phenomenon. But whence this notion of guilt? Just as punishment requires guilt to distinguish it from retaliation motivated by frustration or anger, so guilt must be given content by something other than itself. He who is guilty is *responsible*, again in a moral and psychological sense. We do not hold the insane or men similarly incapacitated guilty for their actions, for we judge that they are not responsible. Thus we might well insist that "he did the deed" and is therefore "responsible" in the sense that he and no other man was the relevant agent, while simultaneously relieving him of responsibility in a moral-psychological sense. And if a man is not responsible in this latter sense, he is not guilty either. The concept of guilt, then, depends on the concept of responsibility. But now consider this notion of responsibility. It no more stands on its own as a concept than do punishment as an institution or guilt as a psychic phenomenon. To be held responsible in the moral-psychological sense an actor must be considered *free*. If I strike a stranger because a stronger man has seized my arm and forced my hand against the stranger's face, or because a malicious neuroscientist has operated on my brain and now controls me so thoroughly that whenever he sends the appropriate signals my muscles contract in such a way that I hit someone—in such cases we would say that I am not responsible because my actions are not self-motivated. Some would even decline to hold me responsible in the relevant sense if I were informed that a kidnapped family member will be executed unless I punch the next man who walks by. If I did indeed strike someone in these circumstances, it would seem natural to some to judge me as having been compelled to do what I did, if not through the direct physical control of another, at least through indirect compulsion. In any case, the point is that the moral-psychological sense of responsibility depends on a prior condition of freedom. If I am not free, I cannot be held responsible for my actions. But am I free? Is it not the case that as a human I am a physical system among physical systems, extraordinarily complex, no doubt, but nonetheless subject to the laws of physics and therefore as thoroughly determined in my actions as every other physical system? At this point the concept of the *will* becomes relevant, in particular the will as a phenomenon of consciousness, as a psychic or spiritual phenomenon. The will being immaterial, it is not subject to the necessities of the laws of nature that operate on matter and physical systems. The will acts spontaneously, which is to say that willed actions are motivated by internal reasons, not determined by external causes.

This, then, is the "entire old psychology" that supports "the doctrine of will," which in its turn legitimizes the institution of punishment on which the ancient priests relied for their power, and on which their spiritual descendants continue to rely to this day. Immaterial wills are attributed to men that we might be accounted free, which we must be in order to make sense of the notion of responsibility that provides the psychic content of the idea of guilt. Guilt is the essential element, for it renders punishment conceptually coherent and institutionally legitimate; and with punishment in place the priests have support for their power.

We have inherited this doctrine of the will; we too regard humans as outfitted with the psychic matter and mechanisms outlined above, which phenomena Nietzsche traces back to their origins through a multiplicity of channels, even beyond the priests at the head of ancient communities. These men worked with mostly preexisting material, but their codification of the elements and the potent uses to which they put them have embedded them in our social-cultural traditions and personal self-conceptions. Thus even Ishmael, when bound to Queequeg by a rope in the present chapter, and reflecting on his situation "metaphysically," even he imagines that since the freedom of his will is impeded, any disaster that might befall him would be a "gross … injustice." In other words, since his bodily movements are not freely motivated, it would be both conceptually incoherent and morally unjustified if he should suffer as a consequence of his—or, really, Queequeg's—actions. Yet when he realizes on further reflection that his situation is analogous to the situation of all men, our well-being and even our lives being dependent on the actions of others over whom we have no control, he at least intimates some doubt regarding the freedom of the will. He does not quite say, with Nietzsche, that "Becoming has been deprived of its innocence when any being-such-and-such is traced back to will, to purposes, to acts of responsibility," but he does suggest a definite sympathy with the idea that the "fatality of [a man's] essence is not to be disentangled from the fatality of all that has been and will be."

Chapter 73: Stubb and Flask kill a Right Whale; and Then Have a Talk over Him

At this point I think it appropriate to examine the intellectual changes that made it possible for a culture once so pervasively faithful to produce individuals as suspicious of religion as Melville and Nietzsche. These changes took place during the course of the modern period, the early phase of which I have discussed in recent chapters on Bacon, Gassendi, and Descartes.

In the present chapter of *Moby-Dick* Ishmael mentions two other important modern philosophers when he likens the heads of two recently captured whales to John Locke and Immanuel Kant. Locke, as I noted earlier, is the first of the three great British empiricists, and Kant is the man who with his *Critique of Pure Reason* put an end to the standard arguments between empiricists and rationalists by radically altering the terms of their long-standing debate. So these men stand at the two ends of the Enlightenment, Locke at its beginning and Kant at its close. And since it was during the course of this period that philosophical thinking about the Christian religion, and even about the very idea of God, underwent significant changes, we will better understand Melville and Nietzsche on these subjects if we survey the relevant philosophical-theological history.

John Locke (1632-1704) was by and large a religious traditionalist. He was certainly a believing Christian, and he identified throughout his life with the Anglican Church. Some, however, have associated Locke with the early-Christian heresy of Arianism, and specifically with denial of the Trinity. Locke apparently persuaded Newton to pen an anti-Trinitarian essay, and he even arranged for its publication (though Newton eventually decided against releasing the piece). But Locke was a passionate advocate of religious toleration, largely on the grounds of man's limited knowledge of specific spiritual truths, so we can easily imagine that he may have entertained eccentricities of belief while maintaining a general commitment to orthodoxy. Interestingly, Locke argued against suicide and murder on the grounds that humans are the property of God, which is the very argument that Socrates offers against suicide in the *Phaedo* when asked why philosophers should not kill themselves if philosophy is training for death. And Locke reasoned in the Aristotelian tradition when he offered a version of the cosmological argument for God's existence. As we have seen, Aristotle argued that an eternal Prime Mover, or first cause, is required to account for the motions of the heavenly bodies; and Locke argued similarly that an eternal being must exist in order to account for the existence of the universe.

In selecting a thinker strictly the opposite of Locke, Melville might have done better than Kant. Locke's contemporary, Baruch Spinoza (1632-1677) was a rationalist and, according to some, an atheist. Spinoza believed in, and argued for the existence of, God; but since he defined God as the one and only existing substance of the universe, and everything else that exists as an attribute or mode of God, Spinoza identifies God and nature in something like a pantheistic sense. *"Deus, sive Natura,"* as he puts it: God, or Nature. This Nature, the world or the universe, is not separate from God, but is rather the externalization or objectification of God. Every individual, an atom, a tree, a person, or a planet, is but an attribute of the deity. Spinoza would like to avoid the usual anthropomorphic conception of God, which may well be a commendable aspiration. But consider the consequences: If God is not a transcendent personal agent who created the universe from nothing; if God does not act from intentions to accomplish purposes or ends, nor intervene in the world through miracles; and if the universe and every event within it exists necessarily as a mode of God, implying a strict universal determinism binding even on the deity itself—if all these things are so, then what is left of the traditional conception of God? Spinoza insists that God exists, God as an infinite, unified, necessary being; and stated solely in these general terms his account is compatible with tradition. But given his radically anti-anthropomorphic elaboration of this general account, Spinoza was regarded in his own day, and has been regarded by many ever since, as an atheist. It did not help that his conception of death and the afterlife (to which Ishmael refers at the end of chapter seventy-five) seems not to include individual survival. Spinoza may or may not have been an atheist, but he certainly was unorthodox, and he was officially excommunicated from the Jewish community of Amsterdam.

Melville might even have selected Locke's fellow empiricist and Christian, George Berkeley (1685-1753), as his opposite. I shall have more to say about Berkeley in the next chapter; for now, suffice it to say that he insisted that to believe in matter, as Locke did, is to prepare the ground for atheism. If material objects exist and act under their own power—as they do according to the tenets of the mechanical philosophy, of which Locke was a proponent—then there is no need to postulate the existence of a deity on which they depend. Berkeley therefore argued that matter conceived as existing independently of mind does not exist. He was an empiricist, but he was the opposite of a materialist. Berkeley was a strict idealist, which is to say that he believed that all that exists is mental, or spiritual. Atoms, trees, people, and planets are but ideas—or collections of ideas—in the minds of perceiving agents, these perceiving agents being nothing other than minds, or spirits. These ideas are caused in minds through the activity of God, himself a spirit, but an infinite one. And since, according to Berkeley, there is no other possible explanation for the existence of our ideas in all their multiplicity and complexity, his idealism amounts to a proof of God's existence.

The first great modern philosopher to offer a serious challenge to a popular argument for God's existence was David Hume (1711-1776). In his *Dialogues Concerning Natural Religion* Hume presents a sustained critique of the so-called "argument from design," which reasons from our knowledge that complex and systematic devices (a pocket-watch, for example), far from being the chance products of random natural events, are designed and constructed by intellectual and intentional agents, to the conclusion that the complex system that is the universe must likewise have been designed and created by the intellectual and intentional agent that is God. Hume's dialogue infamously concludes with some ambiguity as to whether the many objections raised against the argument have decisively refuted it, but this may have been a consequence of Hume's unwillingness to state his theological, or anti-theological (some would say atheistic), views too openly. Indeed, he withheld the *Dialogues* from publication, and they did not appear until 1779, three years after his death. Yet he did publish in his *Enquiry Concerning Human Understanding* (1748) a chapter entitled "On Miracles" in which he argues that testimony to the occurrence of miracles intended to lend credence to religion, as we find for example in the New Testament in support of Christianity, is unworthy of belief. He also argued against the doctrine of personal immortality (in both his *Treatise* and an essay entitled "Of the Immortality of the Soul," the latter published posthumously). In *Redburn* Melville wrote that Hume "died the death of a Christian," but he had in mind only the philosopher's final comportment, not his beliefs: he admitted that "Hume was not a Christian in theory." Scholars to this day debate Hume's personal theological commitments, but it is indisputable that his published and unpublished writings tend toward advocating a skeptical withholding of assent regarding traditional religious doctrine.

Kant was less evasive than Hume when it came to stating his opinions concerning the validity of the many attempted proofs of various elements of traditional Christian doctrine. Whether the time or the place in which he wrote was more tolerant of intellectual dissent, he boldly published thoughtful refutations of each of the traditional arguments for God's existence. In his *Critique of Pure Reason* Kant argues that both the cosmological argument and the argument from design depend on the ontological argument, which exists in several versions, all of them sharing in common the attempt to derive the existence of God from the very idea of God's nature or essence. Think, in short, of the idea that the essence of God includes existence, which implies that God necessarily exists, that he exists by definition, as it were. Kant's most famous objection to the ontological argument depends on his claim that existence is not a predicate, and that therefore existence cannot be included in the concept or essence of a thing. According to Kant, in fact, the existence of God cannot be demonstrated. Yet he also insists that we must assume that God exists, for morality in particular depends on this assumption (as it depends also on the assumptions of immortality and freedom of the will).

Nietzsche liked to appeal to Kant's own description of his work as denying knowledge in order to make room for faith to characterize him as "an underhanded Christian." He insisted that if Kant is right that God is unknowable, then neither can the idea of God play any role in morality or anything else. The very idea is as good as refuted and should, therefore, be rejected. But, as I have said, Kant was significant to Nietzsche's thinking in other than theological terms. Among the most radical of Nietzsche's many novel ideas is his denial of Being, which besides having an ancestor in Heraclitus descends as well from Kant's work. But as Kant was only the last actor in the modern drama of the piecemeal destruction of traditional ontology, in the next two chapters I recount the relevant history in some detail.

Chapter 74: The Sperm Whale's Head—Contrasted View

In this and the next chapter Ishmael continues his description of the heads of the whales he has compared to Locke and Kant. Since, as I have said, developments in modern philosophy from Locke to Kant—beginning, in fact, prior to Locke, with Gassendi and Descartes in particular—since these developments bear directly on the philosophical perspectives of Melville and Nietzsche, it will be worth our while to consider some further account of them. Since in the present chapter Ishmael provides details concerning the head he has compared to Locke, it is fitting that he writes at length of the animal's eyes and ears, for as an empiricist Locke believed that all knowledge comes only by way of our senses. But I do not intend here to examine empiricist epistemology any more closely than I have done already through the discussion of Gassendi above; I shall concentrate instead on ontology, for the changes in assumptions about *what there is* were perhaps the most novel and, eventually, the most radical of all philosophical changes that occurred during the period leading up to Melville and Nietzsche.

Like Descartes, Locke is a dualist, which is to say that he believes that two fundamentally different types of substance exist, matter and mind (or spirit, or soul). He is also a realist, which is to say that he believes that the world exists independently of any mind's perception of it. The world is, and is as it is, quite apart from our experience—our perceptions, beliefs, or knowledge—of the world. As a dualist and a realist Locke agrees with the majority of his ancient and medieval predecessors; yet he diverges from them in other significant ways. Most pre-modern philosophers, excepting the atomists, believed that we perceive the world directly pretty much as it is. Apart from Platonic Forms or souls or divine beings that we may know or have beliefs about without directly perceiving as they are, the physical objects accessible to our senses exist in the world as three-dimensional objects characterized by the properties we perceive them to possess, such as colors, odors, textures, tastes, and sounds. Of course our perceptions, or the beliefs we formulate based on them, may be mistaken as a result of complications with our perceptual apparatus caused by illness, anatomical defects, or neurological problems, also by facts in the external world that interfere with or outright inhibit accurate perception—for example, an object we would like to observe may be in the dark or situated at some distance from us. But a careful observer will be aware of, and take precautions against, these and related complications. The main point is that despite such potential problems, our perceptions of the world are direct: if I am standing near a well-lit medium-sized object such as a tree, and if my eyes, optic nerve, visual cortex, and related systems are functioning properly, then my mind has direct and unimpeded access to the tree. The tree itself, external to my mind, is the very object of my perception.

This sort of direct realism is perhaps the common-sense understanding of our experiential relation to the world. But many modern philosophers rejected this view in favor of the idea that we know the world only indirectly. We have direct knowledge only of our ideas, or sensations, of the world, not of the world itself. Our beliefs about the external world are, roughly speaking, the result of unconscious inferences from subjective experiences. In short, we experience the contents of our minds immediately, but our experience of the external world is mediated through this content. And this raises skeptical concerns regarding the accuracy of these mediated, indirect, inferential experiences, the worry being that we cannot know whether the external world resembles our subjective representations because we cannot step away from these representations to compare them with the world, for this act of comparing, like all intellectual acts, must itself be conducted by way of subjective representations.

Given these assumptions about our necessarily mediated relation to the external world, then, we have reason to doubt that the world is as it appears to us to be. But most modern philosophers went further than this and insisted that we know for a fact that in many ways the world is *not* as it appears to be. When discussing Descartes I mentioned the distinction between primary and secondary qualities of objects. The distinction goes back to long before Descartes, all the way in fact to the ancient atomists; but in the context of modern philosophy it is associated in particular with Locke. I recall the distinction here, but now in Locke's terms: Objects possess primary qualities, which produce ideas in our minds that resemble them, such for example as our ideas of the size and shape of an object. Objects also possess secondary qualities, which produce ideas in our minds that do not resemble them, specifically ideas deriving from our contact with the world through any of our five senses. The qualities of color, sound, scent, taste, and feel exist only as mental phenomena in the minds of experiencing subjects. They are caused by qualities that *do* exist independently of minds, as the sensation of color is caused in part by the surface of an object reflecting light-waves at certain specific frequencies; but the color itself as we experience it is solely a mental phenomenon. But if the secondary qualities of colors, odors, tastes, textures, and sounds do not exist in the external world as we experience them, then the world is quite different than common-sense presents it to be. It is composed of physical objects of particular sizes and shapes in motion; this is true. But the various other qualities that we associate with these objects—this one is blue; that one smells sweet; that other one feels smooth and emits a low, hollow sound—these qualities are not in the world at all, but only in our minds.

This view might strike some as strange, but probably not many, for it is today embedded in the standard scientific image of the world. Most everyone with a basic level of scientific education has encountered this image and, at least to some degree, incorporated it into his or her worldview. Most, however, have not encountered the radicalization of this view developed by

179

Locke's empiricist successor, George Berkeley. As I mentioned in the previous chapter, Berkeley argued against the existence of material things conceived as objects existing independently of perception. We may put this same point in terms of the distinction between primary and secondary qualities by saying that Berkeley collapses the distinction and insists that all qualities are secondary, or mind-dependent. Thus, it is not only the color, odor, taste, sound, and feel of objects that exist exclusively in the mind, but their every other quality as well, including their size, shape, solidity, and states of motion and rest. Every property that we experience of objects in the external world—indeed, even the objects themselves and the so-called "external" world itself—all this exists as internal to, and dependent on, subjective experience. In short, Berkeley rejects Locke's (and Descartes') dualism of matter and mind. There simply is no matter, and therefore of course no material objects—not, anyway, if we conceive of matter as existing independently of mind, which was and is the standard conception. For Berkeley, then, all that exists are minds, or souls, and their ideas. A tree, for example, is an idea, or a collection of ideas (the ideas, for example, of the colors green and brown, the rough tactile feel of bark, the spatial extension of a particular height and breadth, etc.); in any case it is a subjective phenomenon having no existence external to mind. It may exist external to *my* mind, for it may exist in the mind of another; and if it exists in no human mind whatever, it may yet exist in God's mind. But a tree that exists external to every mind, human and divine—well, there simply is no such thing. The very idea, in fact, involves a contradiction and is therefore incomprehensible. At this point it is important to note that Berkeley does not deny the existence of material objects such as trees or rocks. Nor does he regard them, "metaphysically speaking," as "mere optical illusions," as Melville says of Berkeley in *Mardi*. Rather, he argues for a change in our conception of the ontological status of matter and material objects: matter is mind-dependent. But this is not to deny the existence of any particular material object. Therefore, Dr. Johnson's celebrated "refutation" of Berkeley by kicking a stone misses the point entirely.

But even if Berkeley admits the existence of stones and the bodies of the people who kick them, his insistence that these and all other objects are nothing over and above ideas in minds or souls, purely subjective phenomena, is a revision of the traditional common-sense view of the world more radical even than Locke's—sufficiently radical, perhaps, to justify Melville's referring in *Pierre* to "the airy exaltations of the Berkeleyan philosophy." Berkeley's specific version of idealism was not particularly influential, but various other species of the doctrine flourished in the wake of Kant's development of so-called Transcendental Idealism, which, as I have said, influenced both Melville and Nietzsche. But in order to make sense of Kant's motivation and accomplishment we must first understand something of the philosophy of the third and final British empiricist, David Hume. To Hume and Kant, then, I now turn.

Chapter 75: The Right Whale's Head—Contrasted View

In this chapter Ishmael tours the interior of the head of the whale that he has compared to Kant. The multitude of intricately arranged contents that he discovers inside recalls the many "sublimated categories of Kant" to which Melville refers in *Pierre*, and which he first learned of in detail from George Adler on a ship bound for London not long before he began work on *Moby-Dick*. His several conversations with Adler concerning "the German metaphysics" of "Hegel, Schlegel, Kant &c" impacted Melville profoundly, for he had been passionate about questions concerning the nature of reality, and the possibility of our knowledge of reality, since at least 1847 when he began work on his riotously philosophical *Mardi*, and what he learned of Kant must have upset even the wildest of his speculations on these matters. In this chapter I explain those aspects of Kant's philosophy most relevant to our particular concerns with Melville and Nietzsche, but in order to make sense of his ideas some knowledge of the philosophy of David Hume is essential.

David Hume was the last of the three great British empiricists, and he pushed the claim that all knowledge comes only from experience to such an extreme that he wound up at last in a radical and comprehensive version of skepticism. He went so far as to doubt the capacity of reason to justify its own activities, for, he argued, to the extent that reason justifies itself through rational arguments, it begs the question in its own favor. But neither can reason refute itself, for to the extent that it succeeds in arguing rationally against reason, it undermines the force of rational arguments, including of course the very arguments employed to undermine the force of rational arguments. Thus Hume was a skeptic regarding reason. One can imagine the havoc this position might wreck on one's mind, and, indeed, Hume apparently suffered a mental breakdown while formulating the ideas he would include in the book in which he develops these skeptical arguments. But more relevant to the consideration of Kant's philosophy is Hume's skepticism regarding causality. I shall not here attempt to explain every nuance of Hume's argument, but even a brief account will suffice for our purposes.

Causal connections are distinguished from coincidental associations through the regularity of the relation between two events. If event B follows event A one time and one time only (or only rarely or, at best, occasionally), as for example the heat turning on in my home when I began to type this sentence, we conclude that the two events are only coincidentally related: my typing did not cause the heat to turn on. If, on the other hand, event B *always* occurs on the occurrence of event A, as for example the production of fire on the striking of a match, then we conclude that the two events are causally connected. I say "always" even though sometimes fire does not result from the striking of a match, for since we know from experience that such occasional failures result from changes in other relevant factors—the fact that the matches are wet, say, or that there is too little oxygen in the room—we do not count these failures as counter-examples. Thus we may reformulate our original statement as follows: If event B always follows event A, under normal circumstances and all things being equal, we conclude that A is the cause of B.

Hume expresses the regularity of the connection between cause and effect as a *necessary* connection. Whenever the cause is present (all things being equal) the effect *necessarily* appears. It is this necessity that permits us to reason with confidence about the world around us. I don't just hope or expect that a stone will fall when dropped from a height, or that water will freeze when cooled to thirty-two degrees Fahrenheit: I know that these things will happen because the causal connections have long been established and causal connections operate with necessity. But the necessity of causal connections supports more than just our day-to-day practical activities; it grounds the practice of science as well. Universal laws assume the necessity of causal connections. Scientists' claims about events in time or space too distant to be observed—the behavior of gases or the motions of bodies two billion years ago or two billion years in the future, or at the present moment but two million light-years away—depend on the assumption that established causal connections are *always* operational (all things being equal), and this assumption depends in turn on the *necessary* connection between causes and effects. And here we must come to the point: Hume denies that we can in fact establish any necessary connections between events, and hence he denies causality. The denial derives from his empiricism, which is ironic given that most contemporary scientists identify as empiricists even though a strict application of empiricism seems (according to Hume, anyway) to undermine the reliability of causality, and thereby also of science.

Remember that according to an empiricist epistemology all knowledge comes only from experience. With this in mind Hume points out that we have no experience of a necessary connection between events. All we ever experience is one event and then another. We may experience that the second event has followed the first every time the first has occurred, but this amounts only to an experience of regularity-so-far, not necessary regularity. The combined experience of human observation may have marked the regularity a thousand, a million, or a billion times; but this tells us nothing certain about the outcome the next time. The assumption that the observed regularity must hold at all times and everywhere is an inference beyond the evidence, which is to say it is an induction. The question whether, and how, we can justify our confidence in the occurrence of one event (B) given the occurrence of another (A) is known as the "problem of induction," and though many philosophers have tried, no one has solved it to universal (or even to widespread) satisfaction since Hume formulated it so powerfully in the eighteenth century.

Kant famously wrote that his reflections on his encounter with Hume awakened him from his "dogmatic slumbers." Prior to his reading of Hume, Kant took for granted the relation between cause and effect. But since Hume had demonstrated that no necessary connection between the two can be derived from experience, and as Kant was not willing to abandon causality, he determined to secure it in some other way. His solution to the problem revolutionized philosophy, and not just philosophy but the entire European intellectual landscape, for he completely upset the traditional understanding of the relationship between the human mind and the external world. Prior to Kant it had been assumed by everyone but the most radical idealists, anti-realists, and skeptics that the spatial, temporal, and causal properties of objects exist independently of the human mind. There were disagreements (between rationalists and empiricists, for example) as to the manner of our coming to know these features of reality, but there was a general consensus that they were really "out there" in the world quite apart from our knowledge or ignorance of them. But Kant presented powerful arguments that this is not the case, that in fact spatial, temporal, and causal properties do not exist in the world as it is in itself, but are instead imposed on reality as a construct generated by our perceptual and cognitive systems. Consider the case of causality: Kant argued that the concept of the connection between cause and effect is innate to the human mind, and it structures our experience accordingly; or to put the matter another way, he argued that the mind is configured in such a way that whatever enters into it through experience is stamped with causal properties. So our experience of the world includes necessary causal connections, not because such connections exist in the world itself, but rather because the conditions of the possibility of experience include them. We must experience causal relations because the concept of causality is a precondition of experience itself.

Kant's insight has been referred to as his Copernican Revolution in philosophy because, just as Copernicus reversed our conception of the relation between the earth and the sun, so Kant reversed our conception of the relation between experience and the world. We do not derive our concepts of space, time, and causality from experience; rather space, time, and causality are products of experience. To state the matter briefly, if somewhat crudely, the world is as it is because we make it that way. And if we wonder what the world is like in itself apart from its manner of appearing to us in experience as structured by our perceptual-cognitive apparatus, we must conclude that we do not, and cannot, know. Since all that we know we know by way of our perceptual-cognitive system, we cannot know anything independently of that system, including whether the system represents the world accurately. More, some philosophers (Schopenhauer among them) insist that those features of the world-as-experienced, which Kant attributes to the workings of our perceptual-cognitive apparatus, *cannot* exist in the world independent of that apparatus. Therefore, whatever the world is like in itself, it is not spatial, temporal, or causal. The world we experience ourselves inhabiting, then, is in some real sense a construct of our own minds.

Chapter 76: The Battering-Ram

This chapter of *Moby-Dick*, in which Ishmael continues his commentary on the Sperm Whale's massive head, concludes with an allusion to the inarticulable horror that "befell the weakling youth lifting the dread goddess's veil at Sais." Plutarch preserves the ancient account of a cloaked statue of Isis that once stood in the Egyptian city of Sais, but Melville relies more immediately on Schiller's poem "The Veiled Statue at Sais." According to the narrative therein related, hidden behind the statue's veil is nothing less than Truth itself. When a young Egyptian seeker of knowledge learns of this from a priest, he immediately longs to expose the truth so as to learn it, to possess it; but the priest warns him off by appealing to the deity's own prohibition against lifting her veil. Nevertheless, the brash young man will not be dissuaded. He returns to the temple at midnight, and sneaking over the walls he approaches the goddess. Standing then before the Truth incarnate, he removes the veil and gazes excitedly on it. What does he see? No one knows, for when he was found the following morning passed out before the statue, an expression of dread distorting his pallid mask of a face, he refused to speak it. Nor did he ever after disclose the secret. His remaining days he passed in sorrow, and he died the premature death of a wrecked man.

Nietzsche alludes to this story in the first section of the second book of *The Gay Science*. Headed "To the realists," the passage expresses Nietzsche's rejection of realism, realism in this instance being the idea that "the world really is the way it appears to you." Nietzsche mocks the realists' naive belief that reality stands unveiled before them, their refusal to acknowledge the "human *contribution*" to our experience of reality. This human contribution, according to Nietzsche, includes the most fundamental elements of our experience of reality: the "erroneous articles of faith" that "there are enduring things; that there are equal things; that there are things, substances, bodies; that a thing is what it appears to be," also that there are "lines, planes, bodies, atoms, divisible time spans, divisible spaces," and "cause and effect." Now just consider for a moment your conception of the world, then subtract from it all things and even the very notion of thinghood. What is left of a world from which enduring things have been withdrawn, not to mention the atoms of which things—and even the lines and planes of which three-dimensionality itself—are composed? A world without any "arbitrary division and dismemberment" into individual things causally related one to another would be an undifferentiated blur, a field of indistinguishable distortion, a world, in short, without Being, and therefore a radically Heraclitean "continuum and … flux." If the human contribution is indeed so extensive, then, Nietzsche concludes, "There is no 'reality'" independent of it, no more for the realist than for the anti-realist. And notice the scare-quotes in which he encloses the word *reality*: the letters spell out the mere ghost of an idea, an empty concept. The fact is, as I put it at the end of the previous chapter, that the world we experience ourselves inhabiting—otherwise known as "reality"—is a construct of the human mind.

I have labelled this position anti-realism, and the term is unobjectionable in a general sense. But it is standard today to refer instead to Nietzsche's doctrine of "falsificationism." In the second chapter of *Beyond Good and Evil* Nietzsche reflects on the "strange simplification and falsification" in which man lives, and the source of the simplification and falsification is the "human contribution" as I have detailed it just above. The "will to knowledge," Nietzsche writes, is founded on "the will to ignorance," and this latter will he associates with the sort of Kantian categories that construct the world of our experience by way of "the fictions of logic," the "purely invented world of the unconditional and self-identical," and the "constant falsification of the world by means of numbers." In so far as these features of "reality" are contributed by us to experience, and so do not exist independently "out there" in the world as it is in itself, they are fictions, and the world of our experience constructed from them is a falsification.

Since the world of our experience is at bottom a fiction, our knowledge of this world is grounded on a broad base of ignorance, our cherished truths dependent on original falsehoods. This is what Nietzsche has in mind when he traces our will to knowledge back to a will to ignorance. He does not regard this as an objection in and of itself, for he insists that precisely this form of ignorance is "a condition of life," that without imposing the Kantian categories on experience "man could not live," however conceptually illegitimate those categories may be. The relevant matter is not the truth or falsity of our judgments about reality, but the extent to which our judgments are "life-promoting, life-preserving, species-preserving, perhaps even species-cultivating." Remember that as a philosopher Nietzsche is not obsessed with truth; he is in love with life. His chief aspiration is not to be a fact-finder, but rather to be a Yes-sayer.

We are touching now on Nietzsche's suspicions regarding the value of the will to truth in relation to the will to power. The rhetoric of western philosophy has long promoted truth as man's ultimate goal, wisdom as truth, reality as truth, God as truth. But Nietzsche was less interested in the discovery of truth than in the creation of value, or of systems of values, which really amounts to the design and creation of thought-worlds. The Nietzschean philosopher is in the deepest sense also an artist, a philosophical artist of life, and his wisdom resides not in the supposed objectivity of the scholar or the man of science, but rather in the free Dionysian play of the creator.

Ishmael employs the goddess at Sais as an image of the whale as Truth. Only the greatest of men can "own the whale," or acknowledge the truth, without perishing. Others must leave the veil of illusion in place and intact. Recall Nietzsche's asking, in connection with his conception of the philosopher as one who lives among mountains and ice, "how much truth does a spirit *endure*, how much truth does it *dare*?" In *The Gay Science* he wonders "to what extent can truth endure incorporation" and remarks that "that is the question; that is the experiment." This is also Melville's question, as we have seen in connection with his reflections on Shakespeare and Hawthorne. And since, as we have also seen, his conception of truth is, like Nietzsche's, darker, graver, more poetic and existential, than the typical philosopher's or scientist's conception, this is his *experiment* too. *Moby-Dick* is a veil, Ishmael its weaver; but Melville himself—Melville as author, as artist, as living individual—is the abyss from which issues the haunting and only half-decipherable echo of truth.

Chapter 77: The Great Heidelburgh Tun

According to Plutarch the following inscription was carved on the statue of Isis at Sais: "I am everything that has been, that is, and that will be, and no mortal has yet uncovered my veil." Of these words Kant once remarked that "Perhaps nothing more sublime has ever been said, or a thought ever been expressed more sublimely." His appreciation of the thought makes perfect sense given his view that reality as it is in itself is unknowable. But I do not here intend to discuss Kant's philosophy any further than I have done up to this point. Nietzsche received his Kantianism early in his career by way of Schopenhauer, and as Melville was taken with Schopenhauer's work near the end of his life, I should explain the relevant components of Schopenhauer's version of Transcendental Idealism and the philosophical pessimism deriving from it. And since for a time Schopenhauer contemplated applying for an academic post at the university in Heidelberg; and even though as far as I know he nowhere mentions the city's capacious wine vat; but, more importantly, as this is the appropriate occasion to examine the background to

Nietzsche's mature thought as I have presented it so far—considering all this, in this chapter I explain those of Schopenhauer's ideas that are most relevant to Nietzsche first book, *The Birth of Tragedy Out of the Spirit of Music*, the philosophical specifics of which I discuss in the next chapter.

Schopenhauer accepted the basic tenets of Kant's philosophy, in particular the idea that space, time, and causality are modes through which we experience the world rather than features of the world as it is in itself. The world as we experience it, and thus the very world in which we live, has spatial and temporal properties, and the spatial-temporal things within it are causally related to one another, not because the world apart from our experience is like this, but rather because our perceptual-cognitive apparatus imposes these features on the world as we construct it in and through experience. This idea is more or less faithful to the Kantian philosophy so far as it goes, but Schopenhauer diverges from Kant on one important point. Whereas Kant had argued that, because our intellect structures the world of experience by means of innate categories, we cannot know the world as it is independently of these categories, Schopenhauer believed that he had discovered a route to knowledge of the world as it is in itself.

Schopenhauer followed Kant in dividing reality into the world as it is in itself, otherwise known as the *noumenon*, and the world as it appears to us, or the *phenomenon* (*phenomena* in the plural, as often). Kant contends that our experience is strictly limited to the phenomena, the noumenon being forever inaccessible because the very act of experiencing the noumenon subjects it to the categories (space, time, causality) that transform it into the object, or objects, of our experience, which is to say into phenomena. Schopenhauer agreed with this account as applied to every item in the universe but one. Every object external to ourselves we experience through all the categories of our perceptual-cognitive apparatus, and this includes even our own bodies. My body as I experience it is a spatial-temporal object causally related to similar objects. But I have one special mode of access to my body that I do not have with respect to any other object, a mode that bypasses the categories that through the process of experience transform the noumenon into phenomena. *I am acquainted with my body from the inside*. If any other object in the external world should move, if another human should raise his arm, say, or a tree should sway in the breeze or the ocean roll with waves, I feel no internal relation to these events, and to the extent that I do not experience myself as playing any role in their occurring, we may say that I am surprised by them, surprised in the sense that I did not foresee them and do not feel in any way responsible for them. But when my own body moves, I do feel such a connection: I feel as though I am making the movement happen, as if I am the force internal to my body that through its activity generates the movement. The word we commonly use to refer to the source of this generative activity is *will*. I will my body to move, and it moves. This interior relation that we have to our own body, which we have to no other body within the scope of our actual or possible experience, this, according to Schopenhauer, is our route to the noumenon. For consider that we do not experience our willing as a spatial phenomenon: our will is not itself an object extended in space. Nor is our willing a causal activity: my willing my arm to move is not a cause that produces the effect of my arm's movement. Schopenhauer contends that my willing and my moving are one and the same act viewed from two different perspectives, internally (as willing) and externally (as movement). It is true that our willing takes place in time—that I will this action before that one, or one element of an act prior to another element of the same act (I will my shoulder to move before willing my elbow to bend when raising my arm, for example)—and therefore that we do not experience even our willing independently of *all* the categories. So we must admit that we do not have entirely unimpeded access to the noumenon. But we do come close, bypassing as we do in our relation to will the categories of space and causality. And since we may assume that all other objects in the world have an interior side just as I do, I may conclude that they too are filled, as it were, with will. This is not to say that all these objects act with conscious intentions, for will is distinct from conscious intentionality. In humans and other animals with highly-developed nervous systems, the will operates in conjunction with knowledge and intentionality; but the will itself is nothing beyond the pure impulsion toward activity, blind but forceful, as for example the unknowing force of resistance to pressure that maintains the solidity of stone. Even this is an act of will in Schopenhauer's sense.

According to Schopenhauer, then, everything in the world is, in itself, will. As experience, which is to say as phenomenon, the world is people, trees, stars, dogs, molecules, clouds, stones, rivers, mountains, et cetera; but in itself, as the noumenon, the world is will and nothing besides. And I write "will" in the singular, as opposed to "wills" in the plural, because Schopenhauer insists that since the world as it is in itself is neither spatial nor temporal, it must be a unity, a one. Plurality requires either space, in which two objects can occupy different locations at the same time, or time, in which two objects can occupy the same location at different times. But lacking both space and time, plurality is conceptually impossible. Therefore the noumenon must be singular, and specifically a singular will which when transformed into experience by way of the categories of space and time manifests as a plurality of phenomena.

I shall expand on these ideas in the next chapter through an account of the use to which Nietzsche puts them in *The Birth of Tragedy*, but to conclude this chapter I note the pessimistic consequences that Schopenhauer drew from his ontology. If the multiplicity of phenomena that we experience are, in reality—on the interior or back side of things, as it were—only *one* thing, namely will, and if this will is indeed nothing more than a blind, aimless, eternal striving, then all our goals and aspirations, all the hopes and fears of individuals, and all the conflicts between and among individuals, are meaningless, literally pointless. The will can never be satisfied because *its essence* is impulsive striving; striving is literally all that it is. And we who through our intellects provide direction to this striving as it manifests in us as phenomena, we are but the ephemeral physical objectifications of this will, destined to seek one goal after another until we pass away and the particular phenomenon that each of us is evaporates from the scene. Schopenhauer infers from these bleak facts that if there is any purpose to our existence, it is that we should come to learn that it would have been better had we never existed to begin with.

Chapter 78: Cistern and Buckets

The present chapter of *Moby-Dick* concerns the mining of the Sperm Whale's head for its store of spermaceti. It is a precarious operation, and the man performing it hangs from the side of the ship in constant danger of falling into the whale's head and dying there. But considering the dainty fragrance of the spermaceti, Ishmael speculates that to die in this way would be as sweet as the death of "an Ohio honey-hunter" drowning in a load of honey settled in the crotch of a hollow tree. Inspired by this thought he concludes the chapter by enquiring of his reader, "How many, think ye, have likewise fallen into Plato's honey head, and sweetly perished there?"

The first chapter of the fourth and final book of Nietzsche's *Thus Spoke Zarathustra* is entitled "The Honey Sacrifice." In this chapter Zarathustra climbs to the summit of a high mountain and speaks to himself of luring men to his wisdom with the "bait and sweet mucus and mucilage" of honey, "which makes even growling bears and queer, sullen, evil birds put out their tongues." The world away from which he hopes to seduce these men is a world shaped by Christian values, which Nietzsche regularly identifies with Platonism (recall his statement that "Christianity is Platonism for 'the people'"). Melville did not reject Platonism as vehemently as Nietzsche, but he did regard it as honey-like in its sweet seductiveness, tempting but pernicious if consumed in large quantities.

Schopenhauer had no such scruples regarding Platonism. This is not to say that he was an orthodox disciple. Far from it, for he was sure that Platonism required modification in light of the Kantian philosophy. But he did incorporate Platonic Forms (suitably modified) into his ontology, and he acknowledged both "the divine Plato" and "the astounding Kant" as the greatest influences on the development of his thought (Hinduism and the Upanishads came later). A teacher of philosophy had advised the young Schopenhauer to concentrate his philosophical reading on Plato and Kant, and he was happy to follow the man's instruction. Nietzsche too had admired Plato as a young man. Not long before matriculating to university he declared the *Symposium* one of his favorite works of ancient literature. But his opinion would soon change. In his first book, *The Birth of Tragedy*, he identifies Socrates as the arch villain of intellectual history, and throughout his career he tended to associate Plato with the most objectionable aspects of Socrates' philosophical personality.

In *The Birth of Tragedy* Nietzsche attempts to solve the mystery of the origins of ancient Greek tragedy, a long-standing enigma that Aristotle himself had investigated. Nietzsche's own solution involves a distinction between Apollo and Dionysus as divine representatives of two contrary forces operative in nature and, through nature, in the Greek psyche. The distinction as Nietzsche develops it depends on those aspects of Schopenhauer's philosophy that I have outlined in the previous chapter. Nietzsche identifies the essence of the world with the unified and blind, striving, annihilating will of Schopenhauer's metaphysics. This will is the ultimate source of the human suffering that the ancient tragedians exhibit in their depictions of the dreadful fate of figures like Oedipus and Prometheus. The Greeks' insight into the gloomy underside of the world and of life led them to formulate the wisdom of Silenus as the verdict that it is best for mortals never to be born, and second best that they die as soon as possible. Nietzsche labels the aspect of the Greek psyche that attained to this insight "Dionysian." But this insight is terrible and hard to bear; it can lead to a nihilistic renunciation of life. Thus the Greeks revealed this truth to themselves through the elevating mode of poetry. They wove beautiful illusions around the terrible truth so as not to be destroyed by it. This they were inspired to do by the "Apollonian" aspect of their psyche. The dramatic elements of Greek tragedy represent the Apollonian expression of metrical order and harmony, the stately beauty of grounding symmetry. The chorus gives voice to the wild Dionysian insight into the obliterating essence of things. Through a sort of psychological-spiritual intoxication the Dionysian man breaks through the illusions of the phenomena and stands in the presence of the noumenon, the ever-striving will. For a fleeting moment he becomes one with the One, the All, that is this Will, and thereby he comes to realize the unspeakable horror at the core of the world. But soon he returns to his normal Apollonian consciousness and is wrapped once again in the cloak of the phenomena, in which state he expresses his encounter with the ultimately ineffable truth through the inadequate media of words, concepts, and narrative, enhanced by song and dance. This is the tragedy.

For Nietzsche, then, tragedy is the product of a particular period in western history when the Greeks managed to hold together within themselves—as individuals and as a culture—the contrary tendencies of the Apollonian and Dionysian forces. But this period was fleeting, and the art of tragedy perished from the imbalance resulting from an excessive stress on the Apollonian drives. The tragedian Euripides was responsible for this specifically in relation to tragedy, but he was only a vehicle for a deeper intellectual degeneration, expressing on the stage a mindset that Nietzsche labels "Socratism." According to Nietzsche, Socrates disdained the irrational and pessimistic Dionysian worldview. He agreed that men suffer, but unlike the tragedians he thought that suffering could be relieved or avoided altogether. The tragic worldview has it that humans are at the mercy of ultimately unknowable and uncontrollable forces, embodied on the stage as gods. Suffering is our lot and we can neither understand the reason for this nor do anything to prevent it. But Socrates, in Nietzsche's words, "conceives it to be his duty to correct existence," and he will do so by employing reason to attain knowledge of truth. Socrates is an optimist and a rationalist, and through him "*philosophic thought* overgrows art and compels it to cling close to the trunk of dialectic," and "who could mistake the *optimistic* element in the nature of dialectic." If men are sick, reason will heal them; if they are vicious, reason will lead them to virtue. For he who knows the truth will do good, and good men are happy. Recall the stress on ascetic virtue in the *Phaedo*, and then consider this from Nietzsche: "*The dying Socrates* became the new ideal, never seen before, of noble Greek youths: above all, the typical Hellenic youth, Plato, prostrated himself before this image with all the ardent devotion of his enthusiastic soul."

According to Nietzsche, then, the rationalist optimism of Socrates and Plato reflected and simultaneously hastened the close of the greatest phase of Greek culture, and their ideas and practices also prepared the soil for Christianity. Thus in *Twilight of the Idols* Nietzsche condemns them both as "pseudo-Greek, anti-Greek." And since Nietzsche considered "the Platonic drama," with Socrates as its "dialectical hero," the principal source that disseminated throughout the West the influence of an anti-tragic, rational and optimistic worldview, I have no doubt that he would have been happy to adopt Melville's metaphor and declare Plato's corpus the honey pot in which the nobility of the ancient world sank and finally perished.

Chapter 79: The Prairie

Nietzsche's early commitment to the Kantian premises of Schopenhauer's philosophy prepared the way for his later falsificationism, his thesis that the world of experience is a "simplification and falsification" produced by the "categories of reason." If the world as a field of spatial-temporal objects causally related to one another is a world of phenomena, and therefore of appearance or mere illusion, and if the noumenon, the world as it is in itself, is either altogether unknowable or a single eternal and blind metaphysical will, then the world of our experience is in some significant sense *untrue*. In *The Birth of Tragedy* Nietzsche does not employ the vocabulary of untruth or falsification, for in Kantian and Schopenhauerian terms truth and untruth are conditions of things or propositions that obtain within the phenomenal world, not between the phenomenal and noumenal realms. But considering the many differences between the phenomena and the noumenon, it is not hard to detect elements of Nietzsche's later view prefigured in his early position.

Not long after the publication of *The Birth of Tragedy* Nietzsche began to entertain doubts about Schopenhauer's metaphysics. Not the sort of doubts that would lead to his falsificationism, but rather doubts about any division of the world into two distinct realms. With his work *Human, All Too Human*, published six years after *The Birth of Tragedy*, he articulated a new philosophical approach that inaugurated what has since become known as his "middle period." Nietzsche himself regarded this approach as historical and scientific, for his method was to trace the history of traditional metaphysical concepts back to their origins in natural, human perspectives and prejudices. He argued that philosophical and theological notions of such putatively objective entities as Platonic Forms or the Christian God are not the products of insight into the metaphysical truth dwelling within or behind the veil of appearances, but merely the elaborated conceptual misunderstandings and mistakes of millennia. These elaborations have become so refined, and over the centuries so thoroughly settled into our worldview, that they are second nature to us: it seems evident that, for example, evil is the opposite of good, or that an eternal source of being, and absolute truths, exist somehow above or behind this temporary world of contingent and constantly changing facts. But historical philosophy informed by science exposes these notions for the biased and ungrounded assumptions they are, remnants of various periods of man's conception of himself and the universe that have survived, not because they are true, but because they are adaptive, or by chance. In short, Truth (the absolute truth with, as they say, a capital "T") is not a metaphysical reality, but a human, all-too-human delusion.

Nietzsche's middle period is usually regarded as the phase of his career during which he looked to the natural sciences for information about the world, about the contingent and ever-shifting empirical facts. This judgment is uncontroversial, I agree, if confined to the first two of the three books of this period (*Human, All Too Human* and *Dawn*). But by the time of *The Gay Science* Nietzsche is already expressing doubts about, and even outright rejections of, the idea that science has any more access to truth than do metaphysical modes of inquiry. Indeed, while maintaining a keen and informed interest in the natural sciences of his day, by this time he is very much in the way of thinking of science as one more expression of metaphysics, and he is already employing a falsificationist vocabulary to express himself on this theme.

In the present chapter of *Moby-Dick* Ishmael (still discoursing on the head of the whale!) remarks that every human science "is but a passing fable." Scientists tell stories, stories that shift and change with the times, stories that often are forgotten or intentionally erased from the record. These stories sometimes—perhaps usually—have their origins in facts, but so does most every other variety or genre of story, including even the most bizarre of ancient myths and legends. Yet over the course of the past half-millennium we (in the West in particular) have been persuaded to take the stories of science for transparent articulations of truth, and also to dismiss all other stories as quaint or pernicious fantasies. A cherished element of the rhetoric of scientific story-tellers is the conceit that their stories have the special property of being revisable, but in practice these prosaic bards resist revision by every possible means, from the introduction of ad hoc sub-plots to the denunciation of skeptics as unenlightened enemies of the truth-narrative. But this is just a mendacious disguise for what is in fact metaphysics all over again. As Nietzsche noted in *The Gay Science* when first declaring that "God is dead," the shadow of God does not die so easily, and men will project it inside their intellectual caves for millennia. This shadow is composed of a variety of shades, which Nietzsche sometimes sums up in the word Being, or, as in *The Gay Science*, "the God of the Eleatics," a reference to the followers of Parmenides (from Elea in southern Italy) who introduced the doctrine of Being into western philosophy. And as I have noted in the earlier chapter on falsificationism, the scientists' atom is as illegitimate a postulation of Being as the Platonists' Forms or the Christians' God.

In *Beyond Good and Evil*, a work of his "late period," Nietzsche suggests that "physics, too, is only an interpretation and exegesis of the world ... and *not* a world-explanation." Science, in short, is but a passing fable. And in the material he wrote a few months after completing *Beyond Good and Evil*, material he added as a fifth book to a second edition of *The Gay Science*, Nietzsche says that those who have "faith in science *thus affirm another world* than the world of life, nature, and history," and that "it is still a *metaphysical faith* upon which our faith in science rests," namely, the faith that "God is the truth, that truth is divine." Nietzsche implicates himself in this faith, for even he must struggle to overcome the intellectual and psychological pressures of millennia. Yet unlike the majority of his contemporaries who considered themselves "godless anti-metaphysicians"—and unlike our own contemporary "new atheist" types and like-minded disciples of scientism—Nietzsche was able to recognize his own metaphysical entanglements, and also to resist them. He understood these matters more precisely, if not more deeply, than Melville, for he had command of the relevant technical philosophical background. But Melville understood these matters too, if perhaps at a more intuitive level. "I try all things," his Ishmael says, "I achieve what I can." Melville achieved much intellectually that anticipated many of Nietzsche's later insights, and through Ishmael he expressed himself often in terms that Nietzsche would have appreciated, if only he had had the good fortune to encounter *Moby-Dick*.

Chapter 80: The Nut

In this chapter Ishmael finally concludes his tour of the whale's head, and here in conjunction with the previous chapter he conducts an investigation of the whale's face and cranium in a manner that "no Physiognomist or Phrenologist has as yet undertaken." Through his efforts he discovers a blank mask of a non-face concealing a "great genius," and a bulky mass inside of which resides an "indomitable" nature. The true nobility of the "monster" is not externally apparent to the inexperienced landsman, but this is so because the whale, "like all things that are mighty, wears a false brow to the common world."

Ishmael's study of the whale in these two chapters recalls Nietzsche's account of Socrates in *Twilight of the Idols*, for in this work Nietzsche reports the ancient story—most likely recorded in the *Zopyrus*, a Socratic dialogue written by the historical Phaedo—of the philosopher's encounter with a physiognomist who, after studying his face, concluded that Socrates was "a *monstrum*." But unlike the whale, indomitable and genius, Socrates was a monster hiding vices and weakness within. Socrates' external form was a mask for his decadence, but as the man was notoriously ugly, his was a transparent mask, revealing to the world the "anarchy of his instincts." Most mystifying to Nietzsche is the origin of the "Socratic equation of reason = virtue = happiness," and also the fact that Socrates managed to convince others to adopt this "most bizarre of all equations, which," Nietzsche says, "is opposed to all the instincts of the earlier Greeks." Eventually he concludes that the "fanaticism with which all Greek reflection throws itself upon rationality" was a consequence of a nearly universal decadence: Socrates' degeneration "was no longer exceptional," for "no one was any longer master over himself, the instincts turned *against* each other," and "to *have* to fight the instincts—that is the formula of decadence."

Nietzsche's diagnosis of Socrates in *Twilight of the Idols*, one of his last books, is in many ways consistent with his account of the philosopher in *The Birth of Tragedy*. In both works he portrays Socrates as the man who would cure human suffering through reason; he is the rational optimist who assists at the suicide of the tragic age of Greece. And as in *Twilight of the Idols* Nietzsche notes that Socrates' decadence was not exceptional, in *The Birth of Tragedy* he acknowledges that there must have been "an anti-Dionysian tendency operating even prior to Socrates," and that "the enormous driving-wheel of logical Socratism [was] in motion, as it were, *behind* Socrates, and … must be viewed through Socrates as through a shadow." So although, as we have seen, "Euripides was … only a mask" through which the anti-tragic Socrates spoke, Socrates was himself a mask from behind which a spreading decadence manifested itself in the world.

We are dealing now with layers upon layers of masks: decadence operates through a hideous mask of anarchic instincts; this fundamental physiological degeneration expresses itself through the mask of Socrates; Socrates speaks through the mask of Euripides; and through these various masks a single message is projected: reason equals virtue equals happiness, or as Nietzsche expresses the formula in *The Birth of Tragedy*, "Virtue is knowledge; man sins only from ignorance; he who is virtuous is happy." These are the "three basic forms of optimism," Nietzsche says, and in them "lies the death of tragedy." Rational optimism, then, is the Apollonian mask that through Socrates' efforts supplanted Dionysus's tragic mask, and the philosophy developed by the disciples of Apollo and Socrates, with Plato in the forefront, placed a mask of logical-conceptual intelligibility over the inscrutable non-face of reality, simplifying and falsifying it. So the falsificationism that we have considered in the previous few chapters is ultimately connected to the collapse of the tragic worldview as we have detailed it in these same chapters: decadence and reason, reason as a symptom of the elemental sickness of decadence, are the two poles capping this sphere of Nietzsche's analysis.

So far in this chapter we have considered masks almost exclusively as villains' disguises, the whale's case being the sole exception. But we must not forget that Ishmael is a mask through which Melville speaks, as Zarathustra is a mask through which Nietzsche speaks. And in both cases the mask is a medium for communicating exuberant health and power. I would add that the Platonic dialogues—and not just Socrates as a character in the works, but the works themselves *as wholes*—are masks through which Plato expressed his own great health, but, although Nietzsche once wrote that Plato was "really too noble" for "Socratism," and that in fact he had "the greatest strength any philosopher so far has had at his disposal," I am sure that in most of his moods Nietzsche would disagree with my assessment. Melville, I think, would have been ambivalent. Each one of these men might well have been surprised to find himself in company with the other two, but perhaps only so long as he resisted the urge to look behind his fellows' masks. For I can't help but believe that taking the opportunity to explore one another's depths, these men would recognize something of themselves in each of the others, this something being philosophy as art, and artistic philosophy as a manifestation of wisdom.

Chapter 81: The Pequod meets the Virgin

Since I intend in later chapters to discuss Melville's and Nietzsche's existential relation to their philosophical ideas and insights, I should provide some relevant biographical details. Therefore I take advantage of the opportunity provided by Ishmael's mention of a German virgin, and his description of a sickly blind old whale, to say something of Nietzsche's life and the various mental and physical ailments from which he suffered with increasing frequency and intensity from childhood to the moment of his shocking mental collapse, followed some eleven years later by his premature death.

Nietzsche was born in 1844 in the village of Röcken, in Prussian Saxony, and he passed his early childhood on the grounds of the Lutheran church of which his father was pastor, as his two grandfathers had also been Lutheran pastors. His father died young, just prior to his thirty-sixth birthday, when Nietzsche was only five years old, his younger sister three. The exact cause of death is unknown, but he raved at the end and was diagnosed as suffering from "softening of the brain." As one can imagine, the experience was traumatic for the fragile little Fritz. Throughout his life Nietzsche was terrified at the prospect of dying young himself, and also of descending into madness. In his autobiographical *Ecce Homo* he claimed to be "already dead as my father," and he noted that in his own thirty-sixth year, his life "went downward" and he reached "the lowest point of my vitality—I still lived, but without being able to see three steps ahead."

Following the death of her husband, Nietzsche's mother moved the family to the nearby city of Naumburg. Young Nietzsche was bright and talented, becoming particularly proficient at piano improvisation. Despite the pension his mother received from the church, the family was not well off, so it was no insignificant good fortune that Nietzsche eventually earned a scholarship to a renowned boarding-school called Schulpforta. Here he received the best possible classical education; and here, too, he was introduced to Plato, whose *Symposium* became a particular favorite. Apart from his studies of Greek and Latin, Nietzsche read and wrote poetry, studied and composed music. Life at Schulpforta was regimented and rigorous, but Nietzsche performed very well. Yet he cannot be said to have flourished physically. As a child he was slight and often sickly. He suffered from headaches and eyestrain, sometimes so severely that he had to be granted leave from his studies. Such ailments would dog him throughout his life.

From Schulpforta Nietzsche went to the University of Bonn, and from there to Leipzig. Originally intending to study theology, he abandoned his faith early on—perhaps while still at Schulpforta—and turned his attention exclusively to philology, to the study of the languages, literature, culture, and history of the ancient Greeks and Romans. Nietzsche excelled as a scholar, and he was celebrated as one of the best young academics of his generation.

During his time at university Nietzsche happened one day on Schopenhauer's work while browsing among the stacks of a local bookstore. He had already developed an interest in philosophy, though chiefly in a scholarly rather than a creative-intellectual way. His encounter with Schopenhauer brought him eventually to the point of seriously considering the possibility of living as a philosopher himself. Whatever hopes or plans he may have formulated to this end, however, were postponed by the surprise of an offer to join the faculty of the University of Basel, in Switzerland, as Professor of Philology. This was an unprecedented honor, for Nietzsche had not yet completed his degree. But the authorities at Leipzig conferred on him his Doctorate by counting for a dissertation the scholarly researches he had already published, and off he went to Switzerland.

Not long before accepting the post at Basel, Nietzsche met and impressed the great and controversial composer Richard Wagner. Though over thirty years distant in age, the two men developed a close friendship, and Nietzsche often visited the Wagners at their home in Tribschen near Lucerne, not far away from Basel by train. Wagner had been born the same year as Nietzsche's father, and for a time Nietzsche looked to the older man for something like paternal advice and approval. Wagner, for his part, employed the brilliant young professor as an emissary and promoter of his work, sometimes almost as his lackey. At first Nietzsche was happy to subordinate his personal interests and desires to those of the master, yet soon the pull of his own needs, the budding of his own destiny, drove him to assert some measure of independence. The two men eventually fell out, but during much of Nietzsche's decade at Basel the relationship was sound.

Early in his career at Basel Nietzsche published *The Birth of Tragedy*. The book was not well received by the broader philological community, for it was less a scholarly treatise than a philosophical-intuitive meditation informed by scholarship. The harsh reviews all but destroyed Nietzsche's professional philological career. He was only twenty-eight years old. He continued to write, however; but more and more his work was philosophical, and with the publication of *Human, All Too Human* during the end of his tenure at Basel he made the final transition out of philology into philosophy.

Nietzsche's eyestrain and headaches continued throughout his years at Basel, exacerbated by severe stomach ailments. Often he suffered so miserably that he could not work at all; for days on end he lay in bed straining to endure the pain. In 1876 he was granted a temporary leave from his academic duties, and his doctors insisted that he cease reading and writing altogether, or at least significantly curtail his work. This he could not bring himself to do. Although he managed to remain at Basel for a time, in 1879 he resigned for good. The university granted him a pension, and together with small inheritances and the occasional assistance of friends, these funds served him for the rest of his life.

After his relatively stable years as a university professor, Nietzsche lived the rest of his active life as an itinerant philosopher, still quite regularly assailed by "the torments that go with an uninterrupted three-day migraine, accompanied by laborious vomiting of phlegm," also the "eye trouble" that was "at times dangerously close to blindness." He settled into a routine of wintering in northern Italy and summering in Switzerland, with occasional return-trips to Germany, always on the lookout for the ideal meteorological and atmospheric conditions, which he believed to be necessary for contending with his now frustratingly regular bouts of illness. He continued to write and publish despite his many disabilities, but it must be said that no one much read him beyond the circle of his friends and acquaintances. Beginning with *Beyond Good and Evil*, he had to resort to financing the publication of his books from his own meagre store of funds.

Nietzsche's wandering life of voluntary exile from friends and family provoked in him extended periods of loneliness and sadness. He had a few friends in various cities across Europe, but he never remained in any one place long enough to cultivate deep and lasting attachments. Even the two or three friends whom we might regard as legitimate exceptions to this rule he visited only infrequently. He proposed marriage to women on one or two occasions, but the proposals were rash and motivated chiefly by transitory longings for a stable home-life and work-environment, not by love. Nietzsche never married nor engaged in any serious romantic relationship.

In 1881 Nietzsche discovered Sils-Maria, a small village in the Upper Engadine valley in southeast Switzerland, not far from the popular resort town of St. Moritz. He returned every summer from 1883 to 1888, the mountains, lakes, and crisp, clear air inspiring some of his greatest work. Here, while walking one day along the shores of a neighboring lake, he was overcome by the idea of the eternal return, which thought in one way or another informed all the rest of his life and work. Yet even in this idyllic environment Nietzsche was haunted by loneliness and ill health. A friend who sought him out in his room when he failed one day to turn up for lunch found him disheveled and distraught; he described to her the troubling hallucinatory visions that disturbed his sleep, and mentioning the circumstances of his father's death he inquired whether she thought he might go mad himself.

Eventually of course Nietzsche did succumb to insanity. The original diagnosis was untreated syphilis. Nietzsche apparently told one of his doctors that he had been infected with the disease, but a good many scholars active today—physicians among them—dispute the diagnosis. We know from testimony that as a student in college Nietzsche visited a brothel with friends, but he seems to have had no idea of their destination when they set out for the evening, and when he realized where his fellows had brought him he hurried to a piano to improvise songs while waiting for the others to return from the dark interiors of the establishment. I shall have more to say about Nietzsche's madness in a later chapter; for now I note only that after his death a friend insisted that Nietzsche could not have had syphilis, for, he said, he was certain the man had died a virgin.

Chapter 82: The Honor and Glory of Whaling

Taking the present chapter of *Moby-Dick*, in which Ishmael eulogizes "the great honorableness and antiquity" of whaling, for Melville's personal celebration of his own service aboard the whaleship *Acushnet*, I here put down some of the facts of his biography. Given the time and, in particular, the place of his birth, Melville's life in many particulars was utterly unlike Nietzsche's. In a sense they inhabited different worlds. Yet there are a few remarkable parallels and anti-parallels worth recording.

Melville was born in 1819, a full quarter century before Nietzsche, in New York City, a world away from the Nietzsches' little church-house in the village of Röcken. Far from being pastors, his two grandfathers had distinguished themselves as active participants in the Revolutionary War, and various branches of the extended family occupied the highest levels of society. But Melville's father Allan was an undisciplined man, and in 1830 he went bankrupt and relocated the family to the more affordable town of Albany. Not long thereafter he fell ill and soon, "by reason of severe suffering was deprive'd of his Intellect." To those who saw him he presented "the melancholy spectacle of a deranged man," and some feared that even if he managed to survive, he would live as "*a Maniac!*" He died within a month.

Herman Melville was still a child when beset by these traumatic events, and to compound his suffering he was taken out of school and made to work at the age of twelve. His formal education was thus interrupted for several years, during which period he labored at a variety of jobs, for example as a clerk in an Albany bank. He returned to school finally at the age of seventeen, but he stayed no more than six months, for the family could not afford the tuition. Hoping to mend his scattered and spotty education, he joined such groups as the Albany Young Men's Association for Mutual Improvement, the Ciceronian Debating Society, and the Philologos Society, but with no hope of attending university, and no prospects of steady employment, in 1839 he signed on with the crew of the *St. Lawrence* to sail from New York to Liverpool. He was away for four months, and when after a year back home he had still found no way to improve his position ashore, he enlisted to sail out of Fairhaven, Massachusetts, as a crewman on the whaleship *Acushnet*. Thus began his nearly four years of wild adventure on the high seas.

In February 1846, a little over one year after his return from the Pacific, Melville published his first book, *Typee*, in which he recounts his desertion from the *Acushnet* and his time among the cannibal tribe of Typee natives in the interior of Nuku Hiva, one of the Marquesas Islands in the South Pacific. The book was a popular sensation, as was his follow-up companion, *Omoo*. His third book, *Mardi*, began as yet another travel adventure but transmogrified into a strange sort of dense philosophical prose-poem. Melville's friend Evert Duyckinck, editor of the *Literary World*, noted the book's "poetry and wildness," and this formulation captures well the spirit of the work. It was not at all popular with Melville's established audience, and as a result it did not sell. Therefore in his next two books, which he dashed off back to back, each in the span of a mere two months, he returned to his own experiences at sea to construct more straightforward narratives. He wrote these works, he complained, as "two *jobs*, which I have done for money— being forced to it, as other men are to sawing wood." If only he were free to create according to the inspiration of his personal genius! Then he would follow his heart and compose "those sort of books which are said to 'fail.'" Sometime early in 1850 he set out to do precisely this.

Melville wrote *Moby-Dick* while under the various influences of Plato, Shakespeare, and Nathaniel Hawthorne, whose examples inspired him to strive for intellectual and literary greatness, his audience be damned. The book had its admirers, to be sure, Hawthorne among them, but Melville blundered when he declined his friend's offer to write a review of the work. In its day *Moby-Dick* was not regarded as the masterpiece it is now widely acknowledged to be. Melville was of course disheartened, shocked even, but by the time the book was released to the public he was already writing a novel for which he had even higher hopes, *Pierre*. *Moby-Dick* was a Leviathan of a book, but this new work would be even grander, a Krakens, as he put it in a letter to Hawthorne. Unfortunately, *Pierre* was vociferously condemned in the press, with some critics even denouncing the book as the product of a deranged mind. "Herman Melville Crazy," ran the headline of one review. With this disaster Melville's public life as an author came more or less to a close. He continued to write and publish for approximately five more years, but he never recovered the reputation his early works had gained him. He took then to writing poetry, which he released in small volumes later in life, though he produced also the monumental *Clarel*, a long epic poem full of philosophical interest. But more on this later.

Melville married in 1847, and he and his wife Elizabeth eventually had four children. His first child, Malcolm, died at the age of eighteen from an apparently self-inflicted gunshot wound. His second-born, Stanwix, died while away from home at the age of thirty-five. His youngest daughter seems to have despised him. Malcolm's death has occasionally been blamed on his father's absorption in his own work and consequent neglect of the family, also on his bitter severity. Melville had been living in relative obscurity for years by the time of his son's death, and he seems to have been generally morose and discontented. Hershel Parker remarks that a week in July of 1852, not long after he completed *Pierre*, and at only thirty-two years of age, was "the last week he would ever convince himself or anyone else that he was happy." There are reports of drinking and violence, but the stories are not well documented. Some members of Elizabeth's family disapproved of her husband, and they tried on more than one occasion to convince her to leave him. Some even believed that Melville was insane, but we have no good evidence to confirm their amateur diagnosis.

Sane by most every reasonable measure, Melville worked until the end, leaving various poems and an incomplete manuscript of *Billy Budd, Sailor* among his papers. Yet, like Nietzsche, for most of his life he labored in relative obscurity, and he did not live to experience the world-wide recognition of his genius. It is a shame, not only because he merited the honor, but also because if he had received it, we might have received in turn more work as powerful, as challenging, as sublime as *Moby-Dick*.

Chapter 83: Jonah Historically Regarded

Ishmael's playful treatment of naturalized versions of the story of Jonah and the whale recalls a scene from the beginning of Plato's *Phaedrus*. Socrates and his young friend Phaedrus are walking outside the city walls beside the river Ilisos. When they approach a suitable location for relaxing on the bank to converse, Phaedrus asks whether this is the spot from which the god Boreas snatched and carried off the princess Oreithuia, and he inquires also whether Socrates believes this mythical tale (*mythologêma*). Socrates replies that it would not be unusual if he doubted the story and devised some such clever counter-account as that a blast of the north wind (known as Boreas) blew the girl off the stones where she was playing, and since she died in this way she was said to have been taken by Boreas. He notes that this is the sort of revision that "wise men" impose on the tale, but it is clear from the context that his use of *sophoi* here is ironic. These are men who "devise clever (or spurious) accounts," and we might even say that they "play the sophist." In any case, Socrates remarks that although such naturalistic explanations are entertaining, they are the business of crafty men whom we must judge most unfortunate, for having revised this tale they will be obliged to apply the same treatment to the traditional accounts of all the other myths and legends, bringing them into accord with probability by employing a rustic or boorish sort of cleverness. Socrates has no leisure for such undertakings, for, he says, he is not yet able to satisfy the Delphic command to know himself. And how ridiculous to investigate external matters while not even knowing one's own self! Therefore he accepts the common opinions about these things, and rather than investigate them, he investigates himself.

Here we have a straightforward rejection of the project known today as demythologization. It is consistent with Socrates' reputation as the man who redirected philosophy from the study of nature to the investigation of human character. He wants to know, as he puts it in the *Phaedrus*, whether at heart he is a beast more complex and furious than the multiform creature Typhon, or whether he is a gentler and simpler animal, endowed by nature with a divine and modest character. This question is more urgent than all others, not just for Socrates, but for everyone. I should mention, however, that Socrates does not endorse adherence to traditional tales in all of the dialogues. To take just one example, in the *Euthyphro* he says that he has difficulty accepting such stories as those told of Cronos castrating his father Ouranos, of Cronos devouring his own children, and of his son Zeus later overthrowing him. He even speculates that his doubts about such stories are the cause of his being prosecuted for impiety. So perhaps we should say that Socrates', or Plato's, position on demythologization is vacillating, or ambivalent. It may be that Plato was not averse to reforming traditional myths when this involved purifying them of attributions of vice to gods and heroes, as for example in his own critique of Homer and the tragedians in the *Republic*, but that when the myths served to inculcate virtue he was for leaving them be.

Ishmael's take on the naturalizing of myths and legends is also somewhat ambivalent, in part because he presents believers and unbelievers alike as engaged in demythologization. The old man in his story, known as Sag Harbor, cannot believe that a whale could comprehend a man in his belly, or that a man once there could survive submersion in the whale's "gastric juices." But the bishops and ministers and biblical exegetes have formulated rejoinders to such doubts. Some note that Jonah need not have passed into the whale's stomach, and that he could have remained within its capacious mouth; others speculate that Jonah inhabited a dead whale, whose lifeless stomach no longer produced dangerously acidic fluids; still others insist that the biblical whale was not a whale at all, but rather a ship called "The Whale," or maybe it was only an inflated life-jacket to which Jonah swam for safety.

Ishmael denounces the arguments that motivated Sag Harbor's doubts as "foolish," as evidence of the man's "foolish pride of reason." Sag Harbor was "impious" (one of the charges brought against Socrates), and he engaged in an "abominable, devilish rebellion against the reverend clergy." But what of these clergymen themselves? Do they not exhibit precisely the same doubts as old Sag Harbor? They cannot accept the story of Jonah and the whale as related in scripture any more than he can. They too must demythologize the account, bringing it into accord with a rationalist, and naturalist, understanding of probability, before they can permit themselves to believe. If Sag Harbor is impious for doubting as he does, the faithful are as impious for their version of faith. Both trust reason—reason as informed by the assumptions of modern materialist science—more confidently than they believe the words they proclaim to have been inspirationally communicated by God.

In Nietzsche there is no such ambiguity. When he writes that "God is dead," he means it, and he intends "God" under every possible description, from God as a supernatural divine person to God as impersonal Being, from God as Truth to God as truth, God as morality, as purpose, meaning, or order, God as substance, atom, ego, I, God as anything other than the ceaseless play and flux of Becoming. "The total character of the world," Nietzsche writes just after announcing the death of God, "is in all eternity chaos." Belief in anything more is belief in God, or in a lingering shadow of God. But men do believe in more, even the so-called atheists. Thus Nietzsche wonders impatiently when we will "complete our de-deification of nature." He is eager to "*'naturalize'* humanity in terms of a pure, newly discovered, newly redeemed nature." By "redeemed" Nietzsche means "godless," and by "godless" he intends all that I have indicated above. This last point is essential, for it distinguishes Nietzsche from many of those who today imagine themselves his allies. Nietzsche opposed the typical scientific atheist—the naturalist, materialist, or physicalist—as vehemently as he opposed the theist. This fact is somewhat obscured by his appeals to science in the rhetorical war he wages against Christianity in *The Antichrist*. But when read carefully in the context of his other late works (the Third Essay of the *Genealogy* in particular), it is clear that he deploys science here as an enemy of his enemy, which does not make him any more friendly to science than he is to religion. As I have said, when Nietzsche declares that "God is dead," he means "God" under every possible description.

Chapter 84: Pitchpoling

Plato and Nietzsche are usually regarded as opposites: Plato is the paradigmatic philosopher of Being, Nietzsche the advocate of Becoming. But as one element of Nietzsche's inverted-Platonism is a suspicion of all such oppositions, I like to think that he might be persuaded that despite their many apparent doctrinal differences, *as philosophers* he and Plato share a good deal in common. Since the present chapter of *Moby-Dick* contains nothing of either narrative or philosophical interest, and since the topic fits well with the previous three chapters of this book, I shall in this chapter expand on the theme of Plato's and Nietzsche's existential commonalities, relating them both to Melville in this regard in the following chapter.

Plato's *Phaedrus* famously concludes with a comprehensive critique of writing. As Socrates puts it to his young companion, since written discourses cannot speak for themselves, they can neither answer questions nor rebut attempted refutations. Moreover, since they cannot be selective regarding their audience, they are as available to those who understand them as to those who misunderstand and misuse them. Therefore they forever require the aid and assistance of the author who originally produced them. Moreover, written words cannot effectively communicate or teach the truth in and through themselves; they can only remind the man who knows of the knowledge he has previously acquired by way of spoken discourse. From these considerations Socrates concludes that it is a disgrace to a writer to believe that in his work there is any great certainty or lucidity. The truth is that in written words there is necessarily much playfulness, and nothing written in either poetry or prose is worth taking particularly seriously.

This critique is usually read as Plato's indication to his audience that his dialogues are less valuable than face-to-face spoken exchanges between a teacher and a pupil, the sort of exchanges that in the dialogues we see Socrates engaged in, and that Plato himself presumably conducted as a teacher in his Academy. But I myself reject this interpretation, for Socrates goes on to say that the man who writes from knowledge and can defend his written words, and who can moreover explain why writings are trivial—this man, he insists, is a philosopher. And since Plato himself has demonstrated through this very dialogue that he understands and is able to accomplish these very things, he has thereby declared himself a philosopher. By implication, then, his writings must be works of philosophy. And since he has composed his dialogues so that they pose and reply to questions, since they are often sufficiently difficult or obscure to bar access to the uninitiated, and since moreover at their best, as in the *Phaedrus*, they flaunt their playfulness—what else but playful is a written critique of writing?—since all this is so, I for my part consider the dialogues inestimably valuable. Let us admit that by themselves they cannot teach the truth. But philosophy is not the love of truth; it is the love of wisdom. And it is not evident to me that wisdom is identical to knowledge of truth, nor is it evident that Plato equated wisdom with knowledge of truth. In this connection it is essential to keep in mind the distinction I have previously noted between Plato and Socrates. I myself am less interested in what the character Socrates happens to say in this or that dialogue than in the example that Plato the author has set by producing the corpus of dialogues. Socrates may claim on one occasion that writing is inferior to speaking, but Plato shows time and again that writing is worthy of a life-long expenditure of enormous amounts of time and energy. We have no idea of the nature of Plato's activities as a teacher, how much time he spent speaking with students or associates. But we can easily imagine how much work he put into the creative activity of writing, how much time he spent in solitude with his imagination, strolling quietly through gardens lost in thought, or sitting at a table scattered with notes and drafts of his written work. Plato was a philosopher, a lover of wisdom, and it seems to me that his love manifested in the artistry of thought exhibited in his dialogues.

In a book with the telling subtitle *Life as Literature*, Alexander Nehamas characterized Nietzsche as "the most writerly of philosophers." The appellation strikes me as appropriate, but only if we expand it to include Plato as well. For one man as for the other, I believe, "writing [was] ... the most important part of living." Like Plato, Nietzsche was a philosopher-artist, a type he wrote about himself as one who "knows in that he invents, and ... invents in that he knows." This formulation is from an early abandoned essay, but it is consistent with Nietzsche's description of genuine philosophers in *Beyond Good and Evil* as those for whom "'knowing' is *creating*." Note the scare-quotes around the word "knowing." And when in *Beyond Good and Evil* Nietzsche insists that scholars, scientists, and scientific philosophers must be regarded as mere "instruments of the philosopher and for that very reason ... a long ways from being philosophers themselves," he echoes again his earlier work, in which he wrote that science and knowledge must be directed by philosophy as "a form of artistic invention." Nietzsche is more overtly suspicious of the value of truth than Plato ever was, but this just demonstrates that elusive as he is, he is even more insistent than Plato on stressing the creative-artistic nature of philosophy.

In a passage recorded in one of his late notebooks Nietzsche refers to himself as "half artist, half bird and metaphysician." Admittedly, this is an odd formulation, especially since, as we have seen, Nietzsche liked to think of himself as an anti-metaphysician. I make sense of the note by associating the artistry with the metaphysics: Nietzsche is a creator of worldviews, or of thought-worlds. Unlike the typical metaphysician, who seeks insight into the objective and independently true nature of reality, Nietzsche plays with ideas like an artist, spinning "truths" from abysses as a painter summons landscapes from a blank canvas. This is not to say that he recognizes no constraints on his thinking, but rather that his constraints are self-imposed, like the conventions the Greek poets adopted in order to demonstrate their ability to master and overcome them, to "dance in their chains." Thus Nietzsche can describe himself also as possessing "an anti-metaphysical but artistic worldview." Here he places the emphasis on the act of creation, which implies the ultimate contingency of the created object, in contrast again to the typical metaphysician, who is after necessary truths.

To return once again to Nietzsche's early formulation of the philosopher-artist, we can in light of his later notes understand his attraction to the idea of "*indemonstrable* philosophizing." The philosopher as Nietzsche conceives the type is not primarily motivated by a desire to discover the truth; he is not moved to join with the scientist in generating testable hypotheses. When Nietzsche remarks that the "poorly demonstrated philosophy of Heraclitus possesses far more artistic value than do all the propositions of Aristotle," he does not fear the objection that Aristotle's propositions possess more empirical value and are therefore more valuable overall. By "artistic value" Nietzsche means to indicate the *highest* value. As he writes in *Beyond Good and Evil*, immediately following the assertion that the genuine philosopher's knowing is creating, the philosopher's "will to truth is—*will to power*."

Nietzsche had the bad habit of running together Plato the man, the philosopher-artist, with Platonic doctrine, with Platonism, and with what I have called *Phaedo*-Platonism in particular. The problem is not exclusive to Nietzsche, however, as we have seen. To this day scholars confuse Socrates' words with Plato's thoughts, and from these words they formulate the doctrines of Platonism and attribute this dogma to Plato himself. But if Plato was not a philosopher in the traditional mode, but rather a philosopher-artist, like Nietzsche himself, then we must be cautious when attempting to specify his personal beliefs. I contend that Plato's decision to compose dialogues as high art indicates that he identified the essence of philosophy with an activity distinct from Socrates' practice of public spoken dialectic. Plato practiced philosophy as a creative thinker and writer, which is to say as a philosopher-artist. He had this in common with Nietzsche, and with Melville too.

Chapter 85: The Fountain

In this chapter Ishmael wonders aloud whether whales discharge water or vapor from their spouts. He also shares details concerning his activities as a writer. This latter theme provides Melville the opportunity to draw back the narrative veil and permit his readers a glimpse of himself as the creative artist at work behind his protagonist. In the opening paragraph of the chapter Ishmael records "this blessed minute (fifteen and a quarter minutes past one o'clock P.M. of this sixteenth day of December, A.D. 1850)," and it is impossible to read this without visualizing Melville at his writing desk composing this very sentence. We know that he would normally be writing at this time of the afternoon, for he described his working day in a letter to Evert Duyckinck as beginning at 8:00 in the morning with the feeding of his animals in the barn, followed by his own breakfast, then, to quote the man himself, "I go to my workroom & light my fire – then spread my M.S.S. on the table – take one business squint at it, & fall to with a will. At 21/2 P.M. I hear a preconcerted knock at my door, which (by request) continues till I rise & go to the door, which serves to wean me effectively from my writing, however interested I may be." The rest of the day's business taken care of, he spends his evenings "in a sort of mesmeric state" in his room, and we can well imagine his condition, as he must by nightfall have already set sail on the seaways of his mind to plot the course of his next morning's writing session.

This first-hand account of a master-artist at work at the height of his powers is a precious gift. And when in the same letter to Duyckinck Melville reports, "I have a sort of sea-feeling here in the country, now that the ground is all covered in snow. I look out of my window in the morning when I rise as I would out of a port-hole of a ship in the Atlantic," we see the artist superimposed on the figure of Ishmael, who noted the date of his writing just three days after Melville penned this letter. It is of course important to distinguish authors from their literary creations, at least as an initial hermeneutic approach. But to insist on too wide a gulf between them may in some instances be misguided, and this caveat applies, I believe, to Melville and Ishmael. As narrator of *Moby-Dick* Ishmael is the medium through which Melville gave form to his own deep thoughts and expression to his exultant attitude. Writing away snug in an upstairs room on his farm in Pittsfield, snow on the ground outside and falling still, a fire meditatively crackling within, the magnificent Mt. Greylock looming in the distance beyond a frosty window, alone with his thoughts, memories and wild imaginings swirling, Shakespeare and Plato almost as near as Hawthorne in the neighboring village of Lenox, Melville sits and channels his soul into his work. He knows he is creating a masterpiece, a lasting work of art composed of salt-water, wood, and blubber, the whole infused with poetry and philosophy. Ishmael is not so much a creation as a projection: his story is Melville's allegorical account of the universe and our place in it, and his narrative approach is a manifestation of Melville's philosophical perspective.

Like Plato before and Nietzsche after him, Melville was a philosopher-artist, or perhaps in his case "artist-philosopher" would be more accurate. The reversal of word order marks a difference in content, but only on one level, and not the deepest. Melville was every bit as philosophical as Plato and Nietzsche, but philosophy was not his business: he was not trained in the technical terminology of the various schools, the historical passages of the arguments, the subtle nuances of concepts, or the interconnections and detailed implications of specific positions. He read primary and secondary philosophical literature, to be sure; but he read more widely, and with greater attention to detail, in the fiction and poetry of various ages and cultures. Let's not consider him a traditional philosopher then; but let's do acknowledge his place in the top-tier of philosophical novelists. Consider the following review of *Moby-Dick*, published in *John Bull* on October 25, 1851: "Who would have looked for philosophy in whales, or for poetry in blubber? Yet few books which professedly deal in metaphysics, or claim the parentage of the muses, contain as much true philosophy and as much genuine poetry as the tale of the *Pequod*'s whaling expedition." Now your typical professional academic philosopher would likely object that a book critic knows too little of serious philosophy to be trusted on this matter, but this would only demonstrate the spiritual poverty of professional academic philosophy. Melville's philosophy is nowhere near as conceptually sophisticated as Plato's or Nietzsche's, true; but it is as intuitively rich. And if philosophy is the love of wisdom, love as seeking a distant condition or as cherishing a present state, then setting aside extraneous technicalities, Melville was a philosopher.

Like all good philosophers Melville as Ishmael understands that "in this world it is not easy to settle ... plain things," and in fact he finds the plain things "the knottiest of all." But he is concerned as well with matters far other than plain, and when Ishmael mentions that he once composed "a little treatise on Eternity," one is reminded of Hawthorne's report of an evening spent with Melville discussing "time and eternity, things of this world and of the next ... and all possible and impossible matters." What is this but the record of a philosophical conversation? And consider the reflections with which Ishmael concludes the present chapter:

> And so, through all the thick mists of the dim doubts in my mind, divine intuitions now and then shoot, enkindling my fog with a heavenly ray. And for this I thank God; for all have doubts; many deny; but doubts or denials, few along with them, have intuitions. Doubts of all things earthly, and intuitions of some things heavenly; this combination makes neither believer nor infidel, but makes a man who regards them both with an equal eye.

There are elements here of Plato and Nietzsche both. The doubts recall Nietzsche, the intuitions Plato. But the reality resides at a deeper level. The passage rejects belief and unbelief alike, skepticism too. Penetrating beneath these attitudes, one discovers a broader, more encompassing perspective, an experimentally artistic perspective that explores ideas without a care for final destinations. He who rests must die, and the philosopher is a tireless wanderer—not as one who is lost, mind you; rather as one who creates and admires simultaneously, a cultivator of intellectual gardens forever strolling thoughtfully through the blooming byways of his mind.

Chapter 86: The Tail

Having investigated the whale's head with such exhaustive attention to detail, Ishmael in this chapter adverts to the tail, the main point of interest being a grace of movement combined with "a Titanism of power." If matter could be annihilated, this would be the instrument to perform the deed. Ishmael likens the associated beauty and might of a whale's tail to Goethe's chest, which upon viewing the dead man's corpse Eckermann described as powerful, broad, and arched. Goethe and Eckermann: these two names are not so well known today as they once were, but Goethe was famous among all cultured men and women in Europe and America from around the time he published *The Sorrows of Young Werther* in 1774, when he was only twenty-five, until his death at eighty-two. Johann Wolfgang von Goethe was a German novelist, poet, playwright, painter, naturalist, lawyer, and government official. His *Werther* contributed to the rise and influence of the *Sturm und Drang* movement, a precursor to Romanticism, but he is best known perhaps for his *Faust*. In later life he rejected the gloomy excesses of Romanticism, and in Weimar with his friend Schiller he advocated the order and harmony of Classicism. Goethe exercised a tremendous influence on the artistic and intellectual life of Europe for decades, and for many Europeans, Nietzsche included, he served as the paradigmatically complete human being. Nietzsche admired the fact that Goethe "disciplined himself to wholeness, he *created* himself," and he was fond of quoting Napoleon's remark upon meeting Goethe, "*Voilà un homme*," which Nietzsche took to imply "Here is a *great* man!" Over the course of Goethe's last decade of life his secretary Johann Eckermann recorded his talks with the master, which he published under the title *Gespräche mit Goethe* (*Conversations with Goethe*), a work Nietzsche judged the best book in the German language. He respected "Goethe's paganism with a good conscience," and he was particularly pleased that he and Goethe were in agreement "about the 'cross,'" an allusion to a poem in which Goethe completes a list of four things he abominates with the printed image of a cross. Nietzsche lavishes his highest praise on Goethe when he labels his affirmative faith in the whole, his version of *amor fati*, "Dionysian."

Melville was more skeptical of Goethe, even of his spiritual disposition. In a letter to Hawthorne written while he was at work on *Moby-Dick*, Melville ridicules Goethe's pantheistic tendencies. He had read in a collection of the great man's sayings, "so worshipped by his votaries," the line, "Live in the all," which Melville glosses as the claim that "your separate identity is but a wretched one," coupled with the advice to "get out of yourself, spread and expand yourself, and bring to yourself the tinglings of life that are felt in the flowers and the woods, that are felt in the planets Saturn and Venus, and the Fixed Stars." Melville mockingly wonders what good this is to a man with a toothache. The very idea, he says, is "nonsense" and "flummery." He does admit in the postscript that "there is some truth in" Goethe's feeling for the all, but he objects to Goethe's insisting, as men are inclined to do, "upon the universal application of a temporary feeling or opinion."

As is also the case respecting Emerson, Melville is less willing than Nietzsche to overlook the otherworldly tendencies in Goethe. He is, however, more susceptible than Nietzsche to the lure of the unworldliness of Jesus, at least as an ideal. His Ishmael respects "the peculiar practical virtues of [Jesus's] teachings," even while admitting to the Nietzschean thought that there was no "power" in the man besides "the mere negative, feminine one of submission and endurance." Melville's objection was less to the cross than to the un-Christian behavior of the men who profess to revere it. The submissiveness of the Christian ideal is the element that Nietzsche (with Goethe) most despised. To his mind Christianity is a "slave morality" that caters to the weak and the failures among men. "In Christianity," he writes in *The Antichrist*, "neither morality nor religion has even a single point of contact with reality." This, he says, proves that the typical Christian is decadent. For "who alone has good reason to lie his way out of reality? He who suffers from it. But to suffer from reality is to be a piece of reality that has come to grief."

Nietzsche is willing on occasion to regard Jesus's particular version of submission to his enemies a higher form of freedom, a manifestation of a way of life that affirms all events, and to count this as his authentic teaching, his true "glad tidings," having nothing to do with sin, guilt, punishment, or a life beyond this world—the kingdom of heaven is already at hand, in the heart. But this good news was corrupted by theologians and the church, refashioned into "instruments of torture, systems of cruelties by virtue of which the priest became master, remained master." In short, ecclesiastical doctrines of submission have been designed precisely to oppose the lesson that Jesus taught through his actions: he pointed the way to an all-affirming freedom, whereas the church in his name has led men into a new form of slavery. There is something in common here with Melville's disdain for worldly adaptations of the gospel message for the sake of utilitarian benefit and practicality.

Ishmael remarks that a whale's diving beneath the surface of the sea, when "out of the bottomless profundities the gigantic tail seems spasmodically snatching at the highest heaven," may bring to mind devils or archangels depending on one's mood. So it is with Melville and Nietzsche on religion, if we may take "mood" as a synonym for shifting perspectives. Neither man was a simple believer or unbeliever, ally or enemy. Like all subtle thinkers they found both good and bad in, for example, Christianity, depending on the perspective from which they viewed it. Yes, even Nietzsche, who in one place condemns Christianity as "the one immortal blemish of mankind," acknowledges in another that through the "*essentially dangerous*" efforts of the Christian priest "man first became an *interesting animal*," that only through priestcraft did "the human soul in a higher sense acquire *depth* and become *evil*." Christian self-examination generated depth of soul by digging into the human animal's previously thin layer of consciousness, excavating basement levels beneath it. The psychic expansion weakened man as an animal, but precisely in this peculiar form of weakness is his superiority.

Chapter 87: The Grand Armada

There is something of Captain Ahab in Nietzsche, Ahab as the perpetual philosopher; and there is something of Nietzsche in the Captain, the audacious rebelliousness, the unsettled drive to destruction. The agitation is a trait of the philosopher in contrast to the serenity of the sage, and measured against that standard, a failing. But in an age from which wisdom has withdrawn, when seeking is a prerequisite to possessing, the philosopher is an exemplary type. The matter then is the method or mode of one's philosophizing, or rather the existential bearing of oneself as a philosopher, for philosophy is a way of life first, and a technique of rational thinking second, or third, or—

The present chapter of *Moby-Dick* is in places mesmerizingly beautiful. Ishmael recounts his sojourn floating in a placid pool centrally separated from the sea by a vast circling and counter-swimming pod of whales. Towed within the interior of the rotating circuits by a furious whale harpooned by Queequeg, Ishmael and the others aboard his whaleboat find themselves "in that enchanted calm which they say lurks at the heart of every commotion." An idyllic image, this, of a tranquil peace in the eye of every storm. But for all that, a false image. The interior of a frenzied soul such as Ahab's, the soul of a man lost in the labyrinths of philosophy, so long diverted from the winding way leading out of the maze in the direction of wisdom that he neither recalls nor even cares to find it—at the core of such a tempestuous soul howls a still more furious whirlwind.

The purest portrait of serenity in this chapter is a Platonic image of a newborn calf floating beneath the transparent waters just off the side of Ishmael's little boat. Nursing at his mother's breast, the infant whale gazes dreamily toward some distant, invisible reality. It is as if he were "leading two different lives at the time; and while yet drawing mortal nourishment ... still spiritually feasting upon some unearthly reminiscence." The image recalls Plato's description in the *Phaedo* of the process whereby human souls enter at birth the physical world from out of the spiritual realm of the metaphysical Forms, whose Being and Truth they contemplated in their pre-embodied state. The sensory pressures and excitations of corporeal embodiment, beginning from the very moment of birth, distract the infant, which then forgets the truth it formerly beheld in the Forms. But knowledge of reality is still present, submerged in the soul, and through proper philosophical training the purified soul may raise and recollect it. Plato stresses forgetting and remembering, whereas Ishmael imagines an embodied soul somehow still in touch with its former spiritual abode, reminiscing after a change of location and state, but having forgotten nothing. It is an image of a soul never finally severed from wisdom, and thus perhaps in no need of chasing after it.

Ahab represents the radical contrast to Ishmael's Platonic vision of an eternally binding spiritual connection to truth. As the *Pequod* in this chapter is pursued by pirates, while itself in frantic pursuit of a vast herd of whales, Ahab is "both chasing and being chased to his deadly end." Here we have a man engaged in a feverish activity resembling, but actually other than, seeking as the philosopher seeks. The Captain is not moved by a love of wisdom; he is motivated by hatred. He pursues no Platonic recollection of past communions with sublime truth; he is rather running away from such memories, fleeing from his previous encounter with Moby Dick, foolishly attempting to forget the great whale-God by murdering it. It is one thing to believe with Nietzsche that God is dead; it is quite another to believe in a living God yet lust to kill him. Ahab's forehead reveals his tormented condition: it is "gaunt and ribbed, like the black sand beach after some stormy tide has been gnawing it, without being able to drag the firm thing from its place." Ahab is both beach and tide—dark, raging, suffering; simultaneously battering and battered, tearing and torn. His soul is not at peace; he lacks even the relative calm of the agitated seeker. He does not love wisdom; he rages against it. Therefore he will find no eternal life, neither of the Platonic nor the Nietzschean variety. Nor will he succeed in vanquishing his God. Having transmogrified his divinity into a beast through the workings of his own monstrous thoughts, he will suffer and die by it too.

Ishmael is altogether different: as narrator of *Moby-Dick* he has attained the tranquility of the sage. As a sailor he was a seeker, and he shares with his audience the wildest of those adventures that led him to wisdom. But introspective as he is, he also provides insight into the nature of his present psychic condition: "amid the tornadoed Atlantic of my being," he writes, "do I myself still for ever centrally disport in mute calm; and while ponderous planets of unwaning woe revolve round me, deep down and deep inland there I still bathe me in eternal mildness of joy." This is a description of one who refuses to ignore the bitter actualities of life, and the inexorable advance of death, because he possesses the inner fortitude to confront reality square on. As I have expressed the matter previously, Ishmael regards the accursed questions without regarding them *as* accursed. In Nietzschean terms, he fights monsters without becoming a monster himself.

Nietzsche's Zarathustra considers significant the insight that mountains arise from the sea, for this teaches the lesson that "it is out of the deepest depth that the highest must come to its height." Nietzsche aspired to reach his

217

personal summit, to live continuously the joyful wisdom that occasionally he
expresses in his work, but it is hard to determine whether he succeeded to his
own satisfaction. His Zarathustra was no unalloyed projection of himself, of a
state he had attained. Zarathustra was an ideal that Nietzsche held up to
himself as a goal. Perhaps he could have embodied it, one day; but he died
too young, twice. Melville managed to live his joyful wisdom, for a time.
Ishmael's narrative voice is an expression of Melville's personal perspective.
But Melville lived too long. He scaled his summit from out of his sea, but
gravity proved too strong, and he fell back to earth.

Chapter 88: Schools and Schoolmasters

"Now, as the harem of whales is called by the fishermen a school," Ishmael
explains, "so is the lord and master of that school technically known as the
schoolmaster." Melville and Nietzsche were schoolmasters, as I have noted,
though their charges were not harem girls but "young and vigorous males."
The identity of title vaguely expressed should not mislead us, however;
teachers or schoolmasters they were, but while Melville was only barely
credentialed to teach in a small district schoolhouse, Nietzsche was as
thoroughly credentialed as a European academic could be.

I have mentioned the death of Melville's impoverished father in early
1832, when Herman was but twelve years old. His widowed mother could not
support her eight children, and Herman was forever in search of profitable
work. Although his education had been "irregular" and "spotty, to put the
matter in the best light," he somehow managed to secure a position in the
Sikes District School, near Pittsfield, Massachusetts, from 1837 to 1838. He
was only eighteen years old, and his students were "of all ages, sizes, ranks,
characters, & education," as he explained in a letter to an uncle. They seem to
have been an uneducated lot, many of the teenagers being unable even to
perform simple arithmetic. And unruly, too: a story perhaps originating with
Melville himself relates an actual physical altercation between the teacher and
two of his older pupils. All in all, his experience at Sikes was not particularly
educative for anyone involved.

Returning home at the end of his term, Melville attempted to reconstitute
the moribund Philologos society, and when the members deposed the
president and elected Melville in his place, he became embroiled in a

controversy that played out by way of letters printed in a local paper, letters that Melville signed "Philologean." He was at least still trying to fill the gaps in his spotty education.

In the fall of 1839, following his voyage to Liverpool, Melville was hired to teach once again, this time at the Greenbush & Schodack Academy, near Albany. There was some hope in the family that he might earn a living at the school, but by 1840 the academy was faltering financially. Melville received no pay, and eventually the school itself disbanded. From Greenbush he went to Brunswick to teach, but once again the authorities neglected to reimburse him for his services. Unable to find any other work near home, he travelled west to an uncle's farm in Illinois. When this adventure also failed to pay off, he abandoned his hopes for employment and sailed to sea on the whaleship *Acushnet*.

Melville's failed career as a teacher opened and closed before Nietzsche was born. He went to sea early in 1841 and returned in October of 1844, the very month of Nietzsche's birth. Not long thereafter he began his career as a popular author, which started out so promisingly with the success of his first two tales of seafaring adventure, but eventually declined, precipitously, and concluded altogether well before Nietzsche began his own life as a teacher. His last prose work, *The Confidence-Man*, appeared in 1856; and when Nietzsche accepted the position of Professor Extraordinary of Classical Philology at Basel University in 1869, Melville was all but forgotten.

Nietzsche, for his part, was thriving: he was an officially credentialed philologist, and a nineteenth-century German philologist at that, which is to say an academic trained to a height and breadth of humanistic learning that few other academics have attained in the history of universities. Melville's signature of "Philologean" is touching by comparison. He had attended a "Latin School" for a time, but he knew nothing of rigorous philology. As Nietzsche moved to Basel, Melville was laboring as an inspector at the Customs House in New York City, a reliable but dreary post he accepted in 1866 and would maintain for almost two decades.

In the end, Nietzsche's academic career was no great success; other academics would consider it a failure. But Nietzsche was expanding intellectually beyond the confines of university life. He was bursting his mold of academic philologist and making himself into a "free spirit," a philosopher. By the end of his university career he was excitedly writing to friends of his determination to be a philosopher, whereas formerly he had only admired philosophers and sages from afar.

I should not conclude this chapter without making clear that although Melville finally admitted the truth that had become evident to others well before *The Confidence-Man*, namely that he could not support himself and his family as an author, he did not give up writing altogether. He abandoned prose for the most part, to be sure; but he gradually refashioned himself as a poet. He completed a book of poetry in 1860, but to his dismay the publishers rejected the manuscript. In 1866 he published a collection of Civil War poems entitled *Battle-Pieces and Aspects of the War*, but no other work followed this until *Clarel* appeared a full decade later in 1876. Melville formulated the idea for this epic narrative poem in 1869, the year Nietzsche began teaching at Basel, but to complete the work required four years or more of attention and labor. He privately printed the collection *John Marr* in 1888, Nietzsche's final active year as an author, and *Timoleon* in 1891. For the most part Melville's contemporaries ignored his published poetry, and his failure as a poet exacerbated the anger, confusion, and depression that cast such long shadows over his later years. From the height of *Moby-Dick* Melville sank to the depths of utter anonymity. Nietzsche was no more publically accomplished, but he struggled with some success to resist the bleak moods to which he too was susceptible.

Chapter 89: Fast-Fish and Loose-Fish

In this and the following chapter Ishmael humorously explains the legal niceties involved in the distinction between a "Fast-Fish," which by law "belongs to the party fast to it," and a "Loose-Fish," which "is fair game for anybody who can soonest catch it." The terms are specifically applicable to the fishery, but Ishmael is happy to stretch their signification. For instance, he employs the category Loose-Fish to comprehend such various phenomena as "America in 1492," "all men's minds and opinions," and even "the great globe itself." And we humans, we are "Loose-Fish and Fast-Fish, too," he says. Availing myself of the semantic latitude provided by Ishmael's expansive understanding of these terms, in this chapter I discuss Melville as a man fast to his family, and then, in the next chapter, Nietzsche as an unmarried individual loose in the world.

Melville came of age at a time when it was expected by every relevant party that he would marry and raise a family. Even after his exposure to a blooming diversity of social arrangements during his wanderings abroad in foreign cultures, he seems to have fallen into thinking in conformity with traditional familial customs immediately upon returning home. He took up courting his future wife Elizabeth Shaw the very month his ship made port in New York. The two were engaged at the end of August 1846, when the success of *Typee* convinced Melville that he might at last have found a way to earn a steady living, and they married eleven months later, after his second novel, *Omoo*, proved another hit. Elizabeth was a lively and popular young woman, well-educated and prosperous, daughter of the Chief Justice of the Massachusetts Supreme Court. She and Herman cared deeply for one another, and they stayed together through many grim days. Melville's last book of poetry, left just barely incomplete at his death, was a collection of verses dedicated to his wife. As devoted as they were, however, and to state the matter bluntly, Melville's life as a family man ruined him as an artist.

Melville's mother and four sisters were dependent on him as the oldest male in the family (following the premature death of his brother Gansevoort in 1846). The entire brood moved with him and Elizabeth into their first home, a residence on Fourth Avenue in New York City. To afford the place Melville borrowed money from Elizabeth's father and his own younger brother's new bride (this brother and sister-in-law moved into the new house with everyone else). When in 1850 he bought the farm in Pittsfield, Massachusetts, which he named Arrowhead and on which he wrote the majority of *Moby-Dick*, his mother and three of his sisters followed him there. He borrowed money for this expense too, a loan he was never able to repay from his personal resources. He kept these dealings secret for years, and the stress he suffered from repeated defaults on his payments was psychologically debilitating. Finally, in 1856 he confessed the facts to his father-in-law, who generously loaned him money once again, but even with this aid, in order to square his finances Melville was forced to sell off one-half of his beloved property. These events occurred as he was writing the novel that would turn out to be his last, *The Confidence-Man*, from which he earned no money whatever.

In a letter he wrote to Hawthorne while working on *Moby-Dick*, Melville complained of the deleterious effects of his finances on his art. "Dollars damn me," he confessed, "and the malicious Devil is forever grinning in upon me, holding the door ajar… What I feel most moved to write, that is banned, – it will not pay. Yet all together, write the *other* way I cannot. So the product is a final hash, and all my books are botches." Melville believed—I should say that he *knew*—that he was composing a great book, and it agitated him that he was unable to dedicate to his craft the energy and attention the work required. His farm was in need of various repairs, the land and livestock required attention, he had a wife and son to care for, a second child on the way, and of course there were also his mother and sisters to look after. As he summed up his situation to Hawthorne, he simply had no access to the "calm, the coolness, the silent grass-growing mood in which a man *ought* always to compose."

After finally settling the finances relating to his farm, Melville sailed to Europe, toured Italy and Greece, and journeyed on horseback through the Holy Land. All this on funds borrowed from his father-in-law, who loaned him the money primarily because the family was worried about his health, his mental health in particular. After crossing the Atlantic Melville stopped in Liverpool, where he visited Hawthorne (serving in the city as United States Consul) for the first time in years. Later in his journal Hawthorne wrote that Melville appeared pretty much the same as he remembered him, but "perhaps a little sadder." He noted also that Melville's recent writings "indicated a morbid state of mind." Two years later, in the spring of 1859, two young admirers (a rare breed in those days) paid Melville a visit on his farm in Pittsfield. One of the two reported that Melville's "countenance [was] slightly flushed with whiskey drinking," and he added that Melville was "evidently a disappointed man, soured by criticism and disgusted with the civilized world." The other noted in a letter to his parents that Melville's "air is that of one who has been soured by opposition and criticism … and his attitude seemed to me that of a man whose hand is against every man's and every man's against him."

I shall have more to say about Melville's biography throughout the remainder of this book; it will not reveal a man particularly contented with his life. His failure to support himself by writing in accord with his personal genius was part of his problem; another was the fact of unrelenting obligations to his family that distracted him from the solitude and leisure he required as an artist. As Melville's niece Charlotte Hoadley concluded from the testimony of her aunts and other uncles, Melville "was absolutely unfitted for prosaic marriage life, but was expected to fill that role." In this connection

I find it illuminating to regard Melville as an example of a Nietzschean "higher type" brought low by the pressures of his time and place, living among people with values contrary to his needs as a thinker and an artist. Thus we might say in Nietzsche's terms that Melville succumbed to the bad-conscience of his time: it was then at least marginally acceptable to wander at sea, but to remain a bachelor ashore was all but intolerable; eventually one had to settle down and abide by customary usages. But the presuppositions and the consequences of a bourgeois life tend to impede the growth and free expression of a mind and spirit such as Melville possessed. Nietzsche once observed that "there are few pains as sore as once having seen, guessed, felt how an extraordinary human being strayed from his path and degenerated," and he expressed his dismay at "what wretched things have so far usually broken a being of the highest rank that was in the process of becoming, so that it broke, sank, and became contemptible." Melville did not become contemptible, but probably it would have been better for his art had he lived as Nietzsche lived, if not necessarily isolated—for Melville was good in company, and being in company with literary-intellectual peers was good for him, when he indulged, which was infrequently—if not necessarily isolated, then, at least as a bachelor, certainly as a bachelor for more years than he managed. The business of being a husband, father, and caretaker of an extended family interfered too much, and too perniciously, with Melville's intellectual and creative energies. At a bare minimum he required an inheritance or some other such source of labor-free income sufficient to support a large family, and also perhaps his own taste for travel. Nietzsche, unmarried, with a pension and inherited funds, and content with modest accommodations, was not so encumbered. He was lonely, and he suffered, to be sure. But as a loose-fish he enjoyed many hours alone in the silence of those grass-growing moods that enabled him to create as he wished without distraction.

Chapter 90: Heads or Tails

Elizabeth Förster-Nietzsche, the philosopher's sister, wrote a two-volume biography of her brother. She entitled the second volume *Der einsame Nietzsche*, the *lonely* Nietzsche. The book is notoriously unreliable, but Elizabeth managed to capture a truth in the title. She dates the beginning of

Nietzsche's years of isolation to the breakdown of his relationship with Wagner, who had for so long served not only as a father-figure to the much younger Nietzsche, but also as an intellectual and creative inspiration. But Nietzsche eventually came to regard the composer as a self-serving egotist dedicated to an unhealthy style of music founded on a tenuous grasp of philosophical principles. He had an especial distaste for the numerous acolytes and lackeys who surrounded Wagner, sacrificing their independence to further the mission of the master. Nietzsche's feelings for Wagner began to change most radically in 1876, the year the composer inaugurated the Bayreuth festival with the first performances of his *Ring* cycle. Nietzsche had accompanied Wagner in his personal carriage on the day he laid the cornerstone of the *Festspielhaus* on the site the grand new edifice now occupied. Here at last was the culmination of Wagner's efforts over the course of many years, efforts that Nietzsche had supported with all the enthusiasm of a young believer. But by 1876 he was no longer the awed enthusiast he once had been. He attended a few of the festival rehearsals, but he could stomach neither the dramas themselves nor the atmosphere pervading the event. Therefore he fled Bayreuth before the official commencement of the performances, nor did he return to attend them. He had published a predominately laudatory essay, "Richard Wagner in Bayreuth," timed to coincide with the festival, but the piece included early indications of his disillusionment. In fact it concluded with the judgment that Wagner was not "the seer of a future, as he would perhaps like to appear to us, but the interpreter and transfigurer of a past." Wagner had conceived of his music-dramas as *Zukunftmusik*, music of the future, so Nietzsche's remark is especially cutting. Later he would claim for himself the role of prophet of, perhaps even inaugurator of, the "Philosophy of the Future," which expression he used for the subtitle of *Beyond Good and Evil*.

Near the end of 1876 Malwida von Meysenbug, desiring to facilitate Nietzsche's recovery from the anxieties associated with his separation from Wagner, invited him with his friend Paul Rée and others to join her for an extended vacation in Sorrento, Italy. During their stay Nietzsche began the book that would become *Human, All Too Human*, a work he regarded as an expression of a philosophical perspective opposed to all that had bound him to Wagner. Wagner and his wife Cosima stayed in Sorrento for a time during this period, in a hotel not far from Nietzsche's residence in the Villa Rubinacci. Malwida and her guests visited the Wagners on several occasions, but Nietzsche and Wagner could no longer relate on the intimate and easy terms that had characterized the earlier phase of their friendship. After Sorrento they never met again.

Though Nietzsche repudiated Wagner's work and said so publically time and again—for instance in two anti-Wagner tracts, *The Wagner Case* and *Nietzsche Contra Wagner*—nevertheless he could neither forget nor regret the time he spent in Wagner's company. Late in life he recalled these years as by far his happiest period. He would, he said, let all his other friendships go for one day of his relationship with Wagner. To come into his own Nietzsche had to reject Wagner, but the pain of separation never subsided.

Though Nietzsche never again would be so close to another individual as he had been to Wagner, he suffered from other failed relationships. Recollecting in *Ecce Homo* the period during which he conceived his *Zarathustra*, he writes of melancholy, sickness, despair, and loneliness. He is thinking most likely of his tumultuous relationship with Lou Salomé, a brilliant young Russian whom he regarded for a time as a student and disciple, and potentially even a wife. The two were drawn together immediately upon meeting, bound in particular by intellectual affinities, but their fast friendship soon degenerated into a melodramatically torturous ordeal of misunderstanding and hurt feelings. Nietzsche was thirty-seven when they met, but he was altogether innocent of romance, and he seems not to have understood his own emotions. When Lou showed a preference for Paul Rée, Nietzsche felt abandoned, scorned even. Brooding on the tangled affair, he occasionally succumbed to embarrassing fits of self-pity, bitterness, and rage. He had lived a nomadic, solitary life since leaving Basel in 1879, but in the aftermath of this relationship he felt more alone than he ever had before; he suffered terribly and regarded himself thereafter as a pagan hermit.

In contrast to the suffering and solitude that attended the birth of *Zarathustra*, in *Ecce Homo* Nietzsche stresses "the Yes-saying pathos" that, he says, "was alive in me to the highest degree" in the period leading up to his writing the first of the book's four parts. His relationship with Salomé laid him low, but his Zarathustra understands that great men ascend to their heights by way of their depths. Throughout his career Nietzsche insisted that art is born of suffering, that art redeems, provides solace, and can manifest as an expression of power through which a fundamentally healthy man overcomes every onslaught of illness and depression. In Nietzsche's case "art" means his own books. He wrote straight through his many physical, psychological, and financial hardships, to some extent despite them, but also in a sense because of them, in a way that Melville could not manage. Gloomy bouts of loneliness and suffering attended Nietzsche's existence as a Loose-Fish alone in the world, but his freedom from the sort of responsibilities that burdened Melville enabled him to manage his pressures differently. He was at liberty to channel most all of his energy into his thinking and his art, and "thus there seems a reason in all things," as Ishmael says, even in philosophy.

Chapter 91: The Pequod meets the Rose-bud

The next two chapters of *Moby-Dick* revolve around the noxious stench of blasted whales, which is to say those whales that have "died unmolested on the sea," and also whales that have died "with a sort of prodigious dyspepsia, or indigestion," with the result that little or no blubber can be boiled out of them. The odor of such whales is at times so unbearably pungent as to stink worse than "an Assyrian city in the plague, when the living are incompetent to bury the departed." Ishmael's concern with malodorous smells in these two chapters recalls Nietzsche's fondness for writing about the extraordinary capacity of his nose to sniff out base and corrupted souls. He writes in such terms particularly in *On the Genealogy of Morals* and *Ecce Homo*, in connection with his analysis of an historical event that he sometimes calls "the slave revolt in morals," and which we may think of in broad terms as the genesis and establishment of the Christian world on the wrecked foundations of the ancient Greek and Roman cultures.

In the first essay of the *Genealogy* Nietzsche complains that "Europe is beginning to stink" of a "surfeit of ill-constituted, sickly, weary and exhausted people." He is thinking of European man as shaped by almost two thousand years of Christian culture, which has managed over the course of many long centuries to displace the ancient "master morality" with the presuppositions and doctrines of "slave morality." According to Nietzsche's account in the *Genealogy*, the ancient Greek and Roman nobles lived by a code of conduct suitable to warriors overflowing with health and strength, men who expressed their power through warfare, adventure, athletics, and the hunt. These men displayed consideration, tact, friendship, and loyalty to their equals, but among inferiors they were careless, taking so little notice of others that often they were brutal and cruel to outsiders. Not from hatred, mind you, but from indifference. In their lives and activities they stood so far above the lower ranks of society that usually they simply took no notice of them, and thus they had no regard for them. Nietzsche terms the ancient nobles "masters" or master-types, in contrast to the "slave" or slave-types of the lower orders. These two designations are somewhat figurative, for although they encompass literal masters and slaves, they are not limited to them. They are really short-hand labels for members of different classes or castes who embody different systems of value, and who by living in conformity with their different values live as different types of men.

Members of the master caste of the ancient warrior nobility act spontaneously for self-generated ends; they seek admirable enemies the better to express their own greatness; they do not hate their adversaries so much as affirm themselves through their dealings—even hostile dealings—with them. These master-types evaluate men in terms of "good" and "bad." The concept "good" is the originary concept of master morality, and it derives from the masters' self-affirmation. It is not a moral but a social-political term designating in the first place the individual who speaks it and in the second place the other members of his caste. With the word "good" a noble intends little else than, "I myself and those who are like me in being well-born, powerful, beautiful, and free." The concept "bad" is to the nobles an afterthought, a belated acknowledgement of the fact that lesser men live among them, anonymous ignoble men who scrape by in life as servants of their needs, their appetites, or their masters. The bad are "contemptible" and "base," and these bad men constitute the class of "slaves."

Among the men of the lowest caste there eventually arises a mode of evaluation formulated in terms of opposition to the masters. This is the so-called slave morality. As servile men the slave-types are unhappy with their lot in life, but they are incapable of ameliorating or overthrowing the conditions that keep them down. Foremost among these conditions is the existence of noble warriors against whom the lower orders are powerless to rebel by force. Stewing long in their impotence and resentment, these lower orders eventually denounce their oppressors as "evil," and with this concept slave morality is born. This origin of slave morality in a radical condemnation of the other illustrates the fact that the action of the slave-type is always a reaction; he defines himself primarily through rejecting his opposite, whom he hates as a villain. Whereas master morality originates in the "good" of self-affirmation, slave morality springs from the concept "evil" that functions to vilify others, these others being precisely the good of master morality, the masters themselves. The "good" of slave morality comes last; it designates the weak, cowardly, and powerless members of the lowest social caste, though of course they do not themselves employ such pejorative terms: they make virtues of their vices with words like "patient" and "forgiving." This alteration in the meaning of value terms, whereby for example "impotence which does not requite" is termed "goodness of the heart," and "subjection to those one hates" is labelled "obedience"—Nietzsche calls this the manufacturing of ideals, which is to say the generation of a new code of values through which a new culture, and a new type of man, come into being. Imaginatively peeking through a window of the workshop in which such moral-alchemical transformations are accomplished, Nietzsche's sense of smell is offended. He must, he says, "*close* my nose."

I have recently reported the observations of two young men who visited Melville in 1859, one of them describing the author as "disgusted with the civilized world." He went on to add that Melville was disgusted also with "our Christendom in general and in particular," and he further summarized Melville's stated views as follows: "The ancient dignity of Homeric times afforded the only state of humanity, individual or social, to which he could turn with any complacency. What little there was of meaning in the religions of present day had come down from Plato. All our philosophy and all our art and poetry was either derived or imitated from the ancient Greeks." Here Melville sounds very much like Nietzsche, for whom the ancient Greeks represented the pinnacle of western civilization, and who shared Melville's assessment of the Platonic influence on Christianity (though to his mind there was nothing to admire in this, the Christians having adopted almost exclusively the most objectionably anti-natural elements of *Phaedo*-Platonism). Melville of course did not express contempt for the Christian ideal as radically as Nietzsche did. It is true that on his passage to Europe in 1856, he relished his "many long talks" with the "philosopher" Colonel George Campbell Rankin, author of *What is Truth? or, Revelation Its Own Nemesis*, a "heavily and sarcastically anti-clerical" book that the Colonel himself characterizes in the preface as arguing that "its internal discrepancies, and unpropitious results, [seem] clearly to indicate that Christianity, at least, is not Truth." But Melville would never publish an "eternal indictment of Christianity" as "the one great curse" and "innermost corruption" of mankind, as Nietzsche did in *The Antichrist*. Melville regarded the Christian life in its fullest expression as impractical, and Christians themselves as inconsistent and all too often hypocritical, but he was influenced sufficiently by both his Christian upbringing and American democratic values to respect at least the aspiration to moral equality among men. Nietzsche for his part condemned the idea of equality as a delusion deriving from the falsehood that all souls are equal in the eyes of God, as I have noted previously.

In *Ecce Homo* Nietzsche complains that since "the inmost parts, the 'entrails' of every soul are physiologically perceived by me—*smelled*," he is constantly affronted by the sickly odor of the ill-constituted souls of the Christian slave-types who populated Europe in his day. As a result he suffered from a type of nausea and weariness of man that amounts almost to nihilism. In this connection he writes that "whoever can smell not only with his nose but also with his eyes and ears, scents almost everywhere he goes today something like the air of madhouses and hospitals." These sanitaria are the so-called "cultured" areas of Europe, for as they house the weak, sickly, decadent type of man; as indeed they *produce* such men through the inculcation of Christian slave morality, manufacture these types and celebrate them as the human ideal—serving in this way to debase the human type, European culture is the breeding ground of distrust in man, pessimism regarding the future of man. Thus do all our "instruments of culture" function in fact as instruments of nihilism.

Soon I shall have more to say about nihilism in another of its manifestations, as an expression of, and a reaction to, the death of God. Melville suffered from this form of nihilism, or from a condition similar to it; and Nietzsche struggled against it too. As for nihilism as weariness of man, Nietzsche called this "*our* greatest danger." And although, as I have noted, Melville was not so hostile to man under the rule of Christianity as Nietzsche, we learn not only from his work but from the testimony of the young men who spoke with him in 1859 that he was "disgusted" with Christendom and modern civilization specifically in contrast to the ancient pagan ideal. In this he was not too far from Nietzsche's own assessment.

Chapter 92: Ambergris

"My genius is in my nostrils," says Nietzsche in the first section of the last book of *Ecce Homo.* He smells out lies, he adds, and thereby he is the first man to discover the truth. The discovery he has in mind is his realization of the falsehood of what we might call the Platonic-Christian thought-world, which is informed in particular by Platonic metaphysics and Christian ethics. Of course the ethical implications of the radical denial of the body in *Phaedo*-Platonism, and the metaphysical assumptions behind the Christian view of God, the soul, free will, and the after-life, are equally influential, and in fact all these things are inextricably bound up with one another on a conceptual level; but in the trends of history of interest to Nietzsche that gave shape to the modern western mind, metaphysics is usually cast in Platonic terms and ethics taught in a Christian vocabulary. In any case, in this part of *Ecce Homo* Nietzsche is speaking principally of his rejection of traditional western morality. He begins the paragraph that concludes with reference to the genius of his nostrils with a distinctive formula: *Revaluation of all values*. This has to do with the historical dialectic operative between the master and slave moralities that I introduced in the previous chapter, as I explain below.

By "values" Nietzsche understands in the first place such terms as "good," "bad," and "evil." There are also the more specific notions of, say, faith, forgiveness, and love, but it will do for our purposes to concentrate on the more general terms. With the word "revaluation" Nietzsche refers to the act of altering the connotations and denotations of value terms. So, for example, among the nobles of ancient Greece (excluding the philosophers in the Socratic-Platonic tradition), the word "good" designated physical strength and beauty, social and political authority, directness of speech and action. The noble men themselves were "the good." Among the early Christians, on the other hand, "good" designated the typical characteristics of the downtrodden and the poor, the socially displaced and politically anonymous, men compelled to dissemble or hide in the shadows to survive. These impoverished and uncultured men were "the good" according to the early Christians and their sympathizers. The long, slow process through which the nobles' conception of good was displaced in the popular mind by the Christian conception is an example of a revaluation of values. In fact it is a central component of the most significant revaluation in western history to date, a revaluation that effected nothing less than the final destruction of the ancient world and the generation of the modern.

The lower orders of the ancient world, the "slave" classes of men, could never throw off the yoke of their warrior oppressors by force of arms. Therefore they waged against them a type of psychological-spiritual warfare.

To state the matter briefly, the oppressed conquered their oppressors by promulgating the idea that the highest type of man does not oppress his fellows but aids the oppressed and perhaps even abases himself before them. The meek and lowly of spirit are not contemptible and "bad." No, they are actually "good," and they shall inherit the earth. Whoever denies this, whoever resists this by daily grinding the lowly into the dust of debasement and helplessness—he is in fact "evil," an enemy of the One True God, and he will suffer righteous punishment upon the coming of His Kingdom. Through the teaching of these and similar doctrines the lower orders of men substituted slave morality for the morality of the masters. We must imagine that first they persuaded the members of their own caste of the superiority of the values they held; they need not admire or long to emulate the values of their masters, as doubtless many had done for much of their lives alienated from their true selves and station. Then they persuaded those middling classes of men, neither slaves nor masters themselves, but apes of their superiors' manners and morals. Finally they persuaded even the masters themselves. This last would have been the most difficult phase of the revaluation, for few men will voluntarily abandon the conditions of their social, cultural, and political superiority. But the numbers of the master class are necessarily limited relative to the overall citizenry, and on Nietzsche's telling the population of masters declined in the ancient world through a natural—we might say, evolutionary—process of degeneration. As he describes the situation in *Twilight of the Idols*, with reference specifically to the collapse of the ancient Athenian nobility, "degeneration was quietly developing everywhere: old Athens was coming to an end... no one was any longer master of himself, the instincts turned *against* each other." Since "anarchy of the instincts" is for Nietzsche a formula for decadence, we may conclude that the decadence of the nobles provided the opportunity for the lower orders to supplant master morality with their own slave morality. This reinforced the decline of the nobility, for after the substitution of slave for master morality, even those who were genetically suited to mature into nobles under the right conditions came of age in a culture that condemned the presuppositions of ancient nobility as "evil" while celebrating equality, peace, and loving-kindness as "good." In short, individual adherents of the original master morality died out, and every new generation was inculcated from childhood with the assumptions of slave morality. Thus arose the European Christian civilization that so "disgusted" Melville and offended Nietzsche's refined sense of smell.

Melville was no philosophical legislator of values. He commented critically, sometimes caustically, on the state of the modern world, and he indicated alternatives he judged superior, as historical exemplars or imaginative constructs; but he did not intentionally attempt or advocate the overthrow of contemporary realities. Nietzsche for his part did aspire to change the world as a philosophical legislator; therefore he campaigned for a counter-revaluation. The "revaluation of all values" is the formula for his attempt to overcome Christian slave morality. Just prior to his mental collapse Nietzsche was planning a book or series of books on precisely this theme. "The self-overcoming of morality, out of truthfulness," he characterized his task in *Ecce Homo*, and "the self-overcoming of the moralist, into his opposite—into me," which is to say into the "first immoralist." Here Nietzsche writes against morality itself, making no distinction between master and slave morality. He writes this way more often than not, for usually he adheres to a strict definition of morality as involving three distinct features in particular: first as being grounded on or derived from a metaphysical source like the Platonic Forms or the Christian God; second as applying universally to all men regardless of station or circumstances; and finally as involving such metaphysical, spiritual, and psychological mechanisms as freedom, sin, guilt, and punishment. Master morality does not satisfy these conditions and therefore technically does not qualify as a morality. It is a code of conduct, but it is not strictly a *moral* code. Thus whenever Nietzsche refers to himself as an *immoralist*, we must understand him in this sense. He rejects morality in the technical sense as I have defined it; he does not advocate "immorality" in the popular usage of the term. His preferred code of conduct may well include much that to modern sensibilities seems violent and harsh, modelled as it is on ancient pagan ideals and a Renaissance conception of *virtù*—"virtue that is moraline-free," as he puts it in *The Antichrist*—but it is a strict code nonetheless, and Nietzsche had no use for advocates of anarchic, self-indulgent, or criminal violations of noble decorum. The goal of his revaluation, then, is not a state of moral chaos, a disordered society in which every petty thief and perverted murderer is judged to be as good as any other man. He longs for the reestablishment of a *noble* European culture. Of course he knows that we can never revert to a condition identical to the best period of the ancient world, but he does aim for the institution on earth of a similar state.

So the revaluation of all values is a project through which Nietzsche hopes to set the West on the path toward a new ideal, an ideal beyond the slaves' good and evil, but not beyond the masters' good and bad: in the *Genealogy* he explains that the "dangerous slogan ... inscribed at the head of ... *Beyond Good and Evil* ... does *not* mean 'Beyond Good and Bad.'" To achieve this ideal future state men must burrow into the stench of modern western culture, root around in its entrails and remove the diseased organs, and thereby soil their hands and heads for a time, but eventually, in some bright future, a new generation will emerge into the light of a transfigured and superior world, a reward more eagerly to be desired than even the fragrant ambergris that whalemen dig out from the belly of a rotting, stinking Leviathan.

Chapter 93: The Castaway

Nietzsche's attempt to revalue Christian values in a book like *The Antichrist* is easy enough to follow. He pitches his rhetoric at a very high level, and although there are subtleties at play beneath the surface, the surface itself attracts most of one's attention. In some of his other writings, however, Nietzsche's presentation is more nuanced, so nuanced in fact that readers tend to overlook the revaluation at work. In the next few chapters I explore an example of this phenomenon, beginning in this chapter with an outline of the Platonic conception of the relation between philosophy, love, and madness, followed in the next two chapters by a survey of Nietzsche's subtle revaluation of Plato's account.

In the present chapter of *Moby-Dick*, Pip, a slight young African-American sailor, tumbles out of Stubb's whaleboat and is left alone on the sea. The "awful lonesomeness" he experiences while abandoned on the deep, the "intense concentration of the self in the middle of such a heartless immensity," drives him mad. Ishmael's description of Pip's condition is fascinating and beautiful. It is also evocative of Plato's account of philosophical madness in the *Phaedrus*, a dialogue that Melville almost certainly read. I quote the relevant passage from *Moby-Dick* in full:

> The sea had jeeringly kept his finite body up, but drowned the
> infinite of his soul. Not drowned entirely, though. Rather carried
> down alive to wondrous depths, where strange shapes of the

unwarped primal world glided to and fro before his passive eyes; and the miser-merman, Wisdom, revealed his hoarded heaps; and among the joyous, heartless, ever-juvenile eternities, Pip saw the multitudinous, God-omnipresent, coral insects, that out of the firmament of waters heaved the colossal orbs. He saw God's foot upon the treadle of the loom, and spoke it; and therefore his shipmates called him mad. So man's insanity is heaven's sense; and wandering from all mortal reason, man comes at last to that celestial thought, which, to reason, is absurd and frantic; and weal or woe, feels then uncompromised, indifferent as his God.

In the *Phaedrus*, Socrates delivers two speeches concerning the nature of Love (*erôs*). His first speech he disowns as inadequate and, worse, impious. To atone for the latter offense he delivers a second speech as an act of purification. He had covered his head while delivering his first speech; now he uncovers it. And thus we encounter once again the theme of covering and uncovering that appears in Socrates' death scene in the *Phaedo*, another dialogue pervaded by references and allusions to purification. Socrates begins his second speech with the assertion that the greatest of good things come to humans through madness whenever it is given as a gift from the gods. He then proceeds to describe four different types of god-given madness: the madness of the prophet, of the mystic, of the poet, and, finally, the madness of the philosopher. Philosophical madness overtakes a man whose winged soul prior to its physical embodiment through birth has ascended the high rim of heaven and gazed out from there on the colorless and immaterial Forms of true reality revolving in circuits beyond the heavens. These are the originals on which the natural kinds of this corporeal realm are modelled. Thus does Pip's soul in a counter movement descend into the depths of the sea and look on the "strange shapes of the unwarped primal world [that] glided to and fro before" him. Wisdom is revealed to Pip when his soul sinks down among the coral insects, as those souls that soar up on bird-like wings to acquire knowledge of reality are born as lovers of wisdom in the *Phaedrus*. And as Pip sees God and is called mad by his shipmates for articulating his experience, so the philosophical souls in Plato, having come near to the divine, are denounced by the many as disturbed. Pip has become as indifferent as his God, and his fellows confuse his heavenly sense with man's insanity, just as people according to the *Phaedrus* fail to understand that philosophers stand outside all human pursuits not because they are unstable, but rather because they are possessed.

Before proceeding I should note that in the above paragraph I have not altered Plato's descriptions to match Melville's expressions more closely than they do in fact. I have employed direct or nearly direct translations throughout, and the relevant passages may be found between 247b and 250b of the *Phaedrus*. That Melville was familiar with the *Phaedrus* is suggested (I might say *confirmed*) by, for example, his mention in *Mardi* of "the winged soul" that encounters "eternities," and more definitely by his likening men in *Moby-Dick* to "oysters observing the sun through the water, and thinking that thick water the thinnest of air." I have discussed this image in a previous chapter and demonstrated there that Melville borrowed it from the *Phaedo*. I did not then explain the reference to "oysters," however, for it has no direct relation to the relevant passage in the *Phaedo*. But now we're in a position to determine its origin: the "oyster" appears in the very section of the *Phaedrus* that we have been considering in this chapter. Discussing the winged soul's vision of eternal reality beyond the revolving rim of heaven, Socrates says that men in their mortal condition prior to purification are imprisoned in the body like an oyster in a shell. Melville's grafting of this idea onto the image he borrowed from the *Phaedo* is appropriate, for the notion of the soul imprisoned in the body prior to purification is a principal theme of that dialogue.

Socrates' second speech relates love to madness through associating the sight of physical beauty in the bodily form of other men and women with the soul's desire to behold the metaphysical source of every corporeal instantiation of the beautiful. Bodily love, expressing itself as lust, restrains the soul from mounting on its wings to a vision of that authentic beauty, the immaterial and eternal Form of Beauty itself that alone is worthy of pure love. The philosopher is one who learns to resist the downward inclining seductive lure of the body, and to nurture instead the soul's natural inclination to ascend to the vision of reality itself. He loves true Beauty, unchanging and everlasting, and he disdains the grubby lusting after ephemeral physical bodies that constantly disturbs and disrupts the lives of other men. But this is to say that the philosopher's ideas and activities with respect to such matters are uncommon; and this explains why common men tend to regard him as mad.

Plato writes at length of Love not only in the *Phaedrus*, but also in the *Symposium*, another dialogue that Melville read. Although there is mention in this work of "the madness of philosophy," the stress is less on philosophical mania than on the nature of philosophical love—Platonic love, as the Renaissance Florentine Marsilio Ficino christened the phenomenon. Since Nietzsche's revaluation of Plato's account of the nature of philosophy engages with both the *Phaedrus* and the *Symposium*, I discuss the relevant material from this latter dialogue at the beginning of the next chapter as a preliminary to relating the details of Nietzsche's revaluation.

Chapter 94: A Squeeze of the Hand

In this chapter Ishmael reports his opinion, arrived at, he says, from personal experience, that "in all cases man must eventually lower, or at least shift, his conceit of attainable felicity; not placing it anywhere in the intellect or the fancy; but in the wife, the heart, the bed, the table, the saddle, the fire-side, the country." Some have attempted to extract from these words Melville's own philosophical solution to the problem of modern nihilism, but there is nothing beyond this single passage in the whole of Ishmael's narrative, nor anything in Melville's life or work, to suggest that this is right. Melville found no lasting tranquility in his home and family, nor does he seem to have shifted his conceit of attainable felicity; certainly he never lowered it. He lived in and for his intellect and his fancy until the end, and only those whose knowledge of Melville's biography is limited to the popular but false legend of his retreat from authorship into the quiet life of a customs inspector following the failure of *Moby-Dick* could believe otherwise. Melville loved his wife and family, to be sure. But like the philosopher as described in Plato's *Symposium*, he channeled his love into ideas and his art, always seeking happiness in some far off place, or non-place, beyond the boundaries of his mundane surroundings.

The most famous image in Plato's *Symposium* must be the so-called "ladder of love." The ladder illustrates the true philosopher's disposition to redirect his erotic energies from the earthly to the celestial or, better, from the physical to the metaphysical. Like most other mortals susceptible to the allure of beauty, the philosopher when young is stimulated by erotic desire for individual physical bodies. He longs to give birth through the medium of another's body to still other physical bodies, which activity he regards as his only available route to immortality. Of course reproduction is a mere imitation of eternal life, but it is the most a mortal man may reasonably hope for. With the proper education the aspiring philosopher will eventually transcend his desire for individual bodies and develop an aesthetic appreciation for the human form in general. Further education will then reveal the still greater beauty of the human soul, beside which the beauty of every body must appear insignificant. Mounting even higher on the educational ladder, the philosopher will experience the beauty of the knowledge that provides souls with the pursuits, laws, and customs that inform them, and through this he will understand the beauty of knowledge in general as it exists in "the vast sea of the beautiful." At this point the mature philosopher may finally attain the summit of his ascent, the knowledge of beauty itself, which is to say knowledge of the metaphysical essence of beauty, the Form of Beauty that always is as it is, eternal, unchanging, and perfect, the immaterial source of the many transitory material instantiations of beauty. Having arrived at this ultimate reality, contemplating and communing with it, the philosopher's soul swells with a spiritual pregnancy until at last he gives birth to his most authentic offspring, true virtue. In this way the philosopher may win the love of the gods and so hope for genuine immortality, not the paltry imitation of endurance through future generations of physical offspring, but the actual eternality of the living soul.

The immortality achieved by the proper philosophical education, through which the soul traverses the ascending stages of desire from the lowest manifestation of physical lust to the highest mode of intercourse with reality itself, this is the summit of happiness, *eudaimonia*, the best life available to humans and therefore a *telos*, an end, our ultimate goal. The supreme state to which a man may aspire, then, is the philosophical life as the life of authentic knowledge and virtue. And this account, derived from the *Symposium*, is compatible in every essential with the content of the *Phaedrus*. Here we have the image of the ladder of love, there the image of the winged soul gazing on reality from the revolving rim of heaven; but in both cases the true philosophical drive manifests as the mastering of lust for physical bodies and the transformation of this eros into a passion for metaphysical reality, the reward being virtue, happiness, and immortality.

This, then, is the account of the philosophical life that I have said Nietzsche revalues, albeit so subtly that no one has noticed. His revaluation

237

takes place in sections seven and eight of the Third Essay of *On the Genealogy of Morals*, where he discusses the philosophers' relation to the ascetic ideal. That he has the *Phaedrus* and *Symposium* in mind, and that he means to retain some of Plato's concepts while subverting their Platonic meanings, I shall demonstrate in the remainder of this and the whole of the next chapter.

In the first place Nietzsche eliminates the role of an immaterial soul by stressing the animal nature of the philosopher, who like every animal is moved by natural instincts. As in Plato, the philosopher strives for a state superior to the condition sought by other animals, including other human animals, but this has nothing to do with the soul in any traditional sense of the word, nor does it involve communion with realities beyond the mundane sphere. The philosopher seeks his highest *natural* condition. This is not happiness, *pace* Plato, not even happiness as eudaimonia. No, the philosopher seeks rather "an optimum of favorable conditions under which it can expend all its strength and achieve its maximal feeling of power." In pursuit of this goal Nietzsche's philosopher, like Plato's, avoids the physical entanglements involved in the traditional relationships of marriage and fatherhood. They do not find their felicity in the wife or the fire-side. To them a child is a "fetter" and the home "a place of impurity," which expressions unmistakably recall the *Phaedo*, though Nietzsche here associates them with the Buddha. In any case, the philosopher's shunning of familial bliss, though compatible with Platonism in the effect, springs from altogether different motives: the Nietzschean philosopher has as little use for virtue as he has for happiness. His goal is the "highest and boldest spirituality," and the "spirituality" here is a figure for the activity of natural animal instincts. Philosophers as Nietzsche describes them in this context are dominated internally by those instincts that propel them toward the "most appropriate and natural conditions of their *best* existence, their *fairest* fruitfulness." And though the "fair" here may recall Plato's interest in the beautiful, and the "fruitfulness" his concern with spiritual pregnancy, both of which notions relate to his explorations of the sublimation of physical sexuality, Nietzsche develops these ideas in another direction, which is to say he revalues them. But I stop at this point, for, as we shall see, the subject of sexuality is more suited to the next chapter of *Moby-Dick*.

Chapter 95: The Cassock

Among the crew of the *Pequod* there is a curious laborer known as the "mincer." This man is charged with slicing the whale's blubber into pieces of a size to fit into the pots for boiling. What makes him curious is not his business, but rather the outfit he wears while conducting it, for he is clad from head to toe in a long black robe fashioned from the stripped skin of a whale's penis. Melville makes a joke of this, writing that when "invested in the full canonicals of his calling" the mincer appears a religious authority wrapped in the mantle of his office, or a "candidate for an archbishoprick." One can see how the faithful among Melville's readers might find him at times intolerably irreverent. But be that as it may, this crudity will serve to introduce the following examination of philosophy and sensuality in Plato and Nietzsche.

Nietzsche's account of the philosopher in *Genealogy* 3.7-8 follows Plato's accounts in the *Phaedrus* and *Symposium* by taking off from the problem of human sexuality. He is interested in the role of the ascetic ideal in the life of the philosopher, and he aims to clarify the benefits philosophers derive, *as* philosophers, from ascetic practices involving abstinence from sensual indulgences. There "unquestionably exists," he admits, "a peculiar philosophers' irritation at and rancor against sensuality." In this connection he mentions Schopenhauer in particular, but later he refers to other philosophers as well, Plato included. Socrates of course is an exception to the rule, for he took a wife and fathered children. Yet Nietzsche insists that Socrates "married *ironically*," that he married in order to demonstrate the proposition that philosophers are unsuited for family life. In any case, returning to the example of Schopenhauer near the conclusion of his exposition, Nietzsche writes, echoing Plato, that "the sight of the beautiful" released "the *chief energy* of his nature." But he then speculates contrary to Plato that the element of sensuality aroused by beauty "is not overcome ... but only transfigured and no longer enters consciousness as sexual excitement." The difference here between Plato and Nietzsche is subtle, for Nietzsche admits that the sensual impulse is transfigured. Yet he also denies that it is overcome, as it is in Plato's account. In Plato the impulse begins as an excitation of the bodily element but ends up as a stirring of the soul, and as soul is altogether different and distinct from the body, there must be a real essential difference between the original sexual excitation and the final spiritual intercourse with metaphysical reality—and, yes, Plato does employ language implying sexual intercourse in this context, for the lexical identity brings out all the more the radical difference of fact between body and soul. In Nietzsche there is only a difference of experience; the underlying phenomenon remains bodily through and through.

In the *Phaedrus* Plato illustrates the sublimation of sexual excitement into a spiritual aspiration to know the truth through images of the soul growing wings. The philosophical soul takes flight, rises up, and looks out over the field of eternal Being that stretches away beyond the boundaries of the temporal realm of Becoming. Nietzsche plays with this image of the winged philosopher, but as usual he employs the notion for anti-Platonic purposes. The philosopher, he says, seeks the very conditions under which "all animal being becomes more spiritual and acquires wings." He employs the ascetic ideal as "the cheerful asceticism of an animal become fledged and divine, floating above life rather than in repose." As the "fledged" in this last quote means "winged," here again Nietzsche alludes to Plato's winged souls. But while alluding to Plato's account he intends to subvert it, for when writing of spirituality, divinity, and floating above life, Nietzsche employs figurative expressions for purely natural states. His philosophers grow wings by securing for themselves "freedom from compulsion, disturbance, noise, from tasks, duties, worries; clear heads; the dance, leap, and flight of ideas, good air, thin, clear, open, dry." There are no metaphysical implications in this. Nietzsche is thinking of the conditions required by a philosopher-artist to think and to write, as is clear from his mention of his own "most beautiful study—the Piazza di San Marco" in Venice, Italy.

So Nietzsche's images of the divinity of winged philosophers are symbols for the highest states of the philosophical animal's natural physiological health; they have nothing to do with the spiritual condition of disembodied souls. And though the state to which Nietzsche's philosopher aspires relates, as in Plato, to the matter of the philosopher's offspring; and though Nietzsche agrees with Plato that "this type of spirit clearly has its fruitfulness somewhere else than in children"; nevertheless, he does not accept Plato's account of the philosopher's offspring. Nietzsche's philosophers have their "periods of great pregnancy," their "states of great spiritual tension," as philosophers are said in the *Symposium* to be "pregnant in their souls." But whereas Plato's philosophers give birth to true virtue, Nietzsche's philosopher-artists give birth to their ideas as recorded in books. They abstain from women not in order to liberate the soul by chastising the body, but rather because "their 'maternal' instinct ruthlessly disposes of all other stores and accumulations of energy, of animal vigor, for the benefit of the evolving work."

Nietzsche engages with Plato's ideas in most of his works. Often he does so explicitly, but sometimes he subtly conceals his intentions. In this way he develops and works through familiar themes, yet his ideas unfold in surprising directions. This is one manifestation of his inverted-Platonism. He does not avoid Plato altogether by, say, writing on topics utterly foreign to Plato's concerns; he rarely simply ignores Platonism as a philosophical tradition. Rather, he works within but against this tradition. In this he is similar to Melville, who was drawn to Platonism but could never fully adopt its fundamental assumptions. Melville developed his own version of inverted-Platonism. The similarities between Melville and Nietzsche manifest in other ways as well, for example in their conceptions of the best way to deal with the accursed questions. How might a man stare into the abyss without falling in and perishing there? Melville addresses this problem in the following chapter of *Moby-Dick*.

Chapter 96: The Try-Works

In this chapter Ishmael falls asleep at the helm of the *Pequod* in "the blackness of the sea and the night." Recall Melville's fascination with the "mystical blackness" of Hawthorne's work, the dark shadow cast over his pages by a sense of original sin so palpable as to manifest almost as substantial form. Melville's feeling for such things ran deep too, deeper even than in his friend. He sensed beneath all talk of sin the darker void of the absence of sin, not from innocence or redemption from sin, but rather from the absence of God as the arbiter of depravity and salvation. Melville never declared himself an atheist or stated outright that God is dead, but that he was skeptical of theism in general and Christianity in particular is evident from his work and his behavior. "Silence is the only Voice of our God," he wrote in *Pierre*. No wonder his readers, neighbors, family, and friends worried about the state of his soul.

Asleep and dreaming of hell at the helm of the ship, somnambulistic Ishmael spins himself around with his back to the tiller, which upon his sudden waking seems to him "inverted," like Melville's own Platonism. His carelessness has placed the ship in danger of capsizing. "Nothing seemed before me but a jet gloom," he remembers. "Uppermost was the impression, that whatever swift, rushing thing I stood on was not so much bound to any haven ahead as rushing from all havens astern." Ishmael here is contemplating Nietzsche's "horizon of the infinite," which opens up before all men for whom God has died. "We have left the land and have embarked," Nietzsche writes in *The Gay Science*, just a few pages after his initial announcement that God is dead. "We have burned our bridges behind us— indeed, we have gone further and destroyed the land behind us. Now, little ship, look out! Beside you is the ocean … [and] hours will come when you will realize that it is infinite and that there is nothing more awesome than infinity." Like Ishmael on "the rushing Pequod …. plunging into that blackness of darkness," Nietzsche wonders whether we who have killed God are not "plunging continually," speeding into the blackness "away from all suns" and "straying as through an infinite nothing."

When Nietzsche pronounces God dead he means by "God" something like "Truth" or "the metaphysically Real" under every possible description. The Christian God may well be foremost in his mind, but really he intends every variety of supernatural entity or metaphysical reality postulated to date by philosophy, theology, science, and even common sense. Thus Parmenides' Being, Plato's Forms, Aristotle's Prime Mover, Plotinus's World Soul, Gassendi's atoms, Descartes's ego, Kant's *noumenon*, and Schopenhauer's Will are all substitute divinities. We may, then, read "metaphysics" when Nietzsche writes "God" in this context, keeping in mind that even the scientists' atoms, the psychologists' "I," and the common man's seemingly mundane "thing" are supposed to be substances, independently existing realities that underlie and anchor activity and change. From God as the fount from which the universe flows, through the ego as the self-identical cause of thought, to things as the unified, continuous grounds of the transitory attributes that characterize particular physical objects: all are fictions generated by the illusion of Being. When Nietzsche writes that "Heraclitus will remain eternally right with his assertion that being is an empty fiction," he includes in the category fiction "unity … thinghood … substance … permanence." And if there are no unified things, no permanent substances, no stable Being within the flow of Becoming, then the world as we think we know it is a "lie," and God is dead indeed.

Nietzsche is perhaps the first major western philosopher to reject—or anyway to aspire to reject—every possible manifestation of metaphysics. Schopenhauer before him had publically declared his atheism, but he believed in a metaphysical truth at, and *as*, the heart of all physical appearances. Schopenhauer did not go far enough, then; but the fact of his atheism is telling. Nietzsche came of age in the wake of a century of Enlightenment denunciations of religious tradition, and in an environment in which scholars had recently begun to turn their critical tools—originally developed to study ancient pagan texts—on the very writings that for millennia had supplied the tradition its aura of authority. Biblical criticism of the sort that Melville's Colonel Rankin engaged in was popular in Nietzsche's day, and it generated doubts that the Bible was in any plausible way the unambiguous revelation of God's word. As from at least the time of Galileo in the early seventeenth century the western conception of "the book of nature" had undergone a steady process of demythologization, even of de-deification, culminating in the explosion of Darwinian evolution, so in the late eighteenth and early nineteenth centuries, the standard conception of that other book, "the Good Book," was revised as well. Formerly everyone thought they knew that Moses himself had written the first five books of the Old Testament, and that Jesus's own disciples had composed the Gospels; but in the academic world that Nietzsche inhabited very few men continued to endorse these attributions. This, then, is the meaning of the "is dead" in Nietzsche's "God is dead." There never has been a God, never has been a metaphysical "true world" behind, beneath, or above, the "apparent world" of our experience. But men have had faith in these gods, these "idols," have even formulated arguments to prove their existence. But this long era of belief was drawing to a close by the middle of the nineteenth century. Belief in other worlds and other beings, personal or impersonal, was dying out—more rapidly, and radically, in Europe than in America, and more in the intellectual circles of Europe than among the common folk; but the decline was underway. The deed itself had already been done in fact, but still it would take some time for everyone to perceive and comprehend what had happened. Thus, like his "madman" in *The Gay Science*, Nietzsche understood that "this tremendous event is still on its way, still wandering; it has not yet reached the ears of men."

But news of God's demise had most definitely reached the ears of some men. If the phrase "God is dead" in Nietzsche's mouth amounts to the observation that "We pondering men of the nineteenth century are dubious of divine or metaphysical postulates," then the news had reached Melville even before Nietzsche proclaimed it. In *Clarel* Melville writes of "Europe's grieving doubt / Which asks *And can the Father be*?" and he describes the young Clarel, in terms he well knew applied to himself, as no longer a "student of the sacred lore" but rather "a traveler—no more." In the journal he kept on the Mediterranean tour that inspired this work, Melville noted the following unsettling experience: "Went towards the cemeteries of Pera … Saw a burial. Armenian. Juggling & incantations of the priests – making signs &c. – Nearby, saw a woman over a new grave – no grass on it yet. Such abandonment of misery! Called to the dead, put her head down as close to it as possible; as if calling down a hatchway or cellar; besought – 'Why don't you speak to me? My God! – It is I! – Ah, speak – but one word!' – All deaf. – So much for consolation. – This woman & her cries haunt me horribly." Melville at times was deeply troubled by the absence of God, as was Nietzsche, who wondered "who will wipe this blood off us," God's murderers, and "what water is there for us to clean ourselves? What festivals of atonement, what sacred games shall we have to invent?" Nietzsche feared that "the greatness of this deed [is] too great for us," for he understood the implications of the act, felt in advance the destructive intellectual reverberations. By comparison, our contemporary atheists are objectionably facile in their unbelief, for they imagine that we can eradicate God from our store of beliefs while retaining most every other item intact. Thus they believe in human rights, political equality, social progress, freedom, goodness, peace, and truth. Above all, of course, they believe in reason as expressed in science. But Nietzsche saw more deeply beneath the surface of our beliefs; he traced the tangled subterranean systems that bind all these beliefs to God as their foundational root. Hack at this Ash Tree and the world as we know it must eventually wither away.

Melville and Nietzsche looked into the blackness of the void of God's absence, and neither man mistook for real the hallucinatory images that play before one's eyes in utter darkness. They confronted the abyss *as an abyss*, declining to pretend to see light where none exists. But I discuss sunlight and lamplight together in the following chapter.

Chapter 97: The Lamp

Despite the blackness of darkness in which Melville and Nietzsche lived and thought, neither man succumbed to spiritual blindness, not anyway during their best, their healthiest, periods. They both aspired, for some time successfully, to live in such a way as to echo Zarathustra's "I invented a brighter flame for myself." And when Ishmael writes with reference to the oil-lamps burning in the forecastle of the *Pequod* that "in the pitchiest night the ship's black hull still houses an illumination," I cannot help thinking of the interior brilliance that lighted the shafts of Melville's and Nietzsche's deepest descents of philosophical exploration.

Melville employs a stirring image of the power of self-illumination at the conclusion of the previous chapter. There is, he writes, "a Catskill eagle in some souls that can alike dive down into the blackest gorges, and soar out of them again and become invisible in the sunny spaces." Here we have a portrait of the philosopher as Nietzsche conceives of the type, as a man who attains the height of his creative-intellectual powers by descending into his depths. Or, to revert to my own formulation, we may take this as an image of the man who engages with the accursed questions without regarding them *as* accursed. This is the philosopher as the possessor of *la gaya scienza*, the joyful wisdom, who can say with Zarathustra, "I live in my own light."

But dangers do lurk in the depths, and there is no guarantee that those who descend will find their way out again. Melville acknowledges this when he writes in *Pierre* that "it is the not impartially bestowed privilege of the more final insights, that at the same moment they reveal the depths, they do, sometimes, also reveal—though by no means so distinctly—some answering heights." When the final insights reveal the depths, they *sometimes* also reveal *some* answering heights, and then only indistinctly. There is less hopefulness in this formulation than in the Catskill eagle passage, and the decline reflects the waning of Melville's Ishmaelean high spirits only a short time after *Moby-Dick*. Ishmael possesses a power of internal illumination that allows him to experience even his depths as heights, which comes out explicitly when immediately following his mention of the eagle that flies out of the gorge into the sun, he adds that "even if he for ever flies within the gorge, that gorge is in the mountains; so that even in his lowest swoop the mountain eagle is still higher than other birds upon the plain, even though they soar."

In *Thus Spoke Zarathustra* Nietzsche praises the man who "sees the abyss but with the eyes of an eagle; who grasps the abyss with the talons of an eagle." The idea in Melville and Nietzsche both is of a man so sound of body and mind as to face life's gloomiest mysteries without either flinching, wishing them away, or clinging to facile solutions. Standing before his "highest mountain," Zarathustra plots his course of ascent by judging that he must "go down deeper than ever [he] descended." He knows, as we have seen, that "it is out of the deepest depth that the highest must come to its height." Similar figures of depth interblended with the highest heights appear throughout *Zarathustra*, for Nietzsche valued the vigor of health that empowers a man to celebrate life even from the pit of suffering. His own ability to love his fate in spite of prolonged illnesses, in spite of the loneliness of isolation and misapprehension, in spite of bad weather and worse moods— this seemed to him evidence of his own "great health," a condition that "one does not merely have but also acquires continually, and must acquire because one gives it up again and again, and must give it up." Some men are sickly at bottom, and therefore ultimately incurable; some are sufficiently sound to beat back even the most obstinately recurrent of ailments.

In the previous chapter I wrote of the death of God, of all that must perish along with him, and at least indirectly of the melancholy that darkens the souls of those who have witnessed or received word of his passing. In this context I quoted from the first edition of *The Gay Science*, in which Nietzsche refers to man as a murderer who by killing God has untethered our earth from its orbit, blotted out the horizon, and set us straying through the infinite boundless as homesick wanderers forever lost in the bitter cold of empty space. The passing away of God is an ominous affair, and no serious man will pretend otherwise. Yet Nietzsche begins the new fifth book he added to the second edition of *The Gay Science* with a section entitled "The meaning of our cheerfulness," in which he acknowledges the "approaching gloom" but insists that he is not gloomy himself. To the contrary: the Nietzschean philosopher—the philosopher as a *free spirit*—experiences the death of God as the coming of "a new and scarcely describable kind of light, happiness, relief, exhilaration, encouragement, dawn." And with a Melvillean touch Nietzsche rejoices that now "our ships may venture out again," and that "the sea, *our* sea, lies open again." The homesick wanderers have been transformed into Zarathustra's "bold searchers, researchers" who "embark with cunning sails on terrible seas ... drunk with riddles, glad of the twilight." This is their Ishmaelean character.

In the previous chapter when Ishmael pronounces Solomon "the truest of all men" and *Ecclesiastes* "the truest of all books," he is echoing Melville's judgment that Solomon was "the truest man who ever spoke." The Preacher's words are notoriously bleak, but Ishmael does not suffer from meditating on their significance. He knows the difference between a "wisdom that is woe" and a "woe that is madness," which is to say that he knows the underbelly of life from experience, but he will not lie down to be crushed beneath it. Ishmael understood these matters because Melville himself understood them. At the time he wrote *Moby-Dick* he shone with the great health more brightly than he ever would again.

Chapter 98: Stowing Down and Clearing Up

Ishmael concludes this chapter, in which he details the sailors' laborious cleaning of the ship after capturing, butchering, and boiling a whale, by noting that often as soon as they have completed their chores a man on the mast will spy another whale and they must begin the routine all over again. "Yet this is life," he observes. We mortals toil to extract from this world whatever there is of value in life, then we purify our soul from the vices and corruptions that have stained it in the process; but when at last we think to settle down to enjoy our success—then we die, and we must begin the round again in some other world. "Oh! the metempsychosis," Ishmael exclaims at the thought. "Oh! Pythagoras." And he closes the chapter by stating that although Pythagoras died a sage two thousand years ago in Greece, he sailed with him recently in the guise of a young sailor.

Pythagoras is a shadowy figure in the history of philosophy, but we can say with some confidence that he lived in southern Italy in the sixth century BCE. Although later generations of Pythagoreans attributed to the master a dizzying variety of doctrines, many contemporary scholars believe that the single dogma we can be sure he taught is the transmigration of souls. According to some he was the first man to introduce the notion of reincarnation into Greece. Stories were told among the ancients of Pythagoras's being the hyperborean Apollo in human form, and of his having been spotted—like Moby Dick—in two distant locations at one and the same time; but most famous of all was the report of his claim to possess knowledge of his previous incarnations. It was said that Aithalides, son of the god Hermes, having been granted by his father any gift other than immortal life, requested to remember his experiences all through life and death. This man was then reborn as Euphorbus, a warrior who fought against the Greeks at Troy. Euphorbus was reborn as Hermotimus, who proved his knowledge of his previous incarnation by identifying Euphorbus's shield, which hung as a dedication in Apollo's temple at Branchidai. Hermotimus then returned as Pyrrhus, a fisherman who hailed from Apollo's birthplace of Delos. And, finally, upon Pyrrhus's death his soul was reborn as Pythagoras, who retained memories of all these past lives.

The Pythagorean doctrine of metempsychosis is alien to modern western minds, but stranger still is a related teaching sometimes attributed to Pythagoras or his disciples. Plotinus's student Porphyry reported that Pythagoras himself taught that after certain intervals of time the cycle of the universe begins again and nothing new occurs. His followers were reported by a student of Aristotle to entertain the more specific idea that numerically identical events recur time and again, so that every event is repeated in every one of even its minutest details. Nietzsche refers to this Pythagorean teaching in the second section of an early essay entitled "On the Uses and Disadvantages of History for Life." This is noteworthy because Nietzsche would later declare his own doctrine of eternal return, or eternal recurrence of the same, the central teaching of his philosophy.

In August of 1881, while walking along the shores of Lake Silvaplana in Switzerland, just a mile or so from his summer residence in Sils-Maria, Nietzsche approached a large pyramidal stone and was suddenly overcome by the thought that all the events of a man's life, indeed every episode in the history of the universe, repeats eternally. Every single event in time, from the cosmic orbits of the heavenly bodies to the subtlest twitching of a grasshopper's antennae, recur in precisely the same manner and in the same order an infinite number of times. Hence I have already typed these words while sitting in this chair beside this window listening to that car rumble down the road across the way, and you have already read these words while doing and experiencing exactly whatever it is you are presently doing and experiencing—we have each already lived and known all this an infinite number of times in the past, and we shall live it all again an infinite number of times in the future, every detail precisely the same and in the identical order. This, in brief, is Nietzsche's teaching of the eternal return.

Nietzsche introduced this idea in *The Gay Science*, most famously in the penultimate section of the first edition, written not long after his experience on the lake near the so-called "Zarathustra Stone." In this passage he invites us to imagine our reaction if we should sincerely come to believe in the eternal recurrence of all events. "Would you not throw yourself down and gnash your teeth?" he asks. Or perhaps we might rejoice at the thought and reply, "never have I heard anything more divine." Nietzsche is asking his readers to diagnose the condition of their existential fitness. The principal diagnostic question is, "how well disposed would you have to be to yourself and to life *to crave nothing more fervently* than this ultimate eternal confirmation and seal?" The decadent man will recoil at the thought of the eternal return, for as one who suffers from life he will have no desire to repeat it. The healthy man, on the other hand, the spiritually powerful man, the noble and free individual who revels in the lows of life as well as the highs, who loves his dark abysses for driving him on and leading him up to his highest heights and sunniest summits—this type of man will affirm the eternal return.

There is no evidence that Melville had ever heard of the eternal return, much less that he believed it, though it is at least possible that he encountered the idea in connection with the Pythagorean tradition. Not too long before he sat down to write *Moby-Dick*, a critic wrote the following in reference to his most philosophical work to date, *Mardi*: "Mr. Melville seems to lack the absolute faith that God had a purpose in creating the world. He seems to think that the race is in a vicious circle, from which we cannot escape—that what has been must be again forever." It is easy to believe that Melville rejected the idea that the history of the cosmos and the particular lives of its inhabitants are infused with divine purpose, at least on some occasions in some of his moods. But since there is no explicit statement of eternal recurrence in *Mardi*, we should take the reviewer's attribution to Melville of the notion that time is a "vicious circle" as symbolic of the thought of purposelessness, the idea that human life and human action are vain. In *Mardi* the philosopher Babbalanja wonders, "Yet if our dead fathers somewhere and somehow live, why not our unborn sons? For," he reasons, "backward or forward, eternity is the same." We may take this to hint at the thought of eternal return, but the intimation is rendered at best ambiguous when Babbalanja concludes with, "already have we been the nothing we dread to be," which suggests a *figuratively* cyclical view of the linear progression of time, in which one passes at birth from non-existence into existence and then at death back into non-existence.

The fact that Melville did not explicitly state and *affirm* the thought of eternal return represents a significant difference from Nietzsche—*if*, that is, we believe that Nietzsche took the idea seriously. Many contemporary scholars find it impossible to accept the idea themselves, so there is a tendency among them to insist that Nietzsche did not really mean it, that he employed it merely as a thought experiment with which to conduct the existential diagnosis I mentioned previously. This strikes me as wrong-headed, for it requires that we ignore Nietzsche's own self-assessment, as when he refers to himself at the end of *Twilight of the Idols* explicitly as "the teacher of the eternal recurrence." In any case, despite the fact that Melville and his Ishmael know nothing of, or anyway make no mention of, the eternal recurrence of identical events, I am convinced that they would have affirmed it. They were well aware of life's various hardships; they knew the darkness of blackness from personal experience; yet as Ishmael announces at the commencement of his story, he has "an everlasting itch for things remote" and he loves "to land on barbarous coasts." He is, he says, social with horrors. And as we know from his later account of his "free and easy sort of genial, desperado philosophy," he absorbs "all events ... all things visible and invisible," and even "death itself," yet "nothing dispirits," and in fact it all seems "but a part of the general joke." Ishmael is a Yes-sayer, as cheerful in the shadows of the world's profoundest mysteries as in the teeth of life's fiercest threats. Melville was too, for a time anyway. During the years immediately surrounding his composition of *Moby-Dick* he was, as I have said, a Nietzschean, Dionysian, Zarathustran *Ja-sager*. He was, in short, a knight-poet of the "*gai saber*," the joyful wisdom. Unfortunately, however, he was unable to sustain himself in the rarified air of these heights. Eventually he tumbled into nihilism, or into an existential condition closely resembling nihilism.

Chapter 99: The Doubloon

Recall that in a previous chapter Ahab nailed a doubloon to the mainmast as a reward for the first man to locate Moby Dick. Now, in the present chapter, various men inspect the coin and impose a variety of interpretations on the images inscribed on its face. The second mate, Stubb, overhearing these many interpretations, eventually remarks, "There's another rendering now; but still one text. All sorts of men in one kind of world, you see." But Stubb does not penetrate as deeply into the matter as does Ishmael, who earlier in this same chapter reflects that "some certain significance lurks in all things, else all things are little worth, and the round world itself but an empty cipher." Stubb observes, at most, epistemological-relativism—different interpretations but still one text, "one kind of world." But Ishmael ponders ontological-relativism—the relativism resulting from a fundamental lack of essences and objective meaning, the possibility that—and here I employ a Nietzschean formulation—there are no facts, only interpretations. Or to express the idea in Melville's own voice by citing a letter he wrote to Hawthorne in the spring of 1851: "And perhaps, after all, there is *no* secret. We incline to think that the Problem of the Universe is like the Freemason's mighty secret, so terrible to all children. It turns out, at last, to consist in a triangle, a mallet, and an apron—nothing more!" Melville understands that this sort of universe, a world that is *not* at bottom "one kind of world," would be "an empty cipher," which is to say he understands that nihilism follows from the death of God.

When Nietzsche announces that "God is dead" in the first edition of *The Gay Science*, he does not associate the event with nihilism. But in the second edition he claims at the beginning of the fifth book that the death of God necessitates the collapse of "the whole of our European morality," and he links this collapse three sections later to the advent of nihilism. This is just one of many accounts of nihilism that appear in Nietzsche's publications of the late 1880s, but he nowhere writes about the phenomenon at length. In the *Genealogy of Morals* he stated his intention to publish an analysis of European nihilism, but he never managed to follow through. However, among the material in his unpublished notebooks there is a series of sixteen numbered passages headed "*European Nihilism*. Lenzer Heide, June 10, 1887." The heading dates the notes to the period when Nietzsche was in transit to Sils-Maria, the town in which he wrote his *Genealogy*, from which we may infer that he had these notes in mind when he wrote the promise of a work on nihilism into the *Genealogy*.

In the Lenzer Heide notes Nietzsche reflects on the "Christian moral hypothesis" that once infused human suffering with meaning and significance by situating life in the context of a perfect world and freedom of the will.

According to this account, we suffer because we voluntarily misuse our will. Therefore we have only ourselves to blame. A gloomy explanation, to be sure; but even so it is better than no explanation at all. As Nietzsche would later insist in the *Genealogy*, we humans can endure even extreme suffering so long as we believe there is some meaning in it; any explanation will serve to ward off the "suicidal nihilism" that may follow from despair at meaningless suffering.

But besides providing an explanation for human suffering, the Christian moral hypothesis "posited that man had a *knowledge* of absolute values and thus *adequate knowledge* precisely regarding what is most important." The belief that we possess such knowledge enables humans not only to comprehend suffering, but also to take comfort in the thought that we know the good. Suffering may be our birthright given the events in the Garden, but we know the way out of it—whether in this life or the next—and we also know that beyond suffering there is redemption. Thus we may have hope. Our knowledge of value and of the "moral order" of the world gives us reason to endure and maybe even to aspire.

Eventually, however, this Christian moral hypothesis was undermined by drives generated by Christian morality itself, the will to truth in particular. Motivated by our will to know and revere the truth, we uncovered the origins of the Christian worldview in the human need to relieve suffering by giving it meaning through explanation. And having unmasked the Christian moral hypothesis as a psychological stratagem for coping with pain, we lost faith in its validity. To expose and reject the Christian account of morality and value in this way renders one vulnerable to existential and psychological trauma, but the will to truth is insistent. However terrible it may be to admit the truth about these matters, it is worse to continue to deceive ourselves. Therefore we reject the Christian interpretation of reality, conclude that our sufferings are meaningless and our lives valueless, and thereby add to our suffering a weightier burden of woe.

Nietzsche investigates the origins, expressions, and consequences of nihilism in many other notes collected in Book 1 of *The Will to Power*, but he employs such a variety of formulations, and he approaches the subject from so many different angles, that it's impossible to summarize his conception in a single simple formula. Probably he had no unified conception in mind, and he seems to have conceived the condition of nihilism as by nature a multiform thing manifesting variously as philosophical, psychological, social, political, and cultural disorders. One of his more penetrating accounts characterizes nihilism as a rejection of metaphysical explanations and interpretations of the world and our place in it, coupled with a radical devaluation of the worth of existence. I explain this bipartite conception of nihilism in the following chapter.

Chapter 100: Leg and Arm • The Pequod, of Nantucket, meets the Samuel Enderby, of London

The first of the two manifestations of nihilism mentioned at the end of the previous chapter we may call "metaphysical nihilism." It amounts in brief to the rejection of belief in any metaphysical reality or truth. The second, which we may refer to as "existential nihilism," is the psychological condition of despair or depression resulting from the assumption that if there is no metaphysical truth, then the world is valueless and life is not worth living. Nietzsche approves of the first type of nihilism, metaphysical nihilism, and we may, I believe, fairly label him a nihilist in this sense of the word. Of the second type of nihilism, existential nihilism, Nietzsche vehemently disapproves, and he struggled to resist it himself. When he writes in a late note that he had been "the first perfect nihilist of Europe," but that he has "lived through the whole" of it, "leaving it behind, outside himself," I read him as claiming to have lived through and conquered existential nihilism. It could not have been easy, for even Zarathustra comes perilously close to succumbing to nihilism in its manifestation as nausea at the eternal recurrence of small and despicable men. Nietzsche's desire, often expressed, to be a Yes-sayer involves his striving to affirm every aspect and element of the world rather than nihilistically to deny or disparage anything or anyone. It is, as I say, a struggle, which is why Nietzsche must remind himself repeatedly that this is what he is after.

The believer who retains his metaphysical beliefs (the faithful Christian, for example) need not fear this particular manifestation of existential nihilism, but anyone who has reasoned his way into metaphysical nihilism will have to contend with its existential consequences. In fact, metaphysical nihilism may actually induce existential nihilism. Nietzsche discusses the connection between these two conditions in a note on nihilism "as a psychological state" written not long after the Lenzer Heide notes and the *Genealogy*. In this note he explains that a man will succumb to existential nihilism by believing and then later rejecting the idea that the universe may be characterized in terms of the categories "aim," "unity," and "truth." That the universe has no *aim* means that it lacks an objective *telos*, a goal toward which it is heading through either its own inherent force or a force infused by a deity. In short, universal movement and change do not track any particular course; events just happen; Becoming just is; and all things flow without purpose, plan, or teleological directionality. That the universe has no *unity* means that we are not part of an organizing whole, nor are we modes of the deity, emanations of the One, or the articulate productions of a divine creator. We do not "stand in the context of" or "exist in relation to" any superior structure or system; we do not "fit" into an overarching rational whole, like pieces of a puzzle secure in their proper position. That the universe lacks *truth* means in this instance that there is no "true world," no realm of Being in which the aim and unity missing from this world of eternally cycling Becoming might reside. Some may chase the dream of a transcendent reality of pure Being after losing faith in the aim and unity of *this* world, hoping to discover beyond the void a fullness in some other state of existence, a state attainable either now through meditation or prayer, for example, or after death for those who merit the reward. But when these dreamers realize that they have fabricated this ideal of Being from fear of the reality of Becoming—that is, *if* they realize this; some, perhaps most, will not—then through this realization they will have rejected the imaginary "true world" and will, thereby, have taken the final step into nihilism as a psychological state, which is to say into the depressive condition of existential nihilism. This, as I have said, is the view that the world is valueless, oneself included. One had thought of oneself as having value *precisely through* the aim, unity, and truth of the world of which one is a part, but now that one no longer believes in these categories, one finds no source of value at all. To quote Nietzsche on this subject: "the categories 'aim,' 'unity,' 'being' which we used to project some value into the world—we *pull out* again; so the world looks *valueless*."

I have referred to "losing faith" in these three categories, but the final descent into existential nihilism actually requires that one lose faith in a single aspect of their application only, while continuing to accept another. One must cease to believe that the categories apply to reality—that is, one must become a metaphysical nihilist—but one must retain one's belief that these categories are the sources (indeed the *only possible* sources) of the value of existence.

Without this latter belief as to the source of value, the rejection of one's belief in metaphysics will not generate the conclusion that the world is valueless, will not lead to existential nihilism. Nietzsche stresses this himself, remarking that "nihilism as a psychological state" may be overcome, or avoided altogether, by rejecting the metaphysics of these categories *and also* their supposed existential import. In his own words, we must "give up our faith in [these categories]," for "once we have devaluated [them], the demonstration that they cannot be applied to the universe is no longer any reason for devaluating the universe." In short, we must lose faith not only in the reality of these categories but also in their role as guarantors of value: thus we shall be metaphysical nihilists without succumbing also to existential nihilism.

The distinction is important, for Nietzsche regards metaphysical nihilism as potentially liberating, as providing for the healthy noble man an opportunity for a Dionysian affirmation of life, whereas he regards existential nihilism as the deplorable condition of the life-denying base and timid man. For the right kind of man, then, for the man as Nietzsche admires and aspires to be himself, metaphysical nihilism—as manifested, for example, in the death of God—is a cheerful, liberating event. If all along God was only *apparently* the source of meaning and value, but not *actually* so, then in the nihilistic wake of his death this type of man may recognize in himself the freedom to forge his own, personal and particular, meaning and value. Those who are equal to this effort will affirm this new world—this new life—free of God in all his guises. Hard as it may be, they will with Nietzsche strive to be Yes-sayers. For such men, as we have seen, the nihilistic consequences of God's demise are "like a new and scarcely describable kind of light, happiness, relief, exhilaration, encouragement, dawn."

In the present chapter of *Moby-Dick* Ahab reflects on his endless pursuit of the unobtainable white whale by remarking, "What is best left alone, that accursed thing is not always what least allures." A Nietzschean and Ishmaelean thought, this. But Ahab suffers and finally dies by the accursed thing that so allures him, symbol of the accursed questions that trouble his mind. Ahab succumbs to nihilism. Melville himself stood for a time with Nietzsche and Ishmael in the bright dawn of God's demise. Eventually, however, his sun flamed out, and the world around him, and within him, darkened.

Chapter 101: The Decanter

In the previous chapter Ishmael recalls the *Pequod*'s encounter with a ship, the *Samuel Enderby*, helmed by a captain who had lost an arm to Moby Dick. In the present chapter he reports that he met and boarded that same ship "long, very long after" his voyage with Ahab. Since Ishmael obviously composed his account of boarding the *Samuel Enderby* sometime after the event, and as this meeting took place very long after his voyage on the *Pequod*, the implication is that he wrote the narrative that is *Moby-Dick* many years after the events related in his story. How many years? Some number of years greater than even the number implied by the expression "long, very long after." Surely two or three will not do, nor even, I should think, five. A span of five years does not justify the repetition of the adjective "long" coupled with the intensifying adverb, does it? Shall we say ten years at the least, then, or perhaps even twenty? More? In any case, the matter presently of most interest to me is Ishmael's sustained exuberance. Even after a span of time longer than long, very long after his harrowing entanglement in Ahab's pursuit of the alluring but accursed white whale—even after all this time he is in high humor and good spirits. Ishmael may well be a metaphysical nihilist; he certainly plays with ideas that imply or at least suggest that God is dead. But he is no existential nihilist; he does not suffer from the absence of God. In this, Ishmael is representative of Melville himself at the height of his power, precisely as he was writing *Moby-Dick*. But Melville could not sustain his youthful vigor, his overflowing physical and spiritual health. He could not hold fast to his joyful wisdom.

Given the height of the summit Melville managed to scale in and through *Moby-Dick*, and considering also the apparent effortlessness of his ascent, his later decline is shocking, dispiriting too. But more unsettling still is the rapidity of his descent. Melville once described himself in a letter to Hawthorne as "like one of those seeds taken out of the Egyptian Pyramids, which, after being three thousand years a seed and nothing but a seed, being planted in English soil, it developed itself, grew to greenness, and then fell to the mould." The next short sentence materializes through an almost audible sigh: "So I," he writes. Having lived through a period of rapid development after many years of dormancy, he feels that now he too has "come to the inmost leaf of the bulb, and that shortly the flower must fall to the mould."

In the *Phaedo* Socrates claims to share the gift of prophecy granted by Apollo to dying swans, as he himself is so near to death. Melville would live a good many years yet, but his career as a successful writer would soon pass away. Apart from a brief flurry of moderate success with a few magazine stories in the mid-fifties, he was dead as an author after *Moby-Dick*. Perhaps he too was visited by the prophetic god?

I have previously mentioned the widely unpopular and vociferously denounced *Pierre*, which immediately followed *Moby-Dick*, and for which Melville had such extraordinarily high hopes, all dashed. Next came *The Isle of the Cross*, which was most likely a "fictional account of the experience of the real Agatha Hatch, a Nantucket woman deserted by the shipwrecked sailor she had nursed and married." Melville had tried to persuade Hawthorne to write the story, but eventually he undertook the work himself. The book was complete by the summer of 1853, but for some now inexplicable reason Melville felt that he was "prevented" from publishing it. The work never appeared, and for all anyone knows to this day Melville destroyed it. For the next few years he produced shorter works of fiction, some of which he collected in a volume entitled *The Piazza Tales*. He followed this with *Israel Potter*, a light-hearted work of historical fiction based on the adventures of a real figure active during the Revolutionary War. Finally, in 1857 he published *The Confidence-Man*, and with this book his career as a novelist came to a close. He would live another thirty-four years, but the only work of prose fiction found among his papers was the unfinished novella *Billy Budd, Sailor*.

In *The Myth of Sisyphus* Albert Camus identifies Melville as one of the great "philosophical novelists," and he names *Moby-Dick* one of modern literature's "truly absurd works." He might also have mentioned, as an instance of the absurd in fiction, Melville's short piece "Bartleby the Scrivener." Bartleby is a legal clerk, and with the constantly repeated polite but infuriating refrain, "I prefer not to," he resists his superior's requests that he perform his officially assigned duties. Although he is eventually fired, he will not leave; but neither will he work. In the end the authorities haul him off to jail and there he declines even to continue living. Bartleby is a match for Dostoevsky's Underground Man, the nameless civil servant who stubbornly rejects appeals to reason and practical self-interest with the aim of preserving uninhibited the freedom of his self-asserting will. Nietzsche was fascinated by Dostoevsky, whose work he discovered through a French translation of *Notes from Underground*, and I imagine he would have delighted in Melville's perverse creation of Bartleby, a man at odds unto death with the oppressive utilitarian environment of modern urban life. And as for Melville's last novel, *The Confidence-Man*, this work sails over the walls of the absurd and into the chaos of a skepticism so extreme as to amount to nihilism. The mysterious title character appears (and disappears) here and there in a number of guises and costumes, shifting shapes throughout the work to manifest as a series of persons intent on conning the money and beclouding the minds of various passengers aboard a Mississippi steam-boat. The story is sufficiently unsettling, but Melville's prose, backward-turning and halting with parenthetical and subordinate clauses, is a twisting labyrinth of words as disconcerting to readers as the confidence man is confounding to his marks. It is as if Melville intended not only to describe a nihilistic world but to summon such a world into being through his prose style.

In the present chapter of *Moby-Dick* Ishmael recalls an occasion when his study of a list of a whaleship's supplies suggested to him "many profound thoughts ... capable of a transcendental and Platonic application." An odd subject to inspire Platonic meditations, no doubt; but as Ishmael soars in spirit, he can play with any idea and have a grand time doing so. Melville himself eventually lost the capacity for this kind of play, and the flower of his youthful exuberance did sadly fall to the mould.

Chapter 102: A Bower in the Arsacides

Still under the influence of Apollo's prophetic gift, Melville has his Ishmael refer in this chapter to his activities as a poet. Some time after his voyage aboard the *Pequod* Ishmael composed a poem with the intention of tattooing the verses on various parts of his body. He gives no hint as to the theme, but he does imply that it was a long work. In any case, as I have previously noted, Melville in his later years was himself a practicing poet. He seems to have directed all his energies toward this task immediately following the failure of *The Confidence-Man*, and by the summer of 1860 he had produced a volume with which he was content. In the meantime he had decided to circumnavigate the globe with his brother Thomas, captain of the *Meteor*. At the end of May the ship sailed from Boston Harbor toward San Francisco by way of Cape Horn. Before leaving home Melville issued detailed instructions to his wife Elizabeth and his brother Allan regarding the publication and printing of his new work, which he entitled, simply, *Poems*. Throughout the passage he assumed he was at last a published poet, and he expected to find a copy of his work awaiting him in San Francisco, sent there by his wife. Jubilant as he was, however, the gloomy temper of his later years comes through in a letter to his young son Malcolm, to whom he related the news of a sailor aboard the ship who died when he fell from the main topsail yard to the deck below. The young man was travelling with a friend to California with the idea of relocating there, "but," Melville wrote, "you see what happened." That final clause, so unassuming on the surface, implies much that is deep (too deep perhaps to share with a boy of eleven?) concerning not only human mortality but also the worth of mortal expectations. In his journal Melville noted the young man's "fate," which, he observed, "belongs to that order of human events, which staggers those whom the Primal Philosophy hath not confirmed." And thinking of the dead man's mother he wrote, "Not so easily will his fate be washed out of her heart, as his blood from the deck." When Melville arrived in San Francisco to find, instead of a volume of his *Poems*, a letter from Elizabeth explaining that his manuscript had been rejected by more than one publishing house, he fell into a deep despond. Abandoning his plans to continue on with his brother, he returned home to settle uncomfortably into his life as a failed poet.

Melville's next book of poems, the first to be published, took up the theme of the Civil War. In the spring of 1864 he visited the front lines in Virginia, and in the company of the Union Colonel Charles Russell Lowell he rode with an expedition against the wily and dangerous Confederate John Singleton Mosby. Though the troops never managed to confront the full force of Mosby's notorious rangers, Melville witnessed the exchange of fire and saw the mangled limbs of wounded and dead soldiers. He recalls the experience in "The Scout toward Aldie," included in *Battle-Pieces and Aspects of the War*, which appeared in 1866. But well before the book was published, and not long in fact after his return from the front, Melville suffered a more personal loss: Nathaniel Hawthorne died unexpectedly on May 19 in Plymouth, New Hampshire. Elizabeth reported in a letter to her family that Melville was "much shocked" by the death, and years later, in 1869, when Melville stayed in the hotel in whose dining room he had presented a copy of *Moby-Dick* to Hawthorne, to whom he had dedicated the novel, his memories of this cherished friendship, coupled with melancholy reflections on Hawthorne's ever-ascending reputation and his own public neglect, likely contributed to the dark inspiration out of which the long narrative poem *Clarel* was born.

I have made reference to *Clarel* a few times in this book already, and I have quoted from the work too. But since I intend to make more extensive use of the poem throughout the rest of this book, in particular as illustrative of Melville's later condition of spiritual and psychological nihilism, or pessimism verging on nihilism, I here provide a more robust introduction to the poem than I have so far. Clarel is a young American student of theology who travels to Jerusalem full of doubts about his faith. He visits the holy sites and shrines but finds little to inspire belief; the waste of the land reinforces his suspicion that the universe is void of divinity. He meets and falls for a young Jewish girl, Ruth, but when her father is killed by Arabs she is obliged to participate in the ritual mourning, during which time Clarel is forbidden from seeing her. He joins up then with a band of men who trek to the Dead Sea and back, returning by way of a Greek monastery at Mar Saba, and later passing through Bethlehem. Upon his return to Jerusalem, Clarel learns that Ruth has died. The poem ends with Clarel in despair, but the narrator in the epilogue hints at the possibility of a final supernatural salvation.

Among the group of Clarel's travelling companions are two men particularly worthy of mention, Rolfe and Vine. Today there is near universal agreement among scholars that these two characters are representations of Melville and Hawthorne. Rolfe is the more vocal of the two, an intellectually adventurous skeptic, but by no means an outright atheist. Vine is quiet and mysterious, less given than Rolfe to verbalizing his thoughts and moods. We might say that Rolfe is more the thinker, Vine more of an artist. In any case, Melville appears to have intended to explore in *Clarel* his own intellectual-spiritual condition by comparing his mind to Hawthorne's through Rolfe's and Vine's interactions with men of various philosophical and theological dispositions, ranging from monomaniacal religious fundamentalism to materialist atheism, and all of this under the curious gaze of the thoughtful young Clarel himself. In the end there is no resolution, only a hint in the epilogue that despite Darwin, Despair, and Science, despite the "old debate" between "ape and angel" and the possibility that "there be no God," despite all this it may yet be that "death may prove unreal at the last" as it "routes life into victory."

Clarel is so pervaded by doubt that the final intimation of heaven, or of something like it, does not redeem the whole. In the *Phaedo* Socrates claims with confidence that after death he will join the company of the gods, and he urges his companions to believe likewise. Melville was far from confident about these matters, and his uncertainties bedeviled him in the end. When he wrote *Moby-Dick* he was sufficiently full of spiritual vitality to admit every doubt and still say Yes to life. In the present chapter Ishmael speculates that God is deaf to every mortal appeal, yet his speculations, as always, are full of an exuberant good humor. Like Theseus unspooling Ariadne's thread, to whom he alludes in this chapter, Ishmael can stalk through the labyrinth of even the murkiest skepticism and find his way out unharmed by the Minotaur of despair. In this he is an image of Melville young and bright. But Melville grew older, and eventually his mood grew dim.

Chapter 103: Measurement of the Whale's Skeleton

In this chapter Ishmael despairs of communicating faithfully the whale's appearance to those of his readers who have never seen him alive and afloat in his natural element. "Only in the heart of the quickest perils," he says, "only when within the eddyings of his angry flukes; only on the profound unbounded sea, can the fully invested whale be truly and livingly found out." We might apply a similar insight to certain philosophers and artists. Some do more than express their ideas and imaginings abstractly through speech or writing; they live them out in concrete activity. For this type of man, *philosophy is a way of life*. To comprehend this kind of philosopher one must not only read his books; one must observe his life. This is so not only because as an acting individual he may provide an example of a life well or poorly lived, but also because his thoughts are never fully realized until they work themselves into, and play out through, his everyday life.

It is a commonplace that Nietzsche was one of the few philosophers who really lived his ideas. The observation is true in some sense, but not at all in every sense. Consider the details of his biography: Nietzsche was the pious son of a pious family, quiet, small, and studious. For ten years he worked in a university town as a professional pedagogue. Following his early retirement he travelled through Europe by train and carriage from one hotel or rented room to another, roamed the streets and haunted the cafes of each town he visited, alone, jotted down his thoughts and published books that no one read. He rarely saw his few close friends; he never engaged in a lasting romantic relationship. Melville lived a fuller life, especially when he was young. In his early twenties he was an irrepressible wanderer, gathering experience through the sort of free-spirited exploits that a boyish academic like the young Nietzsche could only read about in story-books. In *Ecce Homo* Nietzsche predicts that his philosophy will one day triumph in the sign "*nitimur in vetitum*," which we may translate as "we seek that which is forbidden." This recalls his citation of this same line in *Beyond Good and Evil* with reference to his courage as an "adventurer" who roams through "all future realms." Of course this makes one think of Ishmael, who, as we know, is himself an adventurer who loves "to sail forbidden seas." And here it is worth underlining the fact that Melville himself was a roaming adventurer who encountered in person different peoples with perspectives widely divergent from his own. He learned his skeptical-perspectivist lessons first hand, through concrete experiences. Not only did he live and work aboard a whaleship at an age when Nietzsche was but a schoolboy, a studious scholar-in-training reading ancient history and philosophy books in a cramped apartment by candlelight; he was active even later in life. Well into his thirties he rode across Israel on horseback, with one eye open wide for bandits and the other seeking the tracks of an absent God. He visited Egypt and marveled at the pyramids, toured Turkey, Greece, and Rome as well. Nietzsche never stepped foot in Greece despite living during the period of Heinrich Schliemann's astonishing discoveries at Troy and Mycenae. He doubtless knew of Schliemann's work, which was publicized throughout Europe when Nietzsche was teaching in Basel. He sailed to Sicily once, but this is as far from home as he ever dared to venture.

In *Beyond Good and Evil* Nietzsche writes that the philosopher "must have been critic and skeptic and dogmatist and historian and also poet and collector and traveler and solver of riddles and moralist and seer and 'free spirit' and almost everything in order to pass through the whole range of human values and value feelings and to be *able* to see with many different eyes and consciences." Melville was himself a multiplicity: descendent of prosperous and noble forebears, now impoverished; intelligent and curious, learned even, but with no formal higher education; sailor, whaler, deserter, and mutineer; captive of cannibals and celebrated author; witness to war and son-in-law of a state Supreme Court Chief Justice. He was a pondering man and an active man simultaneously. He had experience of the world well beyond the confines of nineteenth-century American provincialism, beyond the boundaries in particular of established Christianity. He was, in short, a "free spirit" among the hidebound New England faithful.

In *Ecce Homo* Nietzsche laments the bookishness of his upbringing and education, his lack of practical, physical training. As a result of his typically "German education—its 'idealism,'" he complains that as a youth he was "backward to the point of holiness." The problem as he saw it was that the sort of "classical education" to which he was exposed "teaches one from the start to ignore *realities* and to pursue so-called 'ideal goals.'" Melville craved a classical education, but his family's financial privations prevented him from completing a formal education of any sort. For compensation he dove headfirst into the realities that Nietzsche was denied. His worldliness enabled him to be the artist-philosopher that he was, but a life spent shuffling through multiple perspectives may finally descend into nihilism. Nietzsche once observed that "there are many kinds of eyes. Even the sphinx has eyes—and consequently there are many kinds of 'truths,' and consequently there is no truth." I imagine that something similar to this, the potentially deflating consequences of this, combined with various professional failures and family troubles, finally brought Melville down into a condition approaching Nietzsche's "nihilism as a psychological state," or what I have called existential nihilism.

Chapter 104: The Fossil Whale

Moby-Dick abounds with evidence that at the time he conceived and composed the novel Melville was no existential nihilist. He contemplated the accursed questions without regarding them *as* accursed. He did not suffer from the death of God—he celebrated the event. In the present chapter his Ishmael confesses to being "horror-struck at this antemosaic, unsourced existence of the unspeakable terrors of the whale," but we know that Ishmael is quick to be social with horrors. His enthusiasm for recalling and writing about his time on the *Pequod* in pursuit of the great white whale is palpable in this chapter. When he requests a "condor's quill" for writing, and "Vesuvius' crater for an inkstand," we thrill with his infectious excitement. In "penning his thoughts on this Leviathan" Ishmael "expand[s] to its bulk," and we feel ourselves expand with him. Yes, we agree: to produce "a mighty book, you must choose a mighty theme." Ishmael has accomplished this, which is to say that *Melville* accomplished it. He knows it too, and he revels in his success.

It is Melville himself, then, who is social with horrors. He knows the blackness of darkness, but he burns internally with a light of spiritual, intellectual, and physiological health sufficiently bright to illumine every melancholy alcove, transforming all shadows into dazzling images of high-spirited cheerfulness. This fact shines through unmistakably in his writing, and if in the previous chapter I appeared to draw a sharp boundary between writing and living, I should like at this point to erase it. Melville was a man for whom writing was an essential part of living. He did not retreat from life when walking alone with his thoughts, or sitting in solitude at his writing desk. On such occasions he came most fully to life. When he asks his friend Evert Duyckinck to send him "about fifty fast-writing youths, with an easy style and not averse to polishing their labors," because he has "planned about that number of future works & cant [sic] find enough time to think about them separately," we catch a glimpse of the man in his natural form. He was in the middle of writing *Moby-Dick* at the time, yet still his excited mind refused to settle down. He outlined books enough for years.

Melville loved to spin out words as much in his correspondence as in his books. To Hawthorne he wrote that "if the world was entirely made up of Magians ... I should have a paper-mill established at one end of the house, and so have an endless riband of foolscap rolling in upon my desk; and upon that endless riband I should write a thousand – a million – a billion thoughts, all under the form of a letter to you." Melville was always overflowing with thoughts, and anyone familiar with the letters he did in fact write to Hawthorne will believe that with sufficient time he could have put a billion onto paper. His letter of April 16, 1851 is strikingly good evidence of the flow of words of which he was capable. After writing without pause or transition of the tragedy of human thought, of truth and the absence of God, of Being, the devil, the ego, and death, he concludes as if out of breath by wondering why it is that "in the last stages of metaphysics a fellow always falls to *swearing* so?" He could "rip an hour," he says, and I for one believe him.

Melville was as fascinating a talker as a writer. I have already noted Maunsell Field's observation that he had never heard better talking in his life than when Melville and Oliver Wendell Holmes conversed for hours about eastern religion and mythology. I have also quoted an excerpt from Hawthorne's journal in which he recounts the ever-shifting themes of a conversation with Melville. Here I give the relevant passage in full: "Melville and I had a talk about time and eternity, things of this world and of the next, and books, and publishers, and of all possible and impossible matters, that lasted pretty deep into the night." Melville himself must have had such an occasion in mind when he reminisced in a letter to Hawthorne about their bouts of heroic drinking and "ontological heroics," and Sophia Hawthorne was doubtless recalling such evenings the two men spent together in conversation when she described how Melville "dash[es] his tumultuous waves of thought up against" Hawthorne and "pours out the rich floods of his mind & experience to him." Evert Duyckinck experienced Melville in such talkative moods as well. In a diary entry for October 1, 1856, he noted that "Herman Melville passed the evening with me—fresh from his mountain charged to the muzzle with his sailor metaphysics and jargon of things unknowable."

Melville lived a significant part of his life in and through words. In some men this might be a vice, a manifestation of timidity in the face of active living. Not so with Melville. He had lived a physically active life as a youth, but he matured into "a pondering man" who lived for ideas and insights, and for such a man the activity of the mind is no less active than the muscular movements of the body. A deep thinker is not the same as an idle dreamer.

Chapter 105: Does the Whale's Magnitude Diminish? – Will He Perish?

In this chapter Ishmael discourses on the evolutionary history of the whale, though in a general and allusive, as opposed to a strictly scientific, manner. "Leviathan," he says, has come "floundering down upon us from the head-waters of the Eternities," and he pronounces the animal "immortal in his species, however perishable in his individuality." In the course of his discussion he refers to "philosophers of the forecastle," which expression reminds one of Duyckinck's reference to Melville's "sailor metaphysics," and his contrast between immortal species and perishable individuals is an unmistakable allusion to Platonic metaphysics, which contrasts the eternal Forms of natural kinds with ephemeral natural particulars.

Neither Plato nor Nietzsche spent time in the forecastle of a whaleship like Melville, of course; but they did have experience of sailing, Plato in particular according to ancient reports of his making three trips to Sicily. But be this as it may, Plato and Nietzsche were writers every bit as much as Melville. We tend to overlook this fact, for when we think of these two as philosophers we think of them primarily as generating ideas and arguments, and of writing down their thoughts solely for the sake of publication, not for the sheer love of writing. This is less so with respect to Nietzsche, but the need some scholars feel to locate consistent doctrines in his works exposes their neglect of the poetic aspect of his personality. And although some few scholars take note of Plato's life-long commitment to writing, they are misled by his having written dialogues, which are representations of conversations, into judging him by his supposed love of talking.

Plato may well have loved talking, but we have no information about this one way or the other. His characters talk, no doubt; but he created these characters through writing. His creative output varies from simple, short works of straightforward conceptual investigation to artistically moving flights of frenzied imagination; from subtle depictions of character and emotion to long, dense trains of logical argumentation. There is an ancient story that Plato repeatedly revised the first several words of the *Republic*, apparently seeking the perfect word order, in search of the ideal rhythm. Dionysius of Halicarnassus describes him as "combing and curling his dialogues and braiding them in every way." He judges Plato to be the "most daimonic" stylist of all the philosophers and orators, and he notes with evident approval the saying that if the gods speak a human language, then their king must speak in a Platonic style. Plato knew from experience the time and energy that goes into writing. In the *Phaedrus* he describes the composing and revising of a work as involving "turning [it] up and down over a long period of time, fitting [the parts] to one another and separating them." It is obvious to me that Plato wrote, not as a distasteful but necessary means of transmitting ideas, but because he loved the creative activity of writing for itself. Plato's career as an author lasted a full half century, and he was successful. The ancients told stories of people reading his works and then traveling to Athens to study with him. In one famous case, a woman named Axiothea was so taken by the *Republic* that she left her home in the Peloponnese and turned up at the Academy disguised as a man. She stayed there with Plato for years. The Academy itself survived for centuries. To inspire this sort of passionate commitment requires more than just the intellectual insight of a thinker; the beauty of an artist is necessary too.

Nietzsche was as passionate about writing as Plato and Melville. He was particularly fond of writing while walking along the coast of the sea, or through the winding lanes of an old Italian city, or in the mountains of Switzerland. It was from years of personal experience, then, that he judged that "only thoughts reached by walking have value." In a letter to a friend Nietzsche reports that he wrote *The Wanderer and His Shadow* in several small notebooks while walking through the forests of St. Moritz, and in *The Gay Science* he writes of his "habit to think outdoors—walking, leaping, climbing, dancing, preferably on lonely mountains or near the sea where even the trails become thoughtful." More than one account of his daily routine during his annual summer residence in Sils-Maria describes him as rambling thoughtfully around the local lakes or hiking high into the mountains with a pencil and notebook at the ready.

In the previous chapter I wrote of Nietzsche's isolation, of his infrequent contact with friends through years of solitary wandering. He was often lonely, by his own admission; but he insisted that solitude was necessary to the success of his task as a thinker and writer. In this connection, consider the following brilliant observation from *Twilight of the Idols*: "To live alone one must be a beast or a god, says Aristotle. Leaving out the third case: one must be both—a philosopher." For Nietzsche, writing is not a distraction or escape from life; to write well is to live. I am sure that his Zarathustra speaks for him when he says, "Of all that is written I love only what a man has written with his blood. Write with blood, and you will experience that blood is spirit." In a letter to a friend Nietzsche claimed that in his *Zarathustra* he "brought the German language to perfection," surpassing even Luther and Goethe as a prose stylist. And in this same letter he insists that he is "a poet, in the most radical sense of the word."

It is only a modest exaggeration to say that in his day no one read Nietzsche's books. He had an audience beyond the circle of his friends and acquaintances, but it was a very small audience. I suppose Nietzsche would have preferred the word "select" to "small," for he had confidence that in time the right sort of readers would find him. He would be, he wrote, "born posthumously." In any case, so meager was the population of Nietzsche's contemporary readers, and so great was his self-confidence, that he paid from out of his own pocket for the publication of all of his books beginning with *Beyond Good and Evil*. And although there was absolutely no public demand for it, he brought out a second edition of his works, complete with new prefaces—and in the case of *The Gay Science*, an additional part (Book Five)—after completing *Beyond Good and Evil*. Compare this with Melville, who once lamented in a letter to Hawthorne that if his work by chance survived his death, only his early romances of adventure would survive, and only for one generation.

As much as Melville loved the artistry of writing, he despised the business of being an author. Recall his lamenting that dollars damned him. He complained that he could write the Gospels and still die in the gutter. When he was offered an insultingly low percentage of royalties for *Pierre*, the follow-up to *Moby-Dick*, he disfigured the already completed manuscript by inserting several sections portraying his protagonist as an author, seemingly for the sole purpose of venting his spleen against every aspect of the book industry, from the publishers to the critics and the general reading public. He is doubtless writing of himself when as the narrator he says of Pierre that the "brightest success, now seemed intolerable to him, since he so plainly saw, that the brightest success could not be the sole offspring of Merit; but of Merit for the one thousandth part, and nine hundred and ninety-nine combining and dovetailing accidents for the rest." Indifferent to success or failure, Melville scorned all but his own judgment and the judgment of a select few others, such as Hawthorne. For the most part, as for Pierre, "all panegyric, all denunciation, all criticism of any sort, would come too late" for him. Today we know how mistaken was Melville's assessment of his prospects for future recognition, and how right Nietzsche was regarding his own posthumous influence. Strange to think that the god Apollo might have deceived Melville on this point while bestowing his gift of prophecy on the atheist Nietzsche.

But I was writing about writing. Plato, Melville, and Nietzsche were philosophers, artists, and poets—hybrid types. Each of them inclined more nearly toward one particular style of thinking and writing than did the other two, which is why we tend to distribute them among different taxonomical categories. But if we employ Nietzsche's expression "philosopher-artist," or my own more general "thinker-artist," then we can bring out their commonalities. And it seems to me that when thinking about the nature and practice of philosophy as the love of wisdom, we would do better to look beyond their superficial differences to concentrate on the similarities.

Chapter 106: Ahab's Leg

Early in this book I referred to Ahab as a perpetual philosopher, by which I mean a man lost in the labyrinth of philosophy, never to find his way through to wisdom. He suffers so from the problem of the universe, from the blackness of darkness, from the accursed questions, that eventually his suffering must kill him. In the present chapter, for example, in which we learn of the various torments to which Ahab is prone from his prosthetic leg, we learn as well of his belief that "all miserable events do naturally beget their like" and then some, which is to say that misery is more fertile than felicity, for "the ancestry and posterity of Grief go further than the ancestry and posterity of Joy." Ahab has begotten a son, but he has abandoned the boy and his mother to hunt Moby Dick. And Ishmael's mention of Ahab's accident ashore in Nantucket, not long before the *Pequod*'s departure, when as the result of a twisted tripping collapse his ivory leg screwed round and "all but pierced his groin"—this event intimates an impotence in the Captain respecting the good things and joys of life. Whatever natural human fertility Ahab once enjoyed has somehow turned monstrously spiritual, and the offspring of his seed are no bouncing babes but melancholy thoughts and infernal, fatal, deeds.

The loss of his leg was the beginning of Ahab's end. Doubtless there lay at the base of his soul instinctual and psychic preconditions that primed him to recoil from sanity in reaction to the violence inflicted on him by the whale. But we know nothing of the man's deep past, and besides, a thorough search for root causes would carry us back to the Garden. We must work with the facts provided concerning more immediate events, from which I conclude that Ahab's experience in the jaws of the whale transformed the man into a living symbol of human rage at an indifferent, at times even hostile, universe. Personal God or impersonal nature, it makes no difference in the deed itself: suffering man suffers, and neither intellect nor mechanism responds to his cries for help. This is the thought-world Ahab inhabits, its skies heaving with storm-clouds forever lowering, roiling and booming and flashing with terrible lightning.

Ahab's "pervading, mad recklessness" pilots his every decision and act, and even though he has his moments of clarity, he inevitably enlists his lucid thoughts in the service of the schemes of his "monomaniac mind." He speaks of God and wonders aloud about divine intentionality; he inquires into the perennial problems of personal identity, sin and salvation, the fate of man in life and death; he ponders time and eternity and is full of a jargon of things unknowable. In all this Ahab resembles Melville. There is this difference, however: Ahab is an objectification of the morbid elements of Melville's mind. These elements would surface in time to challenge Melville's own sanity, but when he wrote *Moby-Dick* he had his demons firmly under control. His intellectual vision penetrated beneath the surface waters of his mind to spy the sharks circling in the murky deep, but his health was such that he possessed the power to absorb and transform their dark energy into light. He was, moreover, aware of his condition. Recall Ishmael's image of the Catskill eagle that descends into gorges in the summits of high mountains. His depths are in the heights. And consider this similar thought, from *Pierre*: "The intensest light of reason and revelation, can not shed such blazonings upon the deeper truths in man, as will sometimes proceed from his own profoundest gloom. Utter darkness is then his light, and cat-like he distinctly sees all objects through a medium which is mere blindness to common vision." Melville surely arrived at this insight through self-reflection. His Ahab is a reflection too, but he generated the image by intentionally distorting his mirror.

Unfortunately for Melville, even "the gods themselves are not for ever glad." As the "ineffaceable, sad birth-mark in the brow of man, is but the stamp of sorrow in the signers," Melville's forehead over the years displayed ever more starkly the features of this melancholy seal. For a time he overcame philosophy, transcended the love of the seeker of wisdom to attain the love of a partner and friend. He arrived at a joyful wisdom. Ishmael is an externalization of Melville's contemporary internal condition, a condition for which Nietzsche employed the labels "Dionysian" and "Zarathustran." Ahab is a ghostly projection of Melville's worst potentialities, a tempestuous future looming on the horizon which could either roll in to batter him down or disperse, depending on the direction and force of the winds of his life. In Nietzsche's terms, Ahab is Melville's decadent side. He resisted the approach of the storm for a time, even managed to harness the crackling energy of the thunderbolts firing in the distance. But eventually he was struck, and he burned.

It seems to me that Nietzsche only sporadically attained the summit of cheerfulness to which he aspired, atop which Melville stood, even danced, for a time. But neither did he ever fall so low as Melville. Melville and Nietzsche lived complicated and, perhaps, ultimately unfulfilled lives. They were men after all. What then should we call Ishmael and Zarathustra: idols or ideals?

Chapter 107: The Carpenter

In this chapter Ishmael introduces the *Pequod*'s carpenter, who is charged with carving for Ahab a new leg, his old one having suffered "a half-splintering shock" when he dismounted the *Samuel Enderby*. This carpenter will later construct a coffin for Queequeg, which device is central to the plot as the Captain's leg is not, as we shall see. For now I examine the observation with which Ishmael brings the carpenter onto the stage, for it sounds a theme of interest to Melville and Nietzsche both.

"Seat thyself sultanically among the moons of Saturn," Ishmael writes, "and take high abstracted man alone; and he seems a wonder, a grandeur, and a woe. But from the same point, take mankind in mass, and for the most part, they seem a mob of unnecessary duplicates, both contemporary and hereditary." This is an expression of the character Ishmael's sentiment, of course; but Melville in his own voice once "confess[ed] a dislike to all mankind – in the mass." Even so, he simultaneously "assert[ed] unconditional democracy in all things." He understood that some men have insisted on there being "an aristocracy of the brain," and he even sympathized with the "man of superior mind" who, through "intense cultivation" of intellect and taste, has brought himself into "a certain spontaneous aristocracy of feeling" and so recoils in the presence of intellectual and cultural inferiors. Still, he maintained a "ruthless democracy on all sides." Melville acknowledges hierarchy while advocating democracy in this way from a belief that greatness can arise anywhere, a belief founded on observation, self-observation in particular. Melville's family in the generation of his grandparents included impressive individuals, but theirs were military accomplishments, not intellectual or literary; and in the generation of his parents the men in particular were noteworthy primarily for their failures. His own particular branch of the family descended into poverty and anonymity, while various cousins thrived. Yet his older brother Gansevoort made himself into a stirring public speaker; he was headed for a career in public life before his early death in 1846. His older sister Helen was remarkable too: she "had been capable of fulfilling any role in life open to a woman," yet these roles were limited, and as the oldest sister she was burdened with domestic duties in the house. Then of course there was Herman himself. There were no indications that he would become a great writer; he lacked every refinement of traditional cultural education. Yet he took himself in hand and burst out as a popular author and, later, a truly great artist. Melville respected American democracy because it made a story such as his possible, not from any commitment to an equality of worth of each and every individual.

In *Beyond Good and Evil* Nietzsche writes of "heights of the soul from which even tragedy ceases to look tragic," and he doubts whether "rolling together all the woe of the world" would "seduce us and compel us to feel pity." Nietzsche had no love of mankind in the mass, nor did he have any use for democracy. He stood always for the exception, and he believed that the ideological commitments that democracies inculcate in their citizens tend to undermine the production of exceptional individuals. They bind the bad conscience to the preconditions of superiority and thereby teach the best men to suspect and mistrust themselves. In short, Nietzsche understood the forces that necessitated the failure of Melville's writing career even though he knew nothing of the man's existence. "There are books that have opposite values for soul and health, depending on whether the lower soul, the lower vitality, or the higher and more vigorous ones turn to them," he wrote. *Moby-Dick* was no book for lower souls, but the audience Melville required to succeed as an author was composed predominately of inferior men. Superior men are rare. I have previously quoted Melville's own complaints that he could not earn a living writing as he would have liked to write. He well knew, as Nietzsche wrote, that "books for all the world are always foul-smelling books: the smell of small people clings to them." Yet still he admired the small people's social-political system *par excellence*.

According to Nietzsche, "the virtues of the common man might perhaps signify vices and weaknesses in a philosopher." Melville understood this, particularly if we substitute "artist" for "philosopher," or, better, count the two together as one. He shunned many of the common man's virtues, but he was dependent on common men for a living. Nietzsche managed to survive without profiting financially from his books. But Melville had a large family to support, and he had no real income from any other source than his writing—and this source began to dry up precisely when it should have overflowed, if, that is, there had been an aristocracy of the brain and of feeling sufficient to appreciate the value of his work. But American democratic taste was simply not ready for Melville's brand of superiority.

Chapter 108: Ahab and the Carpenter

Ahab approaches the carpenter at work at his vice-bench filing an ivory joist for the Captain's prosthetic leg. He stands still for the man to take his measurements and speaks at length of gods, the soul, and hell. Reflecting on the phenomenon known today as phantom-limb syndrome, Ahab remarks that if he "can still feel the smart of my crushed leg, though it be now so long dissolved," it is not unreasonable to believe that men after death may "feel the fiery pains of hell for ever, and without a body." Ahab is consumed by thoughts of death and hell, and his obsession provides insight into the state of his soul.

I use the word "soul," which according to Nietzsche we need not expel from our lexicon, for we may make good use of such notions as "mortal soul," "soul as subjective multiplicity," or "soul as social structure of the drives and affects." Yet we must, he insists, finally reject the metaphysical or spiritual idea of the soul, the soul conceived as "something indestructible, eternal, indivisible, as a monad, as an *atomon*." This Christian variety of "soul atomism" is pernicious to the extent that it provides the foundation for a supernaturalist system of justice, a perverse scheme that Nietzsche refers to as "a metaphysics of the hangman." The soul conceived as the spontaneously free source of human action, and judged in the context of an eternal moral world order, is susceptible of being pronounced sinful and guilty, and of being condemned to suffer punishment. Thinking of humans as bearers of souls measured by the standards of a divine morality is the means by which the priest acquires power over others, for he claims for himself a special role in the establishment of spiritual justice. Nietzsche sums the situation up as follows: "the concepts 'beyond,' 'Last Judgment,' 'immortality of the soul,' and 'soul' itself are instruments of torture, systems of cruelties by virtue of which the priest became master, remained master." For all of Ahab's mighty splendor, then, his conception of a shadow-self susceptible of pain in hell after death places him at the mercy of even the humblest priest.

As great, as grand as he is, Ahab is not his own man. He has been shaped by the beliefs and valuations of his Quaker forebears. He is a Christian. He may well be unorthodox, even heretical, but to wrestle with God one must believe in God. Not having heard the news that God is dead, Ahab lusts to kill the deity, or at least to exact revenge for his sufferings, and for the numberless sufferings of countless generations of men, for which he holds his God responsible. Ahab, moreover, must even be something of a traditionalist, for only those who conceive of the divine as omniscient, omnipotent, and omnibenevolent can be moved to blame God for the presence of evil; only those whose worldview includes a particular type of *theos* can expect or demand a theodicy.

When early in the novel Captain Peleg, one of the owners of the *Pequod*, describes Ahab to Ishmael as "ungodly," he does not mean to denounce the man as an atheist. Peleg and his co-owner Bildad are Quakers, and they refuse to hire unbelievers—recall their hesitation to put Queequeg to sea unless he can "show that he's converted." It may well be that these pious old men are ignorant of the full extent and significance of Ahab's recent psychological upheavals; had they known that he had no sincere interest in collecting stores of oil for profit, and only the meagerest intention of fulfilling his contracted obligations—and then only if his duties do not interfere with his actual mission—had they known these things they would most definitely have sought the services of another captain. But these are matters relating to Ahab's official functions as commander of a whaleship. As for his theology, if the Quaker owners of the *Pequod* had plumbed the depths of Ahab's soul, they would have been shocked; they might even have judged him an apostate; but they could not have accounted him unambiguously an atheist.

So Ahab is a believer, even something of a traditionalist. Even so, it would be foolish to deny that as a consequence of his encounter with Moby Dick his doctrinal commitments have been distorted and twisted almost as thoroughly as his leg was wrenched from his person. More, we must insist on the distortion. Ahab has inherited the standard canon of Christian beliefs and valuations; yet in many ways he has turned the dogma upside down and thereby so unsettled the whole that formerly compatible elements have been set against one another. Ahab hates what he should love, aims to conquer that to which he should submit. This is hubris in the original sense of the word: not merely excessive pride, but an aspiration to parity with the gods. The punishment for hubris is nemesis, the wrath of the gods, personified by the Greeks as a goddess of retribution. Ahab will be struck down, struck dead, for his overweening presumption, and thus he is a tragic figure. His doctrinal inversions and distortions are essential to his character, for through them he expands beyond the limits of average mortality into the realm of tragedy. Yet for all this, he is still confined. If the tragic depends on a conflict among a certain set of values and rivalry with God, as in Ahab's case it does, then as expansive as the tragic figure is, he cannot expand beyond a restricted field of theological assumptions. Ahab's are the assumptions of Christian dogma, and thus he is ultimately a creation of the ancient priests who formulated this dogma. From this perspective Ahab looks rather small, and impotent, in comparison.

But Ahab's submission to priestly influences is not the worst of his problems. His overriding problem is the perspective on life—or rather *against* life—that has developed in him from living in accord with Christian values. The real problem, in a word, is nihilism. Nietzsche conceives of the will through which the priests seek power as a "*nihilistic* will," for the priestly perspective reverses the life-promoting valuations of good and bad, true and false, healthy and sick, and it thereby encourages decline and degeneration. The belief in immortality, Nietzsche says, deprives the world of value, and the concepts of "hell" and "beyond" "*kill life*." As hostile to life, the Christian worldview is in essence nihilistic. By implication, then, Ahab too must be a nihilist; and not just by implication, for his actions themselves confirm his nihilism. Ahab's pursuit of Moby Dick is evidently bound up, even in his own mind, with a longing for God, and this turning away from the actual world for the sake of the divine beyond is in itself a negation of reality. The fact that Ahab is willing to die for his goal, even eager to die, exposes his own hostility to life. As tragic, and to that extent great, as this is, a life turned against life is nevertheless nihilistically decadent.

Chapter 109: Ahab and Starbuck in the Cabin

The previous chapter concludes with the carpenter soliloquizing on the subject of Ahab's strange character. The Captain's obscure ramblings about "one leg standing in three places, and all three places standing in one hell" confirm for the carpenter Stubb's characterization of Ahab as "queer, queer, very queer." In the present chapter Ahab himself takes up the theme of his own abnormality. In the course of an argument with Starbuck concerning leaky casks of oil in the *Pequod*'s hold, Ahab remarks, "I'm all leaks myself.

Aye! Leaks in leaks!" He is, he says, a leaky ship full of leaky casks. But he will not attempt to plug the leak, for it can't be found, and even if it could be located, one could never plug it "in this life's howling gale." Ahab understands that he is slowly going under, that he must soon sink from structural unsoundness, yet he plows ahead in pursuit of his singular aim, heedless of thereby hastening his end.

Ahab's punctured and seeping soul contrasts with Ishmael's overfullness and Melville's own abundance of life. I have previously applied to Ishmael Nietzsche's "ideal of a spirit who plays naively—that is, not deliberately, but from overflowing power and abundance—with all that was hitherto called holy, good, untouchable, divine." By now we have encountered several instances of Melville's own irreverent play with much that his contemporaries regarded as sacrosanct, particularly respecting religious and moral matters. Perhaps it is worth adding here an acknowledgement of Melville's playing with traditional narrative forms. The present chapter is one of several in which Ishmael relates events or conversations that he could not possibly have witnessed. This is no mistake on Melville's part; his other works, including the books that immediately preceded and succeeded *Moby-Dick*, amply demonstrate his firm narrative command of his material. Nor does Melville mean to portray Ishmael as an "unreliable narrator." No, Melville conceived and composed *Moby-Dick* from the excess of his overflowing abundance; he played naively with form and structure because he occupied an artistic position as far above contemporary literary standards as he was above moral, theological, and philosophical norms. As an artist he sat among the moons of Saturn, as it were. Thus some chapters of *Moby-Dick* are structured like plays; some even include stage directions. One chapter is little more than a song performed by the sailors in the round. Straight encyclopedic chapters mingle among historical mini-treatises, monologues, and narrative action. *Moby-Dick* in many ways is less a traditional novel than it is an unconscious attempt at a *Gesamtkunstwerk*, a total work of art, consisting exclusively of written words. We do not have the letter that Hawthorne wrote to Melville expressing his appreciation of his friend's accomplishment; Melville apparently destroyed it. But we do have Melville's ecstatic reply. There is no statement in Melville's letter, nor even an intimation, to suggest that narrative or stylistic tricks were at issue. Hawthorne understood and praised "the pervading thought that impelled the book," and even though Melville clearly regards "the soul" of the work as more significant than its "imperfect body," that very body, subversive of orthodox style and structure, contributes to the constitution of its soul.

During one of Nietzsche's most productive periods, when he brought out the second editions of his works, adding new prefaces to each and a fifth book to *The Gay Science*, he reflected deeply on pessimism and the existential condition of the pessimist. In his first book, *The Birth of Tragedy*, he had not recognized a fact he later came to regard as essential, namely that pessimism can be an indication of either health or sickness depending on the underlying state of the pessimist. Pessimism, like every philosophy and even every art, presupposes "suffering and sufferers." Yet some men suffer from "the *over-fullness of life*," while others suffer from "the *impoverishment of life*." The former are Dionysian types; the latter are decadent romantics. In *The Birth of Tragedy* Nietzsche had failed to distinguish between "romantic pessimism" and "Dionysian pessimism." Now he understands that when confronted with artistic or philosophical productions he must inquire whether it is "hunger or super-abundance that has here become creative." From hunger proceeds only decadent romantic pessimism. The super-abundant man is Dionysian.

In the "Attempt at a Self-Criticism" that he affixed to the beginning of the second edition of *The Birth of Tragedy*, Nietzsche formulates the distinction between types of pessimism in terms of strength and weakness. The "pessimism of strength" is "prompted by well-being, by overflowing health, by the *fullness* of existence." The pessimism of weakness is "a sign of decline, decay, degeneration, weary and weak instincts." Originally Nietzsche had expressed the nature of Greek pessimism in Schopenhauerian terms, but now he realizes that he had misunderstood Schopenhauer. Like Buddhism, Epicureanism, Christianity, and the Wagnerian music-drama, Schopenhauer's philosophy was born of weakness and a consequent inability to endure, learn from, and *grow* from suffering. It is in fact a manifestation of nihilism. Greek pessimism was altogether different; it was an expression of Dionysian affirmation.

Nietzsche studied and appreciated philosophy prior to his discovery of Schopenhauer, but his encounter with Schopenhauer's work was the catalyst for his eventually becoming a philosopher himself. Early on he was an enthusiastic disciple of Schopenhauer. In *Ecce Homo* he reports in this connection that "I very earnestly denied my 'will to life' at the time when I first read Schopenhauer (1865)." Later, however, as we have seen, he discovered a distinction between Schopenhauerian and Dionysian pessimism that depends on a more fundamental distinction between decadence and "the great health." Then he realized that as a youth he had occupied alien ground; he had not known himself. But eventually he had found his way, his *own* way, to the "soil out of which my intention, my *ability* grows." He understood himself in the end as "the last disciple of the philosopher Dionysus."

I have gone into these details of Nietzsche's intellectual biography because they serve as a reverse image of Melville's intellectual and existential development (or "degeneration," as Nietzsche would most likely put it). As a young author Melville affirmed his life and the wide world in even its gloomiest aspects, and his affirmation flowed from a super-abundance of health and vigor. His Ishmael can, in Nietzsche's words, "afford the sight of the terrible and questionable" because Melville himself was one of those Dionysian types who are "richest in the fullness of life." Later, however, Melville sprung a leak and sunk into a depressive condition very close to, if not identical to, nihilism. In his last years he even discovered Schopenhauer. He owned several volumes of Schopenhauer's works, and he read them closely. His marginalia indicate that he identified with Schopenhauer's pessimism, and thus that he ended his life in a state that Nietzsche conceived as the muck in which he had begun his own life as a philosopher, but which he ultimately mustered the strength to reject, to escape, to overcome.

Chapter 110: Queequeg in his Coffin

In the present chapter of *Moby-Dick* Ishmael plays Phaedo to Queequeg's Socrates by narrating the story of his friend's death, or anyway what had seemed to all the sailors aboard the *Pequod* would be his death. According to Ishmael's account, one day while moving casks of oil in the damp and frigid hold of the ship, Queequeg caught a chill that quickly developed into a dangerous fever, somewhat as Socrates after drinking the hemlock in prison experienced a chill move from his feet up through his body until finally it reached his heart, at which point he died. Phaedo wept as he watched Socrates drink the poison, and though Ishmael does not mention tears, he clearly lamented the fate of "poor Queequeg," his "fast bosom-friend."

So confident is Queequeg that he will die, he lies down in his hammock to await his passing in peace, as Socrates mounted and stretched out on his own deathbed just prior to finally expiring. And as Socrates covered himself with a burial shroud, Queequeg climbs into the coffin he commissions from the carpenter, reclining for a while in his own death-box, acclimatizing himself to his eternal accommodations. Finding the coffin a suitable fit, Queequeg has the surrounding mourners replace him in his hammock, and then, at a "critical moment" recalling "a little duty" ashore that he did not want to leave undone, he "suddenly rallied" and "changed his mind about dying." Ishmael does not specify the nature of Queequeg's duty, and it appears from the text that he does not know it. The situation reminds one of Socrates' uncovering himself at a moment just prior to dying to ask his friend Crito to sacrifice a rooster to Asclepius. To what end? Crito may have known, but we do not. The meaning of Socrates' last words eludes scholars to this day.

So Queequeg recovers from what had looked to be a fatal illness. The sailors are stunned, and when they inquire whether the matter of living or dying depends solely on his "own sovereign will and pleasure," Queequeg calmly replies that, yes, "if a man made up his mind to live, mere sickness could not kill him." He will live as long as he likes, he says, or anyway until "a whale, or a gale, or some violent, ungovernable, unintelligent destroyer of that sort" finally takes his life. Socrates makes a similar point when he insists that a man must avoid taking his own life and continue to live until a god sends against him some unavoidable necessity, as in his own present case.

Ishmael reports that before Queequeg's recovery, as he was wasting away from fever, he seemed to have acquired special insights from the approach of death. His intuitions, Ishmael says, were equal to the insights of any dying Greek, presumably including Socrates, who was himself inspired by Apollo with special prophetic knowledge as death drew near to him. Socrates gave voice to his prophetic insights, speaking at length with his friends about the soul, the afterlife, virtue, knowledge, the true nature of the physical cosmos, and of metaphysical reality too. He spoke, in short, the contents of the *Phaedo*. Queequeg's insights manifest as mysterious shades moving over his face and in his eyes, but he does not speak them aloud. His actions after recovering, however, are pregnant with meaning and doubtless inspired by his near-death insights. Having decided to repurpose his coffin as a storage-chest, he decorates it with carvings resembling the inked images of his many tattoos. Besides his skeletal frame, these tattoos were all that remained of Queequeg during the period of his wasting away, which made visible the Pythagorean analogy between one's body and one's tomb. His tattoos were inscribed on his body by a "prophet and seer" of his native island, and the overall work represents "a complete theory of the heavens and the earth and a mystical treatise on the art of attaining truth." I read this as a summary of the contents of Plato's *Phaedo*, for the dialogue is spoken mostly by Socrates, who declares himself a "prophet"; it concludes with an account of the earth as a spherical body floating unsupported in the middle of the heavens, and details the true nature of the surface of the earth, the ethereal realm above, and a complex system of rivers, lakes, and caverns in the underworld; and in the work, moreover, Socrates discusses the proper method for attaining truth in association with a broader doctrine that in *White-Jacket* Melville explicitly labels "mystic."

At the end of the *Phaedo* Socrates utters his notoriously obscure last words: "Crito, we owe a rooster to Asclepius: repay it, and do not neglect this." Melville wrote about Socrates' death on more than one occasion, and he interpreted the significance of the philosopher's end with his last words in mind. In a short story written two years after *Moby-Dick* he describes Socrates confronting his death as "cheerful." And referring to the sacrifice of the rooster as a "testimony of [Socrates'] final victory over life," he calls Socrates himself a "game-fowl Greek" and says that he "died unappalled." Here, in *Moby-Dick*, Melville portrays Pip as so moved by Queequeg's calm demeanor in the face of death that he calls for "a game cock now to sit upon his head and crow!" Pip wants a celebration, for Queequeg "dies game!" According to Melville, then, Socrates and Queequeg were in a sort of competition with life, and in dying—or almost dying—unappalled and game, they were victorious. Their tranquility when confronted by death was for him a sign of their health, strength, and over-abundant cheerfulness.

Queequeg at his lowest ebb puts Ishmael in mind specifically of the dying "Zoroaster," Zarathustra to the Greeks. He speculates that his friend was then on the verge of beholding the "last revelation," which is disclosed to men at the moment of their death. What could this be? "Only an author from the dead could adequately tell." So Ishmael says; but others have other ideas. In the antepenultimate section of the first edition of *The Gay Science*, Nietzsche says that although Socrates had been a taciturn man (like Queequeg), "something loosened his tongue" just prior to his dying; and Nietzsche scholar Paul Loeb argues that this something was a revelation of the eternal return: we die, but we shall be reborn—not into another world, another form, another body, or another life, but into the self-same world and the identical life. Millennia upon millennia, even millions or billions of years may pass before cosmic time circles round again to the moment of one's birth, but the loop will close eventually. And since after death one does not exist, and therefore experiences nothing of the passing of time, to a man's subjective experience the moment of his rebirth follows immediately upon his death. The temporal threshold is instantaneous, but as we approach it, just prior to dying and stepping across, we somehow learn the truth of the eternal return. There is no afterlife, no new or different life, nor even any respite between lives. Every man, Socrates included, must always return to his identical life immediately upon dying. This is the final revelation, and since Socrates experienced his life as an illness, and since his one overriding goal, as articulated explicitly in the *Phaedo*, was to escape the cycle of rebirth, he could not bear this truth and so was moved to expend his last stores of energy and breath condemning it. Thus his "ridiculous and terrible" last words, which prove, according to Nietzsche, that Socrates "*suffered life*," which proves in turn that Socrates was a Nay-sayer and a failure, that he was, in a word, decadent.

Nietzsche understood Socrates' death and last words altogether differently from Melville. Socrates was not game; he did not die unappalled. Since Asclepius is the god of healing, Nietzsche interprets Socrates' request that Crito sacrifice a rooster to the god as an admission that he conceives of life as a disease, and of death as the cure. This is not an implausible reading, for, as we have seen, Socrates in the *Phaedo* is relentlessly hostile to embodied life, likening the body explicitly to a prison from which the soul must escape to be truly itself; and he even identifies the practice of philosophy with training for death. Nietzsche takes Socrates' condemnation of life as a *self-condemnation*—for what is life ever but *one's own* life?—and therefore as a sign of Socrates' decadence.

Loeb's claim that Nietzsche intends to suggest that Socrates' last words were prompted by a revelation of the truth of the eternal return depends in part on the interrelations among the final three sections of the first edition of *The Gay Science*. Immediately following the section on Socrates' last words is the first substantive account of the eternal return in Nietzsche's corpus. In this section Nietzsche invites his readers to imagine their reaction if "some day or night a demon were to steal after you in your loneliest loneliness" and announce the secret of the eternal return. "Would you not throw yourself down and gnash your teeth and curse the demon who spoke thus?" he asks. "Or have you once experienced a tremendous moment when you would have

answered him: 'You are a god and never have I heard anything more divine.'"
Socrates famously claimed that a *daimonion*, a little demon, spoke to him
from time to time. Loeb argues that Nietzsche means to suggest that this
demon revealed to Socrates the secret of the eternal return, and that the
philosopher's last words were his cursing the revelation and his gnashing of
teeth. The section following this one on the eternal return is the last section of
the first edition of the book. In it Nietzsche introduces Zarathustra, and this
serves in turn as an introduction to his next book, *Thus Spoke Zarathustra*, in
which he provides an example of the type of man who through an over-rich
abundance of life is able not only to grasp the truth of eternal return, but to
proclaim it himself as the most divine of all doctrines. Zarathustra *affirms* the
revelation of his return. His love of life is so profound—hard-won, to be sure,
given his many ordeals of isolation, misunderstanding, and suffering, but
nevertheless so deep and sincere that he can say, "Was *that* life? Well then!
Once more!" Zarathustra's affirmation of the eternal return is as certain an
indication of his great health as Socrates' condemnation is a symptom of his
pitiable decadence.

Chapter 111: The Pacific

Ishmael says in this short chapter that when riding on the "eternal swells" of
the heaving Pacific one "must own the seductive God, bowing your head to
Pan." Pan was generally considered the offspring of Hermes, a god who
among his other duties was charged with guiding the souls of the dead to the
underworld. Hermes the psychopomp. Others thought Pan the son of Apollo,
who, as we have seen, has his own associations with death and the
underworld, particularly in the *Phaedo*. At the conclusion of Plato's
Phaedrus, a dialogue at least in part about seduction, and therefore often
paired with the *Symposium*, but which addresses many themes in common
with the *Phaedo*, Socrates prays to Pan beside the river Ilisos.

Plutarch, priest of Apollo at the oracle of Delphi, Platonic philosopher,
and prolific author, in his essay on the decline of oracles relates the story of
the announcement of Pan's death. Sometime during the reign of Tiberius
(A.D. 14-37), a sailor aboard a ship bound for Italy heard a voice drifting over
the water from an island off the northwestern coast of Greece. "The great Pan
is dead," the voice cried out, "the great Pan is dead!" The sailors spread the

news abroad, to the general consternation and dismay of those who heard their report. The emperor himself was shocked, convinced as eventually he was of the veracity of the sailors' testimony. God is dead!

Of course Pan was only one of many gods in the Greek pantheon, but the story of his death has often been taken to signify the decline of the ancient pagan world in general. The idea is buttressed by the fact that Jesus came of age during the reign of Tiberius. The old gods are dying; may the new god, the One True God, forever reign! In *The Birth of Tragedy* Nietzsche cites Plutarch's story of Pan's dying as a parallel to the experience among the Greeks when tragedy died. "There rose everywhere the deep sense of an immense void," he writes. As we know, Nietzsche believed that the villain who assassinated tragedy was Socrates. His weapon was philosophy, more specifically "optimistic dialectic," which is to say a naive confidence that men can attain knowledge through reason, that he who knows the good will live well, and that whoever lives well is happy. In these ideas, Nietzsche says, "lies the death of tragedy." Socrates taught his version of rational optimism to others as an ideal, and when he died so calmly, superior even to life itself, such an impressive and awe-inspiring death, Socrates' ideal spread. In short, Socrates' manner of dying seduced others to his manner of living. "*The dying Socrates*," Nietzsche says, "became the new ideal, never before seen, of noble Greek youths." More, "the typical Hellenic youth, Plato, prostrated himself before this image with all the ardent devotion of his enthusiastic soul." This Socratic ideal, this anti-tragic optimism, taken up, developed, and spread abroad by Plato, eventually blossomed into Christianity.

So "the art of Greek tragedy was wrecked" by Socrates, and more specifically by the opposition between Socrates and Dionysus, the archetypal god of Greek tragedy. In his late period Nietzsche tends to identify the Dionysian with the Zarathustran outlook, and we may take his late opposition between Dionysus and the Crucified as a version of his earlier opposition between Dionysus and Socrates, and both of these as in spirit identical to an opposition between Socrates and Zarathustra, the very opposition we encounter at the conclusion of the first edition of *The Gay Science*. The historical decline that begins with Socrates' overcoming of Dionysus, which as exacerbated by Plato prepared the soil for Christianity, will finally be set right when Zarathustra overcomes the Christian God. Thus when Nietzsche introduces Zarathustra in the final section of *The Gay Science*, he entitles the passage "*Incipit tragoedia*," the tragedy begins. We might say that with

Zarathustra the tragedy begins *again*, that the tragic worldview is *renewed*. Socrates had been the one great enemy of tragedy, through whose influence the tragic *Weltanschauung* collapsed, dragging the entire ancient world down with it. But now in Zarathustra we have a new ideal. Now we can put the dying Socrates behind us, beneath us, and rise up to receive inspiration from *the living Zarathustra*. Zarathustra lives eternally, but not as a pure disembodied spirit dwelling in an ethereal after-world; rather as one and the same Zarathustra living his identical life again and again, and, more importantly, *affirming* his eternally recurring life.

Melville himself was not devoted either to Christ or to Zarathustra, or rather, having been raised a Christian, he matured into an inverted-Platonism, eventually declined toward existential nihilism, then settled at last into a resigned pessimism. But do not take the "settled" here to imply that Melville's soul relaxed into a state of absolute motionlessness. No: he was himself the "meditative Magian rover" whose presence Ishmael evokes in the present chapter, and when he writes of the "sweet mystery" of the sea, "whose gently awful stirrings seem to speak of some hidden soul beneath," we may take him as describing himself. Melville's interior waves were "ever-rolling," and like the sea itself he could stay put and heave simultaneously.

Chapter 112: The Blacksmith

"Oh, Death, why canst thou not sometimes be timely?" Thus asks Ishmael with the sad fate of the *Pequod*'s blacksmith in mind. The man had once been employed ashore and lived at home with a wife and children; but later he succumbed to the lure of alcohol and lost everything. Death even robbed him of his family and, worse, withheld the gift of a grave of his own. The blacksmith lived too long, outlived his life, and so he took to the sea. The sea, Ishmael says, offers to men with "death-longing eyes," but who "still have left in them some interior compunctions against suicide," an experience in many ways comparable to death. At sea such men as the blacksmith can "bury [themselves] in a life which … is more oblivious than death."

Ishmael understands the commonalities between death and the sea because he went to sea as a substitute for suicide. Melville as a young man had tendencies toward melancholy himself, but we have no indications that he was ever suicidal. He seems to have gone to sea primarily from a lack of regular employment ashore. We do know, however, as I have mentioned, that Melville's father showed signs of madness before dying, that his son Malcolm took his own life, and that Melville himself was declared insane by certain members of his family. Questions linger regarding his dependence on alcohol. Whatever the precise nature of Melville's condition, it is safe to say that through much of the second half of his life he was a grave, disappointed man. Witness the letter to a brother-in-law from 1877, in which he writes that at his age—he was approaching sixty—"a certain lassitude steals over" him at times, and then "the problem of the universe seems a humbug ... and the – well, the nepenthe seems all-in-all." Nepenthe is mentioned in the *Odyssey* as an Egyptian drug that causes humans to forget their ills and sorrows. As a postscript to this letter Melville added that he "gets to care less and less for everything except downright good feeling. Life is so short, and so ridiculous and irrational (from a certain point of view) that one knows not what to make of it." And beneath his signature he wrote, "N.B. *I aint crazy.*" No, he probably wasn't crazy, but he wasn't particularly happy either. I would not suggest that a timely death would have arrived at the moment Melville completed *Moby-Dick*, but one can wish that life—in more than the technical sense—that life as exuberance, abundance, and cheerfulness had stayed near to him longer than it did.

In a discourse entitled "On Free Death" Nietzsche's Zarathustra advocates dying at the right time. "Many die too late," he says, "and a few die too early." Death is not bad in itself, for the right sort of death can consummate life, and "he that consummates his life dies his death victoriously." We have seen that Melville describes Socrates in death as victorious. But from Nietzsche's perspective, to be victorious over life is to be defeated. The healthy man does not struggle *against* life; he celebrates life, affirms it, even *wills* its eternal recurrence. But to Socrates, life itself is a kind of death, and the body is a tomb, or a prison. And though he will not kill himself, and he refuses to escape from the jailhouse even after his friends have bribed the guards, he is eager for the gods to grant him release through death. Socrates wanted out, and although he claims that his death is a consequence of "some necessity" sent by god, as Nietzsche writes in *The Birth of Tragedy*, he "seems to have brought about with perfect awareness" his own death sentence. But in this way he passed sentence on life, on *his* life. Socrates' death was precisely what Zarathustra warns against, "a blasphemy against man and earth." Therefore his "dying ... turned out badly," which is evidence that his life had gone badly too.

Chapter 113: The Forge

The blacksmith understands that his life has gone badly. He is one of those "all-too-many" who live too long according to Zarathustra, who "all-too-long ... hang on their branches." Zarathustra would have a storm roll in to shake such men from their trees, but the blacksmith, daily toiling amid "sparks in thick hovering flights," is inured to the blast of fire. He hangs on his branch of life in spite of every flare, flash, and boom. He is "scorched all over," he tells Ahab, "past scorching." In speaking with the carpenter in a previous chapter, Ahab referred to this blacksmith as Prometheus. But this was just an idle association, linking the man at his forge with Prometheus's fire. The blacksmith is no god, and Ahab was less interested in the man himself than in his fire, and this because the flames set him to thinking of hell.

Ahab more than any man among his crew resembles a dissident chained to stone and gnawed at daily by Zeus's eagle. As he strives against the gods for no one's sake but his own, his sin is greater than Prometheus's. Prometheus tricked and stole from the gods for the good of humanity; the gift of his fire brought civilization to man, or the awakening of conscious awareness if we read the myth with a more spiritual eye. But Ahab is in flight from civilized life, and he is sailing furiously toward the abyss of his own unconsciousness. No Heracles will release him from his suffering; he has no friends even among the demigods.

Observing the blacksmith's wretched condition, Ahab wonders why the man does not go mad. He is, he says, "impatient of all misery in others that is not mad," and he suspects that the blacksmith cannot go mad because "the heavens yet hate" him. So madness strikes Ahab as a therapy for misery, but his own case surely belies this. He is mad himself, precisely because he hates the heavens, and his frenzied state of mind affords him no relief. He is as scorched as the blacksmith, and not from working at a forge but from tangling with the gods. His lightning-scar is a sign of all that ails him, a symbol of his hubris as punished by Zeus the god of thunder. "The thunderbolt pilots all things," says Heraclitus, and Zeus is not yet done with the Captain. But Ahab is no mere puppet of the gods, for as Heraclitus also noted, "a man's character is his fate."

Ahab intends to wage war with the gods as embodied in Moby Dick. A symptom of his madness, no doubt; an invitation to nemesis. But he has his wits sufficiently about him to know that he requires a suitable weapon. Therefore he has come to the blacksmith for a harpoon "that a thousand yoke of fiends could not part." As material for the shaft he has filled a bag with the nail-stubbs of steel horseshoes, which he expects "will weld together like glue from the melted bones of murderers." For the barbs he provides his own razors, which he does not need for himself as he has vowed neither to "shave, sup, nor pray till..." He does not complete the thought, but one suspects it had to do with the death of either man or god. When the harpoon is completed, Ahab will not permit the blacksmith to temper it in water. Instead, he summons his three pagan harpooners, punctures their "heathen flesh," and soaks his weapon in their blood. Then, "as the malignant iron scorchingly devoured the baptismal blood," Ahab intones: "Ego non baptizo te in nomine patris, sed in nomine diaboli!" We have seen that in a letter to Hawthorne Melville cites a version of this line as the secret motto of *Moby-Dick*. The sentiment indicates Melville's artistic "beyond good and evil," his philosophical immoralism in a Nietzschean sense. But Ahab means to invoke the demonic with all the passion and faith he commands. Melville is a free spirit; Ahab is a *believer*. As a man of narrow faith, Ahab could never create Ahab, much less create Ahab and Ishmael and Queequeg and Pip and the *Pequod* and Moby Dick. Melville as author of *Moby-Dick* was expansive, healthy, and playful. Ahab is constricted, sick, and serious. The "black tragedy of the melancholy ship" is Melville's doing in one sense, of course, but chiefly in the highest sense of the creator who stands above his work as master inventor. He occupies a height from which he can see the comic in the tragic. Ahab is author of the *Pequod*'s tragedy in an altogether different sense, as a man imprisoned in his pain, godlike in a way, perhaps, but still somehow too weak to rise above his depths. He is leaking, and he will sink. He is, as I have said, the perpetual philosopher, never to be the sage.

Chapter 114: The Gilder

From Ishmael's perspective afloat in a whaleboat, it was an idyllic day. The surface of the surrounding sea was a still, crystalline smoothness; tranquility rose from the water like meandering clouds, softly infusing his soul with a dreamy serenity. Drifting through the mists of a "mystic mood," he roamed the meadowed plains of a distant dreamy thought-world in which fact interblends with fancy and all things are possible, and all possibilities are sublime.

Ahab was present too of course; he too experienced the "glassy glades," the "ever vernal endless landscapes" of the spirit. Yes, the sea inspired a golden temper even in the moody Captain. Yet his calm was only temporary, for presently a deeper gloom dulled the luster of his day. Ahab is no longer capable of rest, nor can he calmly enjoy the restlessness of his soul. A man like Ishmael is constantly moving, inside and out; but his perpetual motion does not upset or unsettle him. Ahab is altogether different: his every step is a pain. In this world there are two kinds of wanderer: there is the man who rambles through every garden of life and mind, collecting experiences and ideas, exploring his environment and experimenting even on himself. He seeks no particular destination, for his wisdom is in the walking. Then there is the man on the move because he is lost, from himself as well as from home. Unable to make a home of himself, and so rest content wherever he happens to be, he is forever on the hunt for a point just beyond the receding horizon. His every stride is vain, for his journey is not agreeable in itself; it is an aggravating means to a non-existent end.

Ahab cannot enjoy the sea's calm because he suffers from its transience. He longs so for the eternality of Being, even if only from a rage to capture and kill it, that he is blind to the beauty of Becoming. Therefore he laments that "there is no steady unretracing progress in this life," that "we do not advance through fixed gradations, and at the last one pause:—through infancy's unconscious spell, boyhood's thoughtless faith, adolescence' doubt (the common doom), then scepticism, then disbelief, resting at last in manhood's pondering repose of If." No such repose is possible, for "once gone through, we trace the round again; and are infants, boys, and men, and Ifs eternally." For Ahab this is a melancholy admission that his life is an endless pursuit, a labyrinth of thoughts and moods forever bending round and turning back on themselves, winding in circuits away from the center to twist in time inevitably again toward the core. He is lost inside his own mind, and the cosmic obscurities that thrill him also hold him fast to their mystery, to the *trouble* of their mystery. He cannot find his way to the clarity of a solution, much less to that deeper but more brilliant clarity that is peace in the face of insoluble mysteries. Ahab expresses a longing for a lasting calm, but his physical, intellectual, and spiritual actions belie his words. He is a roving seeker with no idea as to the proper object of his search. In philosophical terms, he loves the love of wisdom rather than wisdom itself. Or anyway this would be so if he were still able to love.

The philosopher truly on his way to wisdom, or the philosopher as the possessor of a joyful wisdom, might also deny to the trajectory of life a steady unretracing progress. But this would be no cause for lamentation; it would instead be a stimulus. The philosopher-sage experiences the recurring If as a series of signposts on the circuitous route by which he arrives at the gates to the garden of wisdom, and along which he wanders within it, exploring and admiring every flower of experience and thought. Nietzsche has a similar idea in mind when he writes that "we ourselves keep growing, keep changing, we shed our old bark, we shed our skins every spring, we keep becoming younger, fuller of future, taller, stronger... Like trees we grow ... not in one place only but everywhere, not in one direction but equally upward and outward and inward and downward; our energy is at work simultaneously in the trunk, branches, and roots; we are no longer free to do only one particular thing, to *be* only one particular thing." The Nietzschean philosopher does not suffer from transience, from the unsteady retracing recurrence of life's every path. Such movement is necessary to the task of the existential-intellectual experimentalist, and Nietzsche regarded the "idea that life could be an experiment of the seeker of knowledge" as "the great liberator." He who would experiment with, through, and on his life must understand that he may never rest, and he must experience his profoundest freedom in the prospect of ceaseless motion, even the ceaseless recurrence of identical motions.

Ahab's dirge on the recurring cycles of the thoughtful man's intellectual and spiritual life is not quite an expression of Nietzsche's eternal return, of meaninglessness repeated eternally in a universe devoid of God. But it is an expression of goal-lessness, of an anti-teleological view of life. And the lines immediately following imply something like the death of God, certainly at least the impenetrable obscurity of the divine, and hence also the obscurity of ourselves, our origin, nature, and destiny: "Where lies the final harbour, whence we unmoor no more? In what rapt ether sails the world, of which the weariest will never weary? Where is the foundling's father hidden? Our souls are like those orphans whose unwedded mothers die in bearing them; the secret of our paternity lies in their grave, and we must there to learn it." This idea that the secret of our nature lies in the grave is not the only expression in *Moby-Dick* of the mysteries of reality and of ourselves; many times by now we have encountered some version of the suggestion that there is no solution to the Problem of the Universe, that the microcosm is as unfathomable as the macrocosm, each unknowable because there are no objects of knowledge—no Platonic Forms, no essences. But if there is no end to our pursuit; if there are no answers to the questions we put to the universe, no independently existing objects of knowledge, then there is no God, certainly no god as conceived either by Plato or by traditional Christianity, God as the source and ground of reality and objective truth.

Nietzsche's eternal return underscores the death of God and the consequent absence of truth and meaning traditionally conceived. According to the Christian account, cosmic history has a beginning and an end, a direction and a purpose. The world as we know it was brought into being through a divine act of creation, and it will conclude with the Second Coming and a final judgment of souls. The beginning leads to the end by way of the disaster of the Fall and the long ensuing period of our working toward salvation. There is a story-line here, and every movement of universal history, from the births of men to the deaths of stars, has a role in the story, and thereby a significance and a purpose. Each individual life has meaning as a character in the drama written from the beginning of time by the divine author of the All. This explains the popular belief that when God closes a door he opens another one, or that some good must come from every unexpected reversal or loss. The story of a life is never random or senseless. Not to say that anyone can ever know the precise nature of his role before he is called on to enact it. We receive no script to review in advance. But if there is a personal God, all-powerful, all-knowing, and all-good, a deity who cares for men and beckons us into his embrace, who for his part is working against the dark power of the forces that would draw us away; if, in short, the Christian account of our relation to God is correct, then our lives are infused with purpose and meaning.

None of this is so if Nietzsche is right about the eternal return. If he is right, then no event occurs in accordance with an anterior design, but simply because this is what happens each time the eternally cycling circuit of universal history returns to a particular point on the circle. The collection of events that is the cumulative history of the universe is not leading toward a final consummation, a revelatory denouement of the drama. It is not leading anywhere; it is just happening. There will be no end, much less a conclusion that neatly wraps up and explains all preceding events; there will be only a stoppage, *in medias res*, and a return to a previous state, to the earliest period of cosmic time, but for all that not to a "beginning" in any meaningful sense, but just to another phase *in medias res*. "The eternal hourglass of existence is turned upside down again and again," Nietzsche's demon announces in *The Gay Science*, "and you with it, speck of dust!"

Chapter 115: The Pequod meets the Bachelor

So lost is Ahab in the morass of his discontent that he cannot countenance joy in others. So when the *Pequod* encounters the *Bachelor*, a ship full up with oil and bound for home, its crew jubilant and rejoicing on the deck, Ahab condemns the ship as "too damn jolly" and refuses to have any converse with her captain beyond inquiring after Moby Dick. When the *Bachelor* reports no sightings of the whale, only incredible rumors, Ahab dismisses the ship. "Sail on," he sneers. But he does follow up with one final question: have they lost any men? He is dwelling on death. Only two islanders gone, the captain replies, then he invites Ahab aboard to join the celebrations. But Ahab will not participate; he cannot permit himself a moment of cheer; by this time he is all but impotent of high spirits. And remarking to himself, "How wondrous familiar is a fool!" he dismisses the "glad ship of good luck" once again. As the *Pequod* pulls away struggling against the wind, plunging deeper into the void on the far side of hope and home, Ahab removes a vial from his pocket and broods on a small treasure of Nantucket sand. He is dwelling now on his own death.

Ahab regards the captain of the *Bachelor* a "fool." The man is too genial, his crew too merry, and his ship, outfitted in its "glad holiday apparel," cuts the waves too brightly for dark Ahab to endure. Poor, wounded soul. He does not comprehend that foolishness and light feet are essential to man's well-being, particularly to the man who would transcend existential despair and thereby finally and truly overcome his God. Ahab apparently does not wish to find a way out of his darkness, to emerge victorious from wrestling with the deity, and although his intransigence is necessary to his being a tragic figure, nevertheless it is true that Ahab is tragic because he is sick. Contrast the Captain with Nietzsche's Zarathustra, shining with the great health. Zarathustra has encountered his devil, he says, and he has "found him serious, thorough, profound, and solemn." But this is a description of Ahab. Zarathustra's devil was "the spirit of gravity," through whom "all things fall." And here is Ahab again. Ahab despises the "lively revelry" of the *Bachelor*'s crew, their "wild cries" and their dancing to "the barbarian sounds of enormous drums." He despises the Dionysian life in the men, their frenzy of release, relief, and high spirits. Ahab is no dancer, and his ivory leg is not so much the cause as the symbol of his lameness. His soul is a heavy plummet. Unlike Zarathustra, who is light, who soars to heights from which he sees himself beneath himself, Ahab is forever sinking. He will die because he will drown, and he will drown in spirit even before Moby Dick drags his body beneath the waves.

The problem with Ahab is not his profundity, but his lack of an appropriate counter-tendency. He requires the folly he denounces in the *Bachelor*, but he cannot appreciate this. He cannot look down on himself for glaring up in search of a God to rage against. Zarathustra teaches that "a sage too is a fool," and that this is so because the man of one thing must necessarily be also a man of the whole. Everything—every person, every life, every event and every moment—every individual element is inextricably caught up in the web of eternal return. Therefore in order to say Yes to even "a single joy," one must affirm "*all* woe." But is this not foolishness? Indeed it is, and so it is also wisdom, *joyful* wisdom.

Unlike Ahab, Nietzsche understands that he who lives must suffer; but he knows too that the fabulizing folly of an artist's perspective can transform one's life into "an aesthetic phenomenon" and thereby render it bearable. There is beauty even in woe, if only as a shadow accentuating the light of joy. When praising the innocent playfulness of a creative approach to knowledge and truth, traditionally revered with so grave a countenance, Nietzsche insists that "nothing does us as much good as a *fool's cap*: we need it in relation to ourselves—we need all exuberant, floating, dancing, mocking, childish, and blissful art lest we lose the *freedom above things* that our ideal demands of us." Here we have a characterization applicable to Ishmael. Melville once wrote that he would "rather be a fool with a heart, than Jupiter Olympus with his head." The all-knowing mind may well be impressive, as the mind of a mathematical prodigy impresses; but Melville, like Nietzsche, sought a condition superior to knowledge. They were lovers of wisdom. Zarathustra is a manifestation of Nietzsche's drive to acquire a joyful wisdom, as Ishmael is an expression of Melville's ideal of the sage who is also a light-hearted fool. As narrator of *Moby-Dick* Ishmael looks down on the *Pequod* from lofty heights, which is why he knows more than he should, including the secret effusions of Ahab's heart. Ishmael's height also explains his brightness, for he could well have said, with Nietzsche, that "whatever one casts into us, we take down into our depth—for we are deep, we do not forget—*and become bright again.*"

Chapter 116: The Dying Whale

If ever Ahab was bright, his violent encounter with Moby Dick darkened him for good. In the present chapter he kills a whale, and while sitting in his boat surveying the animal's still, silent death, he is soothed, but "only soothed to deeper gloom." The dying sperm whale floats so as to turn its head toward the sun, but having expired, it drifts around again. The whale appears to worship brilliant Helios, but to what end? The sun does not intercede against the waters' revolvingly towing the corpse away from the object of its devotions. Ahab takes a lesson from this: in vain to revere and expect new life in return.

Ahab suffers from this "in vain," for he has been taught to expect meaning in life. He has been duped by the founders and purveyors of spiritual traditions, ancient men whom Nietzsche calls "the teachers of the purpose of existence." These are the men who have overlaid the world with their religious and moral prejudices, passing off their idiosyncratic interpretations as original text. Through the power of their influence they inculcate a tendentious hermeneutics into generations of minds, all the while professing to reveal nothing more than the simple, naked truth. The blind necessity of every natural event, which is as it is solely because it must be so from the entanglement and recurrence of all things, this natural necessity they reformulate in terms of a metaphysical freedom of will, God's will or man's, and through this act they revise our understanding of the world. Now we read into every act a motivating intention and a final goal. The moon reflects light *in order* to brighten the dark night; a rock falls to earth *so as* to approach the center of the universe; I suffer *as punishment* for my sins. We may call our inherited conception of the world "anthropomorphic," but this word fails to capture the all-pervading influence of the fact. "Theomorphic," then? This is more accurate, but rather than rely on terminology, I quote Nietzsche's account of the state of affairs at issue: "In order that what happens necessarily and always, spontaneously and without any purpose, may henceforth appear to be done for some purpose and strike man as rational and an ultimate commandment, the ethical teacher comes on stage, as the teacher of the purpose of existence; and to this end he invents a second, different existence and unhinges by means of his new mechanics the old, ordinary existence." These teachers have influenced more than our conception of reality; they have shaped our psychological needs as well. Through their influence, Nietzsche says, human nature has acquired "one additional need—the need for the ever new appearance of such teachers and teachings of a 'purpose.'"

Ahab has such needs; he demands a higher meaning, if only as an imposition against which to rebel. In the deepest sense, then, he cannot think his way beyond the confines of the lessons taught by the teachers of purpose. Melville and Nietzsche were born into such a world, a world they were taught to believe is infused with meaning and purpose. But they acquired the intellectual strength to break out, to break free, to appreciate the innocence of Becoming, which is to say the absence of underlying intentionality and meaning. In short, they understood that God is dead. More, they were sufficiently healthy of spirit to celebrate his death and to revel in the dawn of liberation. With Zarathustra Nietzsche imagined a teacher of purpose, the original architect of the moral conception of the world, come back to retract his errors of Good and Evil. And Melville depicted in Ishmael a young inhabitant of a world of meaning eventually maturing into a narrator who looks back, and looks down, on his younger self from a perspective beyond good and evil, beyond the deceptive hermeneutics of purpose. In Ahab he portrayed a perverted figure, a man strong enough to struggle against the divine author of meaning and purpose, but too weak to realize that his enemy is not even real.

Early in his journey around the Mediterranean that would later inspire his *Clarel*, Melville visited Egypt. His reflections on the pyramids as recorded in his journals culminate with doubts about the existence of God and speculations on the power of the priests who taught ancient man to believe. Recalling his encounter with the incomprehensibly impressive pyramid, he writes that "man seems to have had as little to do with it as Nature. It was that supernatural creature, the priest. They must needs have been terrible inventors, those Egyptian wise men. And one seems to see that as out of the crude forms of the natural earth they could evoke by art the transcendent mass & symmetry & unity of the pyramid so out of the rude elements of the insignificant thoughts that are in all men, they could rear the transcendent conception of a God." This is the power of the teachers of the purpose of existence. We have all learned their lessons. Some of us eventually reject their teachings, Melville and Nietzsche for instance, or Ishmael and Zarathustra. Some are pious students throughout their lives: these are the faithful, the loving disciples of God. Some men, like Ahab, inhabit a horrible middle ground: they believe but they hate, and therefore they suffer.

Chapter 117: The Whale Watch

In this chapter the Zoroastrian Fedallah issues prophecies regarding Ahab's death. The Captain has dreamt of two hearses, which he takes for portents of his doom. But Fedallah assures him that he cannot die before seeing two hearses on the sea, which together with his other prophetic pronouncements Ahab takes to be so improbable as to indicate his immunity to death. "I am immortal then," he exults, "on land and on sea."

Ahab's conceit of his own immortality has nothing to do with an insight into the eternal recurrence of his life. Nor is Fedallah a Nietzschean Zarathustran, Zoroastrian though he may be. But a rarified type of immortality does follow from the eternal return, as does the possibility of prophecy, which we may think of as deriving from memories of the future. If time does indeed circle back on itself, so that the future is also the past, and the past simultaneously the future, then it should be possible for a man to remember events he has not yet experienced from the perspective of his present life, but which he has lived through in an infinite number of previous iterations of this same life. Having lived his future already an infinite number of times, he might well remember it, either clearly and specifically or obscurely by way of prophetic signs or previsions. The infinity of recurring cycles, and the identity of each cycle to each, rules out there being an initial cycle or series of cycles in which one has no memory of previous cycles, but which one then recollects in every subsequent cycle. But if in *every* recurrence there is a memory of the previous cycle, then in every cycle one may recall moments that are past in a sense as between preceding and succeeding cycles but future from within the perspective of each individual cycle. One may even recollect events occurring after one's personal death by way of information acquired from others who lived through the events in previous cycles after one's own passing. So, for example, Fedallah could know the facts relating to Ahab's future death by way of memory if this future were also their past, and had *always* been both future and past simultaneously. He would have lived his own future already, as Ahab would have lived his own future; and Fedallah could have insight into Ahab's future, even though the Captain outlives him, because he is acquainted with Ahab and can in a mystical way peer into his soul to access his thoughts, in this case his memories of the future. Similarly, Queequeg's little idol Yojo was gifted with the "judgment and surprising forecast" enabling him to know that Ishmael, after apparently "random inquiries" among the ships sailing out of Nantucket, would "infallibly light upon" the *Pequod* to select for his voyage. Ishmael's choice could be known "ahead of time" if the time of its future occurrence had occurred already in the past.

The phenomenon of eternal return has as a consequence not only the possibility of remembering the future, but also of willing the past. I refer to Nietzsche's notion of "backward-willing," the idea that a man by directing his will backward in time can influence the actions of his earlier self. An extraordinary idea, no doubt—more bizarre perhaps than memories of future time. But consider what happens when one wills to act in the future, for example when Ishmael willed to proceed to Nantucket after waiting out the weekend in New Bedford. Once he realized that he had missed the last ferry to the island, he determined that he would catch the boat the following Monday morning. He *intended* to do this, and his intention was a projection of his will into the future. During the course of the ensuing weekend he did not attend to this resolution; at times, and perhaps for most of the time, his intention resided below the level of his conscious awareness. But when Monday morning arrived, the intention resurfaced and he acted on it. It is as if he had sent a message to his future self from the past, an idea conjoined to a will that travelled insensibly through time to manifest at a specific future moment. Backward-willing would operate in precisely the same manner, only with the temporal directionality reversed. For example, as Ishmael writes *Moby-Dick* he wills his younger self to sign on to the *Pequod*. In that case the thoughts that occurred to him as he stalked the harbor seeking out a suitable ship, together with the motives that induced him to select the *Pequod*, would be no more spontaneous or arbitrary inspirations than the thought to pack and leave for the ferry that manifested upon his waking in New Bedford the previous Monday morning. The ideas and intentions would have occurred to him there on the docks because his older self directed them to his younger self by willing them backward in time. The Monday following a Saturday, or years before in the past: in both cases the subjective experiences are expressions of an act of will operative in the present. If the passage of time is circular, as it is according to Nietzsche's doctrine of eternal return, then we cannot absolutely dismiss the possibility of backward-willing. And if Ishmael had known of the eternal return, he could have regarded his decision to sail on the *Pequod* not as the play of an impersonal fate that misled him to think he had made his choice in the moment, but as the result of his older self's directing his will backward in time to motivate his younger self. And having attained a joyful wisdom in large part through the events he experienced aboard the *Pequod*, he would have transformed that particular "it was" into a "thus I willed it."

Melville's failure to think the thought of eternal return must be a flaw from Nietzsche's point of view, for he considered knowledge of the recurrence of one's life a prerequisite for the supreme affirmation. But Melville's ignorance is not surprising. The teaching of the eternal return in the West has been obscured by two thousand years of Christian history, and before this by hundreds of years of Platonism. Had he known of it, I believe that Ishmael would have affirmed the eternal return, as would Melville during his Ishmaelean phase. Later, however, Melville would have gnashed his teeth at the thought.

Chapter 118: The Quadrant

When Ahab destroys his quadrant in this chapter, he acts from an outraged respect for the sun and an equally enraged realization of the limitations of science. The sky's great glowing Pilot, the sun, which, as we learn from Homer, "oversees all things and overhears all things," must know the location of Moby Dick. But the quadrant does not know; it is merely a "foolish toy," a "babies' plaything," that indicates only "the poor, pitiful point" where it itself happens to be. Ahab will no longer rely on devices that "cast man's eyes aloft to that heaven, whose live vividness but scorches him, as these old eyes are even now scorched with thy light, O sun!" Cursing "science" and its "vain toy," he dashes the quadrant on the deck and tramples it beneath his living and dead feet.

Ahab's rejection of the contrivances of the naturalist's intellect, coupled with his concern for the health of his eyes, recalls the section near the end of Plato's *Phaedo* in which Socrates relates his intellectual autobiography. When he was a young man, he remembers, he had a passion for "that wisdom which they call the study of nature." But his naturalistic investigations into events in the heavens and on the earth "utterly blinded" him; he not only failed to learn anything new, but he forgot all that he had previously thought he understood. When eventually he decided to devise a new mode of investigation, he was careful to avoid an experience similar to that which befalls those who stare at the sun during an eclipse. Some men destroy their eyes this way, and as Socrates did not wish his soul to be similarly "blinded," he determined to study reality by having recourse to Forms through *logoi*, words or concepts resident in the intellect, rather than by directing his bodily senses outward toward physical objects. Ahab's rejection of the scientific mode of inquiry is reminiscent of Socrates' dismissal of naturalistic redescriptions of myths and legends in the *Phaedrus*. Recall Socrates' saying that he is more interested in acquiring knowledge of his own soul than in wasting time on extraneous matters.

In both the *Phaedo* and the *Phaedrus* Plato couples the minimizing of materialist science with a concern for the soul, particularly its immortality and cycles of rebirth. In Book 10 of the *Laws* he employs a version of the argument from motion to demonstrate that soul is prior to what men call nature, and a concise version of this same argument appears in the *Phaedrus* just prior to the discussion of the afterlife existence of the soul, the cycles of its reincarnation, and the possibility of finally escaping the ordeal of rebirth. In the *Phaedo* Socrates says that the thoroughly purified soul will live forever after death without a body.

I advert to Plato's interest in reincarnation here in order to contrast his account of the life of the soul with Nietzsche's doctrine of eternal return. While working on the third part of *Thus Spoke Zarathustra* Nietzsche wrote in a note, "*I have discovered the Greeks*: they believed in *eternal recurrence!* That is the *mystery-faith!*" We have seen that at least some of the

Pythagoreans taught the eternal return, and Plato would likely have known about it through this tradition. But if it was also the secret teaching of the mystery cults, then it may well have been rather widely believed, perhaps even by Plato himself. Paul Loeb has suggested that Nietzsche believed that Plato *did* accept the teaching of eternal return, but that he intentionally obscured it. He publically denied the fundamental fact of eternal recurrence, namely the inescapability of one's present existence, even down to its minutest details, by teaching that humans are reincarnated in different types of being, that within limits we may choose the next life into which we shall be reborn, and that the purified soul may altogether escape the cycle of rebirth. Why would Plato publicize these teachings if he did not believe them himself? Because the eternal return implies the meaninglessness and purposelessness of existence, and meaninglessness is the one thing men find unbearable, either by nature or through the influence of doctrines promulgated by the teachers of the purpose of existence. The majority of men believe in meaning to avoid nihilism, nausea at life, which can be a temptation to suicide ("suicidal nihilism," Nietzsche calls it). Plato denies the eternal return in order to provide men hope for meaning, change, and eventual release, precisely as Christianity would later teach similar ideas from different grounds but for the same reason. Platonism and Christianity were prophylactics against nihilism. Unfortunately, the men they protected from nihilism were inferior men, men too weak to handle radical freedom, and by denying reality in order to comfort such men, they undermined the foundations of their betters, the higher type of man, the Dionysian Yes-sayers and affirmers of life.

Chapter 119: The Candles

The *Pequod* sails on "resplendent Japanese seas," but beautiful as these waters are, they seed and nurse "the direst of all storms, the Typhoon." In this chapter the tempest bears down on the *Pequod* terrible and relentless, an ungodly upheaving of churning skies and thunderous waves. The ship and her crew struggle to stay afloat; howling winds shred the sails; Ahab's whaleboat is struck and stove at the stern, precisely where he stands when on the hunt; and flaming balls of fire, corpusants, burn on the ends of every yardarm and at the tips of the masts, illuminating the *Pequod* with pale fire as if it were a signal ship from hell. As for Ahab, "Old Thunder" as he names himself, he is stalking the deck, raging against the storm, against the universe, ultimately against God. Starbuck urges his captain to yield, to turn the ship around and make for home. "God is against thee," he warns. But Ahab will not relent. Seizing his harpoon from the ruins of his boat, he threatens to slaughter the first man who prepares the ship for retreat. And as his lance has drawn from the circumambient lightning a store of frenzied electricity, and so burns with a flame forking from its razored barb, Ahab bullyingly brandishing the weapon appears a terror to the crew, a diabolical emissary of death. They flee from the man in dismay, leaving him there alone, towering, "a mark for thunderbolts."

Reading this chapter one can almost approve Camus's contention that *Moby-Dick* is an absurd novel. Ahab is a man in full rebellion against the universe. He acknowledges the power of the "clear spirit of clear fire" besieging him; he understands that in the end the "personified impersonal" force will defeat him, and that he must die; yet he resists nonetheless, driven by the conviction that the "right worship" of fire is "defiance." With respect to these matters Ahab seems the paradigm of an absurd hero. But these matters do not exhaust either Ahab or the thought-world he inhabits. The mad Captain strains beyond rebellion into a craving for ultimate destruction, including even self-destruction. He peers through the gale's electric waves of lightning to see the "unsuffusing thing beyond," the nameless source of the cosmic elements, the original author of fire's impenetrable riddle, his own riddle too; and though his speech itself is something of a riddle—not quite the incoherent rambling of a madman, but close, all too close—he seems to suggest that he would unify with the ultimate source of all, rendering himself thereby a brother of its offspring, fire, and yet destroy it too. He would become God and then somehow commit suicide, the omnipotent against the self-same immortal. He would, in short, accomplish a final universal extinction. But this is something other, something graver and darker, than absurd heroism. This is *active nihilism*, a variety of nihilism that, as Nietzsche says, "does not only contemplate the 'in vain!' nor is it merely the belief that everything deserves to perish: one helps to destroy... The reduction to nothing by judgment is seconded by the reduction to nothing by hand."

Ahab insists that he is "darkness leaping out of light," which as a figure of the active nihilist suggests that he imagines himself a central cosmic abyss from which comprehensive annihilation flows. He is more than a rebel, then;

he is a villain, a madman at best. But this implies that *Moby-Dick* is not a work of the absurd. Unlike Camus and the atheist existentialists, Ahab does not believe that God is dead. To him the universe is not benignly indifferent, as it is for example to the protagonist of *The Stranger*. Ahab inhabits a hostile universe, a universe actively and intentionally opposed to his every idea and act. No rush of anger will purify Ahab, nor will he go to his death happy. We cannot even imagine him happy, as Camus would have us imagine Sisyphus at the base of his mountain.

Camus's conception of the absurd hero has much in common with the wise man as I have portrayed him throughout this book: serene in the face of the accursed questions, neither neglecting the questions from ignorance, nor settling into a shallow contentment with superficial answers, nor suffering from the lack of final resolution. But Ahab was no absurd hero. Ahab demands answers, from God or the Devil or the Universe or... From who knows what, exactly? But from some reasoning thing, from something capable of answering, which we might as well call God. Nietzsche would so name it. In any case, Camus overlooked the true sage of *Moby-Dick*, namely the narrator Ishmael—ultimately, really, Melville himself. Unlike gloomy Ahab, Melville-Ishmael could say with Zarathustra—likening himself to such corpusants as burn now on the *Pequod*—could say that "to sit on high masts of knowledge seemed to me no small happiness: to flicker like small flames on high masts—a small light only and yet a great comfort for shipwrecked sailors and castaways." And the fact that Zarathustra's knowledge has nothing to do with possessing the objective universal truth, but is *his* way only, created by himself for himself, for "*the* way—that does not exist," this is an expression of his exuberantly creative philosophy, his intellectual playfulness, of the *gaya scienza* that animates Melville and Ishmael too.

Camus was neither the first nor the last man to be distracted from Ishmael's joyful wisdom by Ahab's agitated philosophy, precisely as scholars are so often distracted by the philosopher Socrates from recognizing Plato the sage at work behind and through him. Even Nietzsche was distracted in this way, which explains his failure to recognize his kinship with Plato. I do not myself insist on their philosophical identity; the doctrinal differences between them are undeniable. But beneath the surface they are close, requiring only the appropriate bonding agent to join them. If we may think of *Moby-Dick* in these chemical terms, then we may regard the compound "Plato-Melville-Nietzsche" as the molecule of wisdom.

Chapter 120: The Deck towards the End of the First Night Watch

The *Pequod* still is brutalized by the typhoon: buffeted by wind, soaked with rain, assailed by thunder and lightning. Ahab implores his crew to press on; he will not withdraw; he will plunge bows-first into the onrushing storm, madly defiant. Starbuck entreats him once again to relent, "in God's name!" But is Ahab now contending with God, or rather with nature, or with the void? I expect that at this point he is none too sure himself. He is babbling, or uttering the murkiest of riddles—either way, he is exhibiting symptoms of a steadily intensifying mental disturbance. Melville wrote in *Pierre* that "with the lightning's flash, the query is spontaneously propounded—chance, or God?" If God in this case, then Ahab is a heretic; if chance, he is a nihilist deluded, for who can contend with the void, the very absence of an adversary?

In the winter of 1876/77, during his stay in Sorrento, Italy, and under the influence of his scientifically-minded rationalist friend Paul Rée, Nietzsche developed the positivist mode of thought that characterizes his so-called "middle period," which was marked by his final break with the metaphysical idealism of Schopenhauer. His intellectual explorations in Sorrento would lead to his book *Human, All Too Human*, which, if not itself an expression of nihilism, certainly marks the beginning of Nietzsche's movement in that direction. See, for example, his reflection on this book in *Ecce Homo* as a "monument of rigorous self-discipline with which I put a sudden end to all my infections with 'higher swindle,' 'idealism,' 'beautiful feelings,' and other effeminacies." Consider also that he associates the book with his later ideas and philosophical projects. In section 37 of *Human, All Too Human* Nietzsche had cited Rée as having written that "the moral man is no closer to the intelligible world than the physical man." In *Ecce Homo* he quotes this passage from his earlier work and adds that "there is no intelligible world," which is a blunt expression of his metaphysical nihilism. He then quotes further from *Human, All Too Human* as follows: "this proposition, grown hard and sharp under the hammer blow of historical insight ... may perhaps one day, in some future ... serve as the ax swung against the 'metaphysical need' of mankind." But here, in *Ecce Homo*, after the phrase "the hammer blow of historical insight," he inserts the following instruction: "read: *revaluation of all values*." And after the reference to "some future" he adds, "1890!" From this passage in *Ecce Homo*, written near the close of 1888, in a section explicitly dedicated to *Human, All Too Human*, it is clear that Nietzsche regards his earlier book as prefiguring his later philosophy, in particular his rejection of metaphysics and his project of revaluation, both of which are directly related to his insights into the death of God and the advent of nihilism.

If *Human, All Too Human* marks the beginning of Nietzsche's middle period, then *The Gay Science* marks its end. By the time he wrote the latter book he had arrived at many of the ideas characteristic of his later works, though he chose not to divulge them in detail. He had, as we have seen, come to accept the eternal return, a thought that he would later present as the core of his philosophy; yet in *The Gay Science* he provides only the briefest glimpse of this doctrine. On the back cover of the first edition of the book Nietzsche declared that "with this book we arrive at the conclusion of a series of writings by FRIEDRICH NIETZSCHE whose common goal it is to erect *a new image and ideal of the free spirit*." When he published *The Gay Science*, then, he understood that with his recent ideas he was headed in a new intellectual direction, which explains his including as a final entry a tantalizing and otherwise inexplicable introduction to Zarathustra. In short, Nietzsche was withholding his freshest ideas for the new phase he saw himself entering, which phase would begin with *Thus Spoke Zarathustra*.

Another new idea, or a new and forceful expression of an idea that was present at least in embryo in *Human, All Too Human*, is the death of God. I have already noted Nietzsche's associating this "greatest recent event" with nihilism in the second edition of *The Gay Science*, but the connection is present in his work much earlier than this, for in *Thus Spoke Zarathustra* he associates nihilism with both the death of god and the eternal return. All this is to say that Nietzsche regarded his middle period as prefiguring the characteristic ideas of his late period, and that *The Gay Science* in particular provides evidence that he was right, that he was not in later years naively or dishonestly reading his mature philosophy back into his middle period.

Melville's *Clarel* appeared in the summer of the year of Nietzsche's winter stay in Sorrento. The work was inspired by his tour of the Mediterranean twenty years earlier, and more specifically by his melancholy reflections on the experience as recorded in the journal he kept at the time. Formerly a bright young romantic, Melville on the Mediterranean was a gloomy realist, or a skeptic, perhaps even a nihilist. Try as he might, he could not project the noble archaic myths and legends onto the modern landscapes he encountered, and he suffered from his incapacity. Delos, for example, the birthplace of Apollo, and site of the celebrated Ionian festivals, once so "flowery in fable," displayed "a most barren aspect." Patmos, too, was equally barren; and when Melville later gazed upon the island's "arid height," his "spirit partook of the bareness." These were "disenchanting isle[s]" indeed, as were all the other islands formerly so inspiring.

Looking about him on his Mediterranean tour, Melville saw only "the decayed picturesque" and "life after enthusiasm is gone." This last phrase is telling, for although he applied it to the Greek islands, we may take it as indicative of the perspective through which he regarded them. Perhaps the bleakest statement of Melville's personal distance from the faith of his fathers is this, written as he sailed past Cyprus: "From these waters rose Venus from the foam. Found it as hard to realize such a thing as to realize on Mt Olivet that from there Christ rose."

More distressing than Melville's unbelief was his inability to muster the old Ishmaelean affirmation, the celebration of uncertainty of which he had been so vibrantly capable in a healthier phase of life, a phase not long since passed chronologically, but an eon gone as marked by the measure of his psychology. Melville on his Mediterranean tour was "afflicted," as he put it, "with the great curse of modern travel—skepticism." For this he condemned the moderns, the Germans in particular, and their disenchanting enlightenment *Wissenschaft*: "Heartily wish Niebuhr and Strauss to the dogs," he writes, "the deuce take their penetration & acumen. They have robbed us of the bloom. If they have undeceived anyone – no thanks to them."

Nietzsche wrote an early essay condemning David Strauss's demythologizing *Life of Jesu*s, which he regarded as a work of cultural philistinism and, worse, philosophical naivety. To Nietzsche's mind Strauss was wrong to think that we can efface the mythological or supernatural elements from Christianity while leaving intact its system of values, moral values in particular. This would later be a recurrent theme in Nietzsche's work: if God is dead, then all our cherished social, political, and ethical ideals are dead as well. It is then the task of the free-spirited philosopher to acknowledge these deaths, indeed to celebrate them, and to set about creating new values. Unlike Melville on the Mediterranean, then, Nietzsche was ultimately thankful for having been undeceived. Compare to Melville's dirge on Mt. Olivet Zarathustra's exuberant, "I run crisscross on my mount of olives with warm feet; in the sunny nook of my mount of olives I sing and I mock all pity." To be free in this way of religious and metaphysical beliefs without suffering from the loss is a symptom of spiritual power and health. Consider in this connection the following passage from *The Gay Science*: "Whoever has a soul that craves to have experienced the whole range of values and desiderata to date, and to have sailed around all the coasts of this ideal 'mediterranean'; whoever wants to know from the adventures of his own most authentic experience how a discoverer and conqueror of the ideal feels, and also an artist, a saint, a legislator, a sage, a scholar, a pious man, a soothsayer, and one who stands divinely apart in the old style—needs one thing above everything else: the *great health*." Melville sailed this ideal mediterranean, and for a time he even flourished with a great health. *Moby-Dick* is evidence of this. But by the time he sailed the actual Mediterranean he had succumbed to a spiritual malaise from which he never fully recovered. We may call it nihilism if we like; it was certainly a state near enough to this to merit at least the adjective *nihilistic*.

Chapter 121: Midnight—The Forecastle Bulwarks

Melville incudes in *Clarel* many of the sentiments he recorded in his journal while touring the Mediterranean. For example, his personal dismay at the demythologizing work of Strauss and Niebuhr is expressed by the Melvillean Rolfe as follows: "All now's revised: / Zion, like Rome, is Niebuhrized. / Yes, doubt attends." And he expands the barrenness of the Greek islands to cosmic dimensions when he has Clarel cry, upon the death of his beloved, "O blind, blind, barren universe!" A barren universe is a godless universe, and whether the divine exists in fact or not, that faith in its presence has declined in the modern era is brought out in *Clarel* through a rhyme recited by Rolfe, which as well as any verse in the poem expresses the death of God:

Flamen, flamen, put away
Robe and miter glorious:
Doubt undeifies the day!
Look, in vapors odorous
As the spice-king's funeral-pyre,
Dies the Zoroastrian fire
On your altars in decay:

The rule, the Magian rule is run,
And Mythra abdicates the sun!

Earlier in the work the character Mortmain expresses a similar thought when
he scrawls on a rock a verse headed, "*By one who wails the loss.*" His short
poem is a lamentation on the death of God by way of a reflection on the
constellation of the Southern Cross. It reads in full as follows:

Emblazoned bleak in austral skies—
A heaven remote, whose starry swarm
Like Science lights but cannot warm—
Translated Cross, hast thou withdrawn,
Dim paling too at every dawn,
With symbols vain once counted wise,
And gods declined to heraldries?
Estranged, estranged: can friend prove so?
Aloft, aloof, a frigid sign:
How far removed, thou Tree divine,
Whose tender fruit did reach so low—
Love apples of New-Paradise!
About the wide Australian sea
The planted nations yet to be—
When, ages hence, they lift their eyes,
Tell, what shall they retain of thee?
But class thee with Orion's sword?
In constellations unadored,
Christ and the Giant equal prize?
The atheist cycles—*must* they be?
Fomentors as forefathers we?

Have the gods declined to mere heraldries? And is religion now a hodgepodge
of empty symbolisms, as existentially vacuous as science? The fear is that the
cross has become a signifier with naught to signify, no living God in his
heaven; and the final two lines of the poem suggest that *we* have killed him.

Recall Ishmael's saying that when afloat on the great Pacific "you needs
must own the seductive god, bowing your head to Pan." In *Clarel* Melville
does not own Pan, for he knows that God is dead. Ishmael knew this too, of

course, but his high-spirited intellectual freedom permitted him to play with ideas at will; unlike Christian and atheist fundamentalists, he was happy to invoke Pan without worrying that such invocations violate deeply personal intellectual commitments. He was beyond adolescent passions for or against; he was the master of his own mind, the artist of his own thought-world. In the years following *Moby-Dick*, particularly at the end of his writing career and during his tour of the Mediterranean, Melville *suffered* from the insights that had so excitedly animated Ishmael, insights we may sum up in Nietzschean terms as the death of God. Over a decade later, when he set to work on *Clarel*, he had not recovered his Ishmaelean health and good humor, but he had attained a sort of spiritual equilibrium. In *Clarel* he does not celebrate the death of God, but neither does he suffer from it. Like Nietzsche after him, he is often less directly concerned with specifying the ontological status of God than with thinking through the potential consequences of a general decline of faith. Regarding the existence of God, Nietzsche was a settled atheist, Melville an agnostic. But the pressing matter for both was the ramifications of belief or unbelief for individuals and civilizations alike. Thus when Melville records in *Clarel* Plutarch's story of the sea-borne announcement of Pan's death, which marked the passing of the pagan "rule and era," he associates it with his own time, unsettled as it is by "that vast eclipse, if slow, / Whose passage yet we undergo, / Emerging on an age untried."

Clarel is the medium through which Melville reflects on the modern passage into an untried age following the death of the Christian God. Considered with an eye to its explicit concerns, it is his most Nietzschean work. Nietzsche once claimed for himself the foresight to "relate the history of the next two centuries," the central event of which period would be "*the advent of nihilism.*" Melville was less confident of future historical developments, but in *Clarel* he undertook a project similar to Nietzsche's, though expressed in the interrogative rather than the declarative mood. What will become of Christendom without Christianity, he wonders: "is faith dead *now* / A petrifaction? Grant it so, / Then what's in store? what shapeless birth? / Reveal the doom reserved for earth? / How far may seas retiring go?" What will become of men raised as Christians who reject their faith, or of future generations reared on no faith at all: "Negation, is there nothing more?" Melville understood, as Nietzsche too would understand, that the rise of modern philosophy and science has undermined traditional modes of belief; but when Melville pondered the question, "Science and Faith, can these unite?" he held out at least some hope for a reconciliation that Nietzsche would later reject. Melville for his part was dubious of the "upstart" attitude, characteristic of Nietzsche's hopeful moods, that "Lodged in power, enlarged in all / Man achieves his last exemption— / Hopes no heaven, but fears no fall, / King in time, nor needs redemption." In short, Melville was less confident than Nietzsche that dead gods remain dead, and that men possess the power to carry on in the future alone and unassisted. As Rolfe observes regarding Rome's role in the history of religion, "Let fools count on faith's closing knell— / Time, God, are inexhaustible."

In the present chapter of *Moby-Dick* Stubb wonders "whether the world is anchored anywhere," and he concludes that "if she is, she swings with an uncommon long cable." Here Stubb anticipates Nietzsche's formulation of the nihilistic consequences of the death of God, as expressed for example in *The Gay Science* through the madman's wondering, "What were we doing when we unchained this earth from its sun? Whither is it moving now? Whither are we moving? Away from all suns? Are we not plunging continually? Backward, sideward, forward, in all directions? Is there still any up or down? Are we not straying as through an infinite nothing?" Straying through an infinite nothing: this is nihilism, a condition against which Melville and Nietzsche both struggled, with varying degrees of success.

Chapter 122: Midnight Aloft—Thunder and Lightning

Since nothing of consequence happens in this, the shortest chapter of *Moby-Dick* (it comprises a mere 36 words, nine of these being the word "um"), I take the opportunity to rehearse in brief the substance of the previous two chapters on Melville's existential condition during the two decades between the collapse of his career as a novelist and his composition and publication of *Clarel*. I have previously mentioned that Melville's father-in-law financed his tour of the Mediterranean because the family was concerned for Melville's mental and physical health. I have also mentioned that Melville visited Hawthorne in Liverpool after crossing the Atlantic. Hawthorne's notes on his time with Melville confirm his friend's debilitated condition: he was "afflicted with neuralgic complaints in his head and limbs"; his "too constant literary occupation" had been "pursued without much success, latterly"; and in general Melville appeared "much overshadowed since I saw him last." That

Melville was suffering from existential nihilism is suggested by his confiding in Hawthorne that he had "pretty much made up his mind to be annihilated." Hawthorne hoped that his old friend would "brighten as he goes onward," but Melville himself "observed that he did not anticipate much pleasure in his rambles."

As for Melville's philosophical perspective during this time, Hawthorne remarks that Melville "can neither believe, nor be comfortable in his unbelief." Here we have a clear indication of Melville's decline from the height of his *Moby-Dick* period. Ishmael is comfortable in his unbelief: as a comfortable believer, or an uncomfortable unbeliever, Ishmael would not be Ishmael. Ishmael "plays naively ... with all that was hitherto called holy, good, untouchable, divine" precisely because he is comfortable in his unbelief; and his condition is a consequence of "overflowing power and abundance," which is to say of physiological and existential wellbeing. Melville as a young man was possessed of this great Ishmaelean health, but by the time he visited Hawthorne on his way to the Mediterranean, though only a little more than five years had passed since *Moby-Dick*, in spirit he had aged tremendously, and he was ill in body and mind alike—hence the recurrence in his Mediterranean journals of the word "barren," which, as I have noted, characterized the state of Melville's soul even more precisely than it described the sites he visited.

Melville on the Mediterranean suffered from a condition similar to Ishmael's before he enrolled to sail on the *Pequod*. Ishmael was haunted by suicidal thoughts; Melville anticipated annihilation. Nor did Melville's literary career improve after he returned to the states. He undertook three lecture tours, delivering addresses on Roman art, the South Seas, and travel in general, but he was no great success on the stage. We have seen that he failed to secure a publisher for his initial volume of poetry; and although his *Battle-Pieces* appeared in 1866, no one much took any notice. His personal life was no better: in the mid-1860s his "domestic situation had become such that [his wife] Lizzie had at last begun to accept the possibility ... that Herman might really be insane," and around this time her relatives were urging her to separate from her husband. Melville was often physically incapacitated, suffering from eye-strain, rheumatism, and neuralgia; in 1862 he finally buckled under years of financial pressure and moved the family out of his beloved Arrowhead; and, the worst blow of all, his eldest son Malcolm committed suicide in 1867.

Melville probably began work on *Clarel* early in 1870, and he labored at
the poem for five years. According to his wife, the "dreadful *incubus* of a
book" had "undermined all our happiness." But the sustained intellectual and
creative activities involved in conceiving and composing the work seem to
have improved Melville's condition, at least somewhat, as compared to his
state in the late 1850s and early 1860s. I refer to his existential-intellectual
condition, which in *Clarel* manifests less as nihilism than as an apprehensive
but bold skepticism. If there is no Ishmaelean play, there is at least a brave
willingness to explore ideas. Not an enormous improvement, perhaps, but an
improvement nonetheless. Nietzsche once wrote that "skepticism is the most
spiritual expression of a certain complex physiological condition that in
ordinary language is called nervous exhaustion and sickliness." But he also
acknowledged the possibility of a "virile skepticism" that manifests as "the
courage and hardness of analysis, as the tough will to undertake dangerous
journeys of exploration and spiritualized North Pole expeditions under
desolate and dangerous skies." In *Clarel* Melville approaches this latter form
of skepticism, expressed in verse as an indefatigable intellectual exploration
through a landscape sunnier than the North Pole, to be sure, but no less
desolate and dangerous. As author of *Clarel* Melville is no longer an Ishmael,
but at least he is no Ahab.

Chapter 123: The Musket

When the typhoon finally abates, Starbuck goes below to inform Captain
Ahab that the "foul breeze" has at last turned "fair." But as he prepares to
knock at the stateroom door, the rack of muskets on the wall nearby transfixes
his attention. In the silence of the outer cabin Starbuck stands unmoving,
contemplating the loaded weapons. Oh, how they shine, gleaming instruments
of death secured in a tight, regimented row. Then this "honest, upright man,"
pious Starbuck, "strangely evolved an evil thought" in his heart. Taking down
one of the guns, he holds it in his hands, brooding on the Captain's mad
pursuit of Moby Dick, his recklessness in the recent storm, his contemptuous
disregard for the safety of his crew. Ahab is "crazed," and he will neither
submit to reason nor heed petitions. If he is not relieved of his command, he
will prove in time to be the "murderer" of everyone on board the *Pequod*.

Starbuck has a wife and child awaiting his return to Nantucket. But between the mate and his family there looms a massive impediment, an obstacle more unyielding than a contract for spermaceti oil, huger than a whale, more expansive than the sea: the Captain's merciless will is a mountain arising from the depths of the ocean, heaving into the sky. No way to tramp around or pass through it. And what Sherpa could scale it? But perhaps a bold man properly armed might obliterate it. Murder, then? But Starbuck is a Christian. True, but he who kills a would-be murderer is not necessarily a murderer himself. To kill an unjust man might in fact be an act of justice. The mate turns over such thoughts in his mind, and for a moment at least he is comforted by the cool steel of the trigger against his finger. Yes, Ahab at present is vulnerable, asleep just beyond the door, his very head level to the gun that Starbuck even now aims in his direction. A slight flexing of muscle and the deed will be done; lives will be saved, loved ones reunited…

At this moment Starbuck doubtless would appreciate the assistance of divine guidance, but apparently his God is distracted by other concerns. The mate seems "wrestling with an angel," but also trembling like a drunkard. Are we in the realm of the sacred or the profane? It's hard to say. Starbuck is a believer, but now he does not pray. To the contrary, he wonders aloud, "Great God, where art thou?" To this he receives no reply, but somehow he resolves against murder and calls out to the Captain. Then unlike the silent divine, Ahab responds. But as he speaks without waking, shouting after Moby Dick from the mists of a dream, perhaps he is like God after all: an illusion hunting the fantastical images of its own creative reveries.

Replacing the "death-tube" in the rack, Starbuck climbs on deck and orders Stubb to rouse the Captain. Ahab's survival ensures the death of his crew, and Starbuck knows this as surely as a man may know the future. Why then can he not act to save himself and the sailors in his charge? This is one aspect of the mystery of life, is it not? The wind is fair, as Ishmael reports; but as Starbuck remarks, the wind is "fair for death and doom," which is to say fair for Moby Dick, "that accursed fish." Moby Dick represents the mysteries that prompt men to ponder the accursed questions, the baffling entanglements of fair and foul, the troubling interweavings of good and evil, life and death, murder and salvation. Confronted with circumstances as loom now before Starbuck, pondering men cannot help but wonder: God or void? Abyss of light or abyss of darkness?

In this chapter we have yet another instance of Ishmael's reporting scenes he could not possibly have witnessed, words he was in no position to hear, and the private thoughts of other men. Are we meant to regard him as omniscient? Must we take him for a fabulist? Neither, I think; not in any straightforward sense. Ishmael is a man, but since he is a fictional being, he is a man as representation of a mind, and more particularly of a thought-world created by a mind. Ishmael is a corporeal manifestation (an incarnation or avatar) of the mental perspective through which Melville contemplates the accursed questions. And I say that he contemplates them, plays with and explores them, rather than that he *asks* and *answers* them, because his curiosity operates in a Nietzschean mode, which is to say that as a "knower" Melville is a *creator*. He is creating himself, his mind, a thought-world to inhabit, and his novel is creature of this grander creation. So Ishmael *knows* all because he *is* all, the all that is the whole of *Moby-Dick*; and he is this all because he is an expression of the source of the all, Melville himself. In brief, then, *Moby-Dick* is less strictly a novel than a projection in narrative form of the contents of Melville's heart and mind, a philosophical expression of Melville's joyful wisdom.

Chapter 124: The Needle

If we think of Melville in relation to the world of *Moby-Dick* as a creative deity in relation to a cosmos, and of Ishmael as the mode of Melville's creative act, the *logos* through which Melville's creativity operates, then however "god-like" Ahab may appear to the characters within the novel, perhaps even to himself, he is a creature all the same. Often mistaken for the hero of the work, and for Melville's mouthpiece, Ahab instead provides the material on which the actual hero and mouthpiece, Ishmael, performs his shaping art. This is not to dismiss Ahab as mere matter, as if any material would do. Ishmael intends a grand production, so he requires a choice selection of marble. The sea is his Carrara, and Ahab's pursuit of Moby Dick is as perfect (and perfectly flawed) a slab of stone as the massive block from which Michelangelo carved the David. Nevertheless, as essential to the work as Ahab and the whale indisputably are, and as much as we learn about these two in the course of Ishmael's narrative, the central teaching of the work does not concern them directly. The principal lesson of *Moby-Dick* is less a teaching than a revelation, a revelation of the narrator Ishmael's thought-world—or, rather, Melville's thought-world manifesting as, and through, Ishmael.

In his dialogue *Ion* Plato likens poets to iron rings attached to magnetic muses. The divine muse is the true author of a poet's work, as a magnet is the original source of magnetism, and an inspired poet articulates the divinity's words within our earthly realm, as an iron ring in contact with a magnet becomes a secondary transmitter of magnetism. If other men recite the poet's words, as professional rhapsodes recited Homer's poems throughout the ancient world, these men receive their inspiration as transmissions from the muse passing through the poet. The rhapsode, then, is like a second ring attracted to the poet as the magnetized first ring. Thus magnetized himself, the rhapsode draws other rings onto the chain, namely the members of the audience present at his performances. In the end a chain of many links is formed, and "the god through all of these [links] draws the souls of humans wherever he wants, suspending one from the other."

When earlier in the narrative Ahab informed the *Pequod*'s congregated crew of his intention to hunt and kill Moby Dick, swearing them all to accompany him even "round perdition's flames," Ishmael described the Captain's life as "magnetic." He attracts the sailors to himself irresistibly, attaches them to his wild scheme even unto death. In the present chapter Ahab magnetizes a needle to repair the ship's ruined compass, and having done this he declares himself "lord of the level loadstone." Ahab's power impresses and frightens the crew, precisely as he intends. And "in his fiery eyes of scorn and triumph, you then saw Ahab in all his fatal pride." Here, then, we have yet another instance of Ahab's hubris. Mistaking himself for a peer of the gods in power, he would usurp their rank and esteem. But Ahab is no god. He attracts the crew and magnetizes a needle, but his magnetism is not his own; he is but a link in the chain. What's worse, he knows this truth but refuses to acknowledge the original source of his power, and not from disbelief in the divine but from prideful contempt.

Within the world of *Moby-Dick*, then, Ahab is a man, a mortal, a creature—a subordinate link on the chain. Within *our* world he is even further removed from the creative center of things. Melville himself is the magnetic muse, Ishmael the first-ring poet, and Ahab is in some sense Ishmael's inspired creation. For even if we trust that Ishmael's story is "true," the manner and mode of his narrative, and his reflections on the events he reports, are all his own. Thus even the Captain as we encounter him is under Ishmael's command, as Ishmael is under Melville's sway. And if in our world, or beyond it, divine poetic muses do exist, if really such "beautiful creative works" as *Moby-Dick* "are not human, but divine and from gods, and the poets are nothing other than interpreters of the gods, each one possessed by whichever god possesses him," then with Melville himself being displaced from the primal creative center, Ahab's apparent power is subordinated even further, and is therefore even less authentically his own. He is *not* the lord of the loadstone, and his declaration to the contrary is a symptom of hubristic madness.

Chapter 125: The Log and Line

Poets in the *Ion* are possessed and inspired by the muses. According to the *Phaedrus* too the poets are possessed, but they are also mad. No one practices poetry well by skill; madness from the muses is essential. And when a poet's soul is aroused to a Dionysian frenzy, when the artist succumbs to divine madness, then his art easily outshines the poetry composed by self-controlled men. The same is true of the philosopher, as I have made clear in a previous chapter. As lovers of the metaphysical, philosophers are gifted with the highest form of madness, namely love of the Form of Beauty, which by shining through beautiful physical objects draws the maddened philosophical soul from its corporeal tomb toward the immaterial originals, among which the soul has its true home and most abundant life.

In the chapter following Ishmael's description of Ahab as "magnetic," the Captain pronounces himself "madness maddened." This is a problem in itself, but what's worse from a Platonic perspective is that Ahab's madness is not a divine gift; he is possessed not by the muses but by rage against God. If god-given madness is superior to human self-control, as in the *Phaedrus* Plato says it is, then it is most definitely superior to human insanity and hatred of the divine. The other mad character in *Moby-Dick*, Pip, is ambiguous, for although his madness derives from his witnessing "God's foot upon the treadle of the loom," and though Ishmael remarks with respect to his crazed utterances that "man's insanity is heaven's sense," Pip shows no signs of poetic or philosophical inspiration. In fact he seems irremediably distraught, and he is forever speaking of himself as a coward lost at sea or, worse, as a dead man.

In the present chapter Pip's madness touches Ahab's "inmost center," but even the Captain seems unsure of the young man's actual condition. He refers to Pip as "that holiness," but also as a "luckless child" abandoned by the gods. Pip's eyes are "vacant," as if his interior self were missing, which moves Ahab to lament the fact that "man should be a thing for immortal souls to sieve through!" It is as though behind the windowed doors of Pip's eyes, the elevator of his soul is stalled between levels on the hierarchy of being. In the *Phaedrus*, after arguing that the soul is immortal, Socrates ranks the various types of human life through which souls sieve in their cycles of reincarnation. The life of the tyrant is the lowest; the philosophical life is the highest. Between these are laborers, doctors, and kings, among others. Pip I suppose before his madness might have been classed with the laborers, which is to say near the bottom of the hierarchy. Now he occupies a transitional state, which is as good as no state at all. Hence his constant feeling of being lost. Ahab perhaps would qualify as a warlike commander or a manager, which would place him near the top. But no matter a man's status, high or low, there is no guarantee that he will advance in his next life. Bad living in this life will bring him down, and what could be worse than living in accord with human, as opposed to god-given, madness? Only exulting in that madness, luxuriating in it, and intentionally acting to intensify it—this is worse. But this is Ahab's condition. The Captain is "daft with strength," but with a strength of will and temper hostile to his own well-being.

Ahab exhibits sympathy for Pip, which one might take for an indication of virtue. But it is hard to say whether he feels for Pip as a being endowed with dignity and worth in himself, or as a reflection of his own insanity and one more excuse to rail against the gods. Ahab points to Pip as an argument against those who believe in "gods all goodness, and in man all ill," for in Pip he sees evidence of "omniscient gods oblivious of suffering man." He is intent on undermining the gods, and not by denying their existence but by diminishing their status. This is another symptom of his madness, for no sane man both believes in gods and opposes them in a contest of honor or might. No one but a hubristic man would dare. And here we have motive to reevaluate the rank of Ahab's life, which may well be nearer to the tyrant's life than to the warlike commander's. In the *Republic* Plato portrays the tyrannical man as coming to be when madness displaces self-control in his soul, and since god-given madness is superior to human self-control, he must have human madness in mind. But if mad Ahab is a variety of tyrant, then he occupies the lowest rung on the hierarchy of human lives, the position furthest from the philosopher.

I have identified Ahab as a philosopher, but more specifically as a type I have deemed the perpetual philosopher, a deep-diving man on the hunt for truth in the profound of his soul, who from one or another variety of degeneration must drown without ever seizing his prey. Ahab is degenerate in that, like a raving and raging tyrant, he lusts for truth in order to ravage and kill it. He is mad with the wrong sort of madness, as even Nietzsche would agree. In *The Birth of Tragedy* Nietzsche cites Plato's observation in the *Phaedrus* that "madness ... brought the greatest blessings upon Greece" in connection with his own view that "Dionysian madness" was responsible for the Greeks' pessimism of strength. When years later he referred to himself as "the last disciple of the philosopher Dionysus," he did so with reference to this earlier account, though reformulated in terms of the "orgiastic" rather than "madness." But despite this difference of terminology, in both cases Nietzsche means to stress the affirmation of life even in the teeth of suffering. Ahab is incapable of this Dionysian madness, this life-affirming philosophy. His suffering consumes him, and he is chasing death.

Chapter 126: The Life-Buoy

Death indeed; death by drowning. This present chapter is pervaded by death and portents of doom. As the *Pequod* approaches the equatorial fishing-ground in the pre-dawn darkness, the men of the watch on deck are shaken by a "plaintively wild and unearthly" cry wafting over the water like the "half-articulated wailings of the ghosts of all Herod's murdered Innocents." The "oldest mariner of all" on board the *Pequod*, whom Ishmael calls the Manxman, insists that the sounds are "the voices of newly drowned men in the sea." When Ahab later learns of this he laughs, blithely attributing the haunting strains to seals resident on nearby islands. But his confident assertion does not reassure the men, for, as Ishmael has reported in a previous chapter, they attribute "preternatural powers of discernment" to the Manxman.

Later that same morning, a sleepy sailor mounting the mast-head tumbles out and falls into the sea. The crew lets down the ship's life-buoy, but as it is old and parched from exposure to the sun, it takes on water and sinks. Nothing more is seen of either the sailor or the life-buoy, two formerly bright things buried now in the dark at the bottom of the ocean. As unfortunate as the sailor's death must seem to every sensitive man, the crewmen are in a way cheered by it, for they interpret the event as fulfilling the portent of the sea-borne howlings that frightened them earlier. But the Manxman rejects their optimism: he sees no fulfillment in the sailor's death but rather a morbid foreshadowing. He anticipates "evil in the future," in accordance, presumably, with his previous decrypting of Ahab's doubloon as presaging the *Pequod*'s destruction. "Ship, old ship!" he had groaned at the time, "my old head shakes to think of thee!" Stubb then referred to the man as "the old hearse-driver," echoing Ishmael's description of him as "sepulchral." Enwreathed with fatal symbolisms, the Manxman possesses special insights into death, much like Apollo's prophetic swans. Best, then, to take his forebodings as "preluding some riotous and desperate scene," as surely as did the "strange calm" that prevailed on the sea before dawn that very morning.

Ishmael does not associate the sailor's sunrise plunge into the sea with ancient Icarus, but I do. Icarus's father Daedalus, imprisoned with his son in the Minotaur's labyrinth, which he himself had designed for Minos, fashioned wings from feathers and wax to effect their escape by air. Daedalus admonished Icarus to maintain a cautious distance from both the sea and the sun as they flew, but the excited boy eventually soared so high that the sun's heat melted the wax on his wings, which dissolved and fluttered away in feathery fragments. Icarus immediately dropped to his death. The story is often read as a warning against hubris. To the Greeks the sun was divine, and no mortal man should presume to rival his status as lord of the sky. The *Pequod*'s hapless sailor was not hubristic himself; he intended no challenge to the sun by dutifully taking his turn at the lookout for whales. Nevertheless, like all the sailors onboard the ship he had bound himself to Ahab's deicidal mission. Therefore even he was guilty and deserving of punishment. He just happens to have been the first to suffer the wrath of divine nemesis.

Now that the *Pequod* has lost its life-buoy, Starbuck is charged with seeing to a replacement. But failing to devise a suitable design, and knowing of no appropriate materials available on the ship, he is about to abandon the task when Queequeg suggests that his coffin will probably serve the purpose.

A strange idea, no doubt, to transform a death-box into a life preserver. But by nailing the lid down tight and caulking the seams, the carpenter just might produce a seaworthy sarcophagus. He is not at all happy with the assignment, which he judges beneath his dignity as an artisan; and if he were superstitious, he would certainly have nothing to do with it. But he does not shrink from irrational fears, for he is, he says, as sturdy as a figure carved from the wood of an old hemlock tree. Therefore he sets to work reconfiguring the coffin for an employment contrary to its nature—an appliance of death in the service of life.

I conclude this chapter by noting that a hemlock tree is unrelated to the plant that produced the poison that killed Socrates. Despite this fact, however, the very name is evocative of death when a man has Plato's *Phaedo* on his mind, as Ishmael surely does; and the association is only compounded when accompanied by references and allusions to death such as Ishmael has packed into this part of his narrative. Nor are we done with the coffin, or with death, or even for that matter with Plato.

Chapter 127: The Deck

Plato's word for the mental state by which we relate to physical objects is *pistis*. According to the ontological-epistemological schematic known as the Divided Line, at the end of Book 6 of the *Republic*, *pistis* is a subjective state only just barely superior to *eikasia*, or "imaging," through which we access images (*eikones*), shadows for instance, or the reflections that appear in water and mirrors. These are the least real objects of our experience, therefore they cannot be known but only perceived or "imaged." The things of which these images are images, physical objects, are more real than their images, but they are not fully real themselves since they both "are and are not," as I have explained in a previous chapter. It is standard to translate *pistis* in this context as "belief" or "trust," indicating a state more reliable than imaging but less stable than knowledge, because that which both is and is not, being unstable itself, can never be grasped by the mind with unwavering certainty.

In a Christian context *pistis* is traditionally rendered "faith." According to Paul in his letter to the Hebrews, *pistis* is "faith" understood as "the assurance [or "the reality"] of things hoped for, the conviction [or "evidence," or even "proof"] of things not seen." On this understanding of *pistis*, then, the

Christian through faith holds fast to that which is beyond all sensory access. Notice the difference from Plato, for whom *pistis* correlates precisely to things *seen*. The unseen realm Plato refers to as "intelligible," indicating thereby that we need *not* rely on faith to access it, for we may comprehend it with certainty through the intellect, which is to say that we may *know* it. In short, for Plato *pistis* relates to unknowable items in the realm of Becoming, physical objects, whereas for many Christians it relates to Being, in other words to God, the soul, and the promise of eternal life, in which we may, and should, believe, but which we can never know.

Nietzsche has the Christian sense of faith in mind when he writes that "'faith' means not *wanting* to know what is true." The man of faith turns away from the actual world of experience to an ideal world, which is in fact an *unreal* world conjured by priests too weak to bear the heavy realities of life, and promulgated by them to the equally impotent and ignorant masses. Since this other world, this beyond, is not only not evident but evidently contradictory of our most immediate experiences, the priest insists that we trust in its reality through faith. But this amounts to insisting that we trust the priest himself, or in other words that we subject ourselves to his authority, submit to his power. We must, that is, deny the evidence of our senses and affirm the word of the priest. But according to Nietzsche this amounts to an outright denial of reality, which is also, and even worse, a variety of *life-denial*. Therefore, to Nietzsche's mind, faith is "a form of sickness," a symptom of decadence.

In the present chapter of *Moby-Dick* Ahab asks, "Faith? What's that?" This question, following as it does on Ahab's denunciation of the gods as "unprincipled" busy-bodies who "do not mean anything" by their actions, but simply "do as [they] do," without a care for the sufferings they inflict on men—this question would seem to suggest that Ahab has no use for faith. Perhaps he doesn't, but he does believe in the reality of things unseen. "Oh!" he exclaims, "how immaterial are all materials! What things real are there, but imponderable thoughts?" If we take "immaterial" to signify *insubstantial*, then the immateriality of material objects is a Platonic notion through and through, as is the implication of Ahab's rhetorical question that material objects are unreal (or anyway less than *fully* real). But this is not to say that Ahab is a Platonist, for he goes on to admit that he is "so far gone ... in the dark side of earth, that its other side, the theoretic bright one, seems but uncertain twilight." It is by no means easy to ascertain the precise significance of these words, I admit, but they suggest an *un*-Platonic attitude. Plato strives for clarity and light, as is evident, for instance, when in the *Republic* just prior to the Divided Line he employs the sun as an image of the Form of the Good, which may well be the supreme principle of his ontology, his version of God. But I suppose it should be apparent by now that Ahab's thoughts are not entirely consistent. Ahab is no Platonist, but neither does he adhere to a consistent version of inverted-Platonism. He resembles more a Platonist who from human madness aches to blot out the sun of the Good. In Christian terms, he believes in God but hates him. Ahab is raving, and when he says to Pip, "I do suck most wondrous philosophies from thee," we have an indication of the madness of his thoughts. Pip is indisputably insane, so a philosophy derived from him is likely to be disturbed itself, unbalanced and incoherent.

Ahab's reflections in this chapter are unsettled by his observation of the carpenter at work on Queequeg's erstwhile casket. He is disturbed by the paradox of a coffin serving as a life-buoy. He would like to meditate on the question whether "in some spiritual sense the coffin is, after all, but an immortality-preserver," but he cannot. He cannot think of life even in the context of death. The carpenter's labors raise a clamor that Ahab describes as "accursed," and Ahab is agitated by accursed things, accursed questions for example. He can no longer think about God and death, for he wants simultaneously to be God and to kill God, to die and to cheat death. His mind is a whirlpool in which his thoughts and moods are tossed about; and dashing against one another they will all be wrecked in time, very soon in fact, and then they will be sucked into the oblivion of life's unfathomable ocean, dragging the mad Captain down with them.

Chapter 128: The Pequod meets the Rachel

Recall that two chapters back the "sepulchral" old Manxman attributed the wailings heard by the night-watch to the voices of men recently drowned at sea. In the present chapter, when the *Pequod* meets the *Rachel* sailing to and fro in search of a lost whaleboat, the Manxman anticipates "bad news." He is right, in more ways than one, as Ahab's meeting with the *Rachel*'s captain soon reveals. Moby Dick is in these waters, and in fact the *Rachel* lowered her whaleboats after him the previous day. One even fastened to the beast, but then he ran, and neither the whale nor the boat has been seen by the mast-head lookouts since. The captain's son was aboard that boat, a child just twelve years old, so the captain himself pleads with Ahab to assist him in his search, even offers to pay a handsome sum for his effort. But Ahab will not hear of it. He is ice cold. He is an unyielding cast-steel anvil. Now that he knows that Moby Dick is near, he can think of nothing but death. The *Rachel*'s captain appeals to Ahab's paternal instincts—he too is from Nantucket, and he knows that Ahab has a son—even invokes the Golden Rule. But Ahab is inexorable. "I will not do it," he says. "Even now I lose time." He appeals to God to bless the captain, and hopes one day to forgive himself, but he must depart immediately. He grants the captain a mere three minutes to heave the *Rachel* out of his way.

Ishmael describes the *Rachel* winding in the *Pequod*'s wake as "weeping for her children, because they were not." This is a reference to the Rachel of the Old Testament, wife of Jacob, whom the prophet Jeremiah depicts as weeping for later generations of Jews conquered and sold into slavery. But more specifically it refers to Matthew's employment of Rachel's tears. In Matthew's gospel it is written that Jeremiah's account of Rachel's weeping was "fulfilled" when Herod slaughtered all the young male children in and around Bethlehem, hoping thereby to kill the baby Jesus. Ishmael, remember, described the wailings of the Manxman's drowned men as sounding like "the ghosts of all Herod's murdered Innocents." Considering, therefore, that the *Rachel* is weeping for her children towed off by Moby Dick, we must conclude that the Manxman was right to identify these wailings as the voices of drowned men. He certainly regards his assessment as confirmed the moment he hears of the *Rachel*'s lost sailors. The captain's child "drowned with the rest on 'em, last night," he declares. "I heard; all of ye heard their spirits."

This episode validates the sailors' belief in the Manxman's "preternatural powers of discernment." Perhaps, then, we should inquire into the substance of the "bad news" he discerns upon the *Rachel*'s approach to the *Pequod*. The disappearance of the sailors in the whaleboat is lamentable, to be sure, especially since the captain's innocent child was among the doomed crew. But this does not concern the men of the *Pequod* directly. The news that Moby Dick is present in these waters does concern them, however; and given the whale's reputation for violence armored with indomitableness, the very thought of engaging him in battle may well strike even the bravest of whalemen as "bad." But the *Rachel*'s captain communicates still other news, though he does not realize it, spiritual news very bad indeed for the sailors aboard the *Pequod*. I have noted that the Manxman long ago interpreted the engraving on the face of Ahab's doubloon as portending the *Pequod*'s destruction, also that he disputed his fellows' judgment that their comrade's fatal plunge was the "fulfillment of an evil" presaged by the ghostly wailings rather than "a foreshadowing of evil in the future." The worst of the bad news brought by the *Rachel*, then, is the confirmation of the veracity of the Manxman's foresight, for if he can divine the future, then the *Pequod* is truly bound for an evil destruction, a doom most likely to be inflicted by Moby Dick, who even now lurks somewhere in the vicinity.

Ahab of course takes none of this as bad news. So dementedly eager is he to confront his nemesis that if he is disturbed at all, it is because the information that another ship has encountered Moby Dick raises the possibility that her crew has already killed him. Thus, as soon as the captain of the *Rachel* reports that he has seen the whale, Ahab ejaculates, "not killed! – not killed!" He attends to the captain's ensuing story only to gather intelligence about his enemy; the subordinate theme of the missing boy does not interest him. Ahab is impatient to be off, and the first word he speaks at the conclusion of the captain's mournful story is "Avast," by which he commands his men to dismiss any thought of preparing to assist the *Rachel*. Ahab cares for nothing beyond his hunt for Moby Dick.

Chapter 129: The Cabin

This chapter begins with Ahab worrying that his attachment to Pip tends to mitigate his madness. As like cures like, Pip's lunacy heals his own. This the Captain cannot allow, for his "malady" is his "most desired health." He admits the fact to Pip: "Ahab too is mad," he says, and he believes that he must persist in his condition to fulfill his destiny. Therefore he will abandon Pip, at least until he is well advanced toward his set purpose. In a way, then, Ahab wills his fate. But this is no sign of a Nietzschean self-affirmation. Ahab's is a nihilistic will that would destroy itself, obliterate the cosmos, and extinguish the light of the divine as well. The mad Captain, an active nihilist, would suck the world into his lungs then hold his breath until the All asphyxiates into Nothingness.

When Ahab leaves the cabin to go on deck, Pip steps forward to stand "in his air," which is to say in the vacuum created by Ahab's desperate departure. Strange, the Captain moves through space trailing an invisible but all-annihilating fire, and wherever he goes he leaves an expanding abyss in his wake. Standing there in the emptiness of Ahab's absence, Pip launches into a typical rant. "Ding, dong, ding!" he chants. "Who's seen Pip? ... Jumped from a whale-boat once," he says, and "shame upon all cowards!" On and on he goes, prattling, babbling, and burbling, drowning in the fancies of his swirling whirlpool mind.

When Pip gives voice to his madness I think of Nietzsche in the years of his insanity, which persisted from early 1889 until his death in 1900. He had begun to exhibit symptoms of a mental disturbance near the end of 1888, around the time of his forty-fourth birthday. Having relocated from Sils-Maria to Turin in September, he was hard at work on several books at once. The strain no doubt was tremendous, but his writing and revising proceeded apace, apparently without effort. By the end of the year, however, he was sending bizarre letters and telegrams to friends and strangers alike. He wrote directly to the German Kaiser, Wilhelm II, and he mailed to Bismarck a copy of *Ecce Homo*, the accompanying note to which he signed, "The Anti-Christian Friedrich Nietzsche." In January of the following year he wrote to a friend, "Sing me a new song: the world is transfigured and all the heavens are full of joy." He signed this note, "The Crucified One." He even sent a telegram to Wagner's widow Cosima, which read, simply, "Ariadne, I love you," and which he signed, "Dionysus." When an old friend in Basel received one of these disturbing notes, he suspected that something was dreadfully wrong. Therefore he travelled at once to Turin, where upon his arrival he found Nietzsche raving in a rented room, alternating between uncontrollable fits of raucous abandon and wilting moods of sadness. He took Nietzsche away to a sanitarium in Switzerland, whence Nietzsche's mother removed him to a hospital in a town near her home in Naumburg. In 1890 she moved him into her own house, and there he remained until her death in 1897, at which time his sister carried him off with her to Weimar.

Nietzsche's mother kept records of her son's condition, including his activities and verbalizations. When he spoke he issued such lunatic statements as, for example, "I swam in the Saale like a whale," "I did not love Friedrich Nietzsche at all," and "Liked whales." Thus it was with Nietzsche in the end. Yet his wretched condition did not prevent admirers from imagining him as inhabiting a summit high above, rather than a chasm far below, rational consciousness. One man who saw him reported that his eyes seemed "Zarathustra's eyes," or "the eyes of the Sphinx." To another he was not "a body from which the mind had fled," but a man who "had risen above little everyday things and withdrawn into himself." To yet another visitor Nietzsche appeared "prophetic," the veritable "Zarathustra Nietzsche." The sad fact is that Nietzsche was hopelessly insane, but there were those who could see in him only a spirit transcendent of mundane realities inhabiting an otherworldly empire of serenity and wisdom.

It is a perplexing irony of intellectual history that so many judged Melville mad during the years he sustained an Ishmaelean "mystic mood," while some mistook Nietzsche insane for a Zarathustran mystic. I have mentioned previously Melville's "earnest desire to write those sort of books which are said to 'fail.'" Beginning with *Moby-Dick* he granted his own wish on a grand scale. When, after the novel's publication, he declared to Hawthorne that "not one man in five cycles, who is wise, will expect appreciative recognition from his fellows," he intentionally excluded from his assessment the multitude of unwise authors who, as he well knew, are often widely, if undeservedly, appreciated. He had no such expectations for himself: he knew that his contemporaries would neither appreciate nor understand the best of his work. Unfortunately, he relied on revenue from his books for a living. Had he had other sources of income, or less need of money, he might have pursued his genius as freely as Nietzsche was able to do. Nietzsche wanted readers, to be sure, but only a select few, men and women of refined sensibilities with serious minds. Even after years of earning nothing from his books, he could still insist that "one does not only wish to be understood when one writes; one wishes just as surely *not* to be understood." Nietzsche deliberately prevented access to his work through his style of writing; he wrote only for his "friends," which is to say actual friends or strangers with sympathetic ears. Few had ears to hear either Melville or Nietzsche as they wished to be heard, as they deserved to be heard, and the misunderstanding persists even to this day. Thus there are those who when reading their books, or when reading about their lives, judge them both to be mad on the crests of their sanity and sane in their troughs of madness.

Chapter 130: The Hat

In this chapter a raging eagle snatches the cap from Ahab's head and carries it off, an uncanny occurrence ominous of the Captain's death. Melville contextualizes the event by looking back to ancient Roman history, or legend, and specifically to the story of Lucius Tarquinius Priscus (Tarquin the Elder). Born in the seventh century BCE, Tarquin was an Etruscan, with a connection through his father to Corinth in Greece. When as a young man he moved to Rome with his wife Tanaquil, an eagle swooped down as he entered the city and seized the hat he was wearing. But soon the bird returned and set the hat back on his head, which Tanaquil interpreted as an omen that one day her husband would be king. And so it was: Tarquin reigned as the fifth king of Rome for nearly forty years.

Ahab will not be so fortunate. Having been hoisted in a basket to a lofty perch to keep watch for Moby Dick, he is assaulted by a "red-billed savage sea-hawk," which, after screaming and circling around his head, jets straight up a thousand feet, descends again in a fury, then takes the Captain's cap in its beak and rushes away. The sable-winged hawk flies so far so swiftly that soon it disappears. Yet, even so, a sharp-eyed man could discern in the distance the slight black figure of Ahab's hat falling into the sea. Ahab will not be king. Like his stolen hat, he will be lost and consumed by the deep.

Though Melville relates this scene to an event in Rome's past, I associate it with a work from Melville's own future, for in his *Clarel* he would employ the same motif to prefigure another man's demise. Recall the character Mortmain, who, moved by somber reflections on the Southern Cross, "wails the loss" of God and dreads the impending "atheist cycles." Sometime after the travelers arrive at the monastery of Mar Saba, Mortmain sits apart from the group brooding on Christ's fate, death and despair, the vanity of earthly knowledge, and the proliferating opinion that there is "*No God*." Perched upon a high crag overlooking the "profound ravine" of the Kedron river, Mortmain is harassed by a "great bird." The shrilly crying "hag" takes the skull-cap from his head, wheels away, and drops it into the riverbed. Clarel later finds Mortmain dead, an eagle's feather settled on his lips.

Inspired by Mortmain's fate, one of his companions tells the story of a man at sea who while on watch atop a mast-head was attacked by "a big bird, red-billed and black / In plume." The bird not only stole the sailor's cap but pecked him on the crown of his head, which caused the man to lose his balance and plummet into the sea. He survived, but he was convinced that the bird had been a devil who "carried off his soul / In the old cap." Later the man required the ministrations of a vicar to recover his soul. The red-billed black bird of this tale is strikingly similar to the eagle that attacks Ahab, as are the circumstances of the assault. There are relevant differences too, of course, the plunge into the sea, for example, and the sailor's survival. But in the bird's seeming "a thing demonic," and its theft of the man's soul, there is, I believe, a recontextualizing allusion to Ahab, as undoubtedly there also is in Mortmain's death. Ahab has baptized his forged harpoon in the name of the devil, and Ishmael has hinted that Fedallah, whose mystic influence over the Captain he stresses in this chapter, descends from the race of devils who once "indulged in mundane amours" with "the daughters of men." Like the melancholy Mortmain, then, gloomy Ahab will be overcome by powers beyond his control, beyond all understanding as well. If there is no God, or if a willful man intentionally antagonizes the living God, then the sudden onslaught of death, with or without purpose or meaning, must come as no surprise. Either way, it does not matter, even a man reclining on a high natural perch, or clinging to the tall mast of a ship in the sun, may be toppled without warning by the beating wings of death.

Ahab dies in full revolt. Mortmain dies despairing. Melville himself was identical to neither, but each man represents a facet of his psyche. During his *Moby-Dick* period the vehemence of affirmative exuberance (in Ishmael) and mad rebellion (in Ahab) predominate. Later, doubt and melancholy intrude. As a young man Melville was closer to Ishmael than to Ahab, the Captain being a circumscribed constituent of Ishmael's thought-world, as Ishmael was an element within Melville's mind. Later in life Melville's mood declined, but however low he sunk for a time into a morass resembling Mortmain's drear despond, he fought his way back to something like tranquility—colored grey by resignation, but tranquility nonetheless. Even if it is true that in *Clarel* Melville intentionally depicted himself in Rolfe and Hawthorne in the mysterious Vine, every character is Melville in a sense. Through the ideas and attitudes of each individual he explores a vein running through his own soul. He encompasses them all, and therefore he exceeds them all. His Ishmaelean side was beaten down through the years; he grew weary and disillusioned. But better to be an Ishmael disenchanted than an Ahab or Mortmain in full form.

Chapter 131: The Pequod meets the Delight

Unlike Nietzsche, at the end of his life Melville was in command of his faculties. Although he suffered from a variety of physical ailments, his mind was sound. Over the course of his final four or five years he composed *Billy Budd, Sailor*, his first prose work in decades, and his last. He had begun the piece originally as a poem entitled "Billy in the Darbies," but through the years he expanded a short prose introduction into the novella we have today. The work was left incomplete at his death—the disorderly manuscript was later discovered among his papers—but it is nearly finished, and since its publication in 1924 it has become an acknowledged classic not only of Melville's canon but of American literature in general.

Billy Budd is evidence not only of Melville's creative powers during his final years, but also of his philosophical commitments, the thought-world he inhabited. We might fairly describe the tone of the work as tragic. Young Billy Budd the handsome sailor, admired by every man but one aboard the ship into whose service he has been pressed by the British Royal Navy during the Napoleonic Wars, is mercilessly harassed by the ship's Master-at-arms, John Claggart. In this Claggart the narrator says there raged "the mania of an evil nature," a wickedness "born with him and innate, in short 'a depravity according to nature.'" When Claggart falsely accuses Billy to the ship's Captain, Edward Fairfax Vere, of conspiring to instigate a mutiny, Billy is stunned, and being unable to reply from a fit of stuttering, he strikes Claggart, killing the man with this one blow. As two mutinies have recently erupted among the British fleet, the captain is constrained to enforce the rule of law with no consideration of leniency, even though he doubts Claggart's charge and cannot fault Billy for a violent act so obviously provoked. But the Master-at-arms was Billy's official superior, and it was indisputably a crime to murder the man. Immediately following Claggart's death the captain encapsulates the tragedy of the affair in the following remark: "Struck dead by an angel of God! Yet the angel must hang!" Billy is hanged indeed, but he meets his fate in a "spiritualized" state, radiating an innocent calm. His last words, "delivered in the clear melody of a singing bird on the point of launching from the twig," are simultaneously portentous and bewitching: "God Bless Captain Vere!" he says.

The details of the narrative of *Billy Budd* exhibit similarities to "The Town-Ho's Story" in *Moby-Dick*—violence aboard a ship at sea provoked by the cruelty of a superior—but here I am interested in the philosophical correspondences to the substance of Schopenhauer's philosophy. For Melville was not only writing at the end of his life; he was still pursuing his old interest in German idealist philosophy. In his last year, 1891, he acquired several volumes of Schopenhauer's works, and he marked such passages as the great Pessimist's claim, in his essay "On the Sufferings of the World," that "the story of the Fall" is "the only metaphysical truth" in the Old Testament. I have previously quoted Melville's observation, which appears in "Hawthorne and His Mosses," that "in certain moods, no man can weigh this world, without throwing in something, somehow like Original Sin," and from the evidence of his volume of Schopenhauer's *Studies in Pessimism* we learn that he preserved this view to the end. Witness his description of Claggart as depraved by nature.

In a letter from 1885 Melville informs a correspondent that he is "neither pessimist nor optomist" [sic] himself, but he adds that he does "relish" pessimism "as a counterpoise to the exorbitant hopefulness, juvenile and shallow, that makes such a bluster in these days." I take Melville at his word on the subject of philosophical pessimism. Though *Billy Budd* exudes no Ishmaelean exuberance, displays no evidence of the joyful wisdom of Melville's younger days, neither does it manifest the bitter nihilism that darkened the years immediately following the failures of *Moby-Dick* and *Pierre*. We might well call Melville disillusioned: this seems fair, particularly considering his manifest appreciation of Schopenhauer's observation that "he who lives to see two or three generations is like a man who sits some time in the conjurer's booth at a fair, and witnesses the performance twice or thrice in succession. The tricks were meant to be seen only once; and when they are no longer a novelty and cease to deceive, their effect is gone." But if we must note that Melville as an older man exhibited signs of resignation, I imagine that he would urge in his defense that he was not deluded by an unrealistically exaggerated pessimism, but was simply resigned to the proven realities of life. He marked Schopenhauer's contention that the "spirit of the New Testament is undoubtedly asceticism" defined as "the denial of the will to live," but though he lived a modest and dignified life himself, Melville showed no signs of a Christian or Schopenhauerian ascetic denial of life.

In point of fact, Melville more often noted Schopenhauer's remarks on the fate of genius in this world than either his metaphysically or ethically pessimistic passages. He doubtless had himself in mind when he approved the insight that if a man "has a soul above the common, or if he is a man of genius, he will occasionally feel like some noble prisoner of state condemned to work in the galleys with common criminals." And of course he was thinking of his own failed career when he marked Schopenhauer's observation in *The Wisdom of Life* that "the more a man belongs to posterity, in other words, to humanity in general, the more of an alien he is to his contemporaries; since his work is not meant for them as such, but only for them in so far as they form part of mankind at large; there is none of that familiar local colour about his productions which would appeal to them; and so what he does, fails of recognition because it is strange." Yet there is after all some connection between these reflections on the neglected genius and pessimism, for the fact that great creative individuals may die in obscurity is further evidence of cosmic injustice. And the sad reality that in this world angelic men like Billy Budd must suffer—and this through no one's autonomous fault, but rather by way of the combined influences of inborn evil, the institution of reasonable laws, and the spontaneous activity of ungovernable instinct—this is just one of the many phenomena that provoke the accursed questions.

A madman like Ahab demonically forges a lance, tempering the weapon in blood and lightning, to take by violence the "accursed life" of the whale of his mind's torment. An innocent like Billy Budd submits. But Melville himself when at his best neither raged nor wallowed in self-pity. With Nietzsche he embraced the liberating idea "that life could be an experiment of the seeker of knowledge," and the equally exhilarating conception of knowledge as "a world of dangers and victories in which heroic feelings, too, find places to dance and play." In brief, Melville at his best was a desperado sage called Ishmael.

Chapter 132: The Symphony

In this chapter Ahab for once acknowledges his own disturbed condition. He is, he says, an "old fool" and, worse, "more a demon than a man." He even sheds a tear into the sea—a single tear, no more, but this one drop contains "such wealth" as even the expansive Pacific does not hold. For a moment, then, Ahab cannot fathom himself, and his internal uncertainties are reflected back to him when, leaning over the side of the ship, he watches his shadow sink recedingly beneath his gaze as he strives "to pierce the profundity" of his own drowning soul. Would that he could say, with Zarathustra, "into your eyes I looked recently, O life! And into the unfathomable I then seemed to be sinking. But you pulled me out with a golden fishing rod; and you laughed mockingly when I called you unfathomable." But Ahab has been marked for death, has marked himself for death, and life fishes no man from the sea who hates and rages against her.

Marveling at his actions, Ahab marvels even through his deeds at the obscure motivations submerged beneath them. What drives the man? What is it, precisely, that has compelled him for these "forty years to make war on the horrors of the deep"? Ahab cannot answer; he does not know. He doubts himself so thoroughly that he begins to lose himself, even to question whether he has or *is* a self. "Is Ahab, Ahab," he wonders. "Is it I, God, or who, that lifts this arm?" And with these questions the Captain approaches the insight that God is dead, that God in every sense is dead because Being itself is a fiction. He approaches in short the Nietzschean idea, inspired by Heraclitus, that in all the world there is only Becoming.

Panta rhei: all things flow. Ahab is a river; Moby Dick is a river; the sea in which they flow together is a river too, a substance-less stream intermingling its waters with the torrent that is the cosmos entire. And you cannot step into the same river twice, as Heraclitus said. Or you cannot step into the river even once, as Cratylus the Heraclitean insisted, for there is no you, and there is no river.

After reading *Moby-Dick* Nathaniel Hawthorne wrote to Melville praising the novel. Unfortunately, this letter no longer exists. But we do have Melville's ecstatic reply, near the end of which he warns Hawthorne that if in the future he posts another letter to Herman Melville, then "possibly … you will missend it – for the very fingers that now guide this pen are not precisely the same as that just took it up and put it on this paper." And with a Heraclitean flourish he wonderingly adds, "Lord, when shall we be done changing?" Melville's sentiment here recalls Plato's discussion of Heraclitus in the *Theaetetus*, in which dialogue Socrates argues that since according to the Heraclitean doctrine of flux all things are always changing in every way, Socrates as a healthy man and Socrates when ill are different individuals. They differ because they do not share identical sets of properties, as Melville conceived as a collection of properties including the property *taking-up-his-pen*, is not identical to Melville conceived as a collection lacking this property but including instead the property *guiding-his-pen*. If sameness requires the precise identity between complete sets of properties, and if all things are always changing in every way, then no two individuals are ever the same from one moment to the next. Recall the ancient puzzle whether the ship of Theseus remained the same after its old planks were replaced by new ones.

Plato pushes Heraclitus's philosophy of flux even further, insisting that no individual is the same as itself at any single moment, and that therefore ultimately there are no individuals at all. "Nothing ever is but always becomes," his Socrates says, and "there is nothing that is one thing in and of itself, nor anything that you could correctly call either something or some type of thing." Now this is a radical reformulation of our common-sense conception of the world, and it would seem to demand as radical a revision of our vocabulary. If there are no individuals, no things, then, Socrates suggests, we should no longer use nouns or pronouns, including for example such words as "something," "this," and "that." And if "nothing is one thing in and of itself," then we shall also have to "remove altogether the verb 'to be'" from our philosophical vocabulary. You cannot step into the same river once, then, not only because there is no you and no river, but also because there is no *is* either.

Nietzsche styled himself a follower of Heraclitus, and like the master he "altogether denied Being." Throughout his career he rejected the common-sense conception of reality that posits "unity, identity, permanence, substance, cause, thinghood, being," all of which notions he dismissed as "errors of reason." According to Nietzsche's Kantian-inspired account of human knowledge, our minds are structured in such a way that we cannot help but perceive and understand the world in terms of enduring substances acting causally on one another. In at least one place he provides a psychological genealogy of our construction of reality from conceptual materials derived from introspection. We experience ourselves as acting from a unified internal source, to which we refer variously as the "self," the "soul," the "ego," or, simply, "I." However much we change throughout the course of our lives, this "I" seems to remain the same, the ground not only of our actions but also of our personal identity. Whenever we act, whether the action be a bodily movement or the thinking of a thought, we experience the action as generated by this self-identical enduring ego, which we take for the core of ourselves, our truest self, our *being*. We then project this self-conception onto the world, which we observe to be filled with other actions, and so we conceive of these actions as united in, and caused by, a self-identical permanent ground or source of activity and identity, a being. We populate the world with such beings, and thereby generate the idea of thinghood, of things themselves. What in reality is a flux of Becoming, flashes of motion or flowing pulses of energy, we gather into a field of beings, of individual substances identical to themselves and distinct from other individual substances.

This way of viewing the world is enshrined in our language, in the nouns and pronouns that designate individual substances, and the verbs that indicate their activities. As we talk about the world in these terms, both to ourselves and to others, we reinforce the "errors of reason" I mentioned just above. When Nietzsche refers to "the basic presuppositions of the metaphysics of language," he intends to indicate this fact that the structure of our language encodes a conception of reality as populated by beings. Sometimes he puts this in terms of "doers" and "deeds." Thus we imagine, for example, that a lightning flash is the activity, the deed, of a substance, the doer. The "lightning flashes," we say, as if the lightning were a substance independent of its flashing, the flashing the activity of this substance. In reality, Nietzsche says, there is only the flashing, which exhausts the reality of the supposed lightning "behind" it. Similarly, we tend to imagine, with Descartes, that "I think," as if there were an "I," a self or soul, a substance, a being, behind my thought as its source. Or we imagine, with Ahab, that "I move this arm," or if not I, then God, or something. There must be some ground or source of the action, we presume, for behind every deed there must be a doer. But according to Nietzsche, this is a misunderstanding generated by the errors of reason and reinforced by the metaphysics of language. Since grammatically every verb requires a noun or pronoun as its subject, we assume that every deed requires an agent. Therefore we conceptualize the world in terms of beings, the lightning behind the flash, the mind behind the thought, the I behind the lifting of the arm, and, ultimately, God behind everything. This last is what Nietzsche has in mind when he writes that "I am afraid we are not rid of God because we still have faith in grammar."

Nietzsche's Heraclitean philosophy of Becoming excludes every enduring substance, all beings, from sub-atomic particles to God. His deepest conception of reality dissolves all things, leaving nothing behind except, perhaps, quanta of energy or power. Plato seems at times to have entertained a similar view, at least with respect to the physical realm of Becoming. Melville never explicitly expresses so radical a view, though I would not insist that it was beyond the reach of his Ishmaelean intellectual experimentalism. But Ahab—Ahab does not reject Being, so although he can imagine that someone or something other than himself might be the source of his actions, he cannot imagine there being no source at all. Even "Fate" he regards as an agent, as a "handspike" turning him round and round. Nietzsche insists that "no one *gives* man his qualities—neither God, nor society, nor his parents and ancestors, nor he himself … no one is responsible for man's being there at all, for his being such-and-such, or for his being in these circumstances or in this environment." This idea he calls "the innocence of becoming," and this is precisely what Ahab cannot imagine, *does not want* to imagine. Nietzsche says, "We deny God, we deny the responsibility in God: only thereby do we redeem the world." But Ahab requires God precisely because he needs to hold God responsible for his suffering. This is why he prolongs the "strife of the chase." He projects the divinity of Being, Being as God, onto Moby Dick so that by killing the whale he may strike at God in retaliation for all that he cannot bear about himself. Unable to see through the errors of reason, he is trapped in the fictional world of Being, of substances as the sources of actions, of responsibility, guilt, and punishment. His pursuit of Moby Dick is a symptom and symbol of his imprisonment in the labyrinth of this false view, and the Minotaur of error will soon be the death of him.

Chapter 133: The Chase—First Day

"There she blows!" and Moby Dick at last swims into view. The "grand god revealed himself," as Ishmael puts it. Ishmael of course does not literally mistake the whale for a god, though Ahab very well might. To the Captain's mind he is in a way God's envoy, a symbol not merely as an intellectual concept resident exclusively in men's thoughts, but a living, breathing symbol through which the divine expresses itself in the physical world. To Ishmael's literary imagination Moby Dick's "mighty mildness of repose in swiftness" surpasses even the divinity of Zeus swimming to Crete as a white bull, Europa mounted on his back. And with this image Ishmael returns very nearly to the beginning of his story. Recall his waking up in the Spouter Inn with Queequeg's arm thrown across his chest: this arm, he recalled, was "tattooed all over with an interminable Cretan labyrinth of a figure." The Cretan labyrinth came to be built through the activities of Minos, son of Zeus and

Europa, who forced Daedalus to construct the maze as a prison for the Minotaur, offspring of his wife and another amorous bull. In later years Athenian children were periodically fed to the Minotaur, seven boys and seven girls devoured, until young Theseus sailed to Crete and killed the beast. The Athenians commemorated this and related events in the festival on the isle of Delos, the celebration of which delayed Socrates' execution, as Plato explains in the *Phaedo*. Now recall that the contents of this dialogue resemble the mysterious meaning encoded in Queequeg's tattoos, the cosmology and mystical epistemology, and that Queequeg carved these images on his coffin, presently serving as the *Pequod*'s life-buoy. The labyrinth expands; it surrounds us. Yes, we ourselves are trapped in a labyrinth stalked by the Minotaur of death, and Ishmael constantly reminds us of our predicament. We are shut in this labyrinth not only as readers but as living individuals as well. We all must face our Minotaur: our decision is whether to confront it madly like Ahab, and die, or to sing, play, and dance like Ishmael, and live.

Nietzsche's Zarathustra reports that although the bottom of his spirit's sea is still, it "harbors sportive monsters." He disports with the terrors of his soul precisely as Ishmael is social with horrors. "Imperturbable is my depth," he says, "but it sparkles with swimming riddles and laughter." The cheerfulness with which Zarathustra and Ishmael engage the accursed questions distinguishes them from Ahab, whose rage alienates him from friends and enemies alike—he is, he says, "alone among the millions of the peopled earth, nor gods nor men his neighbors." Zarathustra knows the type: the man "decked out with ugly truths, the spoil of his hunting," who "has not learned laughter or beauty." Like Ahab, this kind of man has "come home from a fight with savage beasts," and because he lacks the spiritual capacity to transform his combat into joyful play, "out of his seriousness there also peers a savage beast—one not overcome." Zarathustra would have this man "act like a bull," like a "white bull," whose happiness smells of the earth, "and not of contempt for the earth." Ahab's rage—his contempt not only for the earth, but for God and himself as well—prevents him from overcoming the beast within. And if we compare Ahab to Ishmael and Zarathustra, or for that matter to Melville and Nietzsche, then we must conclude that the source of his rage is belief, heterodox to be sure, but *doxa*, belief, all the same.

In the Third Essay of *On the Genealogy of Morals* Nietzsche writes of the ancient "order of Assassins, that order of free spirits *par excellence*," to whose supreme initiates was revealed the teaching that "nothing is true, everything is permitted." He then wonders who among those modern Europeans pleased to regard themselves as free spirits has ever strayed into the "labyrinthine consequences" of this idea, has "ever known the Minotaur of this cave *from experience*." He knows better than to believe that any one of them has. Philosophers, Christians, scientists, and scholars, even the ostensibly godless anti-metaphysicians and anti-Christians among us—they all believe in truth. In this they stand as one with Captain Ahab, and, as in Ahab's case, their "will to truth" is likely "a concealed will to death." To overcome this particular expression of contempt for the earth, Nietzsche insists that the "will to truth requires a critique," that "the value of truth must for once be experimentally *called into question*." Although he conducted this experiment himself through much of his career, he never finally completed his work. He admits that even he at times is still a "pious" adherent of the faith, "which was also the faith of Plato, that God is the truth, that truth is divine." If Nietzsche could not sustain his commitment to his own insight that God is dead, could not always believe it entirely, incorporate the thought into every nook of his soul, and live it in its every manifestation, without occasionally seeking again the maternal embrace of the old faith, then we should not expect Ishmael to state outright that Ahab is deluded because he believes in truth. But this I think is a part of Melville's ultimate message, one element of the secret substance of his teaching. "In landlessness alone resides the highest truth," which suggests to me that there is no truth, or anyway that truth is radically other than we have traditionally taken it to be. Ahab dies for, and because of, his faith; Ishmael lives because he overcomes the petty pairing of belief and unbelief.

Near the end of his active life Nietzsche boasted that he had "discovered happiness" by finding "the exit out of the labyrinth of thousands of years." He succeeded, he said, through a "predilection of strength for questions for which no one today has the courage; the courage for the *forbidden*; the predestination to the labyrinth." And when he wondered aloud who else had found the way out, he meant to insinuate that no one had, certainly no "modern man." It's a shame he knew nothing of Melville, nothing of Melville's Ishmael, who possessed the strength to address the accursed questions, and the cheerfulness to be social with them, who loved "to sail forbidden seas," and who was predestined to sail with Ahab into the labyrinth and find his way out, alone. In Melville Nietzsche had something of a peer, a predecessor even, for Melville intuited the death of God a full thirty years before Nietzsche announced the event, and he came to the insight in an environment much less primed to engender the idea, and much more hostile to it, than the European academic and philosophical circles that Nietzsche inhabited.

Moby-Dick is a labyrinth, as Plato's *Phaedo* and Nietzsche's *Zarathustra* are labyrinths too. Theseus made his way out of his labyrinth, but to escape he had to slay the Minotaur—he lacked the good will, the great health, to befriend it. Socrates escaped through death, but only after convincing himself that eternal life awaited him beyond the walls. He had to believe that he knew the truth, and that truth is divine. In short, Socrates ran from his Minotaur, or he closed his eyes and willed it out of his mind. Zarathustra survives by dying into his identical life; and he lives most fully by intentionally affirming his eternally recurring life. And what of Nietzsche? Shall we take him at his word that he escaped the labyrinth of thousands of years? Perhaps, but in the end Nietzsche went mad and died. Melville also escaped only later to collapse, if not so dramatically as Nietzsche. But for the moment I prefer to concentrate on Melville's literary creations. His Ahab will die, a terrible death, the death of a believer struck down by God while madly attempting deicide. The Captain's Minotaur will devour him, not only because he believes in the beast, nor even because he can neither kill nor tame it. The secret is to tame oneself in the presence of one's Minotaur; to let it live, flourish even, but to match its wildness with a wild tranquility, so that as one rolls, runs, and leaps in unison with it, movements that under normal conditions would express a decadent madness are transformed into a madness divine. Combat then is transmuted into play, frenzy into dance. Ishmael is master of the frenzied dance, which is why he will escape the labyrinth to tell us his story.

Chapter 134: The Chase—Second Day

When Ahab's whaleboat is attacked by Moby Dick on this second day of their confrontation, his ivory leg snaps off, leaving only a splinter in its place. Physically this is inconvenient, no doubt, hence the carpenter immediately sets to carving a replacement from the keel of the Captain's ruined boat. Spiritually, however, Ahab is not moved. "Even with a broken bone," he declares, "old Ahab is untouched." His point is not merely that his prosthetic limb is an alien thing, for even his actual bones are foreign to him now. He says himself that he accounts "no living bone of mine one jot more me, than this dead one that's lost." So his reasons run deeper than any distinction between the natural body and artificial appendages. Ahab's "own proper … being," he says, "is inaccessible." His true self is not composed of flesh, blood, and bones; it is a thing altogether beyond the confines of the physical world, and as such it is unassailable by man, whale, or fiend. Ahab is speaking of his soul, in which resides—or which just *is*—the authentic "unconquerable captain." Unfortunately, however, "accursed fate" has bound this spiritual captain to a "craven mate," which is to say to his body. Ahab conceives of himself as a soul temporarily resident in a body, the soul being his true self, steady and immortal, the body being an ephemeral and cowardly agent.

We have seen that Socrates in the *Phaedo* conceives of his body as a prison in which his soul is temporarily confined. Death will be a release, ideally not merely a restricted parole, but a total liberation. If he has lived well, practicing philosophy correctly as a mode of spiritual purification, then he will escape altogether the cycle of rebirth, live eternally after death without a body, never again to be incarcerated in this realm of Becoming. Near the end of the dialogue, after Socrates has concluded his final conversation, not long before he is due to drink the poison, his old friend Crito inquires how he would have them dispose of his body. Socrates laughs in reply, a gentle rebuke. Crito worries about interring or cremating the man, as if he might suffer. But this is silly, for after he has died Socrates will experience no pain because, quite simply, he will not be. Crito mistakenly thinks that Socrates is "that thing he will soon see as a corpse." But this is not so because, Socrates assures his friends, "after I drink the poison, I will no longer be with you, but I shall go away." Therefore neither Crito nor any one else should say at the funeral that they are laying out Socrates, or carrying him to the grave, or burying him. All this will be done only to the remains of his body, but Socrates will not then be, as even now he is not, his body. Socrates' actual self, now and forever, is his soul.

So Socrates and Ahab agree that they are their souls, and that their bodies are extraneous vessels. But Socrates is at peace with this conception of the self, whereas Ahab is agitated. Socrates welcomes death as a final transition to his true life among the gods. Ahab clings to life from a rage to murder God. He insists that he acts "under orders," that all these events have been "immutably decreed" from eternity. He is, he says, "the Fates' lieutenant."

But Ahab's conception of fate is bound up with doom. Socrates accepts that there are rewards and punishments in the afterlife, and that the future lives of those who return to earth are confined within certain limits by necessity; but he believes that those who while alive acquire virtue and wisdom may have great hope for a beautiful reward. In these matters, then, Socrates and Ahab disagree. Ahab accepts the premises of *Phaedo*-Platonism, but he resists the conclusions. In short, he accepts the distinction between Being and Becoming, even accepts that Being is superior to Becoming; but his unhappiness and rage compel his body to rebel against his soul's beliefs. It is not that he judges the physical sources of pleasure and pain more real than anything else, as Socrates says that some men do. It is rather that he suffers so terribly from pain that he cannot but lash out against everything that wounds him.

Despite their disagreements, Ahab and Socrates stand together when contrasted with Nietzsche. They both believe in the doer behind the deed, the "I" as an enduring substance that acts and thinks. They both subscribe to a "soul atomism" that conceives the soul as "something indestructible, eternal, indivisible, as a monad, as an *atomon*." In a word, Ahab and Socrates both believe in Being. This belief in at least its principal manifestation is, as we have seen, a natural consequence of the "errors of reason." Given the nature and structure of human minds, we necessarily experience the world as a spatial-temporal field populated by substances and their properties and actions. But when systems like Platonism and Christianity spin philosophy or theology out of the presuppositions of reason, these fundamental errors are compounded in conceptions of entities like Forms, souls, angels, and God—metaphysical entities distinct from physical objects, as Ahab and Socrates distinguish their souls from their bodies. Nietzsche rejects all this, hence his inverted-Platonism and his anti-Christianity.

Ishmael may not go so far as to reject Being utterly, but neither does he entirely accept it. As I have said, Ishmael has transcended belief and unbelief. And by this I do not mean to brand him an agnostic suspended between the two states: I employ the word "transcend" intentionally. In this chapter Ishmael refers to the *Pequod*'s crew several times in the third person. "They were one man," he says, "not thirty." And "they still strove through that infinite blueness to seek out the thing that might destroy them." Where then is Ishmael? Early in his story he stressed his personal identification with the crew. "I, Ishmael, was one of that crew," he recalled, "my oath had been welded with theirs ... Ahab's quenchless feud seemed mine." Now his fellow sailors and their Captain have congealed into a unified "they," with Ishmael himself occupying an independent perspective beyond them. But he is still a participant in the events, as we shall see. It appears, then, that on occasion Ishmael attains intellectual and spiritual heights transcendent even of himself. During these times he identifies with neither his body nor his soul. He is not a being, not even an omniscient being. We may call him "all-knowing," but only if we take this as a verb-form, not as an adjective. Ishmael is all deed, floating free of any doer. He is not merely playful, nor is he man become playfulness or play itself. Ishmael is *a playing*. But in the end I suppose I can express this thought most clearly by conforming my words to the experiential possibilities of our minds. Let me say, then, in terms similar to those I have previously employed, that Ishmael is the playing of Melville's mind, the supreme manifestation of Melville's joyful wisdom.

Chapter 135: The Chase—Third Day

During these final days of the *Pequod*'s fatal voyage Starbuck pleads repeatedly with Ahab to relent. It is not too late to call off the hunt, turn around and sail for home. In the present chapter, for example, as Ahab prepares to board his boat, Starbuck urges him, "go not—go not!" But Ahab will not listen. "Lower away," he shouts, and in an instant he is gone.

In these moving scenes Starbuck stands to Ahab as Crito stands to Socrates in prison. In the Platonic dialogue named for him, Crito strains to persuade Socrates to escape from jail and flee Athens. He has collected funds to bribe the guards, and his friends in Thessaly are willing to shelter the old philosopher. Moreover, Crito cannot bear to lose so dear a friend. At the end of the *Phaedo*, when Socrates calls for the poison, Crito begs him to wait just a little while longer. "Do not hurry," he pleads, "there is yet time." But Socrates insists that to delay would be ridiculous; he will gain nothing by putting off his death. Therefore he takes and raises the cup, and after inquiring of the guard whether he might pour a drop as a libation to the gods, he downs the poison "coolly and calmly." Everyone present weeps and wails. Crito in particular cannot restrain his tears; he cries as Starbuck cries when shaking hands with Ahab just before the Captain lowers his boat to confront Moby Dick on this, the third day of his clashing with the whale.

Starbuck is particularly moved by the fact that this is "the critical third day" of the ongoing struggle, for "when three days flow together in one continuous intense pursuit," he reflects, "be sure the first is the morning, the second the noon, and the third the evening and the end of that thing—be that end what it may." Therefore he is convinced that Ahab will not return to the ship, and that he, Starbuck, will never again return to Nantucket to hold his wife and child at home. Sadly, his premonition will prove all too accurate. Just so does Socrates die on the evening of the third day reckoned from his early morning meeting with Crito. When in the *Crito* Socrates sees his friend upon waking at dawn, Crito announces that he bears the bad news that Socrates must die the next day. The old ship of Theseus has been sighted in the harbor at the southernmost tip of Attica, on its way back to Athens from the Delian festival; and since the prohibition against executions will expire when the ship reaches the Athenian port in Peiraias, which it surely will the next day, Socrates must then die. But Socrates himself is not convinced. It seems that he has dreamt, just prior to waking in fact, of a beautiful woman clothed in white who called to him and said, "On the third day you shall come to fertile Phthia." The woman's words echo Achilles' announcement in the *Iliad* that because of his wrath against Agamemnon he will abandon the Achaian army at Troy and sail home to fertile Phthia, the shores of which he will reach with fair weather "on the third day." Achilles' mother, the goddess Thetis, has informed her son that he may choose to remain in the battle at Troy, where he will die young but win immortal acclaim, or sail home to a long but anonymous life in Phthia. For a time he considers returning home, but of course eventually he is provoked to return to the bloody field of combat. It may seem strange that Socrates infers the time of his death from Achilles' words concerning the conditions affording him a long life, but his conception of the afterlife makes sense of it all: he expects through the death of his body to liberate the life of his soul. This is why he scorns Crito's appeal to remove his body from the prison in Athens. Unlawful escape would be unjust, as he argues at some length; but also he would rather abet his soul's escape from the prison that is his body.

Socrates has little choice but to die, in spite of Crito's appeals. He has been lawfully convicted and sentenced. Eternal Justice demands it. Ahab too must die, however eagerly Starbuck insists, crying out to the Captain in his whaleboat below, that "Moby Dick seeks thee not. It is thou, thou, that madly seekest him!" But Moby Dick's head is "predestinating," in his aspect are "retribution, swift vengeance, eternal malice," and the conditions of Fedallah's prophecies of Ahab's death are satisfied one by one. Has Ahab not insisted that "this whole act's immutably decreed"? Indeed; and Ahab is "under orders" as surely as Socrates was.

Socrates' last words are notoriously enigmatic, though they manifestly express the philosopher's respect for the gods. Ahab shouts his final words, spits them at Moby Dick with no ambiguity whatever. And far from conveying a love for the divine, which he does not feel, Ahab barks that from "hell's heart" he lashes out "for hate's sake" against the "damned whale." Then, as the shattered *Pequod* sinks to doom beside him, Ahab darts his lance into the grand god's flesh. To no purpose. The whale surges, unharmed and enraged, jerking the line from the tub in the stern of Ahab's boat. The Captain stoops but cannot finally evade the horrible whale-line, which as towed by Moby Dick catches him round the throat. And in one gruesome instant, noosed old Ahab flies from his boat and disappears beneath black waves, dragged by his nemesis into the void of a bottomless grave. Thus Captain Ahab dies, his mad soul raging even to his last breath. Phaedo avows that Socrates died "the best, and also the wisest and most just" of men. Starbuck on this day addresses Ahab as "noble heart," but his final and more candid verdict is that the Captain is mad. Socrates' friends lament his death because they must live without him. The crewmen aboard the *Pequod* weep because in his madness Ahab compels them to die with him.

This final chapter of *Moby-Dick* begins with Ahab reflecting that "thinking is, or ought to be, a coolness and a calmness; and our poor hearts throb, and our poor brains beat too much for that." The thought contrasts with Plato's account of Socrates "coolly and calmly" drinking the poison in prison, and it recalls Melville's complaint, expressed in a letter to Hawthorne as *Moby-Dick* was running through the press, that "the calm, the coolness, the silent grass-growing mood in which a man *ought* always to compose, – that, I fear, can seldom be mine." Yet as both a thinker and a writer, Melville for a time possessed the power to overcome external agitations, to attain a state of internal tranquility sufficient to his needs as a philosophical artist, and to play on the heights while plumbing the depths of his soul. Melville then became an Ishmael, diving and dancing simultaneously, playing profoundly with the accursed questions, a desperado philosopher animated by a joyful wisdom.

Epilogue

"Alas, destiny and sea!"

In a fascinating letter to Hawthorne, from which I have had occasion to quote several times throughout this book, Melville writes, "From my twenty-fifth year I date my life." He is referring to the conclusion of his four years of Ishmaelean adventure at sea, at which point evidently he experienced himself as a man who in some intellectual-spiritual sense had died and been reborn. He left home aimless and unemployed; he returned a thinker and an artist. In *Moby-Dick* he depicts his rebirth in Ishmael's dying and returning to life. Consider Ishmael's several experiences of death so far: he begins by contemplating suicide and trailing funeral processions; he descends into the underworld where he meets a spirit-guide, his *daimôn* Queequeg; he imagines dissociating from himself by merging his identity with the ocean's heaving soul, or plunging to his death from the mast-head; he relinquishes his will to Ahab; he loses consciousness and his soul leaves his body. And most ominously of all, when the whaleboats are lowered for the first time on the voyage, he falls from his boat into "death's jaws." But Ishmael survives this death, lives through it to emerge into a new life. He reckons himself a Lazarus resurrected from the dead, and through the experience he develops the genial, desperado philosophy that empowers him to face even death itself without feeling dispirited. Now, in this final section of the book, Ishmael has once again toppled out of a whaleboat, but this time he does not die: he confronts but overcomes his death. After the *Pequod* and her crew finally "sink to hell," and the churning ocean becalms, Ishmael finds himself adrift on the sea alone. But then Queequeg's "coffin life-buoy" emerges from the depths, breaches the surface, and settles down beside him. Climbing atop this "dreaded symbol of grim death," as Ahab had called it, serving now as "the expressive sign of the help and hope of most endangered life," Ishmael floats undisturbed by the sharks and sea-hawks until the *Rachel*, still vainly cruising in search of her lost children, encounters and rescues him.

Recall that after recovering from his illness Queequeg decorated his coffin with images of his labyrinthine tattoos, and that a prophet from his native land had encrypted in the design of these tattoos ideas reminiscent of Plato's *Phaedo*. Resembling his body as it does, Queequeg's coffin is a symbol of the Pythagorean identification of the body (*sôma*) with a tomb (*sêma*). Therefore we may interpret the fact that Ishmael survives by surmounting the coffin—rather than by climbing inside, to lie supine like a corpse—as a figure for his overcoming the death-obsessed, life-denying thought-world of *Phaedo*-Platonism. And here I am reminded of Zarathustra, who once had a dream in which a roaring wind "cast up a black coffin before" him; and as a symbol of his advancing toward the giddy affirmation of the eternal return, "the coffin burst and spewed out a thousandfold laughter." Thus it is with Ishmael's overcoming of death. His existential transformation from the philosophically agitated sailor to the playfully sagacious narrator is now fully underway. He is learning to affirm life, even when circling the "closing vortex" of death, around which every man continually wheels until his final end.

In the first chapter of this book I pronounced Ishmael's existential transformation "the secret heart of *Moby-Dick*." But since Ishmael never explicitly mentions this transformation, most readers take the novel for Ahab's story. But Ahab is but a player in Ishmael's grander narrative; and Ishmael's narrative is encompassed in turn by Melville's still more expansive project, the creation of a work of art that I have termed an "intellectual-spiritual autobiography." Ahab, Moby Dick, and Ishmael himself are elements of Melville's psyche personified and projected as a symbolic self-conception, a self-portrait conveyed in narrative form as the allegorical tale of Melville's life, death, and rebirth. Ishmael's transformation, then, mirrors Melville's own existential development. He dated his life from his return from the sea because his experiences there transformed him so profoundly that he thought of himself as having died to his previous life to be reborn as the Ishmaelean pondering man who would conceive and compose *Moby-Dick*. So even if Melville did not attain a Nietzschean experience of the eternal return, we may nevertheless say of him, as Nietzsche used to say of himself, that some men are born posthumously.

I have mentioned the ancient story of the Seven Sages and the tripod assigned by Apollo to the wisest man. The Milesians bestowed the honor on Thales, but he passed it on to another man, who passed it to another, and so it made the rounds as each declined the designation "most wise." Since Thales is traditionally identified as the first philosopher, this story takes us back to the primal boundary separating wise men from lovers of wisdom. That Thales stands with one foot on either side of the divide reveals a fundamental perplexity: What is wisdom? And what, therefore, is the love of wisdom? To understand the nature of philosophy one must reflect on the nature of wisdom and the proper manner of loving it. Having studied the history of philosophy in some detail, with a particular interest in Platonism and nineteenth-century German idealism, and having come to regard himself as a pondering man, Melville explored his personal relation to philosophy and wisdom in and through *Moby-Dick*.

Despite its inverted-Platonism, then, Melville's novel resembles a Platonic dialogue in that *within* the text the characters directly address a variety of philosophical themes, while *through* the text Melville himself reflects indirectly on his own experience and understanding of the philosophical life. The grand god Moby Dick survives in the end, for the accursed questions he embodies and provokes can never finally be resolved, and philosophy conceived as the search for truth is an endless affair; Ahab dies, as the perpetual philosopher lost in the labyrinth of the search for truth, and agitated by the accursed questions, must perish by philosophy; and Ishmael lives as that part of Melville's mind that plays naively with the accursed questions from the abysmal peak of a joyful wisdom.

A little over midway through his story, after contrasting the keenness of the whale's perception with the minuteness of its eyes and ears, Ishmael addresses his audience: "Why then do you try to 'enlarge' your mind?" he asks, and he suggests that instead we "subtilize it." The thought recalls Heraclitus's "much learning does not teach understanding," and it seems to dispute the value of Solon's "as I grow old I am always learning many things." But these two sentiments need not contradict one another, for a properly elastic mind can expand without impeding its power of concentrated penetration. This is precisely the type of mind that ascends the heights by descending into the depths, a mind that thrives on conflict, within and without, yet maintains that state of receptive calm indispensable for the acquisition of insight. Ishmael is such a fecundly contradictory type, learned and subtle, active and contemplative, profound and playful. He is this type because he is a personification of Melville at his best, at the moment of his highest noon. Ishmael represents Melville as a lover of wisdom conceived, not as a philosopher who lacks and searches for wisdom, but as a sage admiring the flowers gleaming in the garden of the wisdom he owns and cultivates.

Melville's British publisher omitted the "Epilogue" from the first printed edition of *Moby-Dick* (under its original title, *The Whale*), which prompted numerous critical complaints that since no one survives the whale's assault, there can be no living narrator to relate the tale of the *Pequod* and its mad Captain. How can a drowned corpse tell a story? Why should we call a dead man Ishmael? It makes no sense. The "Epilogue" appeared in the American edition of *Moby-Dick*, but since in Melville's day many American periodicals reprinted reviews from the London press, or based their criticism on the opinions prevailing therein, he suffered at home for his foreign publisher's mistake. The book did garner a share of adulatory reviews, the most significant to Melville being the private praise he received from Hawthorne, to whom he had dedicated the work. In general, however, and in the near-term, *Moby-Dick* turned out to be yet another of "those sort of books which are said to 'fail,'" and Melville's career and reputation declined more or less steadily from there, sinking ultimately into obscurity. In the twilight of his life the general public, and even many among his literary contemporaries, assumed he was dead. In some quarters there was genuine surprise when news of his actual death was announced in September of 1891. No more. Mistaken for dead while alive, Melville in death has been resurrected. He lives enduringly in, and through, his literary-philosophical masterpiece. As an afterlife this is fitting, given his spiritual identification with his protagonist, for he did not conclude *Moby-Dick* with the whale's violence, or Ahab's death, but rather with Ishmael alive.

FINIS

Source Abbreviations

Works by Plato:

Alc. *Alcibiades*

Ap. *Apology*

Charm. *Charmides*

Cra. *Cratylus*

Euthphr. *Euthyphro*

Grg. *Gorgias*

Lg. *Laws*

Phd. *Phaedo*

Phdr. *Phaedrus*

R. *Republic*

Sph. *Sophist*

Symp. *Symposium*

Tht. *Theaetetus*

Ti. *Timaeus*

*****

Works by Herman Melville:

BB: *Billy Budd, Sailor (An Inside Narrative)*. Harrison Hayford and Merton M. Sealts, Jr., eds. (Chicago: The University of Chicago Press, 1962).

C: *Correspondence*. Vol. 14 of *The Writings of Herman Melville*. Lynn Horth, ed. (Evanston: Northwestern University Press, 1993).

CL: *Clarel: A Poem and a Pilgrimage in the Holy Land*. Vol. 12 of *The Writings of Herman Melville*. Harrison Hayford, Alma A. MacDougall, Hershel Parker, and G. Thomas Tanselle, eds. (Evanston: Northwestern University Press, 1991).

CM: *The Confidence-Man: His Masquerade*. Vol. 10 of *The Writings of Herman Melville*. Harrison Hayford, Hershel Parker, and G. Thomas Tanselle, eds. (Evanston: Northwestern University Press, 1984).

J: *Journals*. Vol. 15 of *The Writings of Herman Melville*. Howard C. Horsford with Lynn Horth, eds. (Evanston: Northwestern University Press, 1989).

M: *Mardi and A Voyage Thither*. Vol. 3 of *The Writings of Herman Melville*. Harrison Hayford, Hershel Parker, and G. Thomas Tanselle, eds. (Evanston: Northwestern University Press, 1970).

MD: *Moby-Dick: or, The Whale*. Vol. 6 of *The Writings of Herman Melville*. Harrison Hayford, Hershel Parker, and G. Thomas Tanselle, eds. (Evanston: Northwestern University Press, 1988).

P: *Pierre: or, The Ambiguities*. Vol. 7 of *The Writings of Herman Melville*. Harrison Hayford, Hershel Parker, and G. Thomas Tanselle, eds. (Evanston: Northwestern University Press, 1971).

PT: *The Piazza Tales and Other Prose Pieces, 1839-1860*. Vol. 9 of *The Writings of Herman Melville*. Harrison Hayford, ed. (Evanston: Northwestern University Press, 1987).

R: *Redburn: His First Voyage*. Vol. 4 of *The Writings of Herman Melville*. Harrison Hayford, Hershel Parker, and G. Thomas Tanselle, eds. (Evanston: Northwestern University Press, 1969).

WJ: *White-Jacket: or, The World in a Man-of-War*. Vol. 5 of *The Writings of Herman Melville*. Harrison Hayford, Hershel Parker, and G. Thomas Tanselle, eds. (Evanston: Northwestern University Press, 1970).

*****

Works by Friedrich Nietzsche:

A: *The Antichrist* in *The Portable Nietzsche*. Walter Kaufmann, ed. and tr. (London: Penguin, 1954), pp. 568-656.

BGE: *Beyond Good and Evil* in *The Basic Writings of Nietzsche*. Walter Kaufmann, ed. and tr. (New York: The Modern Library, 1967), pp. 191-435.

BT: *The Birth of Tragedy* in *The Basic Writings of Nietzsche*. Walter Kaufmann, ed. and tr. (New York: The Modern Library, 1967), pp. 15-144.

EH: *Ecce Homo* in *The Basic Writings of Nietzsche*. Walter Kaufmann, ed. and tr. (New York: The Modern Library, 1967), pp. 671-800.

GM: *On the Genealogy of Morals* in *The Basic Writings of Nietzsche*. Walter Kaufmann, ed. and tr. (New York: The Modern Library, 1967), pp. 449-599.

GS: *The Gay Science*. Walter Kaufmann, ed. and tr. (New York: Vintage, 1974).

HH: *Human, All Too Human: A Book for Free Spirits*. R. J. Hollingdale, tr. (Cambridge: Cambridge University Press, 1996).

KSA: *Sämtliche Werke: Kritische Studienausgabe*.

MM: "Mixed Opinions and Maxims," in HH, pp. 215-299.

NCW: *Nietzsche Contra Wagner* in *The Portable Nietzsche*. Walter Kaufmann, ed. and tr. (London: Penguin, 1954), pp. 661-683.

Ph: "The Philosopher," in *Philosophy and Truth: Selections from Nietzsche's Notebooks of the Early 1870's*. Daniel Breazeale, ed. and tr. (Amherst: Humanity Books, 1990), pp. 1-58.

PTG: *Philosophy in the Tragic Age of the Greeks*. Marianne Cowen, tr. (Washington: Regnery, 1962).

TI: *Twilight of the Idols* in *The Portable Nietzsche*. Walter Kaufmann, ed. and tr. (London: Penguin, 1954), pp. 465-563.

TSZ: *Thus Spoke Zarathustra* in *The Portable Nietzsche*. Walter Kaufmann, ed. and tr. (London: Penguin, 1954), pp. 121-439.

UM: *Untimely Meditations*. R. J. Hollingdale, tr. (Cambridge: Cambridge University Press, 1983).

WP: *The Will to Power*. Walter Kaufmann, ed.; Walter Kaufmann and R. J. Hollingdale, eds. and trs. (New York: Vintage, 1968).

WS: "The Wanderer and His Shadow," in HH, pp. 301-395.

*****

Other sources:

CN: Sander L. Gilman, ed., and David J. Parent, tr. *Conversations with Nietzsche* (Oxford: Oxford University Press, 1987).

DK: Diels and Kranz. *Die Fragmente der Vorsokratiker*.

DNZ: Paul Loeb. *The Death of Nietzsche's Zarathustra* (Cambridge: Cambridge University Press, 2010).

FN: Curtis Cate. *Friedrich Nietzsche* (New York: The Overlook Press, 2005).

HM1: Hershel Parker. *Herman Melville: A Biography, Volume 1, 1819-1851* (Baltimore: The Johns Hopkins University Press, 1996).

HM2: Hershel Parker. *Herman Melville: A Biography, Volume 2, 1851-1891* (Baltimore: The Johns Hopkins University Press, 2002).

MB: Hershel Parker. *Melville Biography: An Inside Narrative* (Evanston: Northwestern University Press, 2013).

PM: Merton M. Sealts, Jr. *Pursuing Melville, 1940-1980: Chapters and Essays* (Madison: The University of Wisconsin Press, 1982).

PP: Arthur Schopenhauer. *Parerga and Paralipomena*, 2 vols. E. F. J. Payne, tr. (Oxford: Clarendon Press, 2000).

SP: Arthur Schopenhauer. *Studies in Pessimism*. T. Bailey Saunders, ed. and tr. (London: Swan Sonnenshein & Co., 1891).

*All other sources are listed in the notes.

*All translations from the Greek are my own.

Notes

Etymology: By "modern logic"—and setting aside for now Nietzsche's deeper critique, which I take seriously—I allude to the contemporary obsession among professional philosophers with, say, reasoning exclusively according to the dictates of propositional logic, prostrating by citation before the shades of Quine and David Lewis, and neither addressing broader cultural, literary, or artistic matters nor thinking of their own work in these terms, which results in mediocre writing on subjects of limited appeal and only professional relevance. It may be worth noting here (for those who know), that apart from the influences explicit in the content of this book, my thinking in relation to contemporary philosophical developments, particularly in the so-called "analytic" tradition, with which I more or less identify, is informed by the critical work of Hume, the later Wittgenstein, Kuhn, Feyerabend, Plantinga, and Rorty in particular. Taken together their work tends to undermine the authority of the empiricism, evidentialism, non-skeptical realism, and narrow scientism that so dominate the philosophical scene today. My differences from Rorty have mostly to do with the fact that, whereas he moves from private irony to liberal hope, my own interest in rewriting philosophy and experimenting with new vocabularies is motivated, not by a desire to expand the "we" for social-political ends, but rather by the romantic goal of self-creation through expanding the scope of my personal intellectual freedom for philosophic-artistic exploration with a good conscience.

Extracts: "The unexamined life" (Ap. 38a); "And yet self-knowledge" (CM, 19); "I am not yet able" (Phdr. 229e); "Active, successful natures" (MM 366); "Those who philosophize correctly" (Phd. 67e); "All that philosophers have handled" (TI "Reason" 1); "Death, though in a worm" (CM, 194); "Plato, I think" (Phd. 59b); "A sick philosopher" (CM, 80); "And as for my long sickness" (NCW "Epilogue" 1); "Those who are not sham" (Sph. 216c-d); "Oh, this mad" (TSZ 3, "The Other Dancing Song" 2); "Life is not by square" (CL 3.11.1-2); "For folly's sake" (TSZ 3, "Before Sunrise"); "Nor was his philosophy" (WJ, 353); "If the things I say" (Phd. 91b); "But truth is ever" (C, 213); "Nothing is true" (TSZ 4, "The Shadow"); "Philosopher, probe not" (M, 415); "This experience of wondering" (Tht. 155d); "Profound aversion" (WP 470); "Common consistency" (M, 459); "In a written discourse" (Phdr. 277e); "And you shall learn" (TSZ 3, "On Old and New Tablets" 16); "No man can read" (PT, 249); "And so I tell" (EH "Epigraph").

Chapter 1: Ishmael and Melville: Walter Bezanson, who also put Ishmael at the center of *Moby-Dick*, was right to warn against "any one-to-one equation of Melville and Ishmael" ("*Moby-Dick*: Work of Art," in *Moby-Dick Centennial Essays*, Tyrus Hillway and Luther S. Mansfield, eds. [Dallas: Southern Methodist University Press, 1953], pp. 30-58). Yet one may well accept his point while nevertheless insisting that in writing of Ishmael Melville was writing very much about himself. The two men do after all share much in common: the substance and formulation of their interests and ideas (Ishmael and Melville are both concerned with "the problem of the universe" [Ishmael: MD, 158; Melville: C, 186 & 452]; they both consider Solomon "the truest" of all men, specifically with reference to the idea expressed in *Ecclesiastes* that all is vanity [Ishmael: MD, 424; Melville: C, 193]; and both are keen to explore "the blackness of darkness" [Ishmael: MD, 10 & 423; Melville: PT, 243]); details of their biographies (generally there is their time at sea, during which [more specifically] Ishmael and Melville both read Owen Chase's account of a whale's sinking of the whaleship *Essex*, of which Chase was first mate, and even met and spoke with his son near the scene of the catastrophe); the date and time of their writing (in the course of composing his narrative Ishmael records a date and time within three days of Melville's describing in a letter his own writing of *Moby-Dick*, including the fact that he would have been writing at the same time of day as Ishmael, and reporting also that on his farm in the country he has "a sort of sea-feeling," and he looks out of his window as he would "out of a port-hole of a ship in the Atlantic" [C, 173-74]); their passion for Platonism in general and for Plato's *Phaedo* in particular; and much else besides. Melville said himself that fine authors almost always provide existential-intellectual self-portraits in and through their works (see the penultimate quotation in "Extracts"); "Pondering man" (J, 35); "beyond human ken" (J, 628); "heroics" (C, 196); "well-pleased" (R. 620c-d); a "life to which" (R. 617e); "truth is in the deep" (DK 68B117); on Plato and water I exaggerate somewhat: for Plato, as for many upper-caste Athenians, the sea had a political meaning in connection with democracy, the navy, and commerce, all of which were associated with the lower orders of society. So the sea represented the element of the people's—the mob's—power, which the more conservative elements of society resented. See the Athenian's remarks on these matters in Book 4 of Plato's *Laws* (Lg. 704d-707d); "mountains for company" (GM 3.8); "everything is in the sea" (TSZ 3, "On Old and New Tablets" 28).

Chapter 2: Death as separation of soul from body (Phd. 64c); Plato's philosophical reformulation: for more on this theme, see my *Plato and Nietzsche: Their Philosophical Art* (London: Bloomsbury Academic, 2014), pp. 133-38, and Radcliffe G. Edmonds III, *Myths of the Underworld Journey:*

Plato, Aristophanes, and the "Orphic" Gold Tablets (Cambridge: Cambridge University Press, 2004); some men are born posthumously (A "Preface"; EH "Books" 1).

Chapter 3: "a mind fitted by nature" (P, 165); "Neither by land nor by sea" (A 1).

Chapter 5: "man is the measure of all things" (DK 80B1); "full of the German metaphysics" (J, 4); "talked metaphysics continually" (J, 8); "talked high German metaphysics" (J, 19); for more on Melville's philosophical conversations with Adler during this trip, see also J, 33 and 34.

Chapter 6: "Fayaway in his face" (MB, 326).

Chapter 7: "a letter from the spring of 1849" (C, 127-29), and for further documentation see Merton M. Sealts, Jr., "Melville and The Platonic Tradition" (page 297, and note 30 in particular) in PM, 278-336; "dwelling in the midst of the depths of the sea" (Phd. 109c); Parmenides' Being as the one and only existent reality: here I present the standard reading, which seems in the relevant sense also to have been Plato's reading; but for another, perhaps deeper and more faithful reading of Parmenides, see Peter Kingsley, *Reality* (Inverness: The Golden Sufi Center, 2003); "turning" of the soul (R. 518c-d).

Chapter 8: to live in the future forever without a body (Phd. 114c); "spiritual withdrawal" (Phd. 83d); exaggerated desires (Phd. 64c-e); Plato's rejection of empiricism and materialism (Phd. 82d-83e); hatred of reason (Phd. 89c-91a); basest of base things (Phd. 83c; cf. 89d).

Chapter 9: "Plato, I think, was ill" (Phd. 59b); Socrates' arguments are incomplete or inconclusive (Phd. 84c-d, 114d-e); *diaskopein* (R. 472a); true nature of the earth as *logos* (Phd. 108d), and as *mythos* (Phd. 110b); "a noble risk" (Phd. 114d); Plato's dialogues as models of the novel (BT 14).

Chapter 11: the soul's release: the body is called a prison twice (Phd. 62b, 82e); "really strange feeling" (Phd. 59a).

Chapter 12: "men who *dive*" (C, 121); "the body and its desires" (Phd. 66c); MD as "inverted Platonism": Michael E. Levin, "Ahab as Socratic Philosopher: The Myth of the Cave Inverted," *American Transcendental Quarterly* 41 (1979), pp. 61-73; Nietzsche's philosophy as "inverted Platonism" (KSA 7:7[156]); "eternal indictment of Christianity" (A 62).

Chapter 14: "unfolded within myself" (C, 193); "Melville in the Berkshires": for the account of Melville in this section I draw on Hershel Parker, "Melville and the Berkshires: Emotion-Laden Terrain, 'Reckless Sky-Assaulting Mood,' and Encroaching Wordsworthianism," in *American Literature: The New England Heritage*, James Nagel and Richard Astro, eds. (New York: Garland, 1981), pp. 65-80. For more on Melville's psychological-existential condition during this period see the relevant chapters of HM1. I cite Hershel Parker throughout this book for specific details, but it is worth noting that Parker and Jay Leyda are responsible for *all* of our best and most reliable biographical information. Parker's two-volume biography is long, but it is very good, and there really is no reason to read any other; "official tour" ("Melville in the Berkshires," p. 66); "expansive" (ibid., p. 68); "Swamps and quagmires" (ibid., p. 67); "young and healthy" (ibid., p. 69); "threw off thoughts" (ibid., p. 70); "Artists ... [know] only too well" (BGE 213).

Chapter 15: "*tuchê tis*" (Phd. 58a); Zalmoxis (Charm. 156d-157c); Parmenides and incubation: Peter Kingsley, *In the Dark Places of Wisdom* (Inverness: The Golden Sufi Center, 1999).

Chapter 16: "prophetic *daimonion* ... abundant evidence" (Phd. 40a-c); "the body is our tomb" (Grg. 493a); the followers of Orpheus (Cra. 400c); "has nothing healthy" (Phd. 68c-69b); "a trick of metaphysical and morbid meditations": Fitz-James O'Brien, "Our Authors and Authorship—Melville and Curtis," *Putnam's Monthly Magazine*, April 1857; "a morbid state of mind" (J, 628).

Chapter 17: "the spirit *is* a stomach" (TSZ 3, "On Old and New Tablets" 16); "turning his mind toward himself" (Symp. 174d); Socrates has this habit (Symp. 175b); prayer to the sun (Symp. 220c-d); Socrates' wisdom (Symp. 220c-d).

Chapter 19: implies that the soul is immortal (Phd. 102a-107b); soul as rational agent of deliberation (Phd. 98c-99b); "wonder" (Tht. 155d; *Metaphysics* 1, 982b).

Chapter 20: "fated" and "journey" (Phd. 115a); purification as preparation (Phd. 114c); "education and rearing," and becoming "good" and "wise" as the soul's "salvation" (Phd. 107d); "make and practice music" (Phd. 60e); "greatest music" (Phd. 61a); "potentially culpable negligence" (Phd. 60e); incantatory charm (Phd. 114d).

Chapter 21: dubious and vulnerable points (Phd. 84a-c); Socrates and the swans (Phd. 84e-85b); Socrates died "unappalled" (PT, 275).

Chapter 22: "thirty days" (*Memorabilia* 4.8.2); "pure of intercourse": the story is told and attributed to Speusippus (among others) by Diogenes Laertius (3.2).

Chapter 23: final version of *Moby-Dick*: for a summary history of these ideas, see section five of the "Historical Note" in MD, pp. 648-659; "shanties" (C, 195); "like most professional authors" (George R. Stewart, as quoted in MD, p. 655); "a strange sort of book" (C, 162).

Chapter 24: "the truth of the thing" (C, 162); "intense feeling of the visable truth." (C, 186); "the tragicalness of human thought" (ibid.); "the Problem of the Universe" (ibid.); "acquire *depth* and become *evil*" (GM 1.6); very good on *Moby-Dick* and Melville's notion of truth is Gustaaf Van Cromphout, "*Moby-Dick*: The Transformation of the Faustian Ethos," *American Literature* 51.1 (1979), pp. 17-32.

Chapter 25: "deep far-way things" (PT, 244); *Zum Lazarus*: see Isaiah Berlin, *The Hedgehog and the Fox: An Essay on Tolstoy's View of History*, Henry Hardy, ed. (Princeton: Princeton University Press, 2013, 2nd edition), p. 13n1. Hardy acknowledges that Mikhailov may have adopted an already current Russian expression for his translation of Heine's German.

Chapter 26: Plato on democracy in the *Republic* (R. 555b-563e); Nietzsche on democracy and Christianity: BGE 202 ("the *democratic* movement is the heir of the Christian movement") and A 43.

Chapter 27: they voluntarily imprison themselves (Phd. 82e-83a).

Chapter 28: "astonishing conception" etc. (PT, 406).

Chapter 30: man who contributes to his own confinement (Phd. 82d-e).

Chapter 31: Socrates' wisdom is ... a dream (Symp. 175c-e); "wisdom" in the cave (R. 516c-d); contending over shadows (R. 520c); the prisoners are like us (R. 515a); Glaucus (R. 611b-612a); Diotima's account (Symp. 210a-211d).

Chapter 33: "contemplate beings" (*Nicomachean Ethics* 1139a); *nous* and *epistêmê* (ibid. 1141a); function or naturally proper activity (ibid. 1139b);

"Platonism in Europe" (BGE "Preface"); "every profound spirit needs a mask" (BGE 40).

Chapter 34: that man is corrupt (A 6); why not rather untruth? (BGE 1); "supposing that those things are true" (Phd. 83d); "most distinct and most true" (Phd. 83c); "binds the soul with nails" (Phd. 83d); hierarchy of reincarnated beings (Phdr. 248d-e).

Chapter 35: fleeing from the body (*to sôma … pheugei*, Phd. 65c-d); flight (*pheugousa*, Phd. 80e-81a); "try to fly" (*pheugein*), flight (*phugê*), and "likeness to God" (Tht. 176a-b); "with wisdom" (Phd. 69a-b); "release from the bonds of the body" (Phd. 67c-d); *lusis … tôn … desmôn* (R. 515c); *lusis … apo tôn desmôn* (R. 532b); as divine … as a human may (R. 500c-d); *homoiousthai theôi* (R. 613a-b); "assimilation to god takes on new meaning": John M. Armstrong, "After the Ascent: Plato on Becoming Like God," *Oxford Studies in Ancient Philosophy* 26 (2004), pp. 171-183 (the quotation is from page 174); quotations from Book 8 of the *Laws* (Lg. 828c-d); deserving of ridicule or reprimand (R. 516e-517a); the World Soul (Ti. 34b-37a); the Good "beyond being" (R. 509b); to *be God* (*theon einai*, *Enneads* 1.2.6); "the All-Pure" (*to katharôtaton*, *Enneads* 6.9.3); for more detail on unification, *henosis*, and *theôsis* see my *Pure: Modernity, Philosophy, and the One* (San Rafael: Sophia Perennis, 2009), pp. 75-84; "gloomy religio-moral pathos" (WP 427).

Chapter 36: Socrates was offered the opportunity to escape from jail (see Plato's *Crito*); "not speaking well" (Phd. 115e).

Chapter 37: wine for the guests to drink (Symp. 213e-214a); Alcibiades on his relationship with Socrates (Symp. 216a-c; 218a); A naturally gifted man corrupted (R. 489d-495b); Aristotle on unmitigated badness (*Nicomachean Ethics* 1126a).

Chapter 38: "passionate desire" (Thucydides 6.24.3); "excessive desire" (ibid. 6.24.4); "Demeter and Korê": Plutarch records the indictment in his *Life* of Alcibiades (section 22). The word "*korê*" literally means "young girl," "maiden," or "virgin." In this indictment it is used, as was traditional, as a title for Demeter's daughter Persephone; "two Spartan kings": from a very early period Sparta was ruled by a pair of kings, one from each of the city's two families descended from Heracles, the legendary founder of Sparta; Socrates meets the young Alcibiades (Alc. 133b). Some scholars argue that Plato is not the author of the *Alcibiades*. The authenticity of the work was not doubted by the ancients, and many contemporary scholars (myself included) see no good reason to doubt it now; "longs for him" (*Frogs* 1425).

Chapter 39: "wise Stubb": for a defense of Stubb as a philosopher, see Alan Dagovitz, "*Moby-Dick*'s Hidden Philosopher: A Second Look at Stubb," *Philosophy and Literature* 32 (2008), pp. 330-346.

Chapter 40: Wisdom in a polis (R. 428a-429a); wisdom in an individual (R. 442c); poets and divine inspiration (Ap. 22a-c); shrine to the muses in the Academy: see Diogenes' *Life* of Speusippus (4.1). Speusippus was Plato's nephew and second scholarch of the Academy; Socrates like figurine of Silenus (Symp. 215a-b).

Chapter 41: "weighed down and dragged back" (Phd. 81c-d); "phenomenality of the inner world" (WP 477).

Chapter 42: "the innate systematic structure" (BGE 20); Aristotle's Prime Mover: in fact there are many such movers in Aristotle's system. For further information about these matters, see Book 12 of Aristotle's *Metaphysics*; "thought thinking of thought" (*Metaphysics* 12.9).

Chapter 43: "By vast pains": included in Sealts's essay, "Herman Melville's 'I and My Chimney,'" in PM, pp. 11-22; Hume on the self: "Of Personal Identity," Book 1, section 6, part 4 of *A Treatise on Human Nature*; "the prejudice of reason" (TI "Reason" 1 & 5); "Deep, deep": also included in Sealts' essay (see above).

Chapter 44: Socrates thought it best to sit in prison (Phd. 98c-99b); the proper explanation involves mind (Phd. 97b-d); "burying Socrates" (Phd. 115c-e); "corpses" (DK 22B96).

Chapter 45: "some vague idea" (C, 219).

Chapter 46: desiring to maintain that which one already possesses (Symp. 200a-e); "auditory hallucinations" (TI "Socrates" 4).

Chapter 47: "as a philosopher" (GS 357); "what so ever comes to pass" etc. (from the Westminster Confession of Faith); "Transcendent Speculation" (PP1, 201-223); "a supernatural guidance" (PP1, 202); "the simultaneity itself" (PP1, 216); "the accidental coincidence" (PP1, 215); "the accidental and the necessary" (PP1, 207); "neither our *action*" (PP1, 205, note); "that which in an event is natural" (PP1, 221).

Chapter 48: even formulated an argument (Phd. 70c-72d); "resurrecting" an argument (Phd. 89b); to live in the future without a body (Phd. 114c); covering-uncovering: for a detailed and thoroughly documented reading of this part of the *Phaedo*, see my *Plato and Nietzsche*, pp. 133-137.

Chapter 49: "how he that says NO" (EH "TSZ" 6); "in the happy condition" etc. (C, 186); "profundity and high spirits" (EH "GS"); "the Provençal concept of gaya scienza" (ibid.); "a cavalier on horseback" (HM1, 852-53); "whispering of eternal things" (TSZ 3, "On the Vision and the Riddle" 2); "the ideal of a spirit" (GS 382).

Chapter 50: Nietzsche's "demand upon the philosopher" etc. (TI "Improvers" 1); "Zarathustra was the first" etc. (EH "Destiny" 3).

Chapter 51: We are told in the *Phaedo* (Phd. 66b-d); In the *Phaedo* it is said (Phd. 81e-82b)—see also Phdr. 249b and Ti. 91d-92c.

Chapter 52: "the plain of truth" etc. (Phdr. 247b-248c); "purification" etc. (Phd. 72e-77a); health (Phd. 69b-c, 90e); Socrates' "bizarre equation" (TI "Socrates" 4); "the Socratic love of knowledge" (BT 18); "the most spiritual expression" (BGE 208); "another and stronger type of skepticism" (BGE 209); "pessimism of strength" (BT "Attempt" 1).

Chapter 53: "taciturn, but genial" (HM1, 571-72); "had always known ... the conversation drifted" (HM2, 230-31); "I am intent upon the essence of things" (M, 352); scholars have detected: see, for example, H. Bruce Franklin, *The Wake of the Gods: Melville's Mythology* (Stanford: Stanford University Press, 1963), p. 216n.1; "the Dialogues of Plato": *Literary Gazette*, April 11, 1857 (quoted in CM, 324).

Chapter 54: Plato's *Phaedo* concludes (Phd. 108c); Only those who have thoroughly purified themselves by philosophy (Phd. 114b-c); Socrates' description of the hollows in the earth (Phd. 109a-b).

Chapter 55: little reliable information available concerning Eastern philosophies and religions: for documentation of the knowledge of Eastern philosophy and religion in Melville's time and place, see Part One of Daniel Herman's *Zen and the White Whale: A Buddhist Rendering of* Moby-Dick (Lanham: Rowman and Littlefield, 2014). The book concentrates on Buddhism but includes information about contemporary knowledge of Hinduism; "the most profitable and sublime reading" (PP2, 397); "dwellings still more beautiful" (Phd. 114c); The monster on this vase: for a picture of the Corinthian amphora and a brief "natural history" of the ancient *kêtos*, see chapter four of Daniel Ogden's *Perseus* (New York: Routledge, 2008).

Chapter 56: "Bacon's brains" (P, 211); "old Greek times" (P, 198); "those philosophies which come home" (CM, 50); "vain ... betray him" (CM, 135); "*Knowledge is power*" (CL 3.28.7-8); "reckless sky-assaulting mood" (P, 347); "But, as to the resolute traveler in Switzerland" (P, 284); "Those legends" (CL 1.36.110-115).

Chapter 57: Achilles in anger (*Iliad* 22.346-7); "two beautiful cities" (*Iliad* 18.490-91).

Chapter 58: "much learning" (DK 22B40).

Chapter 59: Unless otherwise noted, all quotations in this chapter are from BGE 204; like ink from a squid: Friedrich Nietzsche, *Briefwechsel: Kritische Gesamtausgabe*, Giorgio Colli and Mazzino Montinari, eds. (Berlin: de Gruyter, 1975), #690 (April 21, 1886, to Heinrich Köselitz); "the Platonic way of thinking" (BGE 14); "the greatest strength" (BGE 191); "royal and magnificent hermits" (BGE 204); "projected suspension of judgment": *The Hellenistic Philosophers*, vol. 1, A. A. Long and D. N. Sedley, eds. (Cambridge: Cambridge University Press, 1987), p. 440; too "delicate [a] creature" (BGE 208); "despises but nevertheless seizes" (BGE 209).

Chapter 60: "no one comes back from the dead": *Either/Or*, Part 1, Hong and Hong, eds. and trs. (Princeton: Princeton University Press, 1987), p. 26; pure knowledge of truth is possible only after death (Phd. 66e-67a); when we suffer but cannot say why, and suicide by hanging (*Problems* 954b); Socrates and Plato suffered from melancholy (*Problems* 953a); we humans have been fashioned by the gods (Lg. 644d-e); "Between Birds of Prey": see *The Peacock and the Buffalo: The Poetry of Nietzsche*, James Luchte, tr. (London: Continuum, 2010), pp. 268-273.

Chapter 61: Melville refers to Descartes' theory of vortices: David Charles Leonard has demonstrated that Melville likely learned of Cartesian vortices by way of Ephraim Chambers's *Cyclopedia: or, An Universal Dictionary of Arts and Sciences* (1846), which includes entries on "VORTEX" and "CARTESIAN *Philosophy*, or CARTESIANISM." See "The Cartesian Vortex in *Moby-Dick*," *American Literature* 51.1 (1979), pp. 105-109. Melville mentions the vortices again in *Pierre* (P, 267); "By convention sweet" (DK 68B9).

Chapter 65: the best thoughts "are born outdoors" (EH "Clever" 1); "morbidity ... brooding" etc. (GM 1.6); "the salvation of humanity": the quotation marks around this phrase are Nietzsche's own; Nietzsche on the English diet (EH "Clever" 1); "strong doses" (ibid.); "*Water* is sufficient" (ibid.); vegetarians are "*attracted* by what is harmful" (CW 5); "an animal, a species" (A 6); Schopenhauer on eating meat in cold climates: *On the Basis of Morality*, E. F. J. Payne, tr. (Indianapolis: Hackett, 1995), p. 182; "revoltingly crude" (ibid., 175); "a total difference" (ibid.).

Chapter 66: the "Euthyphro dilemma" (Euthphr. 10a-11b).

Chapter 67: Margaret J. Osler, *Divine Will and the Mechanical Philosophy* (Cambridge: Cambridge University Press, 1994); "the differences between" (ibid., 222).

Chapter 68: the philosopher "demands of himself" (BGE 205); "all profound knowledge flows cold" (TSZ 2, "On the Famous Wise Men"); "the level to which modern philosophy has gradually sunk" (BGE 204); whale blubber that must be cooked (C, 162); "of the horrible texture" (C, 206); "clenched teeth" (FN, 485); "sudden sparks" (BGE 296); "a wicked book" (C, 212); "the hell-fire" (C, 196); "Ego non baptizo te": from "Superstition and Knowledge," published anonymously by Francis Palgrave in 1823; "we investigators are" (D 432); "evil art" (C, 209).

Chapter 69: "the wretchedness of the most recent philosophy" (BGE 204); "lukewarm" etc. (TSZ 2, "On the Famous Wise Men"); the spirit's transition (TSZ 1, "On the Three Metamorphoses); "how much truth" (EH "Preface" 3); "those deep far-away things" (PT, 244); "mystical blackness" (PT, 243); "the eternal wound of existence" (BT 18); "meaninglessness of suffering" (GM 3.28); "life ... in its strangest" (TI "Ancients" 5); "Have you never seen a sail" (TSZ 2, "On the Famous Wise Men").

Chapter 70: "forced by circumstances" (PT, 245); "covertly, and by snatches" (PT, 244); "not a frank man" (C, 122); Emerson "a great man" (C, 119); "oscillate in Emerson's rainbow" (C, 121); "thought-divers" (C, 121); "no wisdom ... before Zarathustra": unless otherwise indicated, all quotations from Nietzsche in this chapter come from EH "TSZ" 6; "I love him whose soul is deep" (TSZ "Prologue" 4); Emerson "does not know how old he is already" (TI "Skirmishes" 13); "made obscure" (GS, "Translator's Introduction," p. 12); "transcendentalisms, myths & oracular gibberish" (C, 121).

Chapter 71: "perhaps uncannier" (EH "GM"); "physiological depression" etc. (GM 3.16-17); "*life-inimical* species" (GM 3.11); the ascetic ideal functions to preserve life (GM 3.13); "For every sufferer" (GM 3.15); "psychological-moral" interpretation (GM 3.16); "owing to [a] lack" (GM 3.17); The ascetic priest provides that meaning (GM 3.28).

Chapter 72: All quotations from Nietzsche in this chapter come from TI "Errors" 7, except for the last one ("the fatality of [a man's] essence"), which comes from section 8.

Chapter 73: Locke argued against suicide (*Essay* 2.2.6); the very argument that Socrates offers against suicide (Phd. 61c-62c); Hume "died the death of a Christian" (R, 291); Kant denies knowledge to make room for faith (*Critique of Pure Reason* B30); "an underhanded Christian" (TI "Reason" 6); The very idea is as good as refuted (TI "Fable" 4-5).

Chapter 74: "metaphysically speaking" (M, 63); "the airy exaltations" (P, 267).

Chapter 75: "the sublimated categories of Kant" (P, 267); Melville, Adler, and Kant: Melville mentions Kant in the third chapter of *Mardi*, but only in passing, and without suggesting any deep or detailed knowledge of his philosophy. For his conversations with Adler, see J, 4, 8, 19, 33, 34; Hume apparently suffered a mental breakdown: the book is *A Treatise on Human Nature* (1739). To be fair, I should note that although some scholars attribute Hume's breakdown to his skeptical insights broadly conceived, there is no consensus as to its actual cause; "dogmatic slumbers" (*Prolegomena to Any Future Metaphysics*, "Preface").

Chapter 76: "To the realists" (GS 57); "erroneous articles of faith" (GS 110); "lines, planes, bodies" (GS 112); "continuum and ... flux" (GS 112); "There is no 'reality'" (GS 57); "will to knowledge" (BGE 24); "fictions of logic" etc. (BGE 4); "a condition of life" (GS 110); "life-promoting" (BGE 4); "how much truth" (EH "Preface" 3); "to what extent" (GS 110).

Chapter 77: According to Plutarch: "On Isis and Osiris" 354c. The word I have translated as "uncover" is *apekalupsen*, which is related to the words for cover and uncover at the end of Plato's *Phaedo*; Kant once remarked: *Critique of Judgment*, Werner S. Pluhar, tr. (Indianapolis: Hackett, 1987), p. 185n.51; Schopenhauer accepted: I should note that I make no attempt to employ the relevant technical philosophical terminology as precisely as Kant did himself. For present purposes it will suffice to use such words as, for example, "categories" as they are used by Schopenhauer and Nietzsche, which is to say more broadly, or loosely, than they appear in Kant's own writings.

Chapter 78: Socrates "conceives it to be his duty" (BT 13); *"philosophic thought* overgrows art" (BT 14); *"The dying Socrates"* (BT 13); "pseudo-Greek, anti-Greek" (TI "Reason" 2); "the Platonic drama" (BT 14).

Chapter 79: the scientists' atom (see GS 108-112); "physics, too" (BGE 14); those who have "faith in science" (GS 344).

Chapter 80: the *Zopyrus*: Livio Rossetti, "Phaedo's *Zopyrus* (and Socrates' Confidences)," in *From the Socratics to the Socratic Schools*, Ugo Zilioli, ed. (New York: Routledge, 2015), pp. 82-98; "a *monstrum*" (TI "Socrates" 3); "anarchy of his instincts" (ibid. 4); "most bizarre of all equations" (ibid.); the "fanaticism with which" etc. (TI "Socrates" 9-11); "an anti-Dionysian tendency" (BT 14); "the enormous driving-wheel" (BT 13); "Euripides was ... only a mask" (BT 12); "Virtue is knowledge" (BT 14); Plato "really too noble" for "Socratism" etc. (BGE 190-191).

Chapter 81: "already dead as my father" (EH "Wise" 1); "the torments" (EH "Wise" 1); A friend who sought him out (CN, 164).

Chapter 82: illness and death of Melville's father: I take the quotations from Jay Leyda, *The Melville Log: A Documentary Life of Herman Melville: 1819-1891*, vol. 1 (New York: Harcourt, Brace and Company, 1951), pp. 51-52; "poetry and wildness": Evert Duyckinck to his brother George (March 9, 1848); "two *jobs*" (C, 138); "those sort of books" (C, 139); Plato, Shakespeare, Hawthorne: Charles Olson persuaded most scholars that *Moby-Dick* was influenced by Melville's reading of Shakespeare (Charles Olson, *"Lear* and *Moby-Dick," Twice a Year* 1 [Fall-Winter 1938], pp. 165-189, and *Call Me Ishmael* [New York: Reynal & Hitchcock, 1947]). On the rare occasions that Melville scholars address Plato's influence, they present Plato vaguely as an "idealist," without quite specifying what they mean, then briskly move on to discuss Melville and democratic optimism, or Melville and Emerson's transcendentalism. But Plato influenced Melville much more deeply than through his "idealism," and the facts of Melville's interest in Kant's transcendental idealism and its philosophical progeny expose the inadequacy of "idealism," without further specification, as a term of analysis. Merton Sealts came as close as any Melville scholar ever has to recognizing the significance of Plato's influence on Melville, and indeed he began his "Melville and the Platonic Tradition" with the observation that "Of the various philosophers whose thought was familiar to Melville ... Plato is clearly the preeminent influence on his thinking and writing" (PM, 279). Yet as valuable as Sealts' work is, it is for the most part a cataloguing of verbal or thematic similarities. He details the superficial effects of Platonic formulations on the contents of Melville's works, but he neglects the deeper matter of Plato's philosophy shaping the nature of Melville's mind. The neglect of Plato in Melville scholarship beyond Sealts' work is astonishing: there is *no entry for Plato* in the indexes of Wyn Kelley's *A Companion to Herman Melville* (Malden, MA: Wiley-Blackwell, 2015), Robert S. Levine's *The New Cambridge Companion to Herman Melville* (Cambridge: Cambridge University Press, 2013), or Harold Bloom's *Herman Melville's Moby-Dick* (New York: Chelsea House Publishing, 2007). There is a single page referencing Plato in the index of Michael J. Davey's *Herman Melville's Moby-Dick: A Routledge Study Guide and Sourcebook* (New York: Routledge, 2003), and two pages referenced under the sub-heading "Platonic," listed under the general heading "Idealism," in the index of Giles Gunn's *A Historical Guide to Herman Melville* (Oxford: Oxford University Press, 2005); *Pierre* as "Krakens" (C, 213); "the last week" (HM2, 119).

Chapter 83: the beginning of Plato's *Phaedrus* (Phdr. 229a-230a); "clever (or spurious)": *sophizomenos*, from *sophizô*; Socrates doubts the gods fight among themselves (Euthphr. 6a); "The total character of the world" (GS 109); "complete our de-deification of nature" (ibid.).

Chapter 84: in written words there is necessarily much playfulness (Phdr. 275c-277e); the man who writes from knowledge ... is a philosopher (Phdr. 278b-d); "the most writerly of philosophers": Alexander Nehamas, *Nietzsche: Life as Literature* (Cambridge: Harvard University Press, 1985), p. 26; "writing [was] ... the most important part of living" (ibid., 41); "knows in that he invents" (Ph 53); "'knowing' is *creating*" (BGE 211); "instruments of the philosopher" (BGE 210); "a form of artistic invention" (Ph 53); "half artist" (KSA 13:14[1]); Nietzsche as anti-metaphysician (GS 344); "dance in their chains" (WS 140); "an anti-metaphysical but artistic worldview" (KSA 12:2[186]); "*indemonstrable* philosophizing" (Ph 61); "poorly demonstrated philosophy of Heraclitus" (Ph 61); "will to truth is—*will to power*" (BGE 211).

Chapter 85: "I go to my workroom" (C, 174); "I have a sort of sea-feeling" (C, 173); "Who would have looked for philosophy in whales" (HM2, 134); Melville was a philosopher: Melville's wife Elizabeth evidently accepted the idea, often expressed, that her husband's obsessions with philosophy interfered with the quality and quantity of his literary output (see PM, 212-214).

Chapter 86: Goethe "disciplined himself to wholeness" (TI "Skirmishes" 49); *Gespräche mit Goethe* the best book in German (WS 109); "Goethe's paganism with a good conscience" (GS 357); agreement "about the 'cross'" (TI "Skirmishes" 51); Goethe's poem: see *Venetian Epigrams* 66, included in *Goethe: The Collected Works, volume 1: Selected Poems*, Christopher Middleton, ed. (Princeton: Princeton University Press, 1983), p. 127; Goethe as "Dionysian" (TI "Skirmishes" 49); Melville on Goethe (C, 193-94); "In Christianity" (A 15); "instruments of torture" (A 38); "the one immortal blemish" (A 62); *"essentially dangerous"* etc. (GM 1.6).

Chapter 87: Thus in the *Phaedo* Plato describes (Phd. 73a-77a); "it is out of the deepest depth" (TSZ 3, "The Wanderer").

Chapter 88: Melville's education "irregular" and "spotty" (HM1, 159 & 116); "of all ages" (C, 7-9); Nietzsche's determination to be a philosopher (KGB 729 and 734); Melville refashioned himself as a poet: see Hershel Parker, *Melville: The Making of the Poet* (Evanston: Northwestern University Press, 2008).

Chapter 89: For a concise version of the biographical details related in this chapter, see Hershel Parker's "Damned by Dollars: *Moby-Dick* and the Price of Genius," in MB, 481-497; "Dollars damn me" (C, 191); the "calm, the coolness" (ibid.); "perhaps a little sadder" (J, 628); two young admirers (HM2, 397-399); Melville "was absolutely unfitted" (HM2, 900); "there are few pains" (BGE 203).

Chapter 90: Wagner was not "the seer of a future" (UM, 254); Nietzsche, Salome, and Rée: on this episode of Nietzsche's life, see Robin Small, *Nietzsche and Rée: A Star Friendship* (Oxford: Oxford University Press, 2005). For a more detailed and fully biographical account, see FN (chapters 26-29 in particular); "the Yes-saying pathos" (EH "TSZ" 1).

Chapter 91: "Europe is beginning to stink" (GM 1.11); *"close* my nose" (GM 1.14); Melville "disgusted with the civilized world" etc. (HM2, 398-99); Melville and Rankin: I take the "many long talks" and "philosopher" from Melville's letter to his brother Allan (C, 301). The characterization of Rankin's book as "heavily ... anti-clerical," and the excerpt from Rankin's preface, I quote from the "Editorial Appendix" to J, 534; "eternal indictment of Christianity" (A 62); "the inmost parts" (EH "Wise" 8); Nietzsche constantly affronted (GM 1.12); "instruments of culture" as instruments of nihilism (GM 3.14 & 1.11); "*our* greatest danger" (GM 1.12).

Chapter 92: "degeneration was quietly developing" (TI "Socrates" 9); Nietzsche's formula for decadence (TI "Socrates" 4, 9, 11); "The self-overcoming of morality" (EH "Wise" 3); "virtue that is moraline-free" (A 2); the "dangerous slogan" (GM 1.17).

Chapter 93: a second speech as an act of purification (Phdr. 243a); Socrates uncovers his head (Phdr. 237a, 243b); the greatest of good things come to humans from madness given by the gods (Phdr. 244a); "the winged soul" (M, 230); oyster (Phdr. 250c); Melville's allusion to both the *Phaedo* and the *Phaedrus* in the passage at issue was recognized by H. N. Couch in "*Moby Dick* and the *Phaedo*," *The Classical Journal* 28 (1933), pp. 367-368; Melville and Plato's *Symposium*: Merton Sealts writes that the *Symposium* was "fresh on [Melville's] mind in November of 1851," not long after he completed *Moby-Dick*. As evidence he cites a letter to Hawthorne in which Melville refers to "the ugly Socrates" (PM, 319). This is suggestive, if not conclusive. Much more persuasive is a passage from Book II of *Pierre*, which Melville was writing at the time of his letter to Hawthorne, in which he writes of "two Platonic particles ... roaming in quest of each other, from the time of Saturn and Ops till now" (PM, 320). That Melville was familiar with the *Symposium* even before writing *Moby-Dick* is clear from his mention in *Mardi* of the wise man who can drink all night without getting drunk, and who walks home in the morning as his drinking partners collapse all around him (M, 489; cf. *Symposium*, 223b-d); "the madness of philosophy" (Symp. 218b).

Chapter 94: Some have attempted: See Hubert Dreyfus and Sean Dorrance Kelly, *All Things Shining* (New York: Free Press, 2011). The chapter on Melville, "Fanaticism, Polytheism, and Melville's 'Evil Art,'" is on pages 143-189 (see p. 163 in particular); the most famous image in Plato's *Symposium*: The only possible rival would be Aristophanes' account of the original unity and later division into pairs of humans, to which Melville alludes in the passage from Book II of *Pierre* quoted in the notes to the previous chapter (via Sealts, PM, 329); "the vast sea of the beautiful" (Symp. 210d).

Chapter 95: All quotations from Nietzsche in this chapter are from GM 3.7-8; language implying sexual intercourse: *suneinai, sunontos autôi* (Symp. 211d, 212a); "pregnant in their souls" (Symp. 209a).

Chapter 96: "Silence is the only Voice of our God" (P, 204); "We have left the land" (GS 124); "plunging continually" (GS 125); "Heraclitus will remain" (TI "Reason" 2); "this tremendous event" (GS 125); "Europe's grieving doubt" (CL 1.3.135-36); "student of the sacred lore" (CL 1.9.25-27); "Went towards the cemeteries" (J, 62); "who will wipe this blood" (GS 125).

Chapter 97: "I invented a brighter flame" (TSZ 1, "On the Afterworldly"); "I live in my own light" (TSZ 2, "The Night Song"); "it is the not impartially bestowed" (P, 169); "sees the abyss" (TSZ 4, "On the Higher Man"); "highest mountain" etc. (TSZ 3, "The Wanderer"); "great health" (From GS 382, as quoted in EH "TSZ" 2); "The meaning of our cheerfulness" (GS 343); "bold searchers" (TSZ 3, "On the Vision and the Riddle"); "the truest of all men" (C, 193).

Chapter 98: Pythagoreans and the eternal return: see Porphyry's *Life of Pythagoras*, section 19; a student of Aristotle: Eudemus's report is recorded by Simplicius in his *Commentary on the Physics*, 732.29-33; "Would you not throw yourself down" (GS 341); "Mr. Melville seems to lack": William Alfred Jones, "Melville's Mardi," *The United States Democratic Review*, vol. 25, issue 133 (July 1849), pp. 44-51 (the quotation is from p. 50); "Yet if our dead fathers" (M, 237); "the teacher of eternal recurrence" (TI "Ancients" 5): for a thorough and, to my mind, convincing defense of Nietzsche's commitment to the eternal return, see Paul Loeb's DNZ, also his "Eternal Recurrence" in *The Oxford Handbook of Nietzsche*, Ken Gemes and John Richardson, eds. (Oxford: Oxford University Press, 2013), pp. 645-671; with the "knight-poet" and "*gai saber*" I allude to the final paragraph of *Beyond Good and Evil* 260.

Chapter 99: "And perhaps" (C, 186); "the whole of our European morality" (GS 343); "*European Nihilism*" (KSA 12:5[71]): this note appears as notes 4, 5, 114, and 55 in Book 1 of WP; "suicidal nihilism" (GM 3.28); material on the "Christian moral hypothesis" is from the Lenzer Heide notes.

Chapter 100: "the first perfect nihilist" (WP "Preface" 3); Zarathustra's nihilistic nausea (TSZ 3, "The Convalescent" 2); nihilism "as a psychological state" (WP 12); "like a new" (GS 343).

Chapter 101: "like one of those seeds" (C, 193); Socrates, prophecy, and Apollo's swans (Phd. 84e-85b); *The Isle of the Cross*: I borrow the summary from the indispensable Hershel Parker, "Herman Melville's *The Isle of the Cross*: A Survey and a Chronology," *American Literature* 62.1 (1990), pp. 1-16; "philosophical novelists": Albert Camus, *The Myth of Sisyphus and*

Other Essays, Justin O'Brien, tr. (New York: Vintage International, 1991), p. 101; "truly absurd" (ibid., 113n8).

Chapter 102: "you see what happened" (C, 348); "fate" (J, 134-35); "much shocked" (HM2, 576); Melville's hotel stay in relation to the origin of *Clarel* (ibid., chapter 30, passim).

Chapter 103: *"nitimur in vetitum"* (EH "Preface" 3): the line is from Ovid's *Amores* 3.4.17; Nietzsche as "adventurer" (BGE 227); "must have been critic" (BGE 211); "German education" (EH "Clever" 1); "there are many kinds of eyes" (WP 540).

Chapter 104: "about fifty fast-writing youths" (C, 174); "if the world was entirely" (C, 213); "Melville and I had a talk" (HM1, 853); "ontological heroics" (C, 196); "tumultuous waves" (HM1, 834); "pours out" (HM2, 136); "Herman Melville passed the evening" (HM2, 291).

Chapter 105: "combing and curling" (*On Composition* 25); "most daimonic" (*On Demosthenes* 7); if the gods speak a human language (ibid. 23); "turning [it] up and down" (Phdr. 278d-e); "only thoughts reached by walking" (TI "Maxims" 34); on the writing of *The Wanderer and His Shadow*: letter of 5 October, 1879, to Peter Gast (Heinrich Köselitz), in *Selected Letters of Friedrich Nietzsche*, C. Middleton, ed. and tr. (Indianapolis: Hackett, 1996), p. 169; "habit to think outdoors" (GS 366); accounts of Nietzsche's daily routine in Sils-Maria: see, for example, FN, 451, and Marie von Bradke's reminiscence in CN, especially pages 189-190; "To live alone" (TI "Maxims" 3); "Of all that is written" (TSZ 1, "On Reading and Writing"); "brought the German language to perfection" (Middleton, *Selected Letters*, p. 221); "born posthumously" (A "Preface"); only his early romances of adventure (C, 193); write the Gospels and die in the gutter (C, 192); "brightest success" (P, 339).

Chapter 106: "The intensest light" (P, 169).

Chapter 107: "confess[ed] a dislike" etc. (C, 190-91); His older sister Helen "had been capable" (HM1, 347); "heights of the soul" (BGE 30); "There are books" (ibid.); "books for all the world" (ibid.); "the virtues of the common man" (ibid.).

Chapter 108: "mortal soul" etc. (BGE 12); "a metaphysics of the hangman" (TI "Errors" 7); "the concepts 'beyond'" (A 38); *"nihilistic* will" (A 9); "hell ... beyond" (A 58).

Chapter 109: "ideal of a spirit" (GS 382); Melville's narrative command: *Pierre* appears an exception as a consequence of Melville's angry revisions of the already completed manuscript. For a detailed account of these matters, see Brian Higgins and Hershel Parker, *Reading Melville's Pierre; or, The Ambiguities* (Baton Rouge: Louisiana State University Press, 2006); Melville's ecstatic reply (C, 210-214); "suffering and sufferers": all quotations in this paragraph come from GS 370; "pessimism of strength" (BT "Attempt" 1); Nietzsche misunderstood Schopenhauer (GS 370); "I very earnestly denied" (EH "Clever" 1); "soil out of which" (TI "Ancients" 5); "afford the sight" (GS 370).

Chapter 110: Socrates makes a similar point (Phd. 62c); Socrates as prophet (Phd. 84e-85b); "mystic" (WJ, 155); "Crito, we owe a rooster" (Phd. 118a); short story written two years after *Moby-Dick*: "Cock-A-Doodle-Doo!" in PT, 268-288 (the quotations are from p. 275); Paul Loeb argues (DNZ, ch. 2); "ridiculous and terrible" (GS 340); "Was *that* life?" (TSZ 3, "On the Vision and the Riddle" 1).

Chapter 111: Plutarch on the death of Pan (*De defectu oraculorum* 17, 419a-e); "There rose everywhere" (BT 11); "lies the death of tragedy" (BT 14); "*The dying Socrates*" (BT 13); "the art of Greek tragedy" (BT 12); Dionysus and the Crucified (EH "Destiny" 9).

Chapter 112: "a certain lassitude … *I aint crazy*" (C, 452-454); Nepenthe (*Odyssey* 4.220-221); "On Free Death" (TSZ 1); Socrates refuses to escape: see Plato's *Crito*; "some necessity" (Phd. 62c); "seems to have brought about" (BT 13).

Chapter 113: "all-too-many" (TSZ 1, "On Free Death"); "The thunderbolt" (DK 22B64); "a man's character" (DK 22B119).

Chapter 114: "we ourselves keep growing" (GS 371); the "idea that life" (GS 324); "The eternal hourglass" (GS 341).

Chapter 115: "found him serious" etc. (TSZ 1, "On Reading and Writing"); "a sage too is a fool … *all* woe" (TSZ 4, "The Drunken Song" 10); "an aesthetic phenomenon … nothing does us as much good" (GS 107); "rather be a fool" (C, 192); "whatever one casts" (GS 378).

Chapter 116: "In order that what happens necessarily" (GS 1); "Man seems to have had" (J, 78).

Chapter 117: For backward-willing and memories of the future in connection with Nietzsche conception of the eternal return, I rely on Paul Loeb's accounts in DNZ, chapters 7 and 8.

Chapter 118: "oversees all things" (*Odyssey* 12.323); "utterly blinded" (Phd. 96a-c); Socrates did not want his soul to be "blinded" (Phd. 99d-e); Socrates uninterested in extraneous matters (Phdr. 229b-230a); the thoroughly purified soul (Phd. 114c); "*I have discovered the Greeks*" (KSA 10:8[15]); Paul Loeb has suggested (DNZ, 38-41 & 82-83); "suicidal nihilism" (GM 3.28).

Chapter 119: "does not only contemplate" (WP 24); "*the* way" (TSZ 3, "On the Spirit of Gravity" 2).

Chapter 120: "with the lightning's flash" (P, 111); a "monument of rigorous self-discipline" (EH "HH" 5); Nietzsche associates *Human, All Too Human* with his later ideas and philosophical projects (EH "HH" 6); "with this book we arrive": William H. Schaberg, *The Nietzsche Canon: A Publication History and Bibliography* (Chicago: University of Chicago Press, 1996), p. 86; "flowery in fable" (J, 71); "arid height" (J, 97); "disenchanting isle[s]" (J, 71); "the decayed picturesque" (J, 71-72); "From these waters" (J, 95); "afflicted ... with the great curse" (J, 97); "Heartily wish" (J, 97); "I run crisscross" (TSZ 3, "Upon the Mount of Olives"); "Whoever has a soul" (GS 382).

Chapter 121: "All now's revised" (CL 1.34.18-20); "O blind" (CL 4.30.100); "Flamen, flamen" (CL 4.16.208-216); "*By one who wails the loss*" (CL 2.31.43); "Emblazoned bleak" (CL 2.31.50-70); "rule and era" etc. (CL 4.8.1 & 12-14); "relate the history" (WP "Preface" 2); "is faith dead *now*" (CL 3.5.79-83); "Negation" (CL 1.12.100); "Science and Faith" (CL 3.5.64); "upstart ... Lodged in power" (CL 4.8.19-22); "Let fools" (CL 1.31.264-65); "What were we doing" (GS 125).

Chapter 122: Hawthorne on Melville: the relevant passages from Hawthorne's notebooks may be found in J, 628-633; "plays naively" (GS 382); "domestic situation" (HM2, 585 & 599-600); "dreadful *incubus* of a *book*" (HM2, 792); "skepticism is the most spiritual expression" (BGE 208); "virile skepticism" (BGE 209).

Chapter 124: "the god through all of these [links]" (*Ion* 536a); "beautiful creative works" (*Ion* 534e).

Chapter 125: god-given madness is superior to human self-control (Phdr. 244d); Socrates ranks the various types of human life (Phdr. 248d-e); Plato portrays the tyrannical man (R. 573a-c); "Dionysian madness" (BT "Attempt" 4); "the last disciple of the philosopher Dionysus" (TI "Ancients" 4-5).

Chapter 127: the Divided Line (R. 509d-511e); "'faith' means" (A 52).

Chapter 129: "I swam in the Saale" etc. (CN, 234-235); "Zarathustra's eyes" (CN 246); "a body from which" (CN, 247); "prophetic" (CN, 254); "earnest desire" (C, 139); "not one man in five" (C, 212); "one does not only wish" (GS 381).

Chapter 130: "*No God*" etc. (CL 3.28); "profound ravine" (CL 3.10.1); "hag" etc. (CL 3.25); Clarel later finds Mortmain dead (CL 3.32); "a big bird ... carried off his soul" (CL 3.27); "indulged in mundane affairs" (MD, ch. 50).

Chapter 131: "the mania of an evil nature" (BB, 76); "Struck dead" (BB, 101); "delivered in the clear melody" (BB, 123); "the story of the Fall": from Melville's personal copy of SP, 24; "in certain moods" (PT, 243); "neither pessimist" (C, 485-86); "optomist" is Melville's misspelling; "he who lives to see" (SP, 14); the "spirit of the New Testament" (SP, 26); if a man "has a soul above the common" (SP, 28); "the more a man belongs to posterity": quoted from Jay Leyda, *The Melville Log: A Documentary Life of Herman Melville: 1819-1891*, vol. 2 (New York: Harcourt, Brace & Co., 1951), pp. 832-33; "that life could be an experiment" (GS 324).

Chapter 132: "into your eyes I looked" (TSZ 2, "The Dancing Song"); "possibly ... you will missend it" (C, 213); all things are always changing in every way (Tht. 182a); Socrates healthy and Socrates ill are different individuals (Tht. 159a-c); "Nothing ever is" (Tht. 157d); "there is nothing that is one thing" (152d); "something ... this ... that" (Tht. 157b-c); "remove altogether the verb 'to be'" (Tht. 157a-b); "altogether denied Being" (PTG, 51); "unity, identity" (TI "Reason" 5); "I am afraid we are not rid of God" (TI "Reason" 5); "no one *gives* man his qualities" (TI "Errors" 8); "We deny God" (ibid.).

Chapter 133: "harbors sportive monsters": all quotations from Nietzsche in this paragraph are from TSZ 2, "On Those Who are Sublime"; "order of Assassins" (GM 3.24); "will to truth ... a concealed will to death" (GS 344); the "will to truth requires a critique" (GM 3.24); Nietzsche as still "pious" etc. (GS 344); "discovered happiness" (A 1); "predilection of strength" (A "Preface").

Chapter 134: "that thing he will soon see as a corpse" etc. (Phd. 115d-e); great hope for a beautiful reward (Phd. 114c); some men judge the sources of pleasure and pain most real (Phd. 83c-d); "soul atomism" (BGE 12).

Chapter 135: "Do not hurry" (Phd. 116e); "coolly and calmly" (Phd. 117c); "on the third day" (*Iliad* 9.363); "the best, and also the wisest and most just" (Phd. 118a); "the calm, the coolness" (C, 191).

Epilogue: "Alas, destiny and sea!" (TSZ 3, "The Wanderer"); "From my twenty-fifth year" (C, 193); "cast up a black coffin" (TSZ 2, "The Soothsayer").

Made in the USA
Middletown, DE
14 August 2021